Gorgeous George

The Life and Adventures of George Galloway

Gorgeous George

The Life and Adventures of George Galloway

David Morley

POLITICO'S

First published in Great Britain 2007 by
Politico's Publishing, an imprint of
Methuen & Co. Ltd
11–12 Buckingham Gate
London
SW1E 6LB

1

Copyright © David Morley 2007

David Morley has asserted his right under the Copyright, Designs and Patents Act 1988 to be identified as the author of this work.

A CIP catalogue record for this book is available from the British Library.

ISBN 978-1-84275-185-5

Typeset by SX Composing DTP, Rayleigh, Essex
Printed and bound in Great Britain by Biddles Ltd, King's Lynn, Norfolk

For my mother and father, Mary and Derrick;
for Steve, Amy and Emily;
and for my wife, Bernadette.

Contents

Foreword

I got to know David Morley in 2000 when he asked me to narrate an hour-long biography of Jeffrey Archer for BBC Radio Five Live. I was happy to agree – in fact, I volunteered to write it: years before I'd had a bit of a run-in with Lord Archer, and I felt I knew quite a lot about him already.

So while I set about composing what I regarded as the most interesting script since Ambridge was struck by foot-and-mouth disease, but which David always referred to as 'the links', he set about recording as many people as possible who would speak about the great man's life in fiction and non-fiction. The programme's not wholly original title was *The Real Jeffrey Archer* and it went out an hour or two after he was sentenced at the Old Bailey to four years' imprisonment.

BBC Radio Five Live must have been pleased with our efforts as they commissioned us to make a series of eight more programmes about people like Jeffrey Archer, as and when they were in the news. Gratified as we were to be hired, we did wonder if there were eight people remotely like Jeffrey Archer to make programmes about. Or even one. In the event, rather than look for Archer types we worked our way through the great and the good, the famous as much as the infamous in the first and subsequent series.

So we covered the Queen, Prince Charles, Tony Blair, Gordon Brown (at the time of the Budget) and Michael Howard (at the time he was leader of the opposition). We ventured overseas with George W. Bush, Osama bin Laden and Slobodan Milošević. In the world of sport we looked at Alex Ferguson, David Beckham and Bernie Ecclestone. There was plenty of scandal and human interest in *The Real David Blunkett*, *The Real Michael Jackson* and even *The Real Alastair Campbell*.

None were meant to be hatchet jobs, but were intended as a balanced account of the subjects' lives, peppered with as many personal anecdotes as possible. Strangely enough the hardest person to get people to talk about was

Alex Ferguson – colleagues, friends and associates of this distinguished football manager seemed more worried about giving offence than did those of royalty or political leaders. Nevertheless the programme about Sir Alex picked up a Sony Gold Award, UK radio's highest honour.

When David came up with George Galloway as a suggested subject, we felt that here at last might be our Holy Grail. Here was a controversial politician who has been involved in some unusual scrapes and incidents.

We decided that George Galloway deserved a slightly different format. For all our other programmes we had no direct input from the subject. It was the voice of third parties, friends and family, political allies and foes who told the story. But we felt that *The Real George Galloway* without George Galloway would be *Hamlet* without the Prince, and without the Player King, Polonius and Yorick either. So I recorded quite a lengthy interview with the man himself so that sections of it could be used throughout the transmitted programme. It wasn't the first – or last – time I had interviewed him. George is an invigorating interviewee: ready to pounce on any inconsistency or inaccuracy in a question, prepared to heap ferocious criticism on political and other opponents, all expressed in his possibly unique, certainly rather florid verbal style which combines the techniques of a criminal QC, an evangelical preacher and a stand-up comedian (though he is none of those things).

Some people love him, some people loathe him, but most interviewers would welcome Gorgeous George onto the radio or television if not with open arms, at any rate with open mikes.

We were unlucky with our timing of this programme. Some weeks before, Galloway had shot to even greater fame on both sides of the Atlantic with his bravura performance in front of a US Senate committee. But by the time of our broadcast, interest in him had died down somewhat, only to flare up later with his even more extraordinary performance on TV's *Celebrity Big Brother*.

But, with or without the strange incident of Gorgeous George pretending to be Rula Lenska's cat in the night-time, David obviously felt that even an hour of radio had not done justice to George Galloway's life story and has been inspired to write this full-blown biography. For it he has had to dig considerably deeper, go much further into detail and travel around the country. I don't know if George Galloway, his friends or his critics, will wholly approve of the result – he is perhaps too controversial for that – but the story of his life is certainly worth telling and, in this account by David Morley, well worth reading.

Clive Anderson
July 2007

Preface

This is not a critique of George Galloway's political beliefs. It is simply the facts of his life, such as I've been able to establish them. I've gone to great lengths to remain impartial about his politics, and to try to present his controversial story in an even-handed way, but I'm sure that occasionally my views on his personal behaviour have poked through. I make no apology for that. Of course I have views, but what I have tried to do is leave you enough plain information to make your own judgement.

Galloway is one of the most controversial politicians this country has produced, and trying to keep a distance from the arguments has been tough. He provokes strong opinions from all sides and I will be accused by the right of being to the left, and vice versa. Anyone who's worked in journalism knows that this is a fact of life, if you try to tread the middle ground.

A book does give an opportunity to put on record one's views, and I felt it was appropriate to do that in this preface, as a kind of declaration of interest. In broad terms, I am on the same side as George Galloway regarding the Middle East. I believe that he is right in his campaign to bring a fairer deal for the Palestinian people. In later chapters you'll be able to decide for yourself how effective he has been at this. I also believe he was right to fight against UN sanctions on Iraq.

In 1999 the United Nations Children's Fund estimated that 500,000 Iraqi children had died in the previous ten years, partly as a result of the sanctions. Children under five were dying at more than twice the rate that they had prior to their imposition, though it's difficult to assess exactly how many of those deaths were directly as a consequence of UN policy and how much Saddam's regime contributed. However, a later report by UNICEF states: 'The balance sheet of several years of sanctions against Iraq reveals a minimum of political dividends, as against a high human price paid primarily by women and children.' Galloway and others argued that no Iraqi children should have died, while the UN seemed to be content to allow what the military might refer to as 'collateral damage'. So how many children was it morally right to allow to die as a consequence of sanctions? Ten per cent of that UN figure of 500,000? A Lord's cricket ground and two Royal Albert Halls full of children?

In my view, Galloway was right that invading Iraq was the wrong decision, and that the case we were given for it was, in his words to the US Senate, 'a pack of lies'. Irrespective of whether you agree with him or not about that, his performance was outstanding. Who will forget his punchy delivery when he berated Senator Norm Coleman:

> I told the world that Iraq, contrary to your claims, did not have weapons of mass destruction. I told the world, contrary to your claims, that Iraq had no connection to al-Qaeda. I told the world, contrary to your claims, that Iraq had no connection to the atrocity on 9/11 2001. I told the world, contrary to your claims, that the Iraqi people would resist a British and American invasion of their country and that the fall of Baghdad would not be the beginning of the end, but merely the end of the beginning . . . Senator, in everything I said about Iraq, I turned out to be right and you turned out to be wrong.

Galloway's speech is revealing. 'I told the world . . .' he repeated, as if the whole world had been listening to him, but had chosen to ignore his advice. The truth was different. George Galloway is not listened to by the world. He has spent most of his career hardly listened to at home in the UK. As Neil Kinnock put it to me, 'He is a man who has spent his life in a bubble, mistaking it for the world.'

But it would be wrong to think that George Galloway is just a sideshow. For twenty years or more his knowledge of the Israel–Palestine issue made him a regular contributor to the nation's debate on Middle East policy, despite only being a peripheral figure in Parliament. Since the invasion of Kuwait by Saddam Hussein, the interest in his views has become more intense, and when the Tories and New Labour both supported the US–UK invasion of Iraq, Galloway was a leading voice for the millions who disagreed, even before the Senate appearance.

But there are many more reasons why I wanted to write a biography of George Galloway. He is one of the most fascinating politicians of his generation. His colourful language, often impetuous behaviour, and his phenomenal work-rate make him a biographer's dream, but those aspects of his character pale beside his utter conviction that he is right, which seems to have led him to one heated battle after another. Put a man like that into a political scene populated by shallow career politicians, who take their lines from focus groups, and he becomes an intoxicating refreshment. Partly that's why the media loves him, and loves to hate him. In a 24-hour news environment, when there is a tremendous thirst in journalism to move the story on, George Galloway can be relied on for soundbites, or to build up a row.

But how effective is this confrontational modus operandi? There is no doubt that he responds to the immediate political threat or current story with punchy comments that can take the wind out of the opposition, but is there a long-term strategy at play? Politics needs the intelligence and cunning of a chess grandmaster, but how many moves ahead is Galloway looking? You may read this biography and conclude that his career has been an exercise in haphazardly fighting a series of fires. On the other hand, you may think that he has successfully kept the torch of left-wing politics burning, while others left the temple for their own agendas.

With some justification, his supporters say that if George Galloway could stand for election in the Arab world, he'd walk into high office. In his own country, though, the tale is very different and it is possible to view his career as a disappointment, particularly as in his twenties he told comrades that he wanted to be Foreign Secretary. But those were different times. Tony Benn was a Cabinet minister back then, championing wider state control, and Galloway was a supporter. Both have more or less kept to their convictions, while others who held similar views have moved a long way to the right. Galloway will often refer to New Labour Cabinet members who started on the far left, but no-one knows what he could have become if he'd changed his position too. He is undoubtedly a capable politician and if he'd only wanted power at any price, he might now be standing with the likes of John Reid.

Like Reid, Galloway doesn't suffer fools, and likes to control from the centre of an organisation. While his friends say he is keen to hear the opinions of others and is open to change, others claim he is an autocrat. With Galloway at the helm, Dundee Labour Party was run along democratic centralist lines, as was the charity War on Want, which fell into internal feuding. He fell out with his constituency activists in Glasgow, with Neil Kinnock when he was Labour's leader, and with Tony Blair over Iraq. Make your own mind up if George Galloway is a team player or not, and if that has mattered to his career.

A big slice of team play is self-sacrifice. So did Galloway give up the possibility of high office for the good of the left-wing cause, or could it be that he just backed the wrong horse? Having staked everything so vocally on the return of a socialist government, he would have found it impossible to become a Blairite, even if he'd wanted to renounce his old opinions and move with the times. In fact, he has very skilfully kept himself in the game, while other left-wingers have remained in the long grass of the back benches.

In some ways George Galloway is everything you'd want in a politician. He fights hard for what he believes, and doesn't blow with the wind. However, there is something unsettling about his determination not to moderate those vitriolic attacks on his opponents: to find discord where there might be a little harmony. Most of us discover that we can't get exactly what we want and have to settle for compromise. With Galloway it is very often a point of honour not to bend and that is both his strength and weakness. It makes him occasionally hard to like and more often, compelling.

I would like to thank Clive Anderson for his foreword and for laughing his way through the programmes we've made together. Thanks also to Mike Cockerell and Julia Langdon for the kind words, and to Bruce, Helen and everyone at Above the Title.

Special thanks to Leonie Mather, Lucy Adam and Emilia Sava for their research, and to Claire Paterson at Janklow Nesbitt.

Most of all, I would like to thank everyone who gave their time in interviews with me for this book. They are quoted, directly or indirectly, throughout the text, but rather than attribute each individual quote, I credit them all here:

Burhan Al Chalabi

Sabbah Al Mukhtar

Riad Al Tahir

Anas Al Tikriti

Jimmy Allison

Felicity Arbuthnot

Ziad Aziz

Norval Black

Billy Boyle

Richard Burden

Louise Carmi

Charlotte Cassidy

Andrew Child

Mohammed Chowdury

Frank Clark

Petru Clej

Patrick Colquhoun

Tom Connor

Colin Cooper

Tam Dalyell

Dr Radu Dop

Jim Duncan

George Dundas

Martin Eade

Ann Farquharson

Scott Ferguson

Ray Fitzwalter

Suzanne Franks

Elena Gorun

Fran Hazelton

James Henderson

Julian Hopkins

Azmol Hussein

Dilwar Hussein

Dave King

Glenys Kinnock

Neil Kinnock

Sheila Kujawska

Tim Llewellyn

Iain Luke

John McAllion

Colin McAllister

Brian McCartney

Willie McKelvey

Adrian Manole

James Martin

Christopher Mason

Dr Jaqueline Mok

Gulham Moortusa

Neil Mudie

Tim Nuthall

Graham Ogilvy

Keith Pearson

Josh Peck

Martin Plaut

Oliur Rahman

Lord Rea of Eskdale

John Rees

Ken Ritchie

Glyn Robbins

John Home Robertson

Dr Claudia Ruginâ

Dr Sorin Ruginâ

David Scott

Mark Seddon

Saeed Shah

George Soutar

Bill Speirs

Hans von Sponeck

Dave Stark

Simon Stocker

David Stribbles

David Syme

Bill Walker

Alison Whyte

Bob Winter

Alf Young

Fawaz Zureikat

1

Early days

The George Galloway we see before us now is a creature assembled on the factory floor of Dundee's left-wing politics. Like the backdrop to Mary Shelley's *Frankenstein*, this is a dark, isolated place that can steer intelligent men to misguided endeavours. If you look closely, you can make out that Galloway is stitched together from many parts, including a committed Labour activist father, an attractive and fiery Irish mother, and a variety of union and communist mentors. When he rose from the slab it wasn't from the jolt of a lightning strike, though strikes there were in plenty, but from the high-tension electricity of Dundee's confrontational political past. But what can explain the often angry, sometimes self-pitying and occasionally extreme behaviour with which he has entertained and shocked us for over four decades? What is it that drives him on? Is he trying to help others, or just benefit himself? There is a lot to discover about Mr Galloway.

Over the years many journalists and political enemies have questioned his motives, his finances and his sex life, to such an extent that the story of George Galloway is a catalogue of controversies. He leaps from frying pan to fire and back again, screaming 'Look at me!', and as much as he thrives on this adrenalin, the stress and ugliness of this world increasingly shows through the face of the man his foes ironically dubbed 'Gorgeous George'. There is a 'catch me if you can' game being played here and it's remarkable how he is constantly drawn to the edge, so he can look into the abyss of failure and come back again.

But what is failure to this man? Is there more to him than a desire for attention? Though his acolytes reason that he is fighting for justice, others would be forgiven for thinking that what he fears most is to disappear off our screens, out of our papers, off our radios, and into nowhere. For Galloway the world is a stage, politics is theatre, gestures are grand, emotions are worn on the sleeve. His career has been full of movie-style adventures: secret flights under the radar, sexual innuendo, confrontations with the big guy, high-profile court cases, rabble-rousing speeches. This is a million miles from House of Commons committees, grey suits and the compromise of real political power broking. Galloway doesn't belong in that world now, and he probably never will. Yet he has conjured an image of power that draws some in, and while he has no force to effect any real change, he plays the role of a man who does, beguiling with simple answers to complex problems. Though he declared as a young firebrand that he wanted to be Foreign Secretary, he is a maverick at the margin of government who flirts with powerful men, but will never be one. The terrible truth of our age is that a man like Galloway has become a leading voice of dissent against the horrors of the Bush–Blair–Olmert axis.

Perhaps there is something haunted about George Galloway. His career appears to be a classic tragedy of power and ambition that we will have to watch unfold to its climax. As in *Hamlet,* one can perhaps detect a darkness and something deeper at work here, something that draws him towards the chaos of Lebanon, Palestine, Romania and Iraq, and something perhaps that draws chaos to him.

The lifeblood of his career has been the media, and his relationship with it is deep and complex, almost obsessive. He fights journalists and news-papers as if he hates the profession, yet more than almost any other politician he seems to believe his own press. In his mind he is Gorgeous, he is the Ghost of Labour Past, he did take on the Senate Permanent Subcommittee on Investigations and beat it. Yet his career is littered with high points and low points, not to mention his spectacular performance on *Celebrity Big Brother.* He appears to be the hero as loser and if you want to find a window into his mind, you'd do a lot worse than listen to one of his favourite songs, John Lennon's 'Working Class Hero'. Here is an angry hero, who gives the impression that he expects to be brought down by the Establishment, in relation to which he is always the outsider.

From all aspects, Galloway's ego seems to be enormous, but fragile, like an overinflated balloon. It's not an ego that can cope easily with genuine challenges to his authority, so he will choose to ignore dissenters or make them irrelevant. In every organisation he has led, the story is the same from many of those he left behind: he appears to centralise control, dominating policy decisions to the point where he seeks to be in charge in place of true democracy. His enemies say that if you argue with him he believes you are arguing against the party, against the movement, and against the interests of the working class. These days the arguments take place on a grand scale, with a global working class to fight for. He started small: the self-proclaimed champion of Dundee's poor, followed by the persecuted Palestinians, then Ethiopia's starving, then Romanian children and abused Iraqis. It seems almost as if he is fighting evil the world over.

This is a great story – Shakespearian maybe, Hollywood perhaps, or Dickensian – and certainly it's a tale of two parties. Galloway is right when he says he's the Ghost of Labour Past, but which bits of Labour's past does he want to cling on to? The 1983 manifesto? Strikes without ballots? Through George Galloway's eyes we can see the dramatic evolution of the Labour party from 'Old' to New, at the same time as we watch how the world has turned since the first Gulf War and 11 September 2001. The hitherto unfashionable cause of the Palestinians, which Galloway, to his credit, has been championing since the 1970s, is now centre stage in world affairs.

Galloway's childhood was unremarkable, except that he seemed to show early academic promise but underachieved disappointingly. His time in education is hard to fathom. For example, while Blake's *Parliamentary Yearbooks* of 1988 and 1989 list his qualifications as four Scottish Highers, the other respected reference books which rely on an MP's own submissions don't mention them, as we shall see. While Galloway claims he was a jute mill worker and a tyre maker, these jobs seem to have been for short periods and explain neither his claim in *Who's Who* of 1988 to be 'an engineering worker' nor his comment in the House of Commons that 'I have worked hard all my life with my hands'. Menial jobs maybe, but they were sporadic and dead-end ones that included a stint for the Dundee Council Parks Department, which hardly qualifies him as a son of the soil. But no, the way that Galloway appeared to use his hands was in the murky waters of Scottish politics. Like that of many professional politicians, his employment history prior to becoming an MP would not make an impressive CV. No, it is politics that has sustained him, topped up he says, by his fees as a writer and the winnings from his libel victories. Whatever he may say about his past and present sources of income, whatever his motivation, George Galloway, like many others, seems to be in politics for a living.

Countless profiles of Galloway state that he was 'born in an attic in a slum tenement' or variations on that wording.[1] In fact, George Galloway was born in Dundee Maternity Hospital on 16 August 1954, at 6 a.m., according to his birth certificate. A lot of other 'facts' you can read about his childhood are unreliable. There are stories of penury and struggle, of working-class toil in Dundee factories, of a moustache grown in the image of Che Guevara, of meeting handsome young persecuted Arabs and of iconic Irish rebels. Over the years, in hundreds of interviews, Galloway's past has been spun into a web of tales that bring to mind the ex-Dundee MP Winston Churchill's phrase 'a riddle, wrapped in a mystery, inside an enigma'.

The picture painted has come from a range of different sources and is sometimes more a question of emphasis, or spin, put onto the facts at a later stage, often by a process of Chinese whispers as journalists feed off previous interviews. Middle-class writers, hearing that he was brought up on a council estate in grim-sounding 1950s Dundee, assume he was born poor, a picture that has often suited his purposes. There are tales of his mother's Irish ancestors arriving off the boat with literally only the clothes they stood up in. Stepping off the boat onto a Glasgow wharf shoeless is mentioned often: that's the Galloway family legend and there may be elements of truth in it. Suffice it to say that many thousands of poverty-stricken Irish arrived in Scotland around the turn of the twentieth century, desperate for work, with only what they carried to call their own. Galloway told Michael Tierney of the *Glasgow Herald* in April 2000 that his maternal grandparents 'arrived on the cattle boats at Anderston Quay', Glasgow:

> I was kind of born into this. My maternal grandfather was a leading Irish communist. I came from, as it were, a republican tradition. This helped me form views about imperialism. My father used to say that the reason the sun never set on the British Empire is because God would never trust the British in the dark.

Though he has an Irish name, his father's ancestors had been in Scotland for generations, and were butchers by trade. Incidentally, Galloway told

John Humphrys in his BBC Radio 4 *On the Ropes* programme of 17 June 2003:

> I told my maternal grandfather once that a teacher had said the British had an empire so vast that on it the sun never sets. And my grandfather said that's because God would never trust the British in the dark. And I never had cause to doubt that analysis from that day until this.

Galloway was born into Dundee's depressed industrial area of Lochee, or Eye of the Loch, which sounds picturesque until you realise that the loch was drained centuries ago. These days it's an ugly dip in the landscape, stuck with run-down tower blocks and bounded by unforgiving arterial roads. In the 1950s it was crammed with back-to-back housing and low-rise tenements, but it still had a soul. And the soul was Irish.

Galloway's mother, Sheila, and father, George, had been married on 6 February 1954 and lived in a small Lochee council tenement before moving to a slightly bigger place in St Mary's Lane. Galloway is proud that the Irish rebel James Connolly, who was executed for his part in the Easter Rising of 1916, may have lived in the same street and he certainly identifies very strongly with his mother's Irish ancestry and has always been an advocate of Irish nationalism, even marching with Gerry Adams. He likes to quote Hugh MacDiarmid's description of Connolly's qualities: 'Scots steel tempered wi' Irish fire/Is the weapon that I desire,' and clearly sees himself in that mould.

Historically Lochee was so dominated by Irish immigrants and their families that Dundonians called it Tipperary, so Irish that when the anti-Sinn Fein Winston Churchill tried to speak there in 1922 the crowd had to be restrained by the police, for fear they would take his life. Churchill called the 1922 election 'the worst of my life . . . I was faced by an audience of lions with communist teeth,' and during the campaign some crowds cheered for Lenin when he tried to speak. (He lost his seat and never came back, even refusing the freedom of the city in 1943.) However, it isn't just the Irish question that gets people going in Dundee. This angry political environment is typical of the city and, by and large, of Scottish politics and is key to understanding Galloway's evolution.

There is a long history of working-class political organisation in the city that goes back to the end of the eighteenth century, when the Dundee Friends of Liberty, led by a weaver called George Mealmaker, campaigned against the government and factory owners, with an eye on the recent French Revolution. The subsequent rioting in Dundee was eventually put down by the army and later Mealmaker was found guilty of leading a banned organisation and transported to Australia. This history of socialist campaigning carried on through the nineteenth and twentieth centuries, and in the 1960s and 1970s the local unions were run by a succession of widely respected and openly communist leaders. In contrast, the local Labour Party of the time was relatively right wing, with corrupt elements. It was in this divided working-class environment that the young Galloway cut his teeth politically and literally. His father was a Labour Party man and union shop steward and the infant Galloway was surrounded by politics.

The former Labour MP Willie McKelvey, who later helped expose corrupt practices in Dundee, lived in the area and knew the Galloway family well. 'They lived down the road. Our families were very close and I'd watched him grow up from being a baby. I remember he slept in a drawer, the bottom one, because the room was too wee for a cot.' The story of being too poor to afford a cot is often cited as evidence of Galloway's deprived background, yet in the 1950s and 1960s this was not unusual in poorer areas. In fact Galloway's childhood was relatively comfortable, compared to many in Britain's industrial cities of the time. His father was a skilled engineer at National Cash Registers, or NCR. Though making tills and ATMs for 'The Cash' was not going to make you rich, it was steady work and, unlike many, the Galloway family was not known to have had serious money problems. McKelvey remembers: 'We all used to go off to the coast some weekends, play on the beach and so on. It was a pretty normal working-class family in Dundee.'

Galloway is the oldest of three children; he has a brother, Graham, and a sister, Colette. According to Labour activists at the time, Colette and Graham often turned up to help boost Galloway's support when he needed it. Graham was active in the Labour Party for a short while, giving it up when he went off to Glasgow to university. Graham Galloway is tall and slim, but has kept a very low profile, in contrast to his older brother. According to Galloway's friends and colleagues his brother and sister rarely get a mention, as Galloway has little time for anything in his life except work.

Galloway's mother, Sheila, is recalled as an attractive and charming woman, who still lives in the family council house in Dundee. It's a small, grey, rather characterless terraced house, probably built in the 1950s. Though an estate agent would find it hard to describe the place as 'sought after' now, back in the 1960s getting into a house of that kind was difficult and the Galloways would have been thought very lucky.

George Galloway senior, who died in March 1997, is universally regarded with warmth. John McAllion, a former Labour MSP for Dundee, was a young teacher and activist in the city in the 1970s and remembers:

> George Senior was a very nice man, very unassuming. He worked with me in the local party. He was a very good worker, just got on with it. Sometimes it would be just me and him at the meetings, which is funny looking back at it now. We used to run Bingo at the Silver Cage, a pub down the road, and give the money to the Labour party.

McKelvey, who would later work with the young Galloway to overthrow Labour's right wing in Dundee, recalls that 'his father was a nice man, quite quiet. He was active in the Labour party, but not in a subversive way like us. He was like many who'd come and help. They worked for us. You could count on him 100 per cent.'

Though he may not have been as ambitious as his son, the older Galloway clearly had similar views to George Junior. He was a lifelong member of the Amalgamated Engineering Union, on the left of the Labour Party and remembered by some as having the Marxist views that were common in Dundee Labour and union circles. The young Galloway was often heard describing himself as a Marxist too.

George Senior taught his son the nuts and bolts of Labour. He was well versed in the importance of union sponsorship, in how to gather support and use the party's voting system, in campaigning and fund raising and the mechanisms of internal Labour politics. And crucially, Junior met the key man in his political development through his father. The influence of Willie McKelvey is hard to overestimate. He propelled the young Galloway inside

7

Dundee Labour, championed him in the wider national party, and helped to set him up to take his place as local Labour Party leader when he later left for Westminster.

The McKelveys, the Galloways and others worked hard for Labour, particularly at election time. Galloway has remarked in interviews that his father's campaigning in the 1962 general election was so committed that the windows of their house were covered in posters of Harold Wilson,[2] but another activist had a poster specially made that was so big it covered the entire front of his property and they had to cut out a hole to open the door. There was clearly a great spirit in the area, with whole families involved, and McKelvey recalls that 'Little George helped in the Labour Party from around age five or so. That wasn't so unusual. It was a different era then and children came in droves to help with campaigns. They loved putting leaflets through doors for us. And we'd pay them a shilling sometimes.' Even if the boy Galloway never got a shilling, it seems likely that he may have learned very early on that politics and hard work can be a way to make a bob or two.

Away from his fledgling career, Galloway went to Charleston Primary School in Lochee, where one of his contemporaries, George Dundas, remembers him as 'academically one of the brighter ones' and liking a game of football in the yard. His love of football has stayed with him from that day to this. He used to play for the House of Commons football team, and when he lived in the city he was a fan of Dundee United, though now he's seen more regularly at Celtic.

Charleston was a 'fine school' and they had a 'good education with good sports facilities and a good headmaster', according to Dundas. Miss Littlejohn was their form teacher and she taught them nearly all the way through the school. 'George never caused any trouble at school. He's making up for it now!' says Dundas, who also remembers, as does another contemporary, Ann Farquharson, that for many months the young Galloway was forced to wear an eye patch to correct an astigmatism or squint. Children can be cruel and Farquharson and Dundas recall clearly that Galloway came in for what might now be regarded as bullying over his pirate-style patch. It was nothing malicious, 'just gentle teasing', according to Dundas. As part of the same eye treatment, Galloway also had to wear rather clumsy-looking, thick-lensed glasses.

School and consequent academic qualifications have been largely an irrelevance to Galloway's career. He didn't require them and he has clearly never felt the need either to pass large numbers of exams or to talk much about them. He did, however, pass the exam needed to get into Dundee's prestigious Harris Academy. Harris was founded in 1885, and is one of the top two state schools in Dundee, with a reputation for turning out well-educated, rounded individuals. It was a highly selective grammar school at the time Galloway got in, and all pupils had to sit a qualifying exam at the end of junior school, called 'the Qually'. On the Harris Academy website they describe how this old system fell out of favour eventually. 'Children would be assigned to either senior secondary or junior secondary schools on the basis of the marks attained. By the mid-sixties, the wisdom of such a policy was being questioned. Should a child be designated a "first-class" or "second-class" pupil at such an early age?'

Galloway was in the 'first-class' category, a crucial step on the road to Highers and perhaps even university. Harris is still a good school, full of middle-class boys and girls, in a rather grand and imposing stone building on Perth Road. Whereas someone from a council house in Lochee would have expected to go to the equivalent of Bash Street School from Dundee publisher D. C. Thomson's *The Beano*, Harris was far more upmarket. Getting in was 'like winning the lottery for a working-class boy from that part of town' according to Graham Ogilvy, another ex-pupil.

Ogilvy was a couple of years junior to Galloway at Harris, but would later get involved in local politics with him and remembers that 'at school he was a great individualist. He did stand out, I would have said, and had a great sense of humour, as he always has had.' Former Dundee Labour MP Iain Luke also remembers Galloway very well from school. At lunchtimes they used to 'go down south' to the south playground, where boys of all ages used to play football. 'George was a skilful player who used to play with Derek Addison a lot. He went on to play for Dundee United.'

Looking at his political record, one could be forgiven for thinking that Galloway has two left feet, but that's not the case. As a teenager he was a good football player, and made centre forward for the school first team, according to David Stribbles, who was his PE teacher and is still at Harris Academy. That was no mean feat when you had players in the same team who would go on to become professionals. Though Stribbles has fond memories of Galloway, there was a cheeky side to him too and on one occasion when he forgot his football boots he asked to borrow the teacher's for a match. Stribbles agreed, though he thought he had a nerve at the time. Another of Galloway's teachers was Jack Knight, who was at both Charleston Primary and at Harris Academy. He remembers him as 'an able guy, a bit of a Jack the Lad even at that time, and interested in the girls'. He was 'quite a good runner, but with a deceptive, funny style. It was peculiar because he didn't pick his knees up very high.'

Sport can be a useful window into someone's personality, so these recollections about the young football-playing Galloway are illuminating. George Soutar ran the team at Harris from the mid-1960s to the mid-1980s and though he didn't teach Galloway, he remembers him as 'a likeable young rogue' who had a 'harum-scarum playing style'. When Soutar went round collecting valuables in a bag before games 'there'd be a watch here, half a crown there, but George would often have quite a few notes. "It's the milk money, Sir" was George's explanation, so I assumed he had a milk round.' Galloway has often referred to his job delivering milk while at school and once claimed that he used to deliver to the house of Bill Walker, a Scottish Conservative MP from 1979 to 1997. Walker is annoyed to this day about it because Galloway referred to the dirty bottles he had to pick up.

> He couldn't have been old enough. I was married and moved away from the house in 1956, so unless he worked at two years old, he can't have. If he meant he delivered to my parents' house then I can say now that my mother was the sort of woman who washed her doorstep every day and always left everything spotless, particularly the milk bottles. She was that kind of woman.

It is a measure of the petty sensitivities of Dundee that this has become a bone of contention.

Not everyone has good things to say about Galloway at school. Colin McAllister taught him geography in his first year, when Galloway was aged twelve to thirteen. 'He used to sit at the back of the class in the corner. I didn't realise as a young teacher that is where the troublemakers sit!' You'd think that would be lesson number one at teacher-training college.

> One day we were covering Ghana. I used to ask the boys what the cola nut was used for. When I told them it was used to make Coca-Cola, the wee squirt – because that is how I think of him then – put his hand up and said, 'Did you know that if you drink Coca-Cola with aspirin it makes you drunk?'

McAllister was only at Harris for a year and a half; it was his first teaching post. 'It was his attitude and manner, the "entertain me if you dare" attitude. He was a bit of a know-it-all. Mind you, Galloway would probably say I was a useless teacher as it was my first job, teaching a subject I didn't know, and kids are soon to pick up when you don't know what you're talking about . . . "You can't teach me anything" was the feeling I got from him.' McAllister left Harris for Dundee College, where Galloway would register as a student some years later.

Galloway and McAllister clearly didn't hit it off, but fellow teacher Knight claims he was

> a likeable rogue, with a quick repartee. But he was no bother, and never fell out with the staff. It was a selective academy then and everyone knew he wasn't a fool. I have pleasant memories of him. I remember him often asking 'What do you think of that, Mr Knight?' if he'd done something. He always had an opinion on something, always had something to say, but in a likeable way.

Outside school and football, there was always politics. Most young lads of twelve would have been happy just to be allowed to help their dads leaflet in the local area at election time, but for Galloway that wasn't enough. In 1967 he travelled back and forth to Glasgow to help out in the campaign office for the Labour candidate, Dick Douglas, in the renowned Glasgow Pollok by-election. The election is remembered as a fantastic success, but not for Labour. The Tories just held the seat, while Labour's effort was a minor disaster and they lost 21.2 per cent of their votes. It was the Scottish Nationalists who were celebrating, with a much-increased share that set up their landmark victory in Hamilton later that year, when they grabbed the safest Labour seat in Scotland. Whether or not there are scars from that

11

encounter, over the years Galloway has remained strongly anti-SNP, though he was always in favour of a national assembly. When North Sea oil was first brought ashore, he argued that it should be for the good of the whole UK, which to the SNP was the equivalent of selling your sister into slavery.

After his electioneering efforts, or despite them, depending on how you look at it, the thirteen-year-old Galloway was made a member of the Labour Party. Officially this was two years younger than was allowed, but he was admitted anyway, as Galloway himself has confirmed. This is sometimes referred to as a measure of his ability, or in some of the more reverential descriptions of his early days as implying some kind of 'chosen' status, but it's unlikely that anyone cared exactly how old the new boy was. Scottish Labour Party membership records are notoriously hazy and nobody minded adding members to the list when votes were needed. In the following years Galloway would learn that membership of organisations can be flexible, using this flexibility to his advantage. In some cases, huge rifts would open up over the issue of voting and membership and it's ironic that his own membership of the Labour Party had stretched the rules years before.

Galloway was thought of as ferociously ambitious and Willie McKelvey remembers that he had to console the teenager on the stairs of Dundee Labour HQ after a meeting where he had failed to get nominated to stand for the 1973 local council elections. As we have seen, Galloway would later boast that his ambition was to be Foreign Secretary, and he may have inherited this dynamism from his mother's side of the family. Friends remember that his mother was 'a much stronger personality' than his father and 'ran the house'. Apart from his strong character and love of the Irish, he also inherited a passion for boxing from his mother's side. Harris Academy didn't cater for the sport, but McKelvey remembers that Galloway's mother's family, the Reillys, were boxers and that the young George took coaching from their trainer. 'I never saw him box, but the family said he was good.' As he is only around 5 feet 6 inches tall, he must have been more of a Jimmy Cagney than a Sylvester Stallone.

The truth of Galloway's boxing prowess is hard to gauge, as school contemporaries and political comrades all know very little about it beyond what they have read and what he might have mentioned in passing. Though he is well known for liking a verbal scrap, he can be physically brave as well.

Graham Ogilvy remembers walking down the street with him some years later, when they were in their twenties, and seeing a man beating up a woman on the pavement. 'This brute was knocking hell out of his wife and George pitched in and stopped him. I always remember him saying to me once "Let boldness be thy friend" and I think you can say that he has pretty much lived by that.' However, it was widely reported that a 'tired and emotional' Tory MP landed two punches on Galloway in the House of Commons in late 1988.

Apart from his combative style, another Galloway trademark is his love of a Cuban cigar. When Clive Anderson interviewed him for a BBC Five Live profile in December 2005, Galloway explained that this went back to his schooldays. Though Harris was relatively posh, he didn't mean the boys puffed on large Havanas behind the bike sheds, discussing pork belly futures. While at school Galloway did a little part-time work in a local hotel and he used to swipe businessmen's cigar butts from the ashtrays. He described those businessmen as 'plutocrats' in the Anderson interview, in other words members of the wealthy ruling class, the people he claims he has spent his political life fighting against. You'd think puffing on their cigars would have been anathema to him, but expensive cigars will always be associated with the great working-class hero (and acquaintance of Galloway's) Fidel Castro. So Galloway can reason to himself that his socialist credentials are intact. It's not as if he betrayed his class and took up croquet.

The only thing likely to keep Galloway's mind off schoolwork apart from football and politics was girls. Galloway himself recalls that he met his future wife Elaine Fyffe at Harris Academy, when they both played in the school orchestra. He also met Lilian Grewar there, who would play a significant role in Galloway's life for many years.[3]

His schooldays do hold some nostalgic fascination for him, as they do for most of us, and it seems that Galloway likes to keep in touch with his old school contemporaries, to an unusual extent for someone with such a high profile. For example, there is a listing on Friends Reunited for him which reads: 'I'm a Member of Parliament and a writer, I'm married for the second time, I have a nineteen-year-old daughter. You may have seen some of the work I've been doing over the years. I'm keen for reasons I'm not altogether clear about to contact friends (or foes) from school!' This was entered onto the site in 2001, which is why it is out of date now, but it seems Galloway is content for it to stay there.

The Friends Reunited site is open to abuse, so there is a possibility that the above was not left there by Galloway himself, although it doesn't seem to be a spoof. His entry appears in Harris Academy, in the 'class of' 1972. One interesting aspect of Galloway's entry is that it appears twice. The first time it was put on, it was entered in the wrong year and is only half completed. So if you go to Harris Academy 1973 he's there as well, but the entry reads: 'Member of , writer and broadcaster.' The odd, incomplete entry has also been left there and as of the date of publication of this book, hadn't been changed since it was posted.

It's easy to forget later on what year you left school, but it must have been harder for Galloway to work out what year to put his name in because he left school early. To find the right list of people, he had to work out when he would have left Harris had he stayed on to do his Highers.

Galloway's time at Harris can't be judged as a great success. He might have stood out on the football field, and possibly as a character, but he didn't stand out academically. Galloway left Harris after taking his O-grade exams, though exactly what his results were is not clear. He has never publicly disclosed them, but why should he? They are lost in the mists of time.

Galloway is quoted as being proud that he left school at sixteen as a badge of working-class honour, and to the casual observer this sounds like he probably couldn't afford to stay on and had to get a job. If you are successful, yet left school young, it can be seen to imply that you've fought hard against an underprivileged educational background to achieve great things. But that would be misleading in Galloway's case. Harris Academy is a prestigious institution, and one that gives pretty much the best start you could hope for in Dundee, unless you pay for an education. Leaving early doesn't mean you had a bad start in life.

One can speculate as to the possible reasons that he left school after his O-grades. He may have decided that getting a job was necessary to help the family finances; this, however, seems unlikely, as contemporaries at Harris remember many classmates whose fathers and mothers were laid off in the 1970s, but who stayed on and finished their Highers. It would have been the sensible option, given that Highers only take a year, and your job and pay prospects improve enormously if you have them.

It was rare to leave Harris voluntarily. Getting a place there if you were from a working-class background was an enormous opportunity and it wouldn't make sense to leave when it was as good a state education as you could get. So could it be that Galloway failed to pass sufficient O-grades to enable him to remain at Harris or not? A year or so later he enrolled on a course at Dundee College of Commerce, described by one Harris alumnus as 'a college for failures'.[4]

In between Harris and Dundee College it is also unclear exactly to what job Galloway went. There are few records available of his employment in the early 1970s and many stories from him and others to sift through to get to the bottom of exactly what happened in these years. In interviews he has claimed that he worked in the same jute mill as his grandfather and that while he was there he slipped messages into bales destined for far-flung corners of the globe. These read 'Workers of The World Unite' and other slogans – perhaps an odd way of starting a global Marxist revolution. This mill was probably the Parks works, which closed down in the financial year 1978/9.

Around the same time as Galloway was taking a few faltering steps into the world of work, his father was made redundant from NCR. With Dundee in economic freefall, he had little option but to rebuild his career. At the time there was a scheme called the Academic Studies Course, aimed at mature students out of work, whereby you could get a grant to study full time for Highers or A-levels. Galloway Senior enrolled, but so did Galloway Junior. Whereas Galloway's father is remembered as a model student, the story of Galloway's time at the college is very different.

To get onto the Academic Studies Course you had to be over eighteen on 31 August. Galloway turned eighteen on 16 August 1972, which made him eligible as mature. You also needed 'one Higher or three Ordinary Grades of the Scottish Certificate of Education', according to the Dundee College of Commerce prospectus. These requirements didn't change over the years and so Galloway must have got at least three O-grades.

The two George Galloways went off to college together. Norval Black, a senior lecturer in economics at Dundee College at the time, remembers that the administrative staff were slightly thrown because 'father and son had the same name and the same address and were students at the same time'. It was a remarkable event to have a father and son, both called George Galloway, taking the same course. Sheila Kujawska taught history to both George Junior and George Senior, but they were very different students. Now retired and in her seventies she remembers that 'his father was an exemplary student' but that Galloway himself was hardly ever there. 'His attendance was sporadic, shall we say,' she continues, and by the end of the academic year 'he faded out of the picture'.

Just how much time Galloway spent at Dundee College, what exams he might have taken and why he bothered to enrol in the first place is a mystery. There are more clues from Colin McAllister, who had taught him at Harris and had then moved to Dundee College, where their paths crossed again. McAllister taught Galloway's father modern studies, which included the history of the USSR as part of the course. Although they didn't get on at first, the older Galloway warmed to him towards the end and McAllister believes he earned George Senior's grudging respect when they discussed Marxism. He felt that he was 'able to dent a little his impenetrable belief in communism'. McAllister also recalls that there were a number of Marxist mature students on the Academic Studies Course who he'd heard were only there for the grant. Some would even take A-levels rather than Highers, as the grant lasted until the June exams, rather than ending in May, when the exams for Highers took place. McAllister believes that 'some would turn up for the exam and sign their name and walk out again'.

Keith Pearson taught history and economic history at Dundee College and remembers Galloway Junior very well. 'George was supposed to be in my economic history class. He wasn't particularly outstanding in the class, he didn't attend very often and then he just disappeared.' Like the other teachers, he taught both Galloway and his father, who both took the economic history class. Pearson continues:

> His father was a much better attendee and in light of what George Galloway [Junior] is now, he was surprisingly quiet in class and not at all outspoken. Maybe that had something to do with what we were studying, in that it didn't lend itself to comment. His father was very quiet and didn't articulate his views in front of other people.

Pearson remembers that there were twenty or so people in the class, a lot of them mature students. 'At the time there was something called "special recruitment" for teachers and a lot of left-wing groups used the academic studies course as a vehicle to get people on the student council.' So did Galloway complete the course and take the exam? 'My memory is that he didn't sit the economic history exam.'

In Blake's *Parliamentary Yearbook*s of 1988 and 1989, the years following his election as an MP, Galloway's entry reads that he had been educated at Charleston and Harris, with no mention of Dundee College of Commerce and that his qualifications were Scottish Highers in economics, history, English and economic history. Like the other well-known reference books for MPs' CVs, such as *Dod's Parliamentary Companion* and Roth's *Parliamentary Profiles*, these entries are scrupulously compiled from information provided direct from the MP or their office in writing. Each year they are updated, in case the MPs want to make any changes. Interestingly, Roth's *Parliamentary Profiles* of 1989 does not list Galloway's educational qualifications, and neither does *Dod's*. They also both list his schools as Charleston and Harris, and do not mention Dundee College of Commerce.

So what about Galloway's four Scottish Highers? Why did he not supply the list to *Dod's* and Roth's? Most MPs have degrees, and some cite periods of study at prestigious international institutions, or MAs, MScs, PhDs, and so on. Perhaps he thought listing his Highers was less impressive in comparison.

Details of someone's exam results are confidential, so finding Galloway's qualifications is difficult, but the diligent Kujawska has kept her mark books from every year she taught at Dundee College of Commerce. She dug them out for this biography. In her books the following is neatly noted down: '72–73 George Galloway Senior: B pass in higher history', but for the same year the name George Galloway Junior has no exam result next to it and a line scored through the name. Kujawska did this to every student who dropped out of her class. 'I think he was there to get involved in student politics and he was very active in the union . . . My impression is that George didn't complete the course. His energies were directed elsewhere.'

Galloway's old friend Ann Farquharson also remembers him telling her that he was dropping out of Dundee College. They used to see each other regularly at Tiffany's nightclub in Dundee, when he gave her free tickets for Labour Party dances. 'There used to be one nearly every Thursday night . . . one night I was very surprised when George told me that he was ditching his Highers to become full-time secretary of the Labour Club.' Though she is unclear as to the exact date, it was when she had left Harris Academy, so after 1972. Of course, memories do play tricks and her conversation with Galloway about leaving the college may not be as reliable as his teacher's written record. However, Farquharson was no passing acquaintance and has known Galloway since junior school. Charleston had quite a Victorian attitude to boys and girls and kept them separated in the playground, but even so Farquharson got on well with Galloway and they kept their friendship for many years. She says 'he wasn't so opinionated then' and she thinks Galloway 'had a soft spot for me', but she always fancied his mate (whose name she wouldn't reveal). Galloway even rang her a few years ago when she couldn't attend a school reunion, to say how sorry he was she couldn't be there.

While Galloway Junior was concentrating perhaps on student politics, the diligent and focused Galloway Senior collected his exams, trained as a teacher, and then went on to join Harris Academy, where he taught history and modern studies for many years, liked and admired by his pupils. His son wouldn't have been the first student to drop out of a course and by the early 1970s his plans for a political career were well advanced, which may have made him think he was wasting his time at college. Importantly, after May or June 1973, when his grant stopped, he needed to get a job.

Though there may have been some temporary employment between the summer of 1973 and December of that year, it was certainly winter when Galloway took the most important job of his life outside politics. Ironically, it wasn't in any way an important job in itself, or even a stepping stone into a career in that field, it just opened doors for him: big, powerful, heavy, union doors at the Dundee tyre factory, which is now owned by Michelin. In some ways it is from here that he built his political career. At Michelin he joined the TGWU and they have pretty much backed him ever since. Without them providing funding for his campaigns and voting support in reselection battles, he probably would not have survived as an MP. So what kind of job did he have?

Colin Cooper of Dundee TGWU was at Michelin back in the early 1970s, but only got to know Galloway well a few years later. From the official records Cooper has confirmed that Galloway joined the union on 29 December 1973, while he was working at the tyre factory. By coincidence, Galloway's application was processed a week after his own. It took a couple of weeks for the applications to go through, so Galloway probably started the job in early December. Just how long he spent there is in question. According to Cooper, Galloway was only there for 'a matter of months' and worked in the 'P.N. Department', also known as Curing. Here they took a semi-finished tyre and put it in a large mould, which would pop out the finished article a few minutes later. Galloway recalls this as a seven-minute process, which left him time to read in bursts in between. Michelin (unlike the union) hasn't kept its records from back then, but another ex-colleague recalls Galloway's length of service being around seven weeks. Whether it was seven weeks, or a few months, or a year is neither here nor there, but it did allow the newly elected MP to describe his previous occupation in the 1988 *Who's Who* as 'engineering worker'.

No matter how long it was for, it was hard work and Cooper remembers that Galloway stuck out as 'a skinny laddie' in a man's job. He says this 'wasn't a job for a nineteen-year-old', but thinks that Galloway was probably attracted to it because the money was good and the shift patterns meant you had time to do other things in the day. A lot of the workers took advantage of this. 'Not many young lads in that place. It would usually be given to someone who was fully physically developed. It was also the smokiest and fumiest part of the factory, the least hospitable.' Although conditions in the Curing Department weren't as bad as in the jute mills, by today's standards there were a lot of fumes and it was backbreaking stuff, with a lot of bending and stooping, manhandling the tyres. 'It wasn't a job that they would normally give to a young laddie but they were pretty desperate for workers.' As to what qualifications Galloway needed, the answer was probably none. Cooper remembers that 'jobs were often handed out according to height and whether you were left or right handed'. Galloway may not have excelled at Harris, but he certainly knew his left from his right, and his far left from his far right.

Interestingly, Cooper met up with Galloway many years later at a football match at Celtic Park. Cooper had won tickets to the executive box with a couple of Dundee pals and when Galloway saw him, he came over from Celtic director Brian Dempsey's box for a chat. 'He had no airs or graces. He's the salt of the earth type of bloke,' says Cooper. Galloway stayed with the Dundee group and Cooper remembers that he slipped back into the local accent, out of his 'cultured accent . . . the one he got going at Labour Party rallies and when he was Labour Party secretary in his twenties'. Galloway is well known in Westminster and beyond for his rolled Rs, his indefatigable love of rhetoric and for getting carried away by his extravagant language. It perhaps isn't so well appreciated south of the border that he does not speak with the brogue of a true son of Dundee toil.

Cooper was clearly pleased and impressed to meet his old Michelin contemporary, the now famous George Galloway MP. It had been a long time and a lot of water had passed under the bridge for the celebrated politician. Back in the mid-1970s in small-town Dundee, however, Galloway was clearly finding it hard to make a mark. At one stage he took a job in the Dundee Council Parks Department. Andrew Child, who is land services manager and has worked in the department since 1973, doesn't remember Galloway, but puts that down to the high turnover in seasonal workers, who were just taken on for summer jobs. A later press report on the up-and-coming local politician noted that Galloway's summer parks employment was in 1975, so what would he have been doing? Child believes that any summer worker would have been given only fairly rudimentary digging and weeding, perhaps even on roadside verges and roundabouts, but there was a chance Galloway may have been assigned to some kind of routine office job. Galloway himself has not elaborated on this, but though the job was likely to have been hard work, there are worse ways to spend a summer at age twenty than outside doing healthy exercise.

It's easy to forget, because he had been involved in the grown-up business of politics for such a long time, that he was still very young at this stage: only just in his twenties. But Galloway had been involved in Labour Party rallies and business from way back in his teens, and it was a part of his life through school and college. He was still in that transitional period of coming out of education and entering the real world, but he never seemed motivated to make his real world the one that 99.9 per cent of the population inhabit.

That is to say, get a job, settle down, perhaps be somebody in your own small circle, but live a quiet life. Galloway almost from the off has always wanted to be in the big league and the biggest of the big leagues is politics.

He may have been scraping a living with a spade for the Parks Department, but the mid-1970s was to be a time of great excitement and political involvement for Galloway. He was about to start his rapid climb up the local Labour Party ladder at the time of one of the greatest scandals in Dundee's political history. The enemies he was about to make would dog him for years and have a tremendous impact on his development as a person and politician.

2

Dundee politics

George Galloway's rise in the Dundee Labour Party coincides with a tale of great corruption, but not one involving him in any way.

In the 1960s and 1970s James 'J. L.' Stewart, a Labour councillor, and other Dundee Labour insiders were accused of making small fortunes awarding contracts to building firms in which they had financial interests. Stewart went from being a clerk on £8 a week to a wealthy businessman, and at the same time climbed the greasy pole of Dundee Labour politics.

In the 1960s, as Dundee was clearing some of its 20,000 slums, Stewart was the leader of the council administration. The building firm Crudens hired him as a costing clerk and then the local authority contracts came their way. They were granted around £62m of council business thanks in great part to Stewart, who soon moved from a council house to a genteel Victorian villa. Meanwhile, vast areas of Dundee were scarred with concrete public monstrosities, many of which still stand today, headstones on bulldozed dignity.

Dundee became known as the Chicago of the north, run by the 'Townhouse Mafia', or 'Quality Street Gang', at whose centre were Stewart and fellow Labour friends Tom Moore, the Lord Provost (Lord Mayor), and businessman John Maxwell, who had each sheltered their get-rich capitalist views behind soft left-wing rhetoric. Despite complaints to the police, it wasn't until Ray Fitzwalter of ITV's *World in Action* was tipped off in 1974 that the truth started to come out. Fitzwalter, who later became the editor of *World in Action*, had exposed the corrupt architect John Poulson in a previous programme, which had created such a stink that the *Daily Mail* followed it up over three pages and printed a transcript of the show.

> I got a call from a Labour chap called Charlie Farquhar in Dundee, who said they had their own scandal. I went to Dundee and he introduced me to two

other local Labour men, Willie McKelvey and Jack Martin. They had no hard evidence, but I looked into it. I went back through eighteen years of council minutes, companies records and property sales records and proved it.

Fitzwalter was seemingly more expert in investigating this kind of white-collar crime than the local police, who had botched an investigation some years before. He found that it wasn't just the awarding of the building contracts that was dodgy. 'The council wasn't monitoring the construction properly either. Safeguards weren't there because their own companies were doing the work.' Corners were cut to make even more profit. Incredibly, there is even evidence that to make more money, contractors were reducing the size of buildings from the original plans. Fitzwalter discovered that 'in the Ardler part of the city there was a council residential tower block where the whole development had been made smaller to reduce costs and the lifts ended up too narrow to get a coffin in horizontally'. Bodies had to go down by the stairs, or vertically.

The corruption in local Labour politics had been a source of irritation for honest members for years, but many had turned a blind eye, convinced that the police would never do anything. What gave Willie McKelvey and a small group of colleagues the impetus to act was the deep political differences between the two camps. Council chair Stewart and his crowd were way over to the right, but in an era of high unemployment and growing social division they were more and more out of step with a hardening left-wing element.

Galloway had had nothing to do with contacting Fitzwalter, who confirms he'd never heard of Galloway at the time. It was McKelvey and Jack Martin who publicly took on the 'gangsters', whose web included so many of Dundee's public servants that Stewart and Moore had thrown a drunken party in a council office to celebrate the collapse of the previous police investigation. It's not easy to imagine how much guts that took, but McKelvey recalls now that 'the police paid me a visit over J.L. and accused me of not trusting them. I said, "That's right, I don't," because I had a picture of one of them at the party. They claimed they were there as part of their investigation.'

When *World in Action* asked them to be interviewed for the programme, McKelvey and Martin were so afraid to go public that they insisted on being filmed together, to show their solidarity and give each other strength. Once the programme had aired, they were disappointed, after all the risks they had taken, to find that Stewart, Moore and their buddies clung onto office. 'We couldn't force J.L. out of the party. After the investigation was launched his majority went up.'

It would be over two years before Stewart, Moore and Maxwell were arrested and charged in 1977, to be finally convicted on 9 March 1980. They were each given five years for taking bribes, though Moore and Maxwell were freed on appeal that June because the trial judge had misdirected the jury.

Meanwhile, as the long police investigation and trial progressed, Galloway was moving up the ladder, with McKelvey as his mentor. On the day of Stewart's conviction it was Galloway, by then running Dundee Labour Party, who announced to the press: 'We are glad it is over . . . We can't tolerate this sort of conduct. Over the years these men have cost the Labour Party dearly.' It was Galloway who made political capital out of it all and it was Galloway that Stewart would grow to hate. The fall-out from putting Stewart behind bars would permeate Dundee politics for years, leaving cancers that ate away at the people involved. As in so much of Scottish local politics, infighting was to characterise the political culture from then on in Dundee.

Even before the overthrow of Stewart's regime, Galloway's card had been marked by the men in control. Jim Duncan, a politically moderate and respected former Dundee Labour councillor, remembers his first meeting with him well, despite a distance of over thirty years and the fact that he is now in his late seventies. He recounted the occasion:

> I first met George when I was a political education officer and he came to a talk I was giving in the mid-70s. It was in Kirton Ward 7, as I remember; he was a young lad. I was talking about Labour, Liberals and Conservatives and their policies. He said he was a Labour member and when he got talking it became apparent that he had very left-wing views. I told him he was in the wrong party.

Galloway regarded Duncan and the other moderate Labour councillors in 1970s Dundee 'with hostility', according to Duncan. 'We'd voted for council rents to go up, along with national Labour party policy, and they hated that.' Dundee had a higher percentage of social housing than Warsaw at the time, and of its 70,000 households more than 40,000 were council homes. To add insult to injury, it was the Tories' Housing Finance Act that the Labour Party were obeying. Galloway, McKelvey and the others on the left of the party had wanted to take a stand on rents, and were fed up with councillors following a different line.

Frustrated by the old guard's policies, McKelvey gathered around him a group of young socialists that included the twenty-year-old Galloway. If they couldn't force out Stewart and his right-wingers using the media, they were going to work to make changes from inside the party. They had to get their men selected to stand in the local council elections of 1977, by forcing the sitting councillors off the Labour ticket.

Through 1975, in a room at the Dundee YMCA in Constitution Road, this small group met each week, booking itself under the name North East Debating Society, or NEDS. Galloway and his mates claim they saw the joke in calling themselves 'NEDS', which is a Scottish term of abuse, a bit like calling someone a chav. In it were Tom McDonald, who would later become the city's Lord Provost; Colin Rennie, Galloway's confidant and witness at his first wedding; James Gowans, McKelvey's best man and also later Lord Provost; Ian Leggatt; Jack Martin; and Galloway.

Working in their favour was the fact that the old guard were used to being selected without much bother, so they weren't prepared for a fight. The NEDS, on the other hand, were determined and well organised by McKelvey:

> You knew where people needed more votes. We could give people a Labour membership card and get them to come in on the night. There'd be a joke that the place would smell of fresh cardboard. They'd come in and not know when to vote. They'd just walk in and put up their hands, but we'd tell them they had to wait. We'd get them from the estates, get aunts and uncles, family to come and join. Of course if it was being done to you, you'd have complained. And now they have changed the rules.

The idea is straightforward enough. You bring in large numbers of supporters to pack meetings and vote your men in. The local unions co-operated in this and sent delegates along to vote against the right-wingers. Not only that, the Communist Party was involved too, as journalist Graham Ogilvy, a Communist Party member in Dundee at the time, recalls:

> I was at a meeting of the Communist Party where it was decided whether or not to support this and they did decide to support it. So that gave Galloway and his colleagues the muscle to get rid of a whole raft of old Labour people who were right wing and tainted by cronyism and corruption.

McKelvey would later spend twenty years as a backbench MP, most of it in opposition, but back in the 1970s he had real influence. He was a union convenor in the NCR factory, a powerful base in the Amalgamated Union of Engineering Workers (AUEW). The shop stewards committee was dominated by communists and, even though he wasn't one, McKelvey was respected and supported. He managed to get shop stewards from all over Dundee involved, whereas before they hadn't been interested in local council politics and had concentrated on exerting their power through industrial action.

So, in early 1976, the NEDS moved against their enemies in the party and had seven moderate councillors removed from the list of candidates for the forthcoming elections. They included Ian Faulkner, Agnes Bell, Ian Borthwick and George Beattie, all to the right of the NEDS. Duncan, who'd told Galloway that he was in the wrong party, lost his Labour nomination too. 'I was unseated at a local ward committee meeting that was packed with Galloway's supporters from Kirton Labour Ward 7. They had a no-confidence vote in me and then deselected me.' Duncan wasn't just another Labour councillor; he'd been chairman of the local party in the early 1960s, and was a long-standing union man with the Union of Shop, Distributive and Allied Workers and convenor of the Planning Committee. He wrote to the Labour leader, Harold Wilson, to complain, but got nowhere. He then took his case to the Scottish National Executive Committee (NEC), who didn't help either. There was little he or the others could do. Under Labour Party rules there was no appeal against deselection. If the local party wanted you out, you were out.

The NEDS was pursuing entirely legitimate aims as its members saw it, and Galloway wanted to put the organisation on a more formal footing. He wanted minutes to be taken, which McKelvey and others disagreed with because they didn't want to be seen as a party within the party.

> I said no, but they went ahead anyway and then one of the other side, councillor Ian Borthwick, saw these minutes lying around on the desk. He then took the story to the *Sunday Post*, who put it on the front page. I told them to burn the minutes and they came back with a tiny pile of ash, which obviously wasn't enough. They would have had enough to fill a grate!

Throughout Labour's history it has been infiltrated by other parties, to such an extent that for many years there was a proscribed list of organisations. (Infiltration culminated with Militant, or Tony Blair, depending on your point of view.) Mindful of this legacy of parties within the party, Borthwick didn't just go to the papers with his conspiracy story; in October of 1976 he sent a confidential memo to Labour's Scottish NEC explaining that the NEDS had been 'established for the purpose of ensuring that certain policies would predominate and that officers of the party in sympathy with these policies would be promoted for office'. They wrote back and told him there was nothing they could do, so he resigned from the party in disgust. Some years later he stood as an independent and won his seat back.

Though the discovery of the minutes hadn't been a great problem for the NEDS, now that they were out in the open the reasons for being NEDS disappeared, and they evolved into a larger group of those on the left called, unimaginatively, the Left Group. This is where Galloway started to make more of a mark. With McKelvey he had been a key influence in the policy of building relationships with communist union leaders. John Brown, the leader of the locally very powerful AUEW, together with the communist Harry McLevy, decided to support Galloway and McKelvey's plans to take control. They organised union delegates to turn up at Labour meetings that they had previously thought small and irrelevant.

Mervyn Rolfe, former communist and ex-mayor of Dundee, has commented: 'Labour and Communist Party members would sit round the same table, there were very few boundaries. Historical enmity did exist but I think

27

this was the honeymoon period for the left. People like Harry McLevy built strong links between the two groups.'

McLevy was a key player in all this. He was the Scottish organiser of the Amalgamated Engineering and Electrical Union and worked in Dundee's Caledon shipyard. Galloway later wrote in his obituary for McLevy in the *Guardian* in January 1996 that he had signed him up to the Labour Party. 'Although he left the Communist Party in the early eighties and I myself signed him on in the Labour Party, McLevy was a lifelong communist, of a particularly Scottish type – sufficiently broad church . . .' Galloway's tribute to McLevy recounts his ability to 'find stirring words which moved thousands of workers into strikes, days of action, demonstrations, even on issues like Chile or the presence of unwelcome political visitors'. However, the more cautious McKelvey, Galloway's more senior mentor, was crucial in the cementing of this relationship between communists and Labour left.

The pressure building up from the Left Group was having the desired effect on the moderate Labour members. Many had become disillusioned in Scotland in the mid-1970s. So in some ways Galloway was pushing at an opening door. Alec Neil, who was Labour's Scottish research officer and drew up the party manifesto on Scotland in 1974, defected to the breakaway Scottish Labour and recalls that 'the big divisions were over devolution and North Sea oil. In July 1974 the Labour Party Executive in Scotland voted 6-5 against a Scottish Assembly, which created merry hell.'

Against this national background, Galloway was advancing in local politics. It wasn't being made easy for him, though. The moderates in the party had their eye on him, according to McKelvey:

> They saw the danger in George. They had an organisation too, but we had the unions. I saw George at a Labour meeting one day and he wanted to get on the list of possible councillor candidates. I nominated him to be selected to be on this list of potential councillors. Some complained that he was too young and it was voted out. I saw him on the stairs after and he was gutted. I told him not to worry and he'd get on soon enough.

Nevertheless, he became the secretary of Dundee West, then moved up a rung to Dundee City Labour Party, which oversaw both East and West constituencies, where he became assistant secretary. McKelvey began to pay him a small allowance for his work. He seemed destined to go far, but the enemies he'd made in the deselection process were still in their positions as councillors until the election. They were planning to get a little revenge on the 'young upstart'.

Growing success was not bringing great financial rewards his way and colleagues remember that Galloway never seemed to have any cash. Unlike the dapper figure he cuts now, friends of the time remember him looking scruffy, like a student.[1] He would refer to himself as 'impecunious' and didn't even have anywhere proper to live. He was so reliant on the Labour Party that he had to use a bedsit in their offices at 1 Rattray Street, in the centre of Dundee. He wanted to find a decent council flat, but there was a long waiting list in a city of more than 6,000 official slums. It was surprising to some, therefore, that this unmarried 21-year-old should be allocated a three-room flat. It would prove to be a millstone around his neck.

The first couple of times Galloway had applied for somewhere to live he'd been told he was too young, but it was reported that he persisted and went back to the Housing Department for a third time.[2] On this occasion a Labour colleague put in a good word for him too. That was in July 1976 but again he was refused, because the rules were that no single man under twenty-five qualified. A month later it was reported that Galloway's colleague went back and asked for advice, direct to the department, explaining that Galloway was now cohabiting with his girlfriend, Elaine Fyffe. Under the council guidelines there was no distinction made between a married couple and an unmarried one, so Galloway had to fill in a form and be patient. His patience can't have been tried too greatly, for a few weeks later he was allocated a place in a popular modern tower block called Bucklemaker Court, in Hilton.

Some claim that it is unremarkable that he was allocated one so quickly, as there were hundreds of flats in newly built council schemes, whereas others disagree and claim that 1960s tower block flats were in high demand with so much bad council housing still in use. There is no doubt that there was a long housing waiting list that usually took years to work your way up. In the late 1970s around 13,000 were waiting for a transfer into better housing, with 2,000 registered young couples staying with their in-laws while they waited for a place.

However, instead of simple satisfaction at this result and a quiet move in, there was a photo shoot in the flat for Scotland's *Sunday Mail*, to promote Galloway for the forthcoming local council elections. It was a typical act of self-promotion that was hoped to be a great advert for the young face of Labour politics. It ended up being a PR disaster and a humiliating failure.

The picture paints a thousand words. The unmarried couple are sitting next to each other: George in a casual sweater looks relaxed but determined, but Elaine looks like she's just sucked on a very sour lemon. It may just be a bad picture, but she appears so unhappy to be photographed that one wonders what was said immediately afterwards. If her instinct had been that this was a bad idea, she would have been right, because it stirred up outrage from the good burghers of old Dundee.

Local folk stuck in their insanitary slums after the hottest summer for decades claimed they smelled a rat. They asked how Galloway and Fyffe had been given such a comparatively luxurious pad so quickly, according to Jim Duncan. 'Constituents came to me and complained about Galloway. They were on the waiting list, wanting to be rehoused and he was suddenly in a nice flat, in his early twenties and not married. Their reaction was that we were all corrupt in the council.' Although he had been kicked off the list of candidates for the next election, Duncan was still the planning committee convenor and he complained to the director of housing, saying that he was not satisfied with the answers he'd got about the allocation. In reply, it was stressed that no one abused their position, or exerted any pressure, while Galloway's friends rallied round and Willie McKelvey tried to play down the seriousness of the issue by claiming the row was just politically motivated. Galloway's opponents jumped on the bandwagon and J. L. Stewart called for him to be evicted.

There is no suggestion that Galloway personally intervened or put pressure on anyone or acted improperly in any way, but very quickly the row took off. Though the council rules treated unmarried couples the same as married ones, the town's moral guardians did not. There was outcry that two people 'living in sin' could be allocated a spacious council flat ahead of other more 'righteous' folk. Under extreme pressure, Galloway and Fyffe very quickly announced that they were 'to be married within the month'. This amused his political colleagues (Graham Ogilvy, Jack Martin and others), who claim that they had often heard him denounce marriage and religion as part of his Marxist philosophy.

Then, in a final twist, Galloway turned round and said he didn't want the flat after all. Perhaps he was embarrassed to have been so fortunate, or felt others were more needy, or maybe he'd decided that it was an election loser, or perhaps Fyffe and their families were so upset by the publicity that he thought it wasn't worth the hassle to keep the place. Anyway, he'd backed out of it, but the damage had been done and the tale of the Marxist, his girlfriend and their nice council flat was used by his opponents to undermine him in the local elections the following May.

At the outset these elections looked like a shoo-in for Galloway. Supported by McKelvey and backed by powerful union figures, he had been selected to fight in the safest seat in the city. Gillburn ward had a huge Labour majority of 800. Galloway must have thought he couldn't lose, but he was about to reap the rewards of making enemies of Stewart and the moderate Labour men and of alienating the rather old-fashioned, moral majority. On this occasion he wasn't just being paranoid; everyone really was out to get him. The ousted Duncan remembers: 'It was a united front, you can put it like that. The SNP, Conservatives, we moderates, everyone was involved.'

Clearly, in a ward with such a large majority it was going to be a tough job to boot out a Labour candidate, but in a stroke of genius his opponents found the perfect person to take him on. Miss Elizabeth 'Bunty' Turley of Kirkton was in her mid-sixties and had been an active trade unionist for some forty years. Though she wasn't a Labour Party member at the time, she had been until she'd retired. Spinster Bunty was a prim, grey-haired, slender old lady, who stood around 5 feet 4 inches and is remembered as 'knowing her mind' by Duncan. She was a regular at St Columba's Roman Catholic Church and was a well-known local character, respected and liked. Those last two points are key, for she was going to campaign against Galloway on a 'moral ticket' and as a woman in touch with the ordinary voter.

In April, Turley announced she would stand as an independent and told the local press:

I object strongly to the fact that a few left-wing people in this ward threw out Jimmy Duncan, who has given good service to this area. As far as I can see they had no good reason other than to further the ambitions of a Marxist group. The candidate they have chosen has proclaimed ideas and ideals contrary to those of the majority of the people of the ward. By standing I hope to give them the opportunity to vote for a candidate who owes allegiance to the people of the ward.[3]

Not only were the local political figures all campaigning against Galloway, members of Dundee's Catholic clergy were working behind the scenes to undermine him. Spurred on by the religious Turley, Galloway was denounced from the local pulpit on the Sunday before the election. The Irish priest Basil O'Sullivan (now Canon O'Sullivan) described Galloway as 'living in sin' and 'lying down like the beasts of the field'. This sensational news copy ran in the local papers and rekindled all the bad publicity over the council flat allocation.

In the election campaign itself, Galloway was tireless on the stump, leafleting and door-knocking, backed up by well-known union figures and prominent Labour activists. But it was hard to get his message of no cuts and no rent rises over to people who seemed to have written him off already. When the results came in, it was utterly devastating news and a nightmare for Galloway. He had turned a majority of 800 into a loss of 79 votes. Turley polled 508 votes, Galloway 429, and the Conservatives' John Clinton just 50. The man who had claimed to anyone in earshot that he wanted to be Foreign Secretary couldn't even win a local council election in Labour's safest seat, against a retired old lady who had stood as an independent.

Despite all the efforts of the powerful Labour machine, plus McKelvey and the other union boys, Galloway had failed. People in the town were reminded of the wonderful Ealing comedy *The Ladykillers*, where a little grey-haired old dear, against all the odds, foils a bunch of ugly hard men in ill-advised suits.

The impact of this defeat on Galloway is perplexing. Instead of learning from it, it seems only to have made him more resolute. Having been undone by the enemies he'd made in the conspiracy, he didn't decide to take a more conciliatory approach to politics; it only made him more determined. And though the trouble had started from his impetuous decision to be photographed in the flat, he has spent many of his subsequent years saying and doing things in the heat of the moment, only to have to devote time and effort fighting fires as a consequence. Equally important, he has often been outplayed by elements of his own party, who time and again in his career have been the opposition he has spent most energy fighting.

Another possible consequence of his defeat by Bunty Turley was a realisation that he didn't need to get votes to be in power. There is evidence from his behaviour in the following years to suggest that perhaps Galloway lost his faith in what most would think of as democracy. He told Clive Anderson in a BBC Five Live interview of December 2005:

> Within a few months I became the full-time organiser in Dundee and I didn't need to be a member of the council to be influential in what the council did. At that time the party and the council worked very closely together and I was the key person in the party.

In fact, it would be two years until he took over in Dundee, but he is right in saying that he didn't need to be elected to the council. When he took over the reins as full-time Dundee Labour Party secretary organiser, it looked as if he was determined to take control from the centre. Galloway would never fight an election in his hometown again.

3

Party organiser

In the months following Galloway's 1977 election disaster, Dundee Labour expended a lot of energy fighting itself, rather than the Tories. The moderates blamed the Left Group for scaring the voters away. Willie McKelvey and George Galloway's followers remained convinced that they needed to build up a more left-wing alternative, getting the unions even closer and with an eye on the growing Scottish National Party, who were making the most of Labour's perceived wavering over devolution and North Sea oil revenue.

Although Galloway had helped to put in place some councillors sympathetic to the Left Group's views, Dundee Labour was still divided between those in elected positions and those, like him, who were organisers with no authority to vote in the council chambers. McKelvey and Galloway wanted the councillors to vote as they were told. Jim Duncan remembers that in his day 'party activists like Galloway weren't even allowed to talk in meetings. They had to sit at the back and shut up.'

After he failed to get elected, it became even more important to Galloway to take power away from Labour's councillors. The Left Group came down hard on the dissenters and forced more of them out, with Galloway attacking them in the local press:

> The moderates were democratically removed from the panel of candidates, but they have shown themselves to be completely unwilling to accept the democratic decision of the Labour Party, and they used every section of the media to discredit the party right up to the election . . . The moderates don't have the stamina for a comeback.[1]

You have to remind yourself that he is referring to his own party.

The Tories were onto him too and tried to discredit him by complaining about one of the few jobs he's had outside of politics. From 1976 into 1977, Galloway worked as a researcher in the Tayside Area Council for Alcoholism. It must have suited him, as he was never a big drinker and has been teetotal for years. Friends say that he would merely have a beer, or a glass of wine, in marked contrast to many in an area that had an entrenched drinking culture in the 1970s (and still does to an extent). So when it was known that he was working in an organisation to help fight alcoholism and to understand more about the problem, it must have seemed fitting. However, the local Tory leader, Jack Watson, complained that it was inappropriate for someone so politically active to be in a job where he might have access to files of businessmen with a drink problem. It was a strange suggestion, given that it was unlikely that Galloway could make capital out of something that was widely regarded as a badge of honour, even if he'd had access to files. If that was the best the Tories could do, then they were probably right to give up and just let his opponents in the Labour Party do their work for them.

And Labour was still in turmoil, with other resignations coming thick and fast. Janey Buchan, a former Communist Party member and a prospective parliamentary candidate for Dundee East, stepped down, criticising the Left Group and Galloway personally. Janey, wife of Norman Buchan, the West Renfrewshire MP, would become a bitter opponent of Galloway during his time as an MP in Glasgow, along with her husband.

Bad luck struck the so-called moderates too, as Terry Fagan, prospective parliamentary candidate for Dundee West, was caught committing a lewd act in a public toilet and had to stand down. Despite being considered a 'moderate', Terry was a communist union official for the railwaymen. His son, Ken, was one of Galloway's close circle and would later become the city treasurer, an influential position in the city. Ken Fagan is one of a small group of Labour men who have long associations with Galloway. It includes Dundee councillor Colin Rennie, local MP Frank Doran and to an extent the former MPs Ernie Ross and McKelvey.

As Dundee Labour Party fought itself, the hung council's policies continued to hit the poor of the city hard. Rents kept on going up and with the economy in crisis, unemployment blighted the city. Throughout the

1970s and 1980s there was a hothouse atmosphere in Dundee which is remembered as verging on revolutionary at times. Strikes and mass rallies of 25,000 to 30,000 were not unusual, and from the top of the local hill, 'The Law', one could watch as three columns of strikers approached from the east, the west and the shipyards, to meet up in the city square. These highly charged events would be addressed by communist union leaders, such as Harry McLevy, Jimmy Reid and Mick McGahey. It was at these meetings that Galloway would watch and learn the craft of speech making from the masters.

It was an environment that attracted extremist views and idealistic visions of workers uniting throughout the land. In 1978, as part of protests at 11 per cent unemployment in Dundee, 300 shop stewards from all the local unions met to decide on action. The hard left, through their paper *Militant*, called on the shop stewards to take the news back to their members and 'mobilise a full turn-out' for a day of action. It sent out a rallying call: 'The demonstration on March 15th could be a historic turning point in the struggle of the Dundee labour movement, and a shining example to workers in every other part of Britain!'[2]

As part of this campaign to bring life to their dying city, one of the workers had drawn up a plan to create jobs for everyone in Dundee. A scheme was proposed for a new harbour, a ferry dock and rebuilt shipyard to replace the antiquated Robb Caledon, together with a brand new railway station. With the Winter of Discontent and Thatcherism just around the corner, it was an ambitious plan doomed never to get off the ground.

Dundee was also an environment that fed off the politics of confrontation and local feuding. However, Galloway was about to discover that there is more to politics than the harsh surroundings of cold, depressed Dundee. He was planning a trip to sunnier climes. Lebanon, though, was no-one's idea of a holiday destination at the time.

His first visit to the Middle East has to be seen as a turning point in his life and career. It showed him the misery and injustice suffered by the Palestinians, but perhaps it also showed him how he could lift himself out of a parochial backwater, onto an international stage. He recalled in December 2005 how the Middle East situation has propelled his career:

I'd be wheeled on at the tender age of twenty-one, twenty-two to television programmes to talk as if I was an expert about this issue because so few were ready to stand with the Palestinians and from that grew a wider involvement in the Arab world and the broader Muslim world.[3]

To understand how a local Dundee political activist found himself in the crucible of the Arab–Israeli conflict you have to go back a few years from 1978. While Galloway had built strong links with the working-class unions at NCR and the shipyards, his contacts at the more middle-class Dundee University Students Union would be key to his future. Though he was never a student at the university, he'd hang around there, playing snooker in the National Union of Students bar, chatting about politics and making friends with the students. Crucially, he made friends with some young men from the Middle East, Palestinians and Iraqis. The Iraqis had been sent to the UK by their parents to escape the growing pressure on the Iraqi opposition generally, unionists particularly and communists especially.

Since the 1960s Iraq's Ba'athists had taken the economy into state control and suppressed the trade union movement. In the mid-1970s, when Saddam Hussein was Vice-President and in charge of state security, there was still an element of opposition left, but they could see the writing on the wall. The strong historical links to the UK meant that some sent their children to be educated here. In Dundee a small group were befriended by Graham Ogilvy, who was then doing a PhD in politics. Ogilvy, spurred on by the Arabs, helped form the Dundee University Friends of Palestine Society, which he chaired. The aim of the society was to bring publicity to the cause of the Palestinians, who were continually portrayed as the aggressors in the 1970s press. High-profile PLO hijackings, the murder of Israeli athletes in 1972 and the feared Black September group had all received blanket coverage, as was intended. The trouble was that hardly anyone was reporting on the routine persecution of the Palestinians and their life in the refugee camps.

One of the leading members of the university society was Sa'ad Jabaji, a middle-class Palestinian student from a family in the construction business. Together with Ogilvy and two or three Iraqi students, they made contact with the Glasgow office of the British Anti-Zionist Organisation, which was run by a highly committed Maoist called George Mitchell. Mitchell was tireless in his devotion to the Palestinian cause and was organising a fact finding trip to Beirut, which he invited the Dundee students to take part in. Ironically, despite the fact that the Iraqi lads were sons of communists and no friends of the regime in their country, the funding came from the government of Iraq, which hadn't yet been taken over by Saddam. (Saddam, as head of security, was steadily removing his opponents by having them investigated, tortured and executed, as Stalin had in the Soviet Union.)

At a committee meeting to plan the trip, Ogilvy and Jabaji discussed who they should ask along. They were looking for people with media and political contacts who would promote the cause on their return. Ogilvy suggested Galloway, whom he knew from local politics, and Jabaji agreed that he would go to the local Labour Party office to talk to him. Jabaji and Galloway had never met, so when he knocked on the door of the Labour headquarters at 1 Rattray Street he didn't know who Galloway was and they had to introduce themselves.

Galloway describes the meeting in reverential terms, as if the event was 'meant to be' in some kind of mystical sense.[4] He gives the impression when he tells the story that this was the key moment in the story of George Galloway the international statesman, champion of the Middle Eastern underdog, prophet of Blair's undoing in Iraq. He recounts how he was all by himself in the office. It was as if Jesus had been alone in the wilderness; so was Galloway alone in Rattray Street, Dundee. Then there appeared a beautiful vision of a man, who transfixed him with tales from another world.[5]

'I was alone in the Labour Party office and would normally not have answered the door . . . but I did for some reason that day and there was a very handsome young man, who looked like Omar Sharif to me' – he seems to have cast the drama-documentary re-enactment already in his own mind – 'and he spent the best part of two hours mesmerisingly describing the situation of the Palestinian people.'

There can be little doubt that this was a key event in Galloway's life, and through hundreds of retellings true events can start sounding as though they are being read from a book, but one strange aspect of the tale is Galloway's complete refusal to admit that someone else may have had something to do with it. The mythology has to be that this was directed by some unseen hand of fate, with no human involvement. The fact that it appears to be the consequence of a previous suggestion by Ogilvy he seems to detest and immediately goes on the attack at the mention of his name.

Clive Anderson got this reaction when he asked Galloway the following: 'Now I think it was your friend of the time Graham Ogilvy, was it him who suggested that you go to Beirut and have a look at the Arab world?'

> *Galloway:* No. And he has never been a friend of mine, and I say that because I know that you are obviously going to include him now attacking me. He was never a friend of mine, he has never been a friend of mine, but he's made a handy living pretending that he was once a friend of mine, as he's no doubt enjoying the cheque you've sent him for the interview he's given you.
>
> *Anderson:* Ha ha . . . I doubt there's a huge amount of money to be made out of interviews on Five Live—
>
> *Galloway:* He'll do it for any money . . . He's done it for less than you can pay him . . . But he's a professional pretender that he was once a friend of mine. He has never been a friend of mine. Nor have I ever acted on any advice he's ever given me.
>
> *Anderson:* Ha ha ha . . . you didn't go to Beirut with him?
>
> *Galloway:* I didn't . . . he was on the trip to Beirut that I went on, but he was not the person who suggested it, no. The person who suggested it is sadly now deceased, Dr George Mitchell, who was the leader of the pro-Palestinian movement in Scotland at that time.
>
> *Anderson:* Well, it's not an issue that I feel we have to take a decision on in this programme.[6]

For the record Ogilvy received no money for the interview, though interviewees often do get paid by production companies for this type of appearance. He didn't ask for any money and was pleased to tell what he remembered as the truth about his one-time friend and political comrade. Ogilvy was also interviewed for this book for no fee.

This incident helps to illuminate Galloway's character. Ogilvy and Galloway fell out spectacularly a few years later over Galloway's style of running the Labour Party. Since then, Ogilvy has been an occasional thorn in Galloway's side, as many journalists have been. He now runs a successful news agency in Dundee. Ogilvy is even-handed about his ex-colleague's record, though, and agrees that 'he's done a lot of good for the Palestinian cause'. Ogilvy doesn't want to edit history so as to erase political enemies from his past life.

Back in the late 1970s, the pair ended up working closely in Labour's Left Group and Galloway also had a hand in getting Ogilvy a job as a political researcher for the local council. In 1977 they were both very excited to be off for a week or so to Lebanon. They travelled down to London on the train and it was a bit of an adventure for everyone, as Ogilvy remembers:

> We weren't globetrotters in those days and it was quite an experience. They had an intensive programme for us. We went round all the refugee camps. There'd been pretty horrendous things happen to the Palestinians. Tel Al Zaatar, a famous massacre, had just happened previously. We met the survivors, many of them orphans. This had been a massacre that had happened while the West turned its back . . . it was pretty obvious that the Palestinians were being victimised and neglected. And I think that Galloway took it in and thought it was an injustice, as it is an injustice.

Another key event for Galloway on the trip to Beirut was meeting the journalist Ron McKay. McKay is now Galloway's spokesman and co-ordinates some of his media work. They have been very close for years, 'joined at the hip' as McKay puts it, but he is careful to point out that he doesn't get paid a wage for his work, and is employed on a job-by-job basis. It's not certain just how much McKay is paid by Galloway and what exactly the financial arrangements are between them not that there is any reason why they should be disclosed. The only way that would ever be open to scrutiny would be if McKay was taken on full time as the MP's press officer; then his salary would have to be declared.

McKay didn't go to Beirut with the British party; he was a freelancing journalist and had been assigned the job of covering the trip for the *Sunday Times*. He struck up a rapport with Galloway when they discovered they were both Scottish. 'I guess we both have the same scabrous sense of humour,' McKay says now.[7] Whatever the *Sunday Times* wanted to get from the story, it was the beginning of a strong friendship, which has seen McKay running two newspapers for Galloway over the years. They share the use of Galloway's constituency flat in London and have been on many trips together. McKay was with Galloway when he found Mariam Hamza in a Baghdad hospital, the little girl who became the centre of the Mariam Appeal (see Chapter 17).

The Beirut visit of summer 1977 didn't get off to a great start. When the party arrived at the airport there was a problem with their visas and more money had to be paid, but after that everything ran more smoothly and a lot was accomplished. They met significant figures in the PLO, including Abu Zayyad of the nationalist movement Fatah, as well as leaders and spokesmen of the Democratic Front, the Arab Front, the Syrian-backed Sa'ica and most of the many factions in the PLO, including the communist Popular Front for the Liberation of Palestine (PFLP). The PFLP pioneered aircraft hijackings, with funding from China and the Soviet Union, including the Air France Paris-to-Athens flight that was taken to Entebbe in 1976. To meet with these people less than a year afterwards was heady stuff for the young twenty-somethings.

Richard Burden, now an MP and chair of the Labour Palestine Group, but back then a student, was on the trip too. 'It was the first time I'd been anywhere like it. I'll never forget as we flew in there was a burnt-out tank at one end of the runway. It hits you then.'

Galloway and McKay both witnessed the hardship suffered by the home-less Palestinians. Everyone was impressed with the way that families kept their children clean and fed with little running water, and educated well enough to speak English to their foreign visitors. They were shown around 'Fatahland', a buffer zone in southern Lebanon between the fighting factions, where they saw some tit-for-tat shelling. Ogilvy recalls that 'Fatah ran the PLO at that stage. They controlled some of the old Crusader castles.' Castles or not, it was a dangerous trip and the group of twenty-five or so visitors were guarded at times by young PLO men carrying AK47s. They got on very well with their armed escort and at one stage Galloway suggested they had a picture taken with them. Given the circumstances, the results make interesting viewing. The two guards look a little bemused, presumably not used to British political activists wanting to be pictured next to PLO gunmen just a few years after the Munich massacre. Galloway, though, is

Dundee's George Galloway . . . flanked by Yasser Arafat's military.

PLO PAID FOR MY TRIPS SAYS LABOUR BOSS

Sunday Mail 5/4/8

smiling as if he could be on the Costa del Sol, about to order paella and a round of drinks for everyone. When the picture surfaced in the press a few years later he was certainly left with a little egg on his face. It was another example of how he often seems to present PR coups to his opponents.

The picture was taken in Fatahland, by the bus. Ogilvy recalls that Galloway had asked him to get in shot too, but he'd refused.

> I was a very serious young fella back then, very committed to the cause. I thought this would have been a maverick thing to do, a breach of party discipline, and a gift for anyone who wanted to discredit what we were doing.

When someone remarked to the taller of the two Palestinians that he spoke very good English, he told them he'd gone to Brighton Polytechnic and wanted to become an airline pilot. Given the PFLP's penchant for hijacking airliners, that innocent remark got a wry smile from some.

The trip was a great success and was a confirmation for Galloway of what he thought about the Middle East. When it came to leave Lebanon and return to the UK, Galloway decided to stay on: just how long he spent in Lebanon is not certain, but he has referred in interviews to spending three months there at one stage. More importantly, he has since made dozens of trips and a reputation and name out of his visits to the region. If meeting the attractive Arab in the Labour offices turned his head and lured him into a Middle Eastern love affair, then that first journey was its consummation.

4

A democratic centralist?

'Control freak' or 'control freakery' are overused terms in modern politics, ones so associated with New Labour that you could be forgiven for thinking that Tony Blair invented the concept. But the idea that elected party members are expected to do what they are told by the party leaders is a lot older and goes back at least to Lenin. The Soviets called it democratic centralism, where the 'democratic' part meant that policy came from open discussion of issues, and the 'centralism' part meant that once a central body had decided on the way forward, everyone else had to obey. The difficulty was always keeping the democratic bit going, particularly when you had general secretaries such as Stalin, who encouraged a cult of the individual. The pathological smiler Tony Blair has been accused of the same failing, though no-one would ever be silly enough to compare him to the pathologically grim Stalin.

George Galloway, on the other hand, has often been unfairly described as Stalinist by his enemies. That of course is not to suggest he operates by having his competitors bumped off or sent to the gulag. He may send you to Coventry, or accuse you of being a 'drink-sodden Trotskyist' in the case of Christopher Hitchens, and he does wear a moustache, but that is as far as it goes.

Galloway, it is clear, was very aware of the importance of gaining control from the centre. Back in 1977, when one group of people lined the streets to cheer the Queen in her Silver Jubilee year and another group wore mohican hair, put pins through their noses and sang 'Anarchy in the UK', George Galloway appeared to be on the road to helping bring democratic centralism to Dundee. All he needed was to get into the top job in the local party. He was certainly the anointed one as far as the Left Group was concerned, and luckily Willie McKelvey had been selected to stand for Parliament in

Kilmarnock. When he had to stand down as full-time secretary/organiser this was Galloway's chance.

There was a minor formality to go through first. Under Labour Party rules, the job had to be advertised and any assistant organisers that applied had to be interviewed. They only had one applicant, a young Glaswegian called Ian McCartney, who came all the way up from his day job in Dover. It was a long journey to get to the interview with Dundee's party executive, for which McCartney seemed to have done a lot of preparation. Unfortunately, he didn't get a single vote and the job passed in due course to Galloway. McCartney became the MP for Makerfield in 1987 and for years was at the centre of the Blair New Labour regime. One of Dundee's Executive Committee of the time, who prefers to remain nameless, recalls: 'Our group decided it. It was an important position and we weren't going to let an outsider have it.'

So Galloway could be seen as 'inheriting' the top job in Dundee Labour from his mentor, the man who had championed him and would stay close to him throughout both their parliamentary careers. As secretary/organiser Galloway would help co-ordinate the general election in Dundee and later plan the campaign for the forthcoming 1980 local elections.

Galloway was severe on councillors' dissent from party policy. James Martin, one of Galloway's inner circle in the late 1970s and early 1980s, recalls that there was little flexibility if you wanted to get on in Dundee Labour. 'Liaison officers conveyed what was decided from the party to the Labour group. It was made clear that if they didn't do what they were told there would be consequences at reselection time.' It is hard perhaps not to speculate as to whether Galloway's failure to be elected as a councillor may well have focused his determination to take their power away from them.

The social and political divisions in the country as a whole were mirrored in Labour and in Dundee's small corner of the party. Galloway, McKelvey and the other NEDS, who were now the core of the Left Group within the Dundee party, had wanted to control their wayward moderate councillors for some years and, like Blair's project to take over the party years later, there was some sense in trying to get a unified approach to policy. The question was where to draw the line on dissent. How much leeway should they give their elected comrades to pursue their own views and their electors' views? It was a question of judgement.

Galloway and McKelvey's Left Group still had moderate opponents to attend to, many of whom were still determined not to let the group take over completely. To force them out other recruits were needed. The local unions and elements of the Communist Party were under the umbrella, but there was another group of left-wingers that might come over with persuasion: Scottish Labour. The breakaway Scottish Labour Party had been formed by Labour MP Jim Sillars in 1976 when he and others in Labour had become frustrated at the slow progress towards a Scottish Assembly. As well as campaigning for home rule, they were to the left of the Labour establishment and this made them drawn to Galloway when the rebels' experiment started to fall apart.

John McAllion, who would later become Labour MP for Dundee East, was a teacher in the city and a member of Sillars's Scottish Labour.

> George Galloway recruited me to the Labour Party from Scottish Labour in 1977. The SLP was disintegrating and when George turned up with Tom McDonald and Colin Rennie he convinced me to join, mainly because he was much more left wing than the central Labour Party. He was very different all round to the Labour party hierarchy.

McAllion became the chair of Labour's local branch in Gillburn, which was the ward that Galloway had lost to Bunty Turley. Galloway also recruited another SLP member with McAllion, and over the years until its winding up in 1981, there was a fight between Labour and the Scottish National Party to pick up the strays, one that the SNP tended to win. Galloway had always strongly opposed the SNP, something he made great play of when he later became chair of Labour's Scottish Executive. He'd woken up to the threat they posed a little earlier than many and it was fitting that he would be involved in a strategic fight with them.

Meanwhile, Galloway's reputation in the wider Labour Party in Scotland was growing, and he was about to get a good chance to enhance it further. The death of the Labour MP John P. Mackintosh in July 1978 led to a by-election in Berwick and East Lothian. Mackintosh had been a leading

Scottish intellectual and the architect of Labour's response to the question of devolution. At the previous election in October 1974 Labour had taken it with a small majority of around 2,700 over a game young Tory called Michael Ancram, and it was by no means safe, particularly as the SNP were sitting in third, threatening to take valuable votes from Labour and give the seat to the Tories.

Berwick is a picturesque rural constituency, dotted with expensive houses and fine golf courses, but with pockets of mining. It was an archetypal marginal constituency and there were serious jitters in Labour about having to fight the Conservatives and the SNP there, at a time when the nationalists seemed to be on a roll. In the second general election of 1974 the SNP had won eleven seats at Westminster, the most they'd ever had. Labour had to retain this seat and had to be seen to make a stand against the rise of the SNP. Galloway was in the thick of it.

Labour's candidate, John Home Robertson, a distant relative of Alec Douglas-Home and now MSP for East Lothian, remembers the campaign:

> It was the Winter of Discontent, so it was a tough time for Labour. We had lost it in 1974 to the Tories, then taken it back in the second election of that year. It was all hands to the pumps and Galloway was drafted in from Dundee, by the Glasgow HQ.

Galloway was allocated the North Berwick area of the constituency, a sedate seaside town, with an electorate of retired civil servants and prim and proper old ladies. 'George was not the most likely of people for that area and it must have been a shock for him, but he coped remarkably well,' says Home Robertson. This was a tough job, in an area that must have felt a million miles from the industrial strife he was used to. The local party activists were a different kind of animal too, but Galloway adapted his style to suit the occasion. Journalist Alf Young, then the Labour Party's Scottish researcher, recalls: 'He sat there, in the shop that Labour had taken over for the by-election, surrounded by all these well-to-do, middle-class women, getting them to do this and that. He charmed them off the trees. He was totally in his element.' And that is another important ingredient in the Galloway make-up. He can be ruthlessly charming, particularly with women. Home Robertson recalls that 'they thought he was wonderful, so it made for great amusement in the constituency in later years when these same ladies were shocked to read all the reports in the papers about his sexual goings on'.

Galloway ran a good campaign, reassuring the voters that they were just as concerned about North Sea oil revenue and devolution as the SNP. However, it was another closely fought contest and when the results came in, Home Robertson had held for Labour with a 3,112 majority. The Tories took second place with 17,418, and the SNP ran in third with 3,799. The nationalist vote had almost halved and the election marked the start of Labour's fight back against the rise of the SNP, who in the general election of 1979 dropped back to a mere two seats.

Fighting the Scottish Nationalists and Labour's moderates had helped Galloway and McKelvey build up the Left Group as well as draw in the unions, with their communist leaders, and some disillusioned Scottish Labour refugees. However, they also needed to build their support among the local folk of Dundee. They were the voters and the next generation of party activists. One way that all parties have done this over the years is to run social clubs. They encourage membership, can spread party propaganda, are a useful venue for meetings and can be used to raise money. Labour, Conservatives and Liberal Democrats all have clubs, but running them is notoriously difficult. 'They have to be well run, by someone that you can trust,' according to Neil Kinnock.

Since 1967 the Dundee party had run a successful club in the Roseangle part of town, which had originally been the RAF Association. The Labour Party had picked it up when the RAF had pulled out. Called Dundee Labour Club, it was a well-run, popular venue for the working people of the community and it had provided funds for the party from bingo, booze and entertainment. Singers of the stature of Tony Christie had played there, though whether he knew that some of the gate money was going to the local Labour Party, or cared if it might have been on its way to Amarillo, we'll never know.

Encouraged by the success of Roseangle's club, McKelvey and Galloway were keen to open more of them, as McKelvey explains, 'to put the party on a firm financial footing'. This was key, as one use of the money raised was to fight elections. Though the Labour Party could rely on union money to some extent, they struggled to keep up with the traditional Tory enemy, whose wealthy backers had deeper pockets. There were local precedents. It was well known that Cathcart Labour Party in Glasgow had run a successful club that had acted as an HQ for electioneering and a good source of income to fight Teddy Taylor, the local Tory MP.

McKelvey approached James Martin, the younger brother of his old mate Jack Martin, who had taken on J. L. Stewart with him. James Martin was secretary of Whitfield Labour Party at the time and had also worked at the Roseangle club some years before, as a barman. McKelvey said that he was working with a local builder to find a suitable site in Whitfield for a new Labour club. Martin thought it was a good idea, as this constituency of some 17,000 people only had one pub and it seemed very likely that there would be plenty of customers. As it was Martin's patch, it was agreed that if it happened he ought to take a big role in running it.

A few weeks later the builder found a site in Lothian Crescent, whereupon plans were drawn up and planning permission sought. Some were sceptical that they would get consent, as the Conservatives were in control of the council at the time and knew very well that the club would be a boost to their opposition. However, it just scraped through the committee meeting by a couple of votes. Tory councillor Stuart Leach voted for it and that helped swing it Labour's way. Because the builder had found the site and was already deeply involved, he was allocated the contract without a tendering process, while the costs of the building work were borne by Lorimer's brewery. As one committee member recalls, 'The beer was indifferent, but they stumped up £63,000.'

When they announced to the public that a new club was being built and membership was available their hunch about the market for a club was proved right. There was massive demand and very soon over a thousand had applied, happy to part with a £5 fee. So Whitfield Labour Club opened on 1 December 1978 and, as with much else, the people who ran it were appointed by the small Left Group cabal at the heart of Labour. There was a manager overseen by Martin, who was made club secretary by a committee chaired by Galloway. The directors authorised to sign cheques were Galloway and the finance controller, Frank Christie, a Labour councillor and one of Galloway's inner circle. Apart from his part-time job behind the bar at Roseangle, Martin had had no experience of running a club; he was a buyer and a shop steward at NCR. His most important qualification was being one of the inner circle. In 1980 he was made full-time manager of the club. Like many examples of management under Labour's leadership, the running of Whitfield Labour Club would cause him problems some years later, but there were worrying signs right from the start.

Just a few weeks into the life of the new club, McKelvey called a meeting to talk about how they were going to use it to bring money into the party. Sitting in the auspicious surroundings of the club's cloakroom, McKelvey, Galloway and their close supporters Ernie Ross and Colin Rennie, found themselves discussing finance: whether the party could take some of the proceeds of the club's fruit machine, which they'd had for a week. Martin claims there was some heated discussion, as he disagreed with the others, complaining that it was 'madness' to act in this way so early. How could they know how much the club could afford to hand over when they had no good idea what they'd take at the bar and had to pay back the brewer's loan on a monthly contract? Despite his protestations, a motion was passed to hand over 50 per cent of the fruit machine proceeds each week.

Another source of revenue for the club was its regular bingo sessions, run five nights a week, plus Sunday afternoon. It was later decided that the profits of two of those sessions would be donated to the Labour Party. Everyone took their turn running the very popular bingo, including Galloway himself, who used to pick out the balls and call them on Sunday nights.

There may have been a slight disagreement over the fruit machine, but that wasn't worrying anyone back then. The bar takings were good, spirits were high and soon more clubs would be in the pipeline, part of grand plans by Galloway, McKelvey and the others to secure Labour funding for the future. But in just a few short years these clubs would all rise only to fall, in circumstances that would leave their mark on nearly everyone involved in them. That was all to come. In 1979 one issue dominated everything: the general election.

There was perhaps no worse year than 1979 for Labour to fight an election. After five years the perception was that the country had not only gone to the dogs, but had lost its shirt on a three-legged mongrel, got hopelessly drunk and was now being hosed down in the gutter by the IMF. Inflation was cripplingly high, and UK unemployment was creeping towards three million. In Scotland it stood at around 300,000. Margaret Thatcher and her henchmen, aided by their propaganda geniuses the Saatchis and their 'Labour isn't working' posters, were about to give the dozy, suicidal socialists a good kicking, for ten years or more. But despite all this, Galloway and Labour in Scotland were on the up, against the trend.

In Dundee West, a safe Labour seat, the sitting MP, Peter Doig, was resigning. As replacement, Galloway had proposed Ernie Ross, a Catholic, who would go on to win by 8,000 votes, in a constituency of 60–65 per cent Catholics. He kept close to Galloway and kept his head down in Westminster for his entire career, making only the occasional foray into the Palestinian issue. Ross's election victory was a certainty to everyone with any sense, but because of a very bad poll a few days before the ballot, which predicted a loss for him, the bookmakers were giving great odds. The Labour in-crowd were betting men and, according to Martin, put thousands on him. They all won lots of cash.

Ernie Ross had it relatively easy in Dundee West. The problem constituency was always going to be Dundee East, which had been SNP since 1974, in the capable hands of Gordon Wilson, who would go on to be the nationalists' leader. Alf Young recalls that

> Galloway was vehemently against the SNP. Oil had just been discovered in the North Sea and there was much argument from SNP ranks about 'Scotland's oil' and the financial potential for Scotland to become a viable small state such as Norway. Along ideological lines, Galloway argued that, yes, oil on the east coast/North Sea would generate significant tax revenue but that this wealth should be harnessed for the good of the working class all over the UK.

When Labour's selection process for the constituency had been conducted a couple of years before, tragedy had struck. The young Catholic university lecturer David Wittick, who they had wanted as parliamentary candidate, had been killed in a car crash on his way to a party selection meeting. In the aftermath, there was great discussion about who their best candidate was likely to be. Galloway wanted the TGWU candidate, Danny Chisholm, while James Martin, his brother Jack and John Henderson had all backed Jimmy Reid. A communist shipyard union leader from Glasgow, Reid had made his name as a charismatic leader on the Clyde; he'd joined the Labour Party and was canvassing for selection. Reid had stood for Parliament in Dunbartonshire Central in February 1974 for the Communist Party, and had done well to come third, even beating the SNP. This was a remarkable achievement for a fringe party and although his vote had been halved in the second election of that year, he was highly thought of. His success against the SNP worked in his favour and Reid was selected.

It was a mistake and even his proponents in the Labour Group thought he let them down: 'We had trouble fighting the election with him because he had a different strategy over meetings and was not always able to turn up,' Martin recalls. Reid lost. Perhaps with good reason, it was said that Labour would have done better with a local boy, and not a well-known communist. Either way, it had been a long shot against a strong front-runner who went on to hold the seat until 1987. Across Scotland the SNP flopped miserably, so it must have been very disappointing to fail to oust them in Dundee East.

It was Thatcher's election and she swept all before her, though Scotland was less vulnerable to the housewife PM's new broom. Overall on 3 May, the Conservatives took 339 seats, Labour 269 and the Liberals 11. In Scotland the Tories increased their number of seats from sixteen to twenty-two, while Labour went from forty-one to forty-four. It was a far cry from 1997, when the Tories were wiped out north of the border. For Galloway, nothing and everything had changed. Labour still held Dundee West and the SNP Dundee East, but Thatcher would go on to fatally wound the Tories in Scotland, and Labour's social democrats would split and form the SDP, which would only help Galloway's left wing to tighten its grip on the party. So, all round 1979 was a pretty good year for him. Oh, and he got married too.

Elaine Fyffe and Galloway had been together for years, and had originally met at Harris Academy. Galloway recalls that he was playing the double bass in the school orchestra and met Fyffe there. Fyffe was a year older than Galloway, having been born on 22 March 1953. Her father James was a joiner, but sadly her mother Phyllis had died before they were married. Elaine worked as a clerk for the Department of Health and Social Security and is remembered by Galloway's friends as rather reserved. Of course, it may have been that Galloway's inner team didn't bring out the best in her. She certainly isn't the only woman to have had reservations about them. Galloway's mates seemed to have the idea that he'd let himself down, but it seems likely that there was a power struggle going on between the close-knit NEDS and the girl that was understandably trying to capture his heart. One of the NEDS claims now that 'he was a good-looking chap who could have had any number of girls'.

Back in 1977 Galloway had announced that they were to be married, in the middle of the furore over the council flat allocation. Then the marriage question had gone away, until the wedding was 'sprung on everyone', according to one of his friends of the time. They tied the knot on 20 December 1979, at Dundee Registration Office, with Colin Rennie as best man and Elaine's sister Gillian as bridesmaid. It wasn't a big event, as money was tight, with just £8,000 coming in from his full-time job as secretary/ organiser. Galloway was still living in the bedsit at Labour headquarters at the time.

Leaving money aside, and despite the arrival of Thatcher's Britain, Galloway was doing well. He was married, was helping to run Dundee Labour as he thought was right, and was getting a good reputation among the party hierarchy. Jimmy Allison, who would later be the Scottish national organiser, a powerful figure indeed, remembered:

> I first met George when he was the full-time Dundee organiser. He was a young guy, a young Turk, who was very aware and wanted to learn. I thought he was a very able young man. He was up and coming at the same time as Gordon Brown and John Reid were, and look at how well they did.

The question was: would George Galloway fulfil his promise, in the same way as Brown and Reid? Looking back now, we know that he made choices that would keep him away from real power, wedded to 'Old Labour', while they decided to pursue New Labour. It's admirable in some ways that he hasn't changed his views, while other former left-wingers have. He often refers to those who did change; for example with Clive Anderson in December 2005 on BBC Radio Five Live he explained:

> I was never a communist or Trotskyist, or any other kind of ist, I was only ever in the Labour Party, whilst they were in all sorts of weird and wonderful fifty-seven varieties of British Trotskyism. I give one example in my book, Alistair Darling, who is . . . actually I have no personal animus against him. In fact I think that he's a very competent minister. He's the transport minister and Scottish secretary and God knows how many offices he holds . . . But when I first met him, I'm not kidding you, he was pressing Trotskyite tracts into the hands of bemused railwaymen at Waverley station in Edinburgh. Now he's the transport minister, denouncing the wreckers of the railwaymen's union, the RMT, for working to rule on the London Underground. Now he has to explain to us when and why and how he changed from being a Trotskyist to being a loyal general in the New Blair Army, but he never has . . . And John Reid is another case in point. When I first met him he was a leading member of the Communist Party. He used to denounce me as a reformist, which I was and still am . . . he's now the complete opposite.

So we get the point that he doesn't admire the way they have changed their spots. But while Galloway's friends say that he made his choices through principle, his detractors claim he just backed the wrong horse. A horse called Benn.

5

Controlling the media

George Galloway learned early in his career that the media can make or break you and, like many politicians, he's tried to manage it as much as he can ever since, through releasing stories, cultivating journalists, writing books and taking legal action. In 1979 he went the whole hog and set up his own left-wing local paper, through the Labour Party. Like others, including the silver-tongued 'Red Ken' Livingstone and 'Red Ted' Knight, who both got fed up with being called Red, Galloway thought he could redress the right-wing bias in the local press by starting up a rival paper. He called his the *Dundee Standard*.

Dundee's newspaper business has been dominated for years by the D. C. Thomson group, a family-owned and -run business whose flagship is the *Dundee Courier*, an immovable right-of-centre daily that was either ahead or behind the times in its attitude to unions, depending on your point of view. Like a 1950s Teddy boy who refused to change his drainpipe trousers and quiff when they went out of fashion, D. C. Thomson held on to its non-union working practices through the 1960s, 1970s and early 1980s, until Rupert Murdoch made them all the rage again in Wapping.

The *Dundee Standard* came out of a glorified leaflet called the *Dundee Free Press*, which had been run by the Labour Party and distributed by shop stewards around the factories.

Following the Thatcher general election victory of spring 1979, Galloway and Dundee Labour decided they needed a propaganda arm, particularly as they had local council elections coming up in May 1980 and they were desperate to take control. Maybe they could make a stand against the Thatcherism revolution. The plan was to fund the paper in part through money from the Labour clubs they ran, as one of the inner circle, James Martin, later claimed to Channel 4.[1]

Galloway and Colin Rennie were the driving force behind it. Initially, they set up the *Dundee Standard* at their headquarters in Rattray Street. Willie McKelvey was still the local party boss at that stage. He recalls: 'It was run out of my office at first. Any newspaper is very expensive and therefore you're running it on a wing and a prayer. You need money and the costs are a huge burden.' Despite the financial risks, it was decided that Labour needed a voice on the streets to combat the right-wing *Dundee Courier* and that they would find the funds through the Labour clubs, the paper's cover charge and advertising. They were also going to rely on a lot of people giving their time for free, writing columns and so on. But they did need professionals in some posts, so Galloway made Ron McKay, his mate from the Lebanon trip, the editor. McKay had some experience of this kind of paper. In the early 1970s he'd been a reporter on the *Scottish Daily News*, which had been launched as a workers' co-operative with £2 million from the Labour government. Like many new newspapers, it had folded fairly soon afterwards, under intense competition.

The *Dundee Standard* was launched in November 1979, and from the start the Labour Party took an interest. McKelvey recalls now that the Dundee constituency Labour Party had to be very careful not to break Labour's rules over involvement with publications. When the Scottish National Executive got to hear, he says, 'I was accused of being part of it. They wanted to know about the content, to make sure it was in line with party policy. Everything in the paper was questioned.' McKelvey assured them he wasn't in editorial control, 'it was all under investigation. George was on trial.' This was the Foot era, during the repercussions of the general election trouncing, and Labour was deeply worried about how they were being portrayed. 'The party sent an organiser from Glasgow, who even criticised me for selling *The Morning Star*. He also had a copy of the *Dundee Standard* with lots of red markings on it, saying this wasn't party policy.'

The *Dundee Standard* was controversial, and not just editorially. It was a left-wing paper, yet there was no National Union of Journalists chapel agreement. David Syme of the NUJ, who would later be involved in a dispute over redundancies at the *Dundee Standard*, recalls:

> We did not have a chapel agreement there because I did not think it would last long enough for us to go through the various procedures to get one . . . You

should understand that the *Standard* was looked upon as a good alternative paper in Dundee against D. C. Thomson and so many persons – such as McKelvey, soon to be an MP – would work for it and do things for it for nothing. I would not see it as being a place for anyone to use cheap labour and make a fortune out of it. I am sure you are aware that there are many newspapers/journals like that in the world today and the NUJ just turns a blind eye to them.

Apart from the journalists' wages, the other major expense for Labour to shoulder was the printing. Galloway took advice from Brian Wilson, who had run the Highland Free Press in the early 1970s. They looked around for a printer and settled on the machines of Fife Free Press. But, Martin remembers, 'it was too expensive. And the other problem was that, as newsagents were reluctant to stock it, we sold it through the unions and the clubs, in factories.' Preaching to the converted, and a small general circulation of reputedly no more than hundreds, meant that its *raison d'être* of redressing the bias in the local media could be questioned from the start. But in the May local elections, it was another way of promoting Labour policy, which arguably helped Galloway win power, in however small a way.

It would be easy to overplay the importance of the *Dundee Standard* in the local council elections, as we are not talking Murdoch-style influence here. The paper may have turned a few voters, but the overriding reason Labour got in was that after 1979, the anti-Thatcher factor kicked in north of the border. Add to that a well-organised campaign with a vote-gathering, if slightly pie-in-the-sky manifesto of freezing rents, increased spending on leisure and the stopping of council house sales, and it was a winning formula. Galloway even had the satisfaction of seeing Bunty Turley lose her seat to Labour. In the end they took 54 per cent of the vote and ended up winning by twenty-five seats to seventeen, with two independents. Rennie had been allocated one of the safest seats, and the other Galloway supporters who either held or joined the council were James Gowans, Frank Christie, James Martin, Ken Fagan, John Henderson and Charles Bowman.

Once they'd taken control of the council, the paper's funding was easier to control, as Martin explains: 'The *Standard* was an alternative paper with a low circulation, but the council were obliged to put ads in it as well as D. C. Thomson's papers. The council chiefs weren't happy about it, but their bosses were the ruling Labour Group, so they had no choice.' This tactic of getting the local council to put ads in their paper, even though it had few readers, was pure genius. If the council advertised for employees, or had statutory announcements to make, like development proposals and so on, they had to put them in the *Dundee Standard* as well as the *Courier*. Much was made of this by Channel 4's *Dispatches* documentary on Dundee Labour years later, when they showed letters from the council complaining about being billed for ads they had never commissioned. There were allegations, not substantiated, that some ads may have been put in without the knowledge of the council, which was later sent a bill. Colin Rennie, one of the Labour controlling group, later told STV that this had simply been an administrative mistake.

As *Dispatches* revealed, on 28 May 1980 Mr T. Renfrew, clerk to the council board, wrote to the *Dundee Standard* complaining about a £329.50 bill and cancelling the account with the *Standard*. On 2 June the director of administration wrote another letter to them over another bill that the council disputed: 'These notices have been published without instructions from myself or my staff . . . and I disclaim responsibility for payment.' Later in June complaints were made by the Conservative opposition leader, Jack Watson. The *Standard* was accused of taking adverts from the local council in unfair circumstances. McKay argued that the decision to take out ads in his paper had been taken after a unanimous vote by the ruling Labour Group of twenty-five people. This group was implementing party policy.

Even with the council's advertising revenue, voluntary work and money raised from the Labour clubs, the paper was running into financial problems. It didn't help that its distribution was adversely affected when the paper printed an exposé of the level of freemasonry in the area. A good piece of reporting it may have been, but Galloway found that the paper wasn't available in the various unions and when inquires were made it seemed that many of the shop stewards were masons.

The poor financial situation led to tensions. There were rumours that McKay was becoming disillusioned with the management committee, but the big issue was cash flow. McKay must have been finding it difficult to run a paper with a budget that had been slashed. When it was suggested that staff were let go, McKay offered to pay their photographer Steve McMillan's wages out of his own salary.[2]

In July 1980 the paper was near collapse. It had to let people go, but there were arguments over just what the terms of their contracts were and what they were entitled to claim in severance pay. McMillan, an NUJ member who'd worked at the paper since its start in November 1979, was told it couldn't afford to keep him. He asked for a meeting with Galloway and Rennie, together with two others who were vulnerable, reporter Barry Wood and printer Colin Dwyer. At the meeting Galloway told them they were all being let go, not just McMillan. Wood, also an NUJ member, had come from the Aberdeen office of the *Sunday Post* only a few weeks before, so was understandably annoyed.

When the details of the running of the paper became public knowledge, it gave plenty of ammunition to Galloway's enemies. Bill Walker, the Tory MP for Perth & East Perthshire, wrote to Watson to complain. 'I just cannot see how the Labour Party in Dundee can claim to represent the working people and the trade unions when they pay below the NUJ rates to journalists and employ non-union labour on their own newspaper.' Galloway's reasonable point was that it was not possible to run a small paper any other way.

The paper folded in September 1980, after just ten months in existence. David Syme, the Scottish organiser of the NUJ, was at the *Standard* when the announcement of closure happened. He'd come to Dundee to talk about the reinstatement of the sacked NUJ members, but it was all too late. Running newspapers is a difficult business and many have very quickly lost their backers piles of cash. Even so, closing in less than a year has to be seen as another failure for the controlling Labour Group. In a couple of years it would be tried all over again and to resurrect the newspaper, but for now he had no choice but to shut everything down and move on. Only McKay wouldn't let it lie and claimed he was a partner in the company Dundee Standard Publications, which would have entitled him to access to the company accounts and anything left over on its winding up.

There were reports of 'disagreements' between McKay and Galloway over the winding up of the first incarnation of the *Dundee Standard*,[3] and it is perhaps testament to Galloway's skill and ability that nowadays McKay does all Galloway's PR and is close to him, describing him as 'a gifted speaker, a natural wit and sharp brained'.

6

In power in Dundee

Under George Galloway's leadership Dundee Labour Party had won a majority on the council, with twenty-five out of forty-four seats now held by Labour. Galloway's 'chosen few' took up key positions. His mate James Gowans got the job of Lord Provost, or mayor; confidant and ex-NEDS member Charles Bowman became leader of the Labour group of councillors; Ken Fagan became treasurer. Fagan is often pictured sheltering behind dark glasses with a grim expression, while the late Bowman is remembered as a rather charmless fellow with a small man's complex and an obvious wig, 'the sort you keep by the bed and just throw on in the mornings' according to an ex-colleague who is keen to pull the rug from over him.

The central committee that took all decisions, the 'Politburo', as their opponents would dub it, was dominated by the old NEDS, but the communists Harry McLevy and Graham Ogilvy also sat on it and they were not yes-men. Now that Galloway was in power, the question was whether the coalition of Labour men and communists that had got him there would survive. There had been internal rumblings of discontent even before McKelvey had left, but they had been put to one side in the elections of 1979 and 1980. After May, squabbles over who was really running the party started to chip away at the previous unity. The industrial and political wings of the Labour movement were supposed to keep working together as a team, but very soon the two sides began to develop a split. According to those involved, this split arose out of differences of personality and style of leadership. But the new administration had only just been formed; there was work to do, and a general feeling of a new era kept the show on the road for the time being.

In common with many left-wing councils of the time, including Liverpool, Sheffield and some London boroughs, Galloway's Dundee felt it had been mandated to take on the Thatcher government over the funding of services and council house sales. Galloway himself likes to characterise his policies of this era as 'never loony left, not Militant. Labour left, but not Trotskyist, or Marxist, not like Liverpool.'[1] The distinction between Marxists and Trotskyists is pretty irrelevant to the ordinary voter. Some of the policies the council brought in were damned in the local press as being of the loony left, but then the local press was firmly on the right. The policies were certainly left wing and some of them had a element of 'lunacy', such as the banning of NATO ships from Dundee's docks in protest at the arms race, when they hardly ever docked in Dundee. Other policies were neither left nor right politically, but served just to put Labour voters' backs up. When Galloway announced that a war memorial was planned to the victims of Hiroshima, the local Burma Star veterans and the members of the Royal British Legion, whose comrades had died in inhuman Japanese labour camps, were incensed and the plans were scrapped. Bill MacKenzie, a Perth Labour candidate, claimed that the young Galloway had once said to him 'all publicity is good publicity', and those kinds of stunt certainly look like the gestures of a publicity-hungry twenty-something. Over the course of his career, he has been involved in countless stories that have only given ammunition to his opponents. It's theatre, not politics, say his critics, and they realise, even if he doesn't seem to, that there is a fine line between a drama and a crisis.

To counter Galloway, the papers gave much coverage to his critics, including a no-holds-barred speech in December 1980 by Conservative councillor Jack Barnet, in which he described the new Labour administration as 'the most extreme left-wing group in Scotland'.[2] He claimed that his constituents referred to City Chambers as 'the Kremlin', the City Square 'Red Square', and that a Labour councillor should be addressed as 'Comrade this or that'. He made much of Galloway's centralised decision making by 'the Politburo' and 'the ruling junta'. While Galloway and his management committee might have dismissed this kind of right-wing copy, the weight of it could build up over time, as it did with 'Red Ken' Livingstone, Derek Hatton and others on the Labour left.

You can have an excellent new, groundbreaking product, but if you don't sell it competently no-one will buy it. Equally, if you have great new, groundbreaking political ideas, you have to prepare the way for them. Galloway likes to think of himself a great media player, and has been described as such by many. In fact his career contains many PR gaffes and badly thought-through campaigns, from his photo shoot in his new council flat to his appearance on *Big Brother*. Some argue that his inability and unwillingness to deal with the local right-wing press's coverage of his 1980s policies helped drive voters to the SNP.

One policy which Galloway himself now agrees was flawed in its delivery was the decision to twin Dundee with the Palestinian town of Nablus. In 2005 he told Clive Anderson: 'We twinned with Nablus too quickly and ought to have prepared the way, to minimise the political bleeding. It was a noble thing to do . . . Violence in the Middle East is against the Palestinians. They are victims.' It's interesting that Galloway accepts that the affair could have been handled better. However, it did put him on the UK map, as Neil Kinnock remembers:

> I first came across him when he was making his name in Dundee and he got a reputation for being energetic, articulate and flamboyant. Flying the PLO flag in the council chambers was regarded with enthusiasm and as evidence of radicalism and authenticity by some, but others were horrified at the bad publicity.

The story of the twinning of Dundee with Nablus is extraordinary and illuminates many aspects of Galloway, the man and the politician. To Galloway it may have seemed a logical progression from his trip to Beirut and Fatahland. He saw this as a way to bring more press coverage to the Palestinian cause, for which there were (and are) strong arguments, but he misjudged the reaction of the people. One could say that his timing was out by about twenty years. In today's world, twinning with a Palestinian town would not cause a similar concern, but back in 1981, the outcry was phenomenal. Unfounded accusations of anti-Semitism were raised by Edinburgh MP Michael Ancram; the Board of Deputies of British Jews (BDBJ) petitioned the Home Secretary, Willie Whitelaw; and the Foreign Secretary was asked in the House of Commons what he was going to do about the situation.

It had all started very quietly in June 1980, when Galloway, Graham Ogilvy, Harry McLevy and other leading lights in local unions had formed the Trade Union Friends of Palestine (TUFP). Its chairman was Ernie Ross, the MP for Dundee West, and Galloway was the secretary. The linchpin, though, was a young member of the PLO called Yousef Allan. Ogilvy recalls:

> We met Yousef Allan on that earlier trip to Beirut and he later came to Dundee. He was just a young man, but he became a leading player in the friends of Palestine that we had there. A very sincere chap, very dedicated. Not a political sophisticate. He was a good contact for Galloway into the PLO.

Allan became the PLO's man in London, then the Palestinian authority's ambassador to Ireland, but died suddenly in 2001.

The TUFP state on their website: 'The organisation was formed with the purpose of mobilising and co-ordinating support for the cause of the Palestinian people within the trade union movement.'[3] They campaign for the right of the Palestinian people to self-determination within an independent sovereign state and over the years a number of trade unions have been involved.

Willie McKelvey remembers that the twinning idea came out of meeting the mayor of Nablus, Bassem Al-Shaka, on a TUFP trip to Palestine:

> I went to the Middle East on several trips, all paid for by the PLO. We went to the West Bank, Gaza and Lebanon. One thing I particularly remember is that despite the shocking conditions they were living under, the children were all spotlessly clean. We met the Nablus mayor before the town was twinned. He'd been blown up by an Israeli bomb and had lost his legs. He needed a good pair of prosthetic legs, which was one reason he came over to the UK.

The bomb that had crippled the mayor had been planted by an extremist Israeli settler whose own government had described him as 'a terrorist', though he was never brought to justice.

Al-Shaka was keen to twin with Dundee and visited the city while he was in the UK getting medical help in November 1980. It is tradition to exchange the flags of the countries, so he presented the Palestinian flag to the

Lord Provost, James Gowans. Gowans then had the flag flown in the council chambers, alongside the flags of other twins from the USA, France, Yugoslavia and West Germany. Dr Albert Jacob, leader of the Dundee Hebrew Congregation, witnessed the handover along with the Conservative opposition leader, Jack Watson. They both objected later, claiming that they hadn't at first realised what the flag was.[4] Although it is often referred to as the PLO flag, in fact the PLO doesn't have one of its own; it uses the flag of Palestine. In any event, it was a symbolic act of union between Nablus and Dundee and the consequent outrage could hardly have been more vociferous if Galloway and Gowans had blown themselves up in the council chambers.

Galloway's opponents made the most of the golden opportunity to stick the boot in. J. L. Stewart, fresh out of jail and determined to get the men who he thought had helped to put him in there, spread a rumour to the papers that Gowans had not only taken the flag, but in return had presented the legless Muslim with a kilt and bottle of Scotch.[5] This was a classic piece of misinformation, designed to rubbish the Galloway faction for being out of their depth, but Al-Shaka was a moderate man, not a political hard-liner, and also not a teetotal Muslim, so the Scotch was very welcome. And there had never been a kilt. That was a traditional gift of a 'belt' or roll of tartan.

To add to the Pythonesque absurdity, soon afterwards the PLO's ambassador in London, Nabil Ramlawi, sent another goodwill gift to all forty-four members of the council, wanting to cement the developing relationship between Palestine and Dundee. Each council member got a nice red 1981 PLO diary. Needless to say, not everyone was happy about this gift. Jack Barnet told the *Dundee Courier*: 'I am obviously greatly worried that I am now on the mailing list of an organisation such as the PLO which contains within its ranks professional killers and international terrorists.'[6] With no irony, he continued: 'My worry is the mailing list could become some kind of hitlist.' All the Tories sent their red diaries back immediately.

A week or so following the presentation, Galloway and Ernie Ross went off to visit the PLO in Lebanon, on a separate trip organised by the TUFP. Another member of the two-week fact-finding mission was Bill Speirs from the Scottish TUC, who would remain close to Galloway for years, including at War on Want. They didn't visit Nablus, but they did meet Yasser Arafat for the first time. This was to be the start of a series of meetings over the years to which Galloway attaches a lot of importance. Arafat's views on Galloway have been variously reported as grateful and admiring or barely tolerant. There is no doubt that Galloway's links with Palestine, Lebanon and the Middle East run very deep and wide. His second wife, Amineh, says that she is a distant cousin of Arafat.

In December 1980 it was hard for the press or opposition figures to attack Galloway over meeting Arafat, as only a few weeks before David Steel, the mild-mannered Liberal leader, had also met him. (The PLO was meeting and receiving politicians from around the world at the time.) The heat didn't get turned up to full until the New Year, when in the first week of January a horrific bomb blast in the Jewish-owned Norfolk Hotel in Nairobi killed sixteen people. This couldn't have come at a worse time for Galloway's trip to Palestine. Much was made of the fact that the man police were looking for in connection with the bombing was an ex-member of Fatah. Qaddura Mohammed ab Al Hamid, of the same Popular Front for the Liberation of Palestine which had shown Galloway around Lebanon a couple of years before, was named as chief suspect.

To try and counter attempts falsely to imply that Galloway was in some way connected with international terrorists, Charles Bowman, the council leader, announced that they did not have 'a link with the PLO, it is a link with Palestine. There is no way we would support terrorism, on either side of the Middle East conflict.'[7] But the row continued to build when Gowans announced that he would be leading a twinning delegation to Nablus in March, at the invitation of the League of Arab States. The BDBJ organised a meeting in Dundee of Jews from all over Britain. More than 400 gathered in Dundee to protest, claiming racist graffiti and other anti-Semitic behaviour as one consequence of the twinning. They petitioned Sir George Younger, the Scottish Secretary, who replied that there was no evidence of an upsurge in anti-Semitism in Dundee. Younger also replied that it was up to the ruling local group in the district council to undo the twinning and was not a national issue.

But the Zionist lobby kept on fighting and in late March the Scottish BDBJ reported Dundee City Council to the Solicitor General, Nicholas Fairbairn, for inciting racial hatred. They demanded the lowering of the

'PLO' flag. Though Fairbairn agreed that flying a flag could be considered to be a breach of the peace in some circumstances, he disagreed that this had incited any racial hatred.

Despite the furore, there was no chance of Labour backing down and at the end of March 1981 the Dundee twinning party, consisting of Gowans, Colin Rennie, Ken Fagan and an independent councillor called Ian Mortimer, left for Nablus to take part in the reciprocal ceremony. Occupied Nablus, riven by factional PLO infighting, must have felt like a home from home to the Labour boys, but the visit was clearly an eye opener for the Dundonians. They met people who told how they had been tortured in Israeli jails and saw how road blocks and security checks made Palestinians' day-to-day lives a misery. Unfortunately, while they were there, their judgement seemed to evaporate in the heat and Rennie was reported by John Finlayson of Scotland's *Sunday Mail* on 5 April as declaring: 'It is the Israelis who are the terrorists . . . under the leadership of the PLO victory is assured. We will be your voice in Scotland, in the UK and the rest of Europe.' The subsequent UK headlines were the icing on the cake for Galloway's enemies. 'Dundee the UK agents for the PLO',[8] 'Probe on pledge to PLO',[9] 'Nablus nonsense',[10] 'We'll be the PLO's voice, say Scots';[11] all added to the hysteria and put a new set of wheels on a bandwagon already big enough for every anti-Labour pundit and politician in the country to jump on.

As the 'Nablus nonsense' continued through early 1981, it was in danger of obscuring the far more serious issue of how Galloway's rebel council was responding to Margaret Thatcher's teething Tory government. There were two big crises in the pipeline, both of which damaged Dundee and, in the final analysis, perhaps Galloway himself.

Thatcher's idea of 'good housekeeping', where the UK only spent what she thought it could afford, had put her on a collision course with left-wing local authorities, who she believed spent too much money and enjoyed generous central government subsidies that primarily benefited Labour voters. She wanted to cut back without damaging her election chances. The upshot of Thatcher's plans was that local councils were told they had to balance their own books better and not rely so much on rate support grants from the Exchequer.

To the idealistic Galloway, or '*Eminence Rouge*', as he was dubbed around the time, this was a blue flag to a red bull. Fagan and Bowman refused to put up council rents, or cut jobs and services. In reply, the Scottish Office cut Dundee's rate support grant by a hefty £7.3 million. In order to keep paying their council workers and keep the buses running, the council had no choice but to raise the rates, which soared from 20p to 30p in the pound. The impact on local business was to make life ever tougher, but it also made Dundee a singularly unattractive place to start up a new firm. Now a prospective company had to weigh up the risks of a militant local labour force, higher rates and no confidence in a Labour administration many believed was 'loony left'.

By backing a stand against Thatcher over balancing the books, the council and the Labour Group hadn't noticeably improved the lot of the Dundee working man. As with other left-wing councils, a mixture of bravado and believing his own propaganda had led Galloway and the council to paint themselves into a political corner.

Fighting the Iron Lady would not prove possible for left-wingers like Galloway, just as it didn't for the proud steel unions and brave miners later on. Galloway's other, rather more spectacular, miscalculation was to choose to fight the right to buy with the woman who'd described council houses as 'socialism in concrete'. When he did it was to be a personal defeat on the scale of losing to Bunty Turley, but it would also seem to undermine him in the party, and some claim it was a factor in his eventual departure from Dundee to London.

In late November 1979 Michael Heseltine, the Secretary of State for the Environment, announced that the government intended to give all local authority tenants the right to buy their homes. The news was greeted with hostility by Labour's Roy Hattersley, who spat: 'We shall fight it very hard in the House of Commons and in the country.' He spoke for many in the Labour Party and opposition to the right to buy remained its policy until 1987, when Neil Kinnock got rid of it. As part of the 1980 Housing Act, or the rather long-winded Tenants' Rights, Etc. (Scotland) Act north of the border, the secretary of state also had the power to intervene to force a council to comply. Perhaps Galloway hadn't appreciated the extent of the ramifications of the Act properly, as the inevitable consequence of taking on

Thatcher over council house sales was that the officials who obstructed were personally liable. But, as he wasn't a councillor, that liability would fall on his mates in the key positions, Fagan and Gowans.

Dundee had over 41,000 council homes, but a lot of them were poorly built, and it also had 12,500 living in officially overcrowded conditions and some 6,000 slums. There was consensus in the Labour Party that it was wrong to sell off the best council housing, leaving just the dregs for those who couldn't afford to buy. However, the arguments for and against the policy were irrelevant by this stage. It was all about whether Fagan and Gowans were prepared to break the law. You didn't need to be a chess grand master to see the way it was going to play out. Move One: they refused to sell. Move Two: in February 1981 the government appointed Hugh Morton QC to hold a public inquiry into Dundee's refusal to implement the Act. Move Three: Fagan and Bowman were threatened with legal action over their refusal to sell. Move Four: they gave in. Checkmate. They had been the only district council to fight, for the obvious reason that it had been a game that councils would inevitably lose.

In a leaflet written by Galloway to explain why he was for turning, he declared:

> In consultation with the broader trade union movement, Labour consider that it is better to stay in control of events – to defend the council house rents freeze, to maintain our 'no cuts, no redundancies' policy – than to risk what might turn out to be a Kamikazi [*sic*] clash in the High Court . . . Starting this weekend, Labour will be mounting a massive counter-attack against the Tories and their mouthpieces in the local press, to defend the District Council and its policies and to resume the offensive against the Thatcher government.[12]

It hadn't been big and it hadn't been clever. They'd had to back down because Fagan and Bowman might well have been fined and barred from office for up to five years if they hadn't.

Galloway's Left Group had been defeated and the broader trade union movement, of which he had spoken in his statement, now began to turn. He was one of those who had led them into a fight they couldn't win and a significant number were fed up of having to take advice from someone whose judgement they now questioned. Graham Ogilvy claims:

> To argue with him was to argue with the party. To argue with the party
> was to be against the interests of the working class. It was a kind of a classic
> cult of the individual. Some people were frightened of him, but of course all
> the old communists had seen it all before. All this histrionics and
> demagoguery and tough-guy stuff, what does that mean to us? We stood
> up to him, no problem, but it did take a while for us to realise what was
> going on.

This civil war would build from then until Galloway left Dundee in
November 1983. It would be played out against the backdrop of fighting the
Tories and to an extent the SNP, but it would also coincide with Galloway
transferring from the Dundee stage to a national one. And the production
he was starring in wasn't a light comedy. Just as meetings had been packed
with voting fodder to get rid of the NEDS' moderate opponents, so the same
tactics were used to try to get rid of the communists. Ogilvy was one of
them. 'Ironically, after we fell out with Galloway, he would employ the
same tactic against us by packing meetings with TGWU members. He
wound them up about AUEW dominance after McLevy broke with
Galloway.'

Since taking over from Willie McKelvey as secretary/organiser, Galloway
had got a reputation among the wider Scottish Labour Party for his energy
and ability to motivate. Mervyn Rolfe, a former Lord Provost of Dundee,
and an ex-Labour councillor and activist, is now chief executive of Dundee
Chamber of Commerce. He remembers how Galloway was thought of back
in the early 1980s: 'George had a good reputation from building up the
Dundee party. Recruitment levels were very high; there was some spin to it
but he'd done a good job. It was a youthful party and he attracted a band of
like-minded people who liked what he was delivering.'

For Galloway, fighting the Tories was second nature. So when the Labour
Party were looking round for a new chairman of Scottish Labour, Galloway
jumped at the chance. Bill Speirs, who would later take the role himself from
1987 to 1988, was a close friend and ally, but is a little dismissive of the
achievement. 'He had the backing of the trade unions and constituency

people that he needed, but it was basically "Buggins's turn".' Despite this comment, Speirs is a great admirer of Galloway as a politician and person. 'He would always be a dominant figure. Your head always turned towards him when an issue came up. You'd look to see what his opinion was. You knew it was important what he'd say.'

Buggins's turn or not, Galloway's stint as chair was remarkable. For a start, when he took over on 14 March 1981, he was the youngest ever, at just twenty-six. Surrounded by hard-bitten unionists and time-serving stalwarts in their forties and fifties, he was not daunted by their experience and his comparative lack of it. He went in with great plans to shake things up, and he certainly did. In retrospect, his year is regarded by many as perhaps the most turbulent in its history and when asked about the infighting, Galloway said at the end of the year: 'I regard it as a sign that the party is alive and kicking. The peace of the graveyard is not for us.'

The Labour Party across the UK was asking itself where it was going and Galloway put forward answers for Scotland as part of that debate. On the eve of his appointment he gave an interview to the *Morning Star*, in which he set out his policies. He talked of his ambitious plans to unite the Scottish people against Thatcher and the job losses across Scotland's industries. He went on to accuse Thatcher and Ronald Reagan of sabre rattling against the USSR, which played well at a time when many Scots felt themselves to be prime targets in a nuclear strike, given the submarine bases in the country. He said he supported devolution and called for a legislative assembly with the power to redistribute wealth through a wealth tax and control the economy through the Scottish Development Agency. At the conference itself, he declared that the reason Labour was shifting to the left was because 'we are winning the arguments'.

Unsurprisingly, the right of the party didn't agree with that and in the year of Galloway's chairmanship there was row after row as Galloway tried to centralise control in the Labour Party in Scotland to dominate policy at national and local levels. John Home Robertson, the moderate Labour MP who Galloway had helped get elected, saw how he worked. 'George was a very impressive operator, but he didn't turn people in debate, he gathered his support before the meetings and would not tolerate anyone deviating from the agreed line.' Jimmy Allison, Labour's Scottish organiser at the time, remembered that Galloway and other members of the left-wing faction the Labour Co-ordinating Committee, or LCC, formed a powerful group within the executive. 'George, Bill Speirs and a few others had little time for anyone who disagreed with them.'

A move was proposed to make all Labour regional and local groups run along the same lines as Dundee, with Labour executives controlling elected representatives. 'Too many Labour councils disregard the views and opinions of the party that put them there,' Galloway said at the time. Their differences didn't stop at local councils. McKelvey, Galloway and others regarded the Labour parliamentary group of MPs as 'undemocratic', because they acted against the policies of the rest of the party when they wanted. Following the Scottish Labour Partty's conference, McKelvey and Ernie Ross put forward a proposal that MPs should be bound by conference decisions as well as the manifesto. This was greeted by 'uproar', according to McKelvey.

> Tony Benn backed us and it wasn't as clear cut as people imagined, but the Parliamentary Labour Party thought we were nutters. Michael Foot talked to us and warned us to be careful. He said it might be what we want now, but what about when there was a right-wing consensus in the future? We'd get stuck with policies we didn't want.

Their idea got nowhere, though McKelvey thinks it did put the issue of party democracy on the agenda. Many MPs were openly scathing. Even the Bennite Eric Heffer remarked: 'We are a democratic party, not a Communist Party.'

The past may be a different country, but in the 1970s and early 1980s the UK seemed to be on a different planet. In 1979 the UK lost 29,474,000 days of work to strikes. In 1980 it fell to a still appalling 11,964,000, whereas since the early 1990s the days lost have generally bumped along around the low hundreds of thousands. In 1981 there was enormous tension between the workers and the bosses, and between the left and right. In Scotland the struggling Linwood car plant, where the Hillman Imp had been badly manufactured, finally closed. Meanwhile, over in Dundee the clock-watching Timex workers were fighting redundancies with strike action.

The monetarist policies that Labour's Chancellor, Denis Healey, had been forced to adopt in 1978 and that had brought down inflation were carried on by Thatcher's administration and one consequence was a doubling in unemployment from 1979 to 1980. Then when the Chancellor of the Exchequer, Geoffrey Howe, brought in more spending cuts it looked as though unemployment was bound to rise still further. A victory for the left was coming, which would raise hopes. In February the National Coal Board (NCB), which had been denied central government cash, announced a schedule of twenty-three mine closures, which would have devastated large areas of the UK. When the NUM threatened to take their 240,000 miners on strike, they forced the government to agree to reduce coal imports and to give a lump sum to the NCB. Keeping the pits open gave encouragement to the left that they could take on Thatcher, but it would be a fleeting Indian summer, with a cold winter coming. The Scottish miners' leader, Mick McGahey, pressed NUM boss Joe Gormley to get more concrete concessions for the longer term, but they never came. The rest, and the British mining industry, would soon be history.

The tremendous arguments among the fractured left over their core values and who should be in charge to fight Thatcherism mirrored the state of Galloway's Dundee Labour Party. The divisions nationally were played out with more subtlety, but were just as bitter. When four of Labour's moderates broke away and formed their own party in early 1981, it sent shock waves through the whole country. After months of plotting, they announced their new Social Democratic Party, which was to fight the next election in a pact with the Liberals. Shirley Williams, Bill Rodgers, David Owen and Roy Jenkins thought they were the future of socialism but things turned out differently. They helped split the Labour vote and added significantly to the misery of Foot's period as leader. While Galloway was more worried about the SNP than the SDP, they still did play a minor role in Scottish politics when Jenkins took Glasgow Hillhead in the by-election of 1982. In the end it would be Galloway who would wreak the sweetest revenge on the SDP by beating Jenkins in the 1987 election.

Labour in Scotland was boosted by the knowledge that the Tories were running a poor third behind the nationalists. George Younger, who'd drawn the short straw and been made Thatcher's Secretary of State for Scotland, was up against enormous hostility from local councils over the reduction in central government subsidies. In June 1981 he gamely visited Dundee, where he was pelted with eggs at City Chambers, before going on to more abuse at the Timex factory, where they gave him three and a half minutes until he was well poached. That same month Galloway addressed the Scottish miners at their annual conference in Inverness, with a wide-ranging attack on the effects of Thatcherism on the working people of Scotland. He claimed that Tory policies were leading to a rise in suicides and a return of diseases of the 1930s.

Unemployment and poverty were affecting inner cities particularly badly and the immigrant communities especially. The consequent tensions erupted into riots through 1981, triggered by harsh policing under tough powers to stop and search on the streets. In April, Brixton had three days of trouble that left 300 injured and £7.5 million worth of damage. In early July Toxteth in Liverpool followed, but worse, with around 450 police injured and 500 arrests. In the aftermath, seventy buildings in the area had to be demolished. In contrast, following a small disturbance in Dundee on 12 July, which was no more than a handful of chanting youths, Galloway was reported as saying 'we are on the Toxteth Road'.[13]

The chairmanship of the Scottish Labour executive had established Galloway on the national map, and it had also given him a profile in the party in London. He would raise that profile further when Foot chose to leave out Tony Benn from the shadow Cabinet. Galloway admires Benn enormously and had supported his failed campaign against Healey for the deputy leadership. When Foot came up to meet the Scottish executive on 14 November 1981, it resulted in what Jimmy Allison called 'an extremely unpleasant meeting',[14] which was well reported in the next day's papers with terms like 'rough house' used. At the end of the meeting, as people milled around the boardroom, someone pushed Galloway's old enemy Norman Buchan MP in the chest during a heated argument. Both he and his wife Janey had been set against Galloway for some years, since they fell out in Dundee over Galloway's controlling style, and ill feeling had been simmering since August, when Janey had written an open letter to *Labour Weekly* criticising Benn and his followers, for an attitude similar to 'those which led to the corruption of Stalinism and the gulags'.

Tempers had become frayed almost from the start of proceedings because Galloway had chosen to use his position as chairman to break with protocol and angrily voice his own personal views to Foot about Benn and the running of the party. The minutes of the meeting, taken by John Reid, who was the party's research officer at the time, set out the internal divisions of the early 1980s pretty well.[15] The trouble was that Foot was using the excuse that Benn wouldn't toe the party line on certain issues as the reason for not including him in the Cabinet, while at the same time tolerating dissent from others. Backed by members of the LCC, Galloway said it was unacceptable to have the pro-nuclear Healey publicly disagreeing with the party's policy to get rid of nuclear weapons. He went on to describe leaving out Benn as 'little short of disastrous'. Foot replied that Benn couldn't be a member of the shadow Cabinet if he wasn't prepared to go along with agreed policy, which led to heated exchanges between him and those around the table who felt that Benn was being victimised and had a right to express views agreed with by many in the party.

The meeting broke up with nothing resolved, but the subsequent bad publicity must have rankled with Foot, particularly as Buchan went to the papers claiming he had been afraid he was going to be physically assaulted. The irony was that this meeting had no real power; the participants could only pass on a view to their Scottish MPs, who did have a vote. One of those MPs, Donald Dewar, told the press: 'I deeply regret that the Scottish executive have been trapped into a counter-productive and totally unnecessary display of factional politics.'

One aspect of the discussion had been about Foot's attitude to the Trotskyite Militant Tendency, which had infiltrated Labour in a few constituencies. At the time he was pressing for an investigation into what he termed the 'pestilential nuisance', but when pressed by a friend of Militant in the meeting he said he was not in favour of having them expelled from the party. Galloway, however, had a novel idea for combating the rise of Militant, which he revealed in an article in *Scottish Marxist* that same month. Bizarrely, he called for the Communist Party to become affiliated to the Labour Party and that it should campaign for the right to send representatives to the Labour Party Conference and General Management Committee. When questioned he claimed it was to protect the party against

Militant. 'The mainstream Marxist-left organisation, the Communist Party, should come inside the Labour Party.'

If there had been doubt in the minds of the moderates of the leadership, this dispelled them. Denis Healey proposed that Galloway should be banned from selection as an MP because the article showed he wasn't a suitable candidate. Benn rallied to Galloway's cause and in the end Healey's motion failed by thirteen votes to five. As time passed and Labour was taken over by people who make Healey look like, well, a socialist, Galloway would become more marginalised and was finally expelled, backing up Healey's instinct that he was probably never going to be a man of the party.

While Galloway was chairman, two issues dominated Scottish politics: devolution and economic stagnation. Galloway presided over a fundamental ideological debate about constitutional change and how to manage the economy. On the economy, Galloway was in favour of government owner-ship and control, spending on services and wealth redistribution through taxation. In January 1982 he wrote in *New Socialist* that the time had come for devolved government for Scotland. At the annual conference in 1982, as outgoing chair, Galloway proposed three motions: to take power away from the Labour leader to appoint the Scottish Secretary and instead to give that power to the annual Scottish conference; to bring in a form of democratic centralism so that more control could be exerted over councillors and MPs by the party; the appointment of political education officers.

The first two points are pretty self-explanatory, but the third is more interesting and aroused some concern at the time from those who worried that these education officers would have another agenda. An 'education officer' sounds like someone in sensible shoes, with a beard and a pedantic manner, but they would have been in place to 'educate' Labour members in the party line. Galloway's critics quickly called them commissars, the Soviet term for Communist Party officials who made sure that policy was being followed and who had tremendous power to make or break careers and lives. Just using the term was a deliberate attempt to conjure dark images and showed the level of divisions in the Labour Party in Scotland at this difficult period. The proposal was never adopted.

Befitting the conference that was the culmination of a year led by Galloway, all the talk was of repairing division. In his opening address he called for party unity and denounced the press, saying it could not be allowed to silence socialist ideas and 'continue to cast party members into the lion's den'. In support of the left wing, he went on: 'Let hunting witches start and there is absolutely no guarantee that the hunters will not stop at the one witch to the left of you.'[16] There were real challenges on the immediate horizon too. In Glasgow Hillhead, the constituency where he would be MP from 1987, there was a by-election coming up on 25 March that needed hard work if the Labour candidate had any chance of winning. He asked the party to rally round this cause and their Hillhead candidate, David Wiseman, who Galloway had put on the top table in the conference hall. These were great words and went down well, but of course Wiseman lost out to Roy Jenkins of the SDP.

7

The Labour clubs

Ardler, Whitfield and Menzieshill is not a firm of Dundee lawyers, though they kept a few busy. They were the working men's clubs that were started up in Dundee in the late 1970s and early 1980s. After great expectations, they each went bust in circumstances that left bitterness in the community towards the local Labour Party, as well as enough questions to warrant a Channel 4 documentary and a fraud trial. Along the way, there were tales of sex on blow-up beds, bullets through the post, a mystery fire at the Labour Party HQ and Galloway calling the bingo. The story of Dundee's Labour clubs is like *The League of Gentlemen* meets *Peter Kay's Phoenix Nights*. At the very best, the Labour clique demonstrated an inability to organise a booze-up in a working men's club.

The success of the Labour club in Roseangle had convinced Galloway and his inner circle that they could support Dundee Labour Party with money from more clubs, perhaps even a chain, which would be run on a not-for-profit basis. Unfortunately, as is often the case, beer and big ideas didn't mix and with so much feuding already going on, the clubs became another arena for Machiavellian conspiracies involving J. L. Stewart and Galloway's followers. Stewart produced a free newspaper called the *Dundee Independent*, which was edited by Tom Donaldson, a local businessman who was angry at the Labour council over a planning application for an amusement arcade he'd had turned down, which was later criticised as being an act of 'maladministration'. Needless to say, the paper spent a lot of time criticising the council. Between the two of them, over the next few years Stewart and Donaldson would constantly attack Galloway over as much as they possibly could, until eventually Donaldson became too preoccupied with legal problems when he was accused of possession of heroin. The case went to trial, but he was found not guilty. In the process, the innocent man lost over two stone in weight and his health was said to have never recovered. He has since died.

At the start Galloway's Labour clubs did very well and so they should have; there was little opposition. Through 1979 the windswept, bleak monstrosity called Whitfield Labour Club, a hideous brick-and-concrete box with less charm than an abattoir, had been bringing home the bacon for Labour. The Labour Party was laughing all the way to the bank and Galloway wrote to the club's manager, James Martin, saying:

> I wish to place on record, Jim, my gratitude to you personally and to the club generally, for the continued magnificent support which the party receives from you. It is a level of support which is unmatched from any other source and which is enjoyed by no other Labour Party in the country.[1]

It was magnificent support that had to stop just a few years later in 1983 when the brewers called in the auditors Arthur Young (now Ernst & Young), who found a shortfall in the accounts of £34,680. After that they imposed new rules on the management, including a ban on giving money to the Labour Party for two years.

A later Scottish Television (STV) investigation into the clubs confirmed that, after three years in business, 'the management were systematically switching club profits into the local Labour Party.'[2] It also revealed that Whitfield 'was taking in over £5,000 a week from the bar. Yet the club was piling up debts and unpaid bills.' For example, in February 1981 the club had failed to make a VAT return and was pursued for £13,500. (This is all covered in more detail in Chapter 12.) There is of course nothing illegal about making donations to the Labour Party, but the priority must surely be not to send money when the club was not dealing with its bills.

However, the club wasn't all about raising money, as Martin recalls now: 'Whitfield was the HQ for four of the local wards too. The club was how we defeated Harry McLevy. We recruited members for votes from the club. We'd just get them in for AGMs.' McLevy had been a union opponent of Galloway and his close circle.

About eighteen months after the Whitfield club had been set up, Eric Neilson found another site for one of his fetching developments, this time on the Ardler council estate. It was a tiny plot in Americanmuir Road, squeezed between the houses. It was so small that no-one thought it was possible to get a club in the space, but it was assumed that planning would not be a problem, now that the council was Labour run. Sure enough, it got through the planning meeting. The locals were happy because, as in many other local residential areas, there weren't enough pubs. Ardler only had one, for a population of around 8,000 of legal age. The resulting building would be as welcoming as an East German crematorium. If it hadn't been for a few slits for windows high up its stark walls, it would have passed for a pebbledashed coffin.

Soon after the thirsty folk of Ardler realised that they were about to get another watering hole, they were given the opportunity to apply for membership. By the summer of 1980, 500 had put their names down and paid over their £18.40.[3] But if they'd thought they were going to get a round in quickly, they were mistaken. A year later building work still hadn't started and Neilson said he was still waiting for the go-ahead from the main financiers, the Labour Party. Jimmy Kidd, the local motor trader who had sold the land, was getting annoyed too, claiming they hadn't paid him.[4] He claimed that he'd only had £1,500 out of the £13,500 he was owed in total, and was thinking of pulling out. The whole enterprise was in danger of alienating the entire community before they'd even been served a dodgy pint, or a lukewarm pie. Word was going around that the Labour Party had cocked it up. To try to appease their potential members, Galloway had to call a public meeting in Dundee's Park Hotel, where he explained that they were waiting for money from the brewers, Ind Coope, before they could start. Galloway was quoted at the meeting as saying that it was all in hand and the money was agreed, though Ind Coope later claimed that they were still undecided. Anyway, by December 1981 the club had opened with Frank Christie as manager, Ernie Ross MP as president, Galloway as vice-president and James Gowans, the Lord Provost, on the committee too. On the face of it, Christie, Labour's chair of housing, had few professional qualifications that entitled him to manage this club. He had no previous experience of running licensed premises but had partly passed his accountancy exams.

Though it was known as the Ardler club, it was officially named Dundee

West Labour Club and was eventually given its proper opening ceremony by Tony Benn on 19 November 1982. There was a free drink on the house for everyone, except the teetotal Benn, who drank tea. The cost of the opening party was £805.00.[5] According to witnesses Benn went round every single person in the club, shaking hands and chatting. Presumably, he was thrilled that this new club could donate money to the Labour coffers and be the focus of working-class camaraderie. That was its mission and according to Labour MP John McAllion, who was a young party activist and teacher at the time, the members were well aware of the club's *raison d'être*: 'I was on the Social Committee. The club was set up to donate money to the Labour Party and at the AGM it was always made clear to the members.'

Some members of the club claimed that they never knew it was giving money to Labour. Graham Dow and Ian Mudie, in interviews for STV, said they had no idea and were unhappy about its financial management. Dow went on record claiming that 'we had no knowledge of that at all'. He also claimed that when the members saw the annual accounts there was no mention of the Labour Party, only a sum for 'Miscellaneous' expenses, which he asked about and was told that it was to cover normal running costs of the club, such as postage and letters. Other more substantial costs, such as the rates and wages, were not included in this, yet the Miscellaneous total when Dow saw it was around £12,000.

One reason for the lack of knowledge of ordinary members was that the men running the clubs were all part of the tight-knit Left Group. According to James Martin, the clubs' rules were that to get onto the committees you had to have been a member of the Labour Party for at least five years.

Ardler had good revenue sources – for example bingo, fruit machines and pool tables brought in over £31,500 – yet under its management, by 1983 it had a deficit of £2,500. In the same year its Labour donations totalled £4,450.10. By 1984 the members were worried and angry and a special meeting was called to discuss why the club's finances were so dreadful. 'People were disgusted with the balance sheets,' Mudie told STV. Dow claimed to STV that he'd asked why no action was being taken against Christie, and the club's secretary, the Labour councillor John Henderson, had replied that the accounts had disappeared. According to Dow and Mudie, Christie quit on the spot. When accountants W. A. Findlay were called on behalf of the members, they found that the cash book had pages missing and that a total of £30,000 was unaccounted for on the balance sheets.[6] The club struggled on, but eventually closed in December 1986 when Henderson, at the time the Labour housing convenor, announced its voluntary liquidation. By then the debts had risen to £213,000. Christie later claimed that the demise of the club was the result of 'crass mismanagement', even though he had been the manager for a considerable part of its life.

Galloway claimed in a local radio phone-in: 'The clubs are run for the benefit of the members. If that was not so, then we would not have such successful clubs.'[7] Yet all the clubs he helped to set up would close in debt. To lose one Labour club may be regarded as unfortunate, but they would also lose a second, and eventually a third. This was particularly galling to one group of residents who had wanted to start up their own club, but couldn't get planning permission. Back in 1981, while the locals of Ardler were complaining about what had happened to the club they'd given money to a year before, in Menzieshill (pronounced 'Mingis-hill', like Menzies Campbell) a group of local residents were trying to get their own social and community club off the ground.

Unlike the Labour Club, which was to be a simple project, based around drinking and associated adult pastimes such as bingo and staged entertainment, the residents were planning a club aimed at children and OAPs as well. They'd had plans drawn up and got outline planning permission to build, but then the Labour Party put together rival plans in November of the same year. The locals were led by shopkeeper Charlotte Cassidy, who became something of a thorn in Galloway's side as they competed for the council's permission to build the club on the same site. The land in Earn Crescent, a few yards from an old folks' home, would remain owned by the council, but run on a lease by whoever got the council's permission.

Cassidy is now in her sixties and remembers the time well. 'There were going to be facilities for kids from five to eight, nine to fourteen, fifteen to eighteen.' She described it as having a bar, but with more of a community centre feel to it:

It was going to be run by local people for local people, that's what I said at the time. I was leader of another community centre for years so I knew what to do. I used to run discos and dances and raffles to raise money for taking kids on coach trips, on holidays, you know.

On 7 February 1982 Cassidy was due to appear on a Radio Tay phone-in with Labour's Ernie Ross, a local Conservative called Joe Barton, and his brother Charles, a Labour councillor and the shadow planning convenor. 'It was odd the two of them being on different sides politically,' she recalls. The programme was going to give both sides the chance to argue their cases in public, live. Then at the last minute Ross pulled out and Galloway came on instead. 'George Galloway arrived with a black Crombie coat over his shoulders. He shook his shoulders and his mate who'd driven him there, Councillor Fettes, took the coat from his back and put it to one side.' Many others from Dundee at the time remember that Galloway had a penchant for wearing his coat, Italian style, over his shoulders with his arms out of the sleeves. There were only a couple of minutes before they went on air, but Galloway had time for one conversation with the shopkeeper before they started. 'He sat down and advised me that if I said anything wrong about him, he'd sue me.' Charlotte says now that she had almost laughed when he had his coat taken off his back by his crony, but that those comments wiped the smile off her face.

The problem with being on a phone-in is that it's hard to know who might ring up and get put on air to confront you. Sure enough, the word had got around and interested parties had tuned in, including J. L. Stewart and his buddy Tom Donaldson. Donaldson and Stewart had picked up on the Menzieshill club, hoping to hit Galloway over the head with it. They ambushed him. During the course of the discussion, the producer put through a call from Donaldson, who cornered the Dundee Labour chief about his track record on running clubs. He asked Galloway how much money was going from Whitfield Labour Club to the Labour Party, to which Galloway replied 'precious little' and went on to challenge Donaldson to come down to his office, where he would show him all the bills he had to pay. James Martin, who was running Whitfield at the time and would later be acquitted of a financial charge in relation to his job at the club, revealed in

Channel 4's 'In the Red' documentary in 1987 that the club had given many thousands of pounds to the Labour Party, as it felt entitled to, because this was what it was set up to do. The programme quoted 'over £18,500 from Whitfield alone in three years'. Whether this is 'precious little' is perhaps open to interpretation. Either way, Cassidy went away from the phone-in determined to carry on the campaign to get the club run by the Menzieshill locals for the locals.

After his phone-in appearance, Donaldson went into print against Galloway. On 8 February 1982 he published a strange little leaflet called 'The Great Menzieshill Gold Rush'. In it he called on the residents of Menzieshill to 'take yourselves, your tents, your caravans, your cars, your bikes – and, like the Gold Rush days, stake your claim on this piece of open ground. After all, morally, it's yours!!' The leaflet also claimed that Ross and Labour councillor Bill Roberts had not supported the local folk sufficiently. Donaldson was tireless in his pursuit. On 14 February in another cheaply printed leaflet, this time titled 'To My Valentine – George Galloway', he complained that Eric Neilson had been awarded the contracts to build the Labour clubs in Ardler, Whitfield and Menzieshill without them being 'advertised in the local press so that other local building contractors could have the opportunity to tender for them'. According to Willie McKelvey and Martin this had been the case, but they were under no obligation to put the contracts out to tender. It had been up to the management committee of the Labour Party to decide, though it is surely preferable not to get competing quotes. The problem was that Neilson had been in at the outset and had found the sites at Whitfield and Ardler.

Meanwhile, Cassidy's team had started well and had a lot of grass-roots support in the area, among the ordinary folk, many of whom were Labour members. Cassidy herself had been a Labour Party member from the age of eighteen, but then left in 1983 after she became disillusioned with politics. She might have become disillusioned with brewers too when the finance deal she had hoped to sign with Dryborough's for the backing to build the scheme. Cassidy believes that pressure may have been brought to bear on the brewers to stay with the Labour Party, with whom they already had contracts. If that was the case, unfortunately for Cassidy and the residents, that's what happens in business. 'A caretaker from the high school, who was an SNP guy, came up to one of our open meetings and said he thought it was appalling. He did leaflets for us and they were going to guarantee us with another brewer.' Oh, the irony. For a time it looked as though Galloway might be driving support from the Labour Party to the SNP, who would end up with a stake in the proposed club.

Only it didn't end up like that. When Cassidy's Menzieshill Social Club Committee went to the council chambers a couple of days later to oppose the Labour Party's application they were unexpectedly met before the meeting by James Gowans. 'James Gowans said: "Watch what you say, because you are ruining Dundee."' Gowans asked them why they were there and told them that what they had to say was not allowable at the night's meeting because they hadn't written in first. Disaster. Their lack of knowledge of council rules meant they hadn't been put on the all-important bureaucrats' shopping list, the agenda. They went to the pub, where a little later two lads on their social committee came up to them.

> Billy Derby and Kevin Brown, who were both members of the Labour Party, . . . said the vote was going to go against us. They'd already counted up the votes before they had the discussion. They said: 'The Labour Party's taking it.' So we knew ahead that we were going to lose.

Knowing that they had been outplayed, they stayed to watch the discussion in the public gallery and later complained to the press that when the item came up for debate they were annoyed to hear Gowans say that their delegation had withdrawn and didn't want to speak, when they had wanted to but hadn't been allowed. In any case, they had missed the key opportunity and Labour got the go-ahead, after the committee recommended the Labour bid to the council's chief executive, Jim Hoey. From then on it was just a matter of negotiating the lease with the council's commercial manager, John Austin, and they got a pretty good deal. They were granted a lease of sixty years and an arrangement to pay the rent in arrears.

Cassidy is still very bitter about how the local folk were treated and believes that her scheme would have been more suited to the area than the Labour Party's. She even told Galloway that the Labour club was doomed, because no-one wanted it. With sadness she had to give back the money they'd raised for the bid.

> We had 500 members signed up for £10 each, and £1 for OAPs. We were running dances and raffles and raised more as well. When we went into liquidation, every member got their money back and we had £140 left over. £40 went to the local autistic children's Saturday club and £100 to Menzieshill High School.

The SNP was nonplussed and on 24 February Gordon Wilson, their MP for Dundee East, raised the issue in the Commons, calling it a 'sordid affair'[8] and asking if Ross should have declared an interest. Scottish minister Malcolm Rifkind replied that only financial interests had to be declared. A formal complaint was also lodged with the city ombudsman, who rejected claims that there had been any abuse of power by Labour bosses. So that was it for Cassidy and her bid. Menzieshill Labour Club opened towards the end of 1982, with Galloway's inner circle in charge. Ken Fagan was made manager, Galloway was vice-president and Frank Christie was on the committee.

So, at the end of 1982 Galloway had three Labour clubs under his wing, at Ardler, Whitfield and Menzieshill. Neil Kinnock even came and officially opened Menzieshill on 14 September 1983. He recalls:

> I was running for leadership and I went round Scotland with a group of MPs. Ernie Ross and Willie McKelvey, I think, were two of them. I was canvassing and I remember meeting Galloway in a Labour club in Dundee, which I opened, in fact. I even kept the rose bowl they gave me.

Rose bowls for Labour's hierarchy in the end wouldn't cut much ice and it wasn't going to be as easy as all that for Galloway. As one of his inner circle of the time now says: 'Menzieshill was doomed from the start because the locals were against it and didn't want to use it. They felt cheated because they'd wanted their own community club.' The treatment of the ordinary folk of Menzieshill was not Labour's finest hour. The resulting financial chaos could be regarded as natural justice, but the only people who lost out in the end were the locals.

The pathos and unhappiness wouldn't stop at Menzieshill. There was a sign of things to come in February 1983 when the Roseangle club, one of the original inspirations for Galloway's plan, ran into financial difficulties. Galloway announced that it would close for refurbishment, with debts of £17,000. 'The club is situated in an excellent area and we couldn't see it going on any longer trying to break even when it should be earning the same as other clubs in the city, which pull in over £1 million a year.'[9] It closed its doors but, contrary to Galloway's upbeat announcement, it never reopened.

8

Leaving Dundee

George Galloway's well-established links with the Middle East still cause controversy at every turn. Time has moved on, leaving the letters PLO less shocking than they used to be, but back in the early 1980s they would have been of similar impact to Hezbollah and at that time the PLO connection was both a positive and a negative factor in his political life. It would undermine Galloway's image, being used time and time again by the press to have a dig at him and at Ken Fagan, Colin Rennie and his other acolytes. But his close ties to the Palestinian issue have proved very useful in making links with students, trade unionists and other Labour Party members, as well as promoting him in the international arena.

On the student side, Galloway was a regular speaker at the local universities, gathering support. He is remembered by those who saw him in their student days as being a great orator and charismatic leader, who brought a lot of new members to the Labour Party. Galloway's ability to motivate is one of his great strengths. Inspired by Galloway, in March 1982 Joan Ingram, a beauty queen and senior vice-president of Dundee University Students Association went to the West Bank as guest of the PLO. This also attracted bad press and Galloway himself had to defend her in the papers.

Over the years Galloway has had to weather various squalls over the PLO, to add to the initial outcry over the twinning decision. In 1982 the Scottish papers were full of 'PLO Tours!'[1] and similar headlines when they found out that the Trade Union Friends of Palestine (TUFP), of which Galloway was a leading member, had invited Labour's Scottish Executive Committee to be their guests and visit parts of the Middle East. The trips were to be funded by the Palestinian Trade Union Federation, which had close ties to the PLO. On this occasion the outcry was so great that the

Labour Party told their members not to go. Despite this instruction, several members went anyway.

Others were also following his lead over twinning of Dundee with Nablus and in May 1982 he fell out with a young medical student called Liam Fox, who was president of the Glasgow University Conservative Club, when Galloway supported the Students' Union motion to twin with Bir-Zeit in the West Bank.[2] Although Galloway has admitted that the Nablus experiment (see Chapter 6) could have been dealt with better, it had certainly been a very useful introduction to the area and had generated a wealth of publicity for him personally and the Palestinian cause.

His links with Nablus continue to today, and he has made many visits over the years, but in 1982 Dundee's twinned town was suffering under Israeli occupation and the whole elected council had been dismissed, so it was a particularly important visit when he went to the town in late spring. He met the now ex-mayor, Bassem Al-Shaka, who had been put under house arrest, accused of terrorism. With Galloway were Hugh Wyper of the TGWU and John Walker of ASLEF, who were both interested in forming links with trade unionists and were also introduced by Galloway to King Hussein of Jordan and Yasser Arafat on the trip. Galloway described Israel's 'brutality and harassment' of the Palestinians when he got back and laid the blame at the door of Prime Minister Menachem Begin.

It was a tense time in the Middle East and they were there just before Israel launched an invasion of Lebanon on 6 June. It was a tumultuous time for the UK too. It was the middle of the Falklands War, with heavy fighting taking place until the Argentine surrender on 14 June, and the British and world papers were full of it. Galloway, who supported military action against General Leopoldo Galtieri's army, believed that Israel had launched the attack on Lebanon under the cover of the Falklands conflict. That's possible, though it was more likely a little bit of luck that they didn't need. The invasion had the effect of galvanising anti-Israeli support in the trade union movement and the TUFP organised a series of meetings to raise awareness of the issues around the country. Meanwhile, Galloway found strange bedfellows in Margaret Thatcher and her Foreign Secretary, Francis Pym, who both openly backed a separate Palestinian state. That, and kicking Galtieri out of the Falklands were about all they would agree on, though, and in the run-up to the 1983 general election, it was becoming ever clearer that there was a yawning gulf between not just the Conservatives and Labour, but between Tony Benn and Michael Foot.

Labour's 1983 election defeat was a disaster waiting to happen. Gerald Kaufman's devastating description of his own party's manifesto as being 'the longest suicide note in history' sums it up pretty well, although in Scotland the picture was different and Labour were in a much better position than across the UK generally. Foot's introduction to the manifesto, which he describes as a 'programme of socialist reconstruction', talks of huge spending using North Sea oil revenues and borrowing: 'We will expand the economy, by providing a strong and measured increase in spending. Spending money creates jobs.' Foot went on to say that Labour would 'begin a huge programme of construction, so that we can start to build our way out of the slump'. They would also 'repeal Tory legislation on industrial relations and make provision for introducing industrial democracy . . . begin the return to public ownership of those public industries sold off by the Tories . . . [bring about] the removal of nuclear bases from Britain, which is to be completed within the lifetime of the Labour government . . . prepare for Britain's withdrawal from the EEC, to be completed well within the lifetime of the Labour government.'

To be fair to Michael Foot, he had been lumbered with a manifesto that the Bennite left had forced on him. They'd carefully placed this last straw, pretty happy that it was likely to break their leader's back. Such were the divisions at the time that many thought an election defeat was what they wanted. Galloway, however, was bullish in the run-up to the vote. In *Radical Scotland* of April–May 1983 he wrote: 'Scotland must play its part in electing a new Labour government to begin the long haul to industrial recovery, and the shorter step towards national renaissance, the establishment of a powerful elected Assembly in Edinburgh.'

As part of the plan to get his inner circle elected in Dundee, Galloway decided to revive the *Dundee Standard*. They needed a voice for their policies and found that they could get cheap printing done if they used the presses of the Workers Revolutionary Party (WRP). They devised a strange system whereby they paid a Labour member to drive from Dundee to the printers in Runcorn, Cheshire every week and pick up the papers. Despite having to pay him £100 a time, it was thought to work out cheaper than using a local printer. The WRP is the far-left group well known for having Vanessa Redgrave as a member. Though small and on the fringe of mainstream politics, they attracted the interest of Colonel Gaddafi of Libya, who seemed to think they were more influential than they were. They are so extreme in their revolutionary views that even members of the left describe them as 'left-wing loonies'.

Their headquarters were in an out-of-town industrial estate, surrounded by high walls and high-tech security cameras. Back in the early 1980s it was unheard of to have this kind of protection and it backed up the reputation of the WRP for being secretive. When they were asked about their use of cameras outside their premises, a representative said it was because 'we have no way of knowing if prying reporters are with the police on assignment, or are in league with the fascists'.[3]

When Galloway went down to Runcorn to meet the WRP and discuss the printing, they were so suspicious of him and the others that they refused to answer the door. After repeated calls on the intercom, and just when they all thought they'd had a wasted journey, they were told that they would be allowed to meet at the house the party used, a few minutes' drive away. They waited and waited, then eventually they were escorted down the road and given a cup of tea, in a 'pig sty' with someone who 'looked like he was out of the film *Deliverance*', according to one of the Dundee men. They talked about the arrangements for the weekly print run. It was all agreed and the deal went ahead.

Though all they were doing was using the WRP's printing facilities, the connection would later raise eyebrows when it came out as part of a BBC TV investigation into the financial links between the WRP and Gaddafi. In *The Money Programme* of 20 March 1983 allegations were made that the WRP was receiving money from Gaddafi. When the BBC found out that Dundee Labour Party had a deal with the WRP, the programme makers travelled up to interview Galloway, who explained something of the way his printing arrangement worked. But when he was asked how much money he saved by using their presses, he refused to divulge the details, claiming that just as Rupert Murdoch wasn't going to tell his financial secrets, so they couldn't expect him to tell.

On the programme Galloway claimed Dundee Labour Party had asked for a quotation from all of Scotland's printers who could produce newspapers, and that the WRP quote was cheapest. When asked if the WRP quote had been considerably cheaper, he replied: 'No, not considerably cheaper, especially not when the costs of getting to Runcorn and back are taken into account, but sufficiently cheaper.' The BBC pressed him to be precise about how much cheaper and he said: 'Well, I think in the region of £100 to £200 cheaper. Now that's a lot of money when you have very little.' They asked how much the cost of the transport was out of the total cost and he went on: 'Well, I mean, I think I told you before we went on air that you wouldn't get Rupert Murdoch giving you all his trade secrets and you'll not get me giving you all of mine.' Straight after the cameras were turned off, Galloway rounded on the BBC's producer, Suzanne Franks, who remembers him 'shouting at me' for allowing that line of questioning, when he felt it had been arranged for him to be asked less searching questions.

For Galloway to compare himself to Murdoch was pretty ludicrous, particularly as this enterprise seemed to be doomed to fail all over again. They couldn't sell many papers and bundles of them were left at the Labour clubs. Other Labour Party members of the time remember the piles were never picked up and were just lying around. When the local newsagents came under pressure not to stock it and were threatened with withdrawal of their other papers if they did, the *Dundee Standard* looked like the walking dead.

The costs of production were hard to assess, but *The Money Programme* established that Dundee Labour had done an unusual deal. The WRP had told the BBC that they would only consider a print run of 20,000 or more for a community newspaper, but Galloway had claimed their print run was just 8,000. It's possible that the WRP were just happy to have their adverts in the *Dundee Standard*, and that had helped swing the deal. When questioned in *The Money Programme* about his links with the WRP, Galloway was unequivocal: 'I'm not a supporter of the Libyan government. I'm not a supporter of the WRP and my only connections to the WRP are that I along with my colleagues tried to get a struggling left-wing publication printed by them.'

Whatever the finances of the *Dundee Standard*, it was canned again in a matter of months. If Dundee Labour Party had hoped it might affect the outcome of the 1983 general election, they were mistaken, as Dundee East was held by the SNP's Gordon Wilson, and in Dundee West Ernie Ross would surely have triumphed without it. By this time the broad left coalition, which had been formed initially to fight the right wing of the party and had seen communist union leaders brought in to boost support, was falling apart. The problem was that Galloway had been discredited among the public sector unions ever since he had tried to convince the party to take on Margaret Thatcher over public spending and the sale of council houses. He'd wanted to take a stand and risk rate capping and jail for councillors. That was all very well for him, they reasoned; his job and liberty weren't at stake, unlike those of their members. When it had come to a vote in the Labour Management Committee, Galloway had lost convincingly. After that, it was 'fratricide', according to several Labour men of the time, and it seemed that the democratic centralism of Galloway's dreams was over.

Add to that the fact that J. L. Stewart was about to be released from jail, having sworn revenge on the men who'd help put him there, and Dundee was not looking such an attractive place for Galloway. Stewart had been behind much of the gossip and scheming against Galloway even from inside prison, and he had openly compared himself to the revengeful Count of Monte Cristo when he had been led away in the first place. As Graham Ogilvy remembers, 'J.L. was a tremendously persuasive, charismatic fellow and very determined to get Galloway . . . A lot of people were afraid of him.'

So for a number of reasons Galloway had been looking for a way out. He had bigger plans than to stay in Dundee, and clearly his next step after being Labour's secretary/organiser, and having been the chair of Labour's Scottish National Executive, was to become an MP. He'd failed to gain selection to stand for Parliament in Rhondda, and he was looking around at other possibilities. He was impatient to leave the city and not long after the general election, he applied for a job with War on Want, the world poverty charity, which had been advertised in the *Guardian*. The job description, which had been written in May 1983 and which was supplied to those interested in applying, included the following:

> The Council of Management is looking for an experienced and mature candidate with the following background: knowledge and awareness of the

politics of aid; understanding of the links between the UK and the Third World, together with a capacity to utilise them; communications skills; administrative ability and experience; experience in campaigning; knowledge of financial management and budgeting.

One of the council of management, Louise Carmi, had helped write the job description and remembers the selection process:

> Other applicants included Anna Ford's husband, [the late] Mark Boxer. And another MP who'd just lost his seat in the 1983 election. The interview panel was me, chair Vivienne Lukey and treasurer Ken Ritchie . . . George did a very good interview, as you'd expect. He said he had good links with the Labour movement and we thought we wanted a younger, up-and-coming person for the job. He did have the right political agenda for us too.

So Galloway was offered the job, at just twenty-nine. It was to be a momentous time for him and the charity, to rival any of the controversies of his career.

War on Want was set up by Harold Wilson, the former Liberal MP Sir Richard Acland and the publisher Victor Gollancz. It had grown out of Gollancz's Association for World Peace, which had produced a pamphlet called *Tanks into Tractors* on the need to link development with world peace. This was groundbreaking stuff and when Wilson came up with the title *War on Want* for a 1951 report on world poverty, the concept for an organisation with peace and an end to poverty as its joined goal was a natural next stage.

War on Want formally became a charity in 1959, though it had been running as a series of committees since that initial report. Small groups around the country raised money and awareness of the issues. The Glasgow committee flourished, with support from the Christian Iona Community, whose members all gave a percentage of their money to charity. Scottish War on Want was the first to use the phrase 'war on want' in a pamphlet. It called for supporters to take political action: 'Wage war on want. Scotland – act now. Public opinion must be roused. A full-scale national effort must be made.'

That call to action hit the streets of Glasgow in the year of Galloway's birth, 1954. Although he wouldn't arrive for almost thirty years, the political nature of that appeal is key to understanding the problems that would face the charity and which would come to a head under Galloway's leadership.

Looking back at War on Want in the late 1970s and early 1980s, before Galloway, we see that its finances were in a terrible state and some of its ideas to raise money were equally lame. They had a few charity shops, which raised around £¼ million, but added to that they had been involved in strange schemes in Manchester such as a vegetarian restaurant called Grapevine, a folk music shop that also sold clogs, and an agency for punk bands, all imaginative, but amateur. So dire were the finances in the early 1980s that in 1982 the general secretary, Terry Lacey, had to agree to redundancies and cutbacks (in that year War on Want had an operating loss of £201,235).[4] Despite having arranged for more funding from the EEC, Lacey felt obliged to leave after a motion at that year's AGM of a 'lack of confidence in the ability of the Council of Management and General Secretary to deal capably with financial and personnel matters'.

Simon Stocker became the acting general secretary, while they tried to find a replacement, and he did a good job of getting the organisation back on an even keel financially and gained the respect of the staff and the council of management. In the end they found Galloway to take over permanently, attracted by his dynamism and aware that there were risks involved. Over the next four years War on Want would go through what the official history diplomatically calls 'a whirlwind of a time'.[5]

9

A War on Want

Controversy has never been far from George Galloway, from the Bunty Turley incident to *Big Brother*, and will probably beset him all his life. But the War on Want years may leave the bitterest taste. Twenty years on, many of the kind people he left spinning in his wake at War on Want are still traumatised by it all.

Galloway took up his new job in November 1983. The War on Want council of management welcomed the vibrant and ambitious 29-year-old with open arms. Their new general secretary appeared to be just the sort of passionate, committed socialist they needed to increase the good work they were already doing for the world's poor. They wanted to expand and Galloway had told them he was the man to do it for them, using his contacts in the Labour Party and unions and his knowledge of fund raising.

Galloway regards his time at War on Want as a great success and it's a line that many have believed, but if you dig you find many different versions. It is claimed that he left staff morale at an all-time low, and there were financial problems which ran so deep that the Charity Commission held up War on Want as a warning to others. In its report it said the 'acrimonious' internal conflicts of Galloway's time 'became the focus of attention of many of those concerned who became distracted in varying degrees from proper consideration of other important financial matters during the period'.[1] There was also to be deep concern expressed about the level of his expenses.

Galloway used his War on Want credit card on many occasions, and in the financial year 1985/6 his expenses totalled over £20,000, when the year before they had been just £3,000. His salary was £22,000.

So how did a peaceful little charity, founded to help the poverty-stricken Third World, end up divided, with opposing factions leaking damaging stories to the newspapers? To understand how War on Want's war on poverty led to its own civil war, one has to examine the clash between the Labour party's methods used in Dundee and those of an organisation where financial and administrative power had always been devolved to a few key workers in the field, and where there was trust and reliance in the general secretary, with only general guidelines laid down.

Four programme officers looked after the four areas of action: north Africa and the Middle East; southern Africa; South and Central America; and the Indian sub-continent. They had a reputation among some of the War on Want staff for being difficult to deal with. Martin Plaut, a member of the council of management, was chair of programmes, overseeing the policy from London. He says: 'The programme officers are the core of the organisation. I was the chair but I never got a programme officer's plan overturned.' Another full-time member remembers that 'the whole problem started because of a lack of cohesiveness. The four programme officers didn't communicate with Galloway; maybe they found him threatening.'

Galloway was fresh down from parochial Dundee, where he had controlled everything from the centre. The idea that decisions involving considerable sums of money could be taken in Africa, or South America say, without agreement from HQ in London, was unlikely to please him. Meanwhile, his determination to be the face of War on Want, in the publicity shots, shaking hands around the globe, would upset the programme officers in return.

When Galloway took up his post, in November 1983, London must have seemed expensive compared to Dundee and he was a stranger in town who had to find a place to rent, while Elaine and his young daughter Lucy were still in Scotland.

Louise Carmi, one of the council of management who had appointed him, said he could stay in the Bloomsbury flat of her mother-in-law, who had recently died. He jumped at the chance of living so centrally. Discussions of money were a bit vague, as Carmi understood that the intention was for him to find somewhere permanent as soon as he could. In fact Galloway stayed there for over a year, paying irregularly. Carmi remembers now that

after six months he offered me £25 a week. I'm sure he ended up paying me what he owed, but he'd give me £100 every now and then. It started me thinking about his finances. He never seemed to have any money . . . When I finally got the flat back there had been a fire and a flood, which had left damage. [No fault of Galloway in either case.]

Galloway was in a new job, in a new city, with big plans. He quickly found common ground with the chatty Ken Ritchie, a fellow Scot, who'd been working for War on Want since 1973. Ken had combined research for a PhD with research for the charity and had then become a council member in 1977. He was totally committed to the ideals and found himself on many occasions talking politics and poverty with Galloway. Ritchie recalls: 'I was Scottish and he saw me as an ally. We'd go out, sometimes with Ernie Ross and Willie McKelvey, who were both MPs down from Scotland. They were older than him, but on so many issues they would turn to him to ask for the position to take.' Whatever their arguments, 'one thing they all agreed on was the threat of a young upstart called Gordon Brown'.

One night Galloway, Ross, McKelvey and Ritchie all had free tickets to see fellow War on Want council member Simon Fanshawe perform in a show called *Three of a Kind* at the Drill Hall, just off Tottenham Court Road. They sat at a table at the front, but at a comedy show that's not necessarily a good thing and so it proved. Ritchie recalls that the show featured the openly gay Fanshawe, a lesbian and a straight male Scottish comic. While Ross, McKelvey and Galloway were clearly uncomfortable with all the gay banter, it got a lot worse when the straight comic suddenly took all his clothes off and came and sat on McKelvey's knee. While the crowd fell about laughing, McKelvey didn't know where to put himself. 'I'd wanted to go because it was Simon Fanshawe, like George had too, but I thought at the time that George was also fascinated by this different London culture. He hadn't long been down from Dundee.' It was all a long way from the traditional working men's clubs of Dundee.

Light relief was to become unusual in the years of Galloway's tenure as general secretary. There was work to be done, fighting for the world's poor. One of the first high-profile campaigns of Galloway's War on Want was the One Hour's Pay campaign. The idea was that every worker should give one hour's pay to the charity. Galloway threw himself into it, even though it was the brainchild of the previous general secretary, Simon Stocker. It was a successful campaign, in that it raised the profile of War on Want further and it was something that Galloway could get his teeth into because he could call on his union contacts to propel the idea into factories around the land.

Galloway had arrived at War on Want with a mission to 'strengthen links with the political world from which he came', according to the official history of the charity, written by Mark Leutchford and Peter Burns. The authors are very careful, but even they don't disguise the differences of opinion that soon emerged between the new boss and the old regime. They went on: 'Galloway came from a tradition of political organising that did not sit easily with the positions adopted by War on Want.' Stocker, who for Galloway's first year or so worked very closely with him in handing over the reins, recalls: 'When he first arrived we talked a lot. He was doing OK at first and was very positive, but he wanted to get more of his own people involved.'

Even the fact that he wore a suit and tie was seen by some as a problem. When he threw a Westminster party to schmooze politicians, journalists and diplomats, some argued that serving free food and wine was inappropriate for a poverty charity, even though the party had been hosted by Harold Wilson, War on Want's founder.

Little things like that began to chip away at the initial good feeling between Galloway and his colleagues. Then the biggest domestic political issue of the day broke into the internationally focused War on Want like a battering ram.

During the 1984 miners' strike Galloway tried again and again to get funding diverted to the pits from War on Want funds, but the council resisted, concerned that British issues were against the objectives of the Third World charity. A key member of staff recalls now that 'he was following his own political agenda . . . he wanted us to get stuck in. He tried over and over to divert resources to the miners' strike, but staff would come and report it to the council. This happened for months, but no significant sums were given.'

Galloway's frustration at the lack of co-operation over such an important issue for him and many in the union movement caused tension with many of the staff and management council and was a hint of the rows to come. Stocker remembers that Galloway decided pretty early on that he needed more support. 'From the outset he'd wanted to bring in trade unionists to build links with the union movement and to change the culture of War on Want.'

Galloway had to get more influence on the controlling management council. What he needed was some other comrades, with Scottish accents as it happens. He decided to import some, as replacements for some of the old guard, starting with Scottish War on Want. At their 1985 AGM strange scenes took place. The normally quiet event involving a few dozen supporters was instead turned into a rowdy affair when thirty or so students from Strathclyde University got involved. The old team were voted off the council of management and supporters of Galloway were installed. Mark Lazarowicz, now an MP, became the new chair, while John Boothman, who had been the full-time organiser of Scottish War on Want, was voted on to the council. Boothman had also been president of Strathclyde University Students' Union. Tom Connor, a former vice-president of Strathclyde Students' Union, became treasurer. Connor, who didn't stay at Scottish War on Want long, is now at the BBC in Scotland and recalls: 'We wouldn't have been naive enough to have let ourselves be used. We wanted to be active and we voted for a positive reason, not to get rid of the old guard. It was about the future. I wouldn't have known who was on the council.'

How the students had become involved is interesting. Just after Live Aid, in November 1985, the BBC and War on Want staged a concert in Glasgow called Classical Aid. Galloway was heavily involved, travelling specially up and down from London to help set it up. A group from Strathclyde University helped out for nothing, in publicity and on the day. There had been a long connection with Galloway, who they had often booked to speak at their meetings. 'I thought he put a lot of effort into Classical Aid. He was someone trying to get a charity more publicity and to be more upfront. We all thought, yes, let's back him. It was very positive. He had good ideas,' says Connor now.

The Scottish War on Want AGM was around the same time as Classical Aid, and although they'd had little to do with War on Want, the students turned up at the AGM to vote for the people who ran it. Subsequently, there were questions raised about their eligibility to vote. Connor doesn't remember ever officially joining and filling in a membership form, but says:

'I doubt we would have been allowed to vote if we hadn't been eligible.' The Charity Commissioners' report into War on Want some years later noted that there had been an 'absence of proper membership records'.

With Scottish War on Want now operating as planned, it was time to get more support at HQ in London. Stocker recalls:

> I had had discussions with George where he talked about adding new members to take part in the elections, but I don't know if that happened. All of which was quite within the rules and in the end the numbers would have been small. He had a lot of credibility with the membership anyway.

Over his years at War on Want, membership would be a repeated source of friction between Galloway's supporters and those in the organisation who opposed his leadership. Often it came down to a fight between the old guard and the new Scottish contingent that Galloway had brought in to help him gain more central control and, as he hoped, more efficiency.

Any organisation operating in the muddy waters of world politics, the arms race and famine was bound to find it tough to keep politically neutral, as a charity had to. Through its history there had been internal disagreements over who War on Want should do business with in war-torn areas. When the only way to get aid to the starving population is through a corrupt regime, or a rebel army, it's a hard call. The key decisions on these matters tended to rest with War on Want's programme officers, who were on the ground, where the trouble was. It was they who had the information at their fingertips, they who understood that theory is all very well, but in the real world the priority is people's lives. It was in some ways a good system but one that a centralist such as Galloway wouldn't like – but, to be fair to him, neither did others.

The programme officers and the Finance Department were often at loggerheads. They were slow to provide information to each other and even their accounting systems differed. Programme officers would bypass Galloway and talk to the other members of the council of management, which quite understandably must have put his back up. Years later, in the Charity Commission report into what went wrong at War on Want, Galloway explained that after a year his relationship with the Programme

Department degenerated and became 'catastrophic'. To try and get control, he appointed Simon Stocker deputy general secretary. Stocker was a programme officer himself, looking after southern Africa. The idea was that he would report to Galloway and keep him abreast of what was going on when Galloway didn't have time.

It's easy to forget just how inexperienced Galloway was at this stage of his career. The Charity Commissioners' report commented that he hadn't 'had any financial training or management experience'. A period in a job at a Dundee tyre factory and working for the local council were the most he'd seen of the world outside politics. It showed in that first attempt to bring the Programme Department under his control. Stocker was too much a programme officer himself to have become an effective right-hand man, the eyes and ears of Galloway.

Galloway's next move was predictable. He went back to the methods he learned in Dundee and in left-wing Scottish politics: if in doubt, take control of the committees. It was key to take away the power of the programmes committee, which controlled much of War on Want's business. Galloway told the Charity Commission in 1990:

> I felt generally that the Programmes Department had erected a pretty impenetrable wall around our work . . . That part which surrounded the Horn of Africa work was the thickest. To continue the metaphor, any attempt to scale that wall risked, and in my case did [*sic*], the bringing about of a vat of boiling oil poured over one's head.[2]

What he did was to restructure the existing seven committees into three, one for finance and general purposes, one women's committee and one programmes committee. 'It was an attempt . . . of mine to set up a countervailing force . . . one powerful committee, a finance and general purposes committee. It is a model I borrowed from trades unions . . . I wanted to shift . . . the axis of power to the finance and general purposes committee.'[3] Clearly, this wasn't going to go down well with the people who thought they ran War on Want, in other words the programme officers. The scene had been set for a showdown, with a backdrop of the dusty famine in the Horn of Africa.

One employee in particular took Galloway on. James Firebrace was War on Want's programme officer for north Africa and the Middle East, which included the Horn of Africa. Since 1977 War on Want had been helping the people of Eritrea, who wanted independence from Ethiopia and whose army had been fighting the Ethiopians for years. The Ethiopians had been supported on and off by the USA and USSR, but in Galloway's time at War on Want they were being backed by the Soviets. A small minority of others at War on Want were drawn to the Soviet Union and this posed a dilemma for them, because Firebrace was putting money into projects to help the Eritreans, using his contacts with the Eritrean People's Liberation Front, who were fighting the Soviet-backed Ethiopian army. Galloway would later say:

> I was always . . . worried, from a political standpoint first, at what I would almost describe as the fanatical orientation of the organisation toward the two liberation movements [the EPLF and its parent movement, the Eritrean Liberation Front] . . . the extent of War on Want's support, totally uncritical support, for these two organisations disturbed me from a political standpoint. I thought it put us out of kilter with . . . substantial sections of the British left, which was, generally speaking, our constituency.

Others on the left disagree fundamentally with that. Glenys Kinnock, the wife of the former Labour leader Neil Kinnock and at the heart of the Labour Party modernising movement in the 1980s, would later chair War on Want's council of management. She saw the support of the Eritreans as 'a natural place for the Left, fighting for freedom. A just cause against a colonising Ethiopian army.'

Despite these differing views in the organisation, Galloway was pragmatic and realised that the Horn of Africa was bringing lots of 'business' their way and was a perfect PR vehicle. How right he was. The famine in Ethiopia was about to become the biggest story in world news. When the BBC filmed thousands starving to death in the dust, it drove Bob Geldof and Midge Ure to form Band Aid for Christmas 1984 and then stage the groundbreaking and enormously influential rock concert Live Aid, the following summer. Giving money to charity suddenly became the coolest thing for a new generation and Galloway's War on Want was right at the centre of it all. Their banners were all over Live Aid. With no religious associations, they were a very hip charity.

Galloway was a powerful advocate for change. In War on Want's annual report of 1984/5 he summed up the obscene situation by asking: 'How is it possible to film people dying and send pictures back live via satellite, yet still impossible to bring them the food and the medicines to keep them alive?' He then went on: 'The organisation has undergone a year of phenomenal growth. Our income has grown faster than any other British agency.' At the back of the report a simple graphic showed the growth in income from £1.7 million in 1983/4 to £7.3 million in 1984/5.

Yet this is only part of the story. In fact, Firebrace had become the key man on the ground in Eritrea and Ethiopia, not just for War on Want, but for all the other charities too. While every other aid group was based in Ethiopia, War on Want was in Eritrea and so everything had to go through them. Several consortia of aid agencies had been formed in 1983, well before Galloway had joined. Firebrace led the consortia. It was a huge undertaking, the financial management of which would later be deeply criticised by the Charity Commission report into War on Want.

Back in early 1985 Band Aid, Cafod, Christian Aid, Oxfam and many others from around the world were involved in War on Want's consortia, but all the money they raised went through just one central account. That's why War on Want's income seemed at first sight to have leapt up so far. In the 1985/6 annual report you have to look at another breakdown of the accounts and notice a small asterisk to find out that the £7.3 million included over £3 million that was just being put through the War on Want books on behalf of other agencies. Julian Hopkins, the finance officer, remembers:

> I was worried because we weren't equipped for this level of work. George Galloway wanted the money because War on Want would get an admin fee based on the turnover. The money came from the Overseas Development Agency [ODA], the EEC and from the other charities . . . Oxfam and so on. Some on the council were worried about the control of things.

Others had never felt comfortable with taking money from the British government and the EEC, a practice which had started under the previous general secretary. Everyone on War on Want's council of management agreed it was important to keep a distance from any government, but the ODA and EEC development funds were too important to ignore. What happened to the money when they'd got it was so badly managed that it brought the charity to its knees a few years later.

Articles by journalists who quoted Galloway's figures without looking deeper helped perpetuate the myths. For example, *The Times* of 29 October 1986 ran a piece that said: 'From an overdraft of £60,000 at his arrival three years ago the charity's income last year had soared to £7,323,000 with a surplus of £416,763.' This is pretty useless information without the context, particularly as War on Want had never had an overdraft. They had made a loss of around £60,000, but that's very different from an overdraft. They'd called on reserves, according to Ken Ritchie, the treasurer of the time. But by comparison with others, *The Times* was a paragon of solid reporting. The *Guardian* had it that War on Want had been £600,000 in the red and now had '£3 million in the bank'.

But you could forgive journalists' mistakes when the War on Want management were happy to exaggerate their success. Vivienne Lukey told the Charity Commission inquiry: 'I was aware that it gave the impression that we were better off than we were, that we had done better at fund raising than we had done. But all of us inside the organisation were aware that that was an artificial impression.'

So when Galloway refers to the big successes under his leadership, you have to look a little closer at what he means. Certainly, as with virtually every other charity doing business in the mid-1980s, there was a marked increase in income, but he was perhaps slow to point out how a lot of that had happened – so slow that the other members of the consortia complained. Over £3 million of their money had made War on Want's figures look amazing and their names hadn't even appeared in the report. They felt that their hard work was being glossed over. The following year War on Want's annual report contained a careful explanation of the way the fund worked, with all the charities listed.

When Galloway's troubles of the time are mentioned now, the emphasis lies on his expenses bill. In fact, War on Want's management council first called for Galloway's resignation over something completely different, which resulted directly from the management of the Horn of Africa consortia.

In 1985 and 1986 money flowed in from all directions, destined mostly for work in Ethiopia and Eritrea. War on Want's total income in 1985 leapt to £7,224,670 and in 1986 it stood at £6,231,943.[4] The vast majority of this income was going straight out again, as it should in a charity, with the little retained for running costs. In 1985 and 1986 the amount of money left over at the end of both years was around £300,000.

The real credit for the enormous boost in War on Want's income had to go in the main to Firebrace. How that money was being managed back at base wasn't his responsibility, but he did see it as his right to make decisions on expenditure that in any other organisation would have required more senior agreement.

The terrible drought of 1984–5 that had led to the famine, Live Aid and War on Want's enormous increase in business, was still killing thousands. The people needed wells, dug deep down to the water table. In March 1986, without consulting Galloway, Firebrace contracted an American firm to provide a well-drilling rig for Eritrea at a cost of £750,000, a vast sum at the time. This had been after much discussion between key members of the consortia, but no discussion with Galloway. Galloway claims he didn't know anything about this until he received a phone call from a British manufacturer complaining that they hadn't been given an opportunity to bid for the work.[5] He was understandably indignant, and staff remember him angrily complaining to anyone in earshot that Firebrace had become 'paranoid', had been on a 'madcap spending spree' and must have been having 'a nervous breakdown'.

Finding that one of your employees has just spent £¾ million without telling you would enrage any reasonable person and in the heat of the moment Galloway said things he later openly regretted and apologised for.[6] Simon Stocker remembers that 'George quite rapidly moved into confrontation mode. He was quite vindictive towards James in private to me. He said something along the lines of he was going to "get him".' But the respect in the organisation for Firebrace was such that Galloway's angry outburst was the final straw for those who had been unhappy with the way he'd been making big changes and his somewhat abrasive management style.

By coincidence, Firebrace had broken his leg skiing and was off work. When Ritchie rang him to check on his health and talk about the situation, he discovered that he was perfectly rational, perhaps just suffering from some concussion. All unrelated to the decision to buy the rig. They discussed Galloway's reaction to £750,000 purchase and the unhappiness of many of the staff at Galloway's management.

Pretty soon it became obvious that elements in the council of management, together with Firebrace and some other staff, were determined that Galloway had to resign. However, they needed to build a case against him to force him out. Stocker recalls: 'James decided to mobilise the management council against Galloway. I thought that was unacceptable behaviour and I had some limited sympathy for George. A boss needs the support of his staff.'

It wasn't long before another classic bit of Galloway management gave his enemies more ammunition. It came after a high-profile visit to the Horn of Africa for War on Want by Glenys Kinnock. 'We'd been to Eritrea to see the aftermath of the retreat of the Ethiopian army. There was terrible carnage, but it was a moment of hope for the displaced people,' she recalls now. A large press pack, including the Kinnocks' friend Alastair Campbell of the *Daily Mirror*, had been on the trip too. There was big popular interest in the work being done to alleviate the famine, after Live Aid the year before.

Glenys Kinnock subsequently wrote a book on the crisis, while War on Want planned to publish an article about the trip in its annual report. It seems such a small thing now, but when Galloway put his own headline, 'Optimism in Ethiopia', over the piece, Firebrace took exception, claiming that it was all part of Galloway's plan to change the strategy over the region and start siding with the Ethiopians. In fact, it's unlikely that Galloway was doing anything other than making the most of a little good news to make War on Want look more effective in the region. However, it was claimed that Firebrace thought it might undermine fund raising and annoy other members of the consortia. Clearly, giving too positive a spin on things might lead potential donors to think they should give money to other causes. However, Galloway was unsurprisingly itching to get the good news out that War on Want's work in the famine areas was paying off. The printing presses were set to roll and a decision had to be made quickly. So a council of management meeting was arranged for Thursday 13 March, where Ritchie, together with Martin Plaut and Louise Carmi, decided unanimously that publication should be delayed for a week to allow for more thought.

When news reached an impatient Galloway, he immediately rang Vivienne Lukey, who had yet to vote because she hadn't been able to make the meeting. According to all four of the management council, Galloway told her she had the deciding vote, even though it was useless against the three already cast.

Not knowing that the vote had already been lost, Lukey said to go ahead with publication, which happened shortly afterwards. When the other three told her what had happened she was horrified and angry. They called Galloway to a private meeting on 22 March 1986, a Saturday morning. At that meeting they put it to him that because of his comments about Firebrace and this latest incident, he should resign and go quietly, or take the matter to the council. Galloway looked shocked, but said he would not go. He also explained that he did have a quick temper and that he was going to apologise to Firebrace, which he did the following day.

Around the same time, Treasurer Ritchie became aware that Galloway's expenses bill was increasing hugely in comparison with the previous year's. Ritchie's duties were to monitor the financial running of the charity, so he asked Julian Hopkins to provide him with details. Hopkins was a full-time employee and ran the finance office, with a small team of administrative staff.

When the finance office collected the separate expenses claims from the various clerks the picture of Galloway's spending became all too clear. It was running into thousands. When Ritchie saw the details he was shocked at what he found and the four senior members of the council of management, himself, Plaut, Lukey and Carmi, decided to consult an expert in charity law at the solicitors Bates, Wells and Braithwaite. The advice was that they had an obligation as trustees to pursue their inquiries so that the accounts could be settled for the year. Carmi also told the Charity Commission in October 1990 that she recalled being advised that they should get Galloway to go as soon as possible.

A week or so later, just before the council of management meeting of 6 April, Plaut, Ritchie, Carmi and Lukey had an informal meeting with Galloway to discuss matters. Carmi recalls that 'we kept it to ourselves what we were doing, to protect War on Want'. The idea was to get him to go quietly. From Galloway's perspective, though, this must have looked like a conspiracy to unseat him.

With only a few minutes to go before the council meeting, they laid it on the line to Galloway. After going over the Firebrace allegations and saying that they had talked to him and all seemed fine with him mentally, Ritchie then raised with Galloway the issue of his expense account. Carmi recalls that 'he went white' and sat back quite shaken as Ritchie put it to him that they were concerned that he might have been using his War on Want credit card improperly. Plaut remembers: 'He was gobsmacked. He didn't think he'd been doing anything wrong. He thought this was his role to wine and dine and believed that if it was an advantage to him, it was an advantage to the organisation.'

Ritchie then said to Galloway that he should take six months' pay and resign. If there were any thoughts in Galloway's head that this was just a bunch of flaky part-timers who would go away, that must have disabused him of them. And for it to come from Ritchie, the fellow Scot who had socialised with him outside the office over the months, was doubly galling.

After Galloway had composed himself, he firmly denied all the unfounded allegations of wrongdoing and left the meeting. The last thing he wanted, within spitting distance of the next election and the chance to fulfil his dream of entering Parliament, was to have to quit this job, leaving rumours behind him. It would be necessary for him to resolve this mess, to win this fight.

Waiting outside the room were Galloway's supporters Bill Speirs, Campbell Christie, Mark Lazarowicz, Laurie Gardner and Christine Hamilton, Galloway's Labour Party agent. He got them in a huddle and spent fifteen minutes briefing them before the meeting proper started. They went on the attack and overturned the agenda quickly. The meeting became a heated discussion over Galloway's alleged misleading of Lukey over the voting procedure and the alleged slander of Firebrace. Members who had come from Wales, Manchester and from War on Want in London were all shocked and surprised to be in this kind of meeting, when they had thought they were there to talk about fighting poverty.

When Ritchie raised the issue of Galloway's expenses, accusing him of spending War on Want's money for non-business reasons, the Scottish contingent erupted. After much shouting and abuse directed towards the four ill-prepared, rather timid accusers, Gardner proposed a motion of no confidence in them all. Carmi now admits that the others at the meeting 'effectively demolished' the complaints, being more experienced than her and her colleagues with this style of conducting business.

Though the vote of no confidence did not get a majority,[7] at the end of the meeting another vote was taken on whether to pursue the matter of Galloway's conversation with Lukey and his treatment of Firebrace. The vote went twelve to five against the 'Gang of Four', as Galloway would like to refer to them later. The only person to support them was Kim Webber from the Manchester branch. It was a terrible humiliation and Lukey walked out, in tears and in disgust. The other three immediately offered their resignations, but Galloway said he didn't want them to go and they were asked to consider this for a month. Carmi remembers that after the meeting the staff 'pleaded with us' to stay on, which they decided they would.

The first battle of the war of War on Want had been won by Galloway, but it was going to be a long campaign. Although the day had seen a victory, one chink in his armour was still the expenses issue.

The 1991 Charity Commission inquiry into the running of War on Want concluded that the feud between the Galloway and 'Gang of Four' group was 'so serious that the attention of staff and members of Council of Management was diverted from the overview of fundamental activities of War on Want and from its financial reporting'. Galloway testified that

> War on Want has long had the reputation on the left as being an extremely divided organisation, even by the standards of the British left . . . War on Want was an organisation which seemed often, and for some periods continuously, at war with itself. I am sorry to say that never really changed in all the time I was there.

By all accounts of those who had been there long enough to compare regimes, things had never been as bad as they were in the middle of 1986. There may have been financial difficulties, there may have been arguments over policy, there may have been resignations of general secretaries, but there had never been open warfare. The well-meaning, hard-working and often badly paid workers, all of whom earned considerably less than Galloway's expense account was worth, were sick of it all. Many felt they couldn't do the jobs they were employed to do. In June 1986 the staff union, the Association of Clerical, Technical and Supervisory Staffs, wrote to the council of management complaining of 'the current divisions and distrust in War on Want and the serious problem of low staff morale'. There were opportunities for a period of reconciliation, but nothing came about, not even the equivalent of a game of football in no-man's land. Instead, positions were retrenched.

While the expenses arguments took everyone's eyes off the ball, Galloway's plans to get more supporters selected was another issue to consume vast amounts of valuable time at War on Want. The staff and the pre-Galloway members of the council of management were unhappy that he seemed to be openly drawing power to himself by bringing in his political friends, people like Christie, Speirs and his Labour party agent, Christine Hamilton. The *ancien régime* had been used to taking decisions through consensus, and the devolution of power away from the centre, whereas these people wanted tight control. The old days of laissez-faire bosses and staff who got their own way were out under Galloway: 'I felt intensely that the organisation was controlled by the workers within it, that that was an unhealthy situation and one of the only ways of altering that were [*sic*] to make the organisation bigger and change the balance of power.'[8]

The lax controls over finances that had led to the difficulties over Galloway's spending were mirrored in the way that War on Want looked after its membership records and voting system. They didn't keep proper records of their membership.[9] In 1986 some members even complained that they didn't receive ballot papers for the annual management elections. People who made donations were treated as active members and could be enrolled and be given the right to vote. They didn't have to sign anything to join up; that could be done for them. They didn't have to attend any meetings, or take any demonstrable interest in the charity at all.

While they were the equivalent of shareholders in a public company, who equally don't have to take any part if they don't wish to, the culture before Galloway's arrival had been that members did take an interest and kept themselves informed of the charity's work. So when this culture changed, the majority of the staff and the pre-Galloway management took issue. The row got so heated that the company secretary, Ben Birnberg, wrote to both sides: 'It is obvious that very strong emotions have been roused, but I for one have absolutely no axe to grind and would like to see a return to the spirit of moderation and comradeship which has been the normal hallmark of War on Want.'[10]

What they were really fighting about was how the War on Want electoral roll was constituted. Galloway wanted more members, as he had declared, to change the power base. His plan certainly bore fruit in the years he was general secretary. Although it's hard to know exactly who was a member because the records were so poorly kept, there are accurate records of who voted for the most successful candidate in the AGM. In 1985 the total was 404, but after a concerted membership 'drive' by Galloway it then tripled the next year to 1,256, then rose again to 1,674 in 1987.[11] After Galloway had left, the voting frenzy abated and just 494 were recorded in 1989.

Because War on Want had never properly defined its policy towards membership and voting rights, the two sides wrangled over it for months. It was decided that outside help was needed on this issue. On 1 August 1986 Lukey asked Simon Stocker to find out how much the Electoral Reform Society (ERS) would charge to oversee their annual poll.

On 11 August Stocker told Galloway just before a finance and general planning meeting that he had been asked to look into the ERS costs. At the end of the meeting Lukey tried to raise the issue for discussion with Martin Plaut and Louise Carmi, but Galloway was reluctant to reopen what he considered to be a closed meeting. He angrily declared: 'Staff will object; no complaints have been received. Are you suggesting that there have been irregularities?' In the end it was agreed that the matter should be brought to the council of management meeting on 6 September.

However, while Galloway was on holiday, it was arranged for a sub-committee to discuss the best course of action for the forthcoming elections. This meeting took place on 26 August, the day after Galloway returned from holiday, which left him little time for preparation. However, the wind was taken slightly out of his fellow council members' sails as the *Guardian* had already been leaked the story of the internal dispute. Accusations of who was behind this got in the way of actually dealing with the matter in hand, but the costs of having the ERS oversee the ballot were presented to the meeting. It was going to be expensive.

Then a minor bombshell landed on Lukey's desk. It was an undated letter from Laurie Gardner, of Scottish War on Want, to Steve Morgan, who'd been appointed to compile the list of members eligible to vote in the forthcoming elections. Morgan's job was key, as a lot rested on who could vote in a contest where Galloway and his four main opponents were going to be battling for control of the council.

Gardner's letter was handwritten on Scottish War on Want headed notepaper and concerned the staff of a whisky distillery called Hiram Walker. It read as exactly as follows:

> Steve,
> Please find attached list of 100+ names from Hiram Walkers. They should be immediately given membership on your computer. I have been given them in this form, i.e. with home addresses. You may wish to remove these addresses before passing on, just in case somebody insists on using them instead of the following:
> C/o Mr W. Moffat
> Convenor, GMB & ATU
> Hiram Walker & Sons
> 3 High Street
> Dumbarton.
> You should let me know before they are sent AGM & proxy forms, so I can alert our man on the inside that they are on the way.
> Laurie.

Attached to the letter was a list of handwritten names, with the heading 'War on Want Contributers [*sic*] Dumbarton 2 Branch – GMB & ATU – Hiram Walker & Sons PLC'. There then followed a list of names and addresses, not compiled alphabetically, but totalling 107. Under that list a line had been drawn, beneath which was written 'Known AUEW Contributors HW&S' and two more names with 'home addresses unknown' alongside. How the letter from Gardner to Morgan was intercepted was never explained, but it was an indication that staff were clearly sneaking around each other's desks, looking for potentially damaging material, even though Gardner's letter had a completely innocent explanation.

It was later minuted that Gardner had explained that

> the procedure he was following was in line with a direct response from the union at Hiram Walker, who wished to follow their normal union procedure . . . As a member of the Scottish WoW Committee works in Hiram Walker, they had requested that he be informed as soon as notification of the AGM had been despatched. The reason for this was twofold. 1) The union concerned wished to be informed to prepare for a shop meeting. 2) Hiram Walker is a large factory with many sites and mail often gets delayed or misplaced.

In the end, the Hiram Walker ballots were allowed, as long as the ballot papers were sent to the individual homes of the workers concerned.

Looking back at the mid-1980s from the merciful sanctuary of 2007, it does seem a very different era. Margaret Thatcher's anti-union legislation had begun to create a society where the use of block votes felt undemocratic. The classic *Not the Nine o'Clock News* sketch where three union bosses sit round a table and show hands on whether they want tea or coffee in their meeting says it all. Two hands go up for tea: 'So it's 4,000 for tea.' That gets a good laugh. 'And for coffee?' The last hand goes up: 'And 5,000 for coffee. Coffee it is then.' It isn't known if the workers of Hiram Walker preferred coffee breaks or tea breaks, but hopefully if a decision had been needed their shop steward would have held a vote, not just gone with what he liked to drink.

At War on Want the staff were getting restless. While their bosses were wrangling over last year's and this year's ballots, they were trying to keep the place running. The union gathered and voiced their disgruntlement. In a memo to Galloway of Friday 5 September they laid it on the line to the man in charge:

> The Union Shop expresses deep concern about the state of disorganisation of the War on Want membership and possible irregularities and misunderstandings on the organisation of the 1986 AGM . . . In view of this, this Shop

SCOTTISH WAR ON WANT

The Campaign Against World Poverty

266 Clyde Street
Glasgow
G1 4JH
Tel: 041-204 1315

Steve,

Please find attached list of 100 + names from Hiram Walkers. They should be immediately given membership on your computer. I have been given them in this form, ie with home addresses. You may wish to remove these addresses before passing on, (just in case somebody insists on using them instead of the following:-

    c/o   Mr W Moffat
          Convenor . GMB&ATU
          Hiram Walker & Sons
          3 High Street
          Dumbarton.

You should let me know before they are sent AGM & proxy forms, so I can alert our man on the inside that they are on the way.

Laurie.

Bank Details: Royal Bank of Scotland, Gordon Street, 83.05.04 No. 268527

50/- per Week Deduction from Wages. "WAR ON WANT" CONTRIBUTERS W/E 7/8/86.

DUMBARTON 2 BRANCH - GMB & ATU. - HIRAM WALKER & SONS PLC.

B. O'BRIEN	18, KEIL CRESCENT, DUMBARTON
W.H. GILLIES.	81, DICKENS AVE., CLYDEBANK
J. NEESON	11, DOVEHOLM AVE., DUMBARTON
A.F. GILLIES	5, MUIR CRESCENT, LEVENVALE, ALEXANDRIA
G. WARDEN	6, OVERWOOD GROVE, DUMBARTON
J.J. HAGGARTY	10, PARK AVE, DUMBARTON
M. CONROY	106, TONTINE PARK, RENTON
G.M. McDERMID	7, LATTA ST, DUMBARTON
D. O'NEILL	8/7, MILTON ESTATE, JAMESTOWN, ALEXANDRIA
T. McMENAMIN	151, ENDRICK HOUSE, ALLAN CRES, DUMBARTON
A.J. CARROLL	36, KILPATRICK VIEW, DUMBARTON
A. BARCLAY	6, GRAHAMFIELD PL. BEITH, AYRSHIRE
G.A. McDERMOTT	61, HIGH ST, PAISLEY.
P.E. FALLON	9, KERSE AVE, DALRY, AYRSHIRE
S. GRIER	63, WELLPARK RD., SALTCOATS, AYRSHIRE
J. COOK	18, NAPIER GARDENS, LINWOOD, PAISLEY
A. CARRUTHERS	21, MEADOWSIDE, BEITH, AYRSHIRE
J. McGINLEY	21, LYNN DRIVE, KILBIRNIE
J. McCOY	18, PLACE VIEW, KILBIRNIE, AYRSHIRE
W. WINTON	15, MAINS RD, BEITH, AYRSHIRE
C. HAMILTON	32, COCHRANE ST, KILBIRNIE, AYRSHIRE
W. MOFFAT	8, OVERBURN CRES., DUMBARTON
Ms. S. HOSIE	13B, SUNDERLAND AVE., CASTLEHILL, DUMBARTON
M.P. KORSEN	81, HIGH MAINS AVE. DUMBARTON
MR J. MATHESON	1/2, BURNSIDE TERR. DUMBARTON
Ms. C. ATKINSON	300, DUMBARTON RD, OLD KILPATRICK
M. BRANNAN	"WOODVALE" 241, LENNOX ST, RENTON
C.A. STEWART	19, WALLACE ST, DUMBARTON
T. O'CONNELL	10, GLENCAIRN RD, DUMBARTON.
MR JMcKPROCTOR	34, HILLFOOT AVE, GARSHAKE, DUMBARTON

Extract from Laurie Gardner's letter (see p. 112)

asks the Council of Management (A) to conduct an immediate inquiry into the current system of membership and the handling of the election and mailings; (B) [to compile] a definitive list of War on Want members with voting rights for the 1986 election and the bringing in of the Electoral Reform Society if that is acceptable to the Council.

So Galloway's view that the staff wouldn't want their elections overseen was proved wrong, but more importantly they were clearly at the end of their patience with the management. When Galloway presented this union resolution to the council of management meeting the next day it was a shock, but there was worse to come.

Incredibly, Galloway also reported that there were serious flaws in the way they had voted the previous year – in fact, in the way they had conducted the vote that had put them all on the council of management.[12] It seemed that they might all have their positions by mistake. The constitutional review group had taken advice from Philip Heslop QC, and he had outlined loopholes in the constitution and mistakes in their procedures. Up until that point, War on Want had been allowing people to vote as 'deemed' members if they had set up banker's orders or covenanted money, even if they had never formally signed up.

The upshot of this was that the people sitting around the table had been elected by ineligible people under the wrong system. It was questionable if the council of management had any right to make decisions about the running of the charity. Managing War on Want was becoming a farce. They'd all been so concerned with their own feuds over balloting that they'd failed to notice that the whole council might be just so much hot air, with no legal rights. They had to work together to find a way forward. They took advice from Ben Birnberg and unanimously decided that they had to continue as they were, conduct new elections monitored by the ERS and set up yet another committee to look into membership.

Towards the end of the meeting Ken Ritchie tried to raise the issue of the Gardner letter and the attached list of Hiram Walker workers' names. He suggested it would be a good idea to discuss this important letter, even though it wasn't on the agenda. This wasn't allowed and instead Bill Speirs suggested that a small committee should be set up to investigate matters and decide who should be given a vote. Martin Plaut took the chair and Christine Hamilton, Charlotte Cornwell, Hermione Harris and Jill Evans sat on the committee.

A few days later, on 9 September 1986, when this committee sat down with Birnberg, as well as Galloway, Morgan and Julian Hopkins, it was decided that an extra fifty or sixty last-minute membership forms should be admissible and those members were to be allowed to vote in the election. These people were admitted to War on Want and were eligible to vote, despite never having filled in or signed a form themselves. Some of them had never paid a penny to the charity prior to their acceptance as members because their £2 student/unemployed member's fee was paid for them. They may well have paid up afterwards, but 'the records are no longer available', as the Charity Commission inquiry explained.

So the voting chaos and internal management oddities of War on Want continued, diverting attention from the thousands of starving that the charity had been set up to help.

10

Found Wanting

Though there were some battles inside under George Galloway's leadership, to the outside world things were going well at War on Want. Its campaigning and aid projects in South Africa, Bangladesh and Central America were making news in the mid-1980s. Galloway has to take credit for this, though of course these were continuing relationships developed over years by the programme officers of the three areas.

In Nicaragua War on Want was giving aid to schools and hospitals, which were struggling to survive under attack from the US-backed Contra rebels. When the Scottish Caterpillar tractor plant was closed down by its US owners, the workers donated the last tractor to War on Want, to send to Nicaragua. They painted it pink and handed over the keys to Galloway in Glasgow's George Square: a typical piece of gesture politics by Galloway, which ended in the tractor being repossessed before it could be sent. Of course, it was never going to get there because the workers didn't own it and didn't have the right to give it away, but that wasn't the point. It made good copy and a bright picture for the papers.

As soon as Galloway had taken his place at War on Want, he had been determined to bring the organisation closer to the unions. A trade union sub-committee had been formed, whose job it was to collaborate with the unions and raise money from them. At the same time, union officials would be powerful allies for Galloway in making changes at War on Want. Over the next couple of years fund-raising campaigns were developed in conjunction with unions. 'Nursing Aid', 'Council Aid' and 'Union Aid' all helped boost the coffers.

At the same time, Galloway was building a closer relationship with CND, with the help of its general secretary, Bruce Kent, who'd been on War on Want's council at one stage. The two organisations shared common objectives in the end of the arms race and stopping the development of nuclear power. In the summer of 1985 Kent walked the 500 miles from Faslane nuclear base in Scotland to the plant in Berkshire where parts for the weapons were made. Galloway went with him, some of the way.

Roughly at the same time, War on Want was also strengthening its work in the Middle East. Palestine has never been far from Galloway's political life and he has been involved with some ground-breaking, controversial and daring work over the years, including during his time at War on Want. In the West Bank and Gaza Strip a health clinic and insurance fund were established as a joint project between Palestinian and British trade unions.

A snapshot of War on Want under Galloway shows a politically aware organisation, as it had been set up to be by Harold Wilson and the others in the 1950s. But the nearer Galloway led them to direct political action, the more likely it was that this would bring them up against the Charity Commission, which took its role of keeping politics out of charity work extremely seriously.

The tense relationship between the Charity Commission and War on Want goes back to the 1960s and came to a climax when the commission issued their scathing report on the charity in 1991 that was critical not only of Galloway but also of almost everyone else who had been involved in the organisation in the 1980s. The trouble was, and is, that a charity involved in work against war and poverty inevitably moves in the world of politics. Yet charities are supposed to be above all that and are not allowed to try to influence political decisions.

In 1977 the commission had complained about a donation made to the strikers of the Grunwick print works. In 1979 it came down heavily on War on Want for acting politically and gave it a list of what it wasn't allowed to do, which included the line 'seeking to eliminate social, economic, political or other injustice'. Given that this was exactly what War on Want was trying to do, this posed a problem for the then general secretary, Terry Lacey, but he neatly sidestepped the commission by creating a separate company called War on Want Campaigns Ltd (WWC), which from then on dealt with the outlawed sensitive work. However adroit this may have been legally, it hadn't gone down well with the commission and it was watching.

In 1987, when Galloway decided to run a series of adverts to boost contributions and support, the Charity Commission came down hard on them again. One of the ads showed a graveyard of headstones, in the shape of US bombs. Over the graphic were the words: 'In Nicaragua 15,000 men, women and children have felt the effect of American aid.' It was a clever image and a succinct message about the cynical meddling in Central America of Reagan's government. When a US-backed right-wing pressure group, Western Goals (UK), complained about the ads, the Charity Commission held that they were 'a clear political statement' and that WWC should have dealt with the contract, not War on Want. They ordered WWC to reimburse War on Want the £36,745.98 paid for the ads. This debt remained outstanding for years, with no interest charged, until the Charity Commission cracked down and it was finally paid off in the early 1990s following threats of legal action under the Charities Act.

There is something more than a little Shakespearian about the Galloway story. Something in the controversy and excitement that he gathers to him that reminds of *Macbeth*, the 'Scottish Play'. And if there had been witches in the woods during his time at War on Want, they may well have seen something coming, particularly once the *News of the World* had run a rather scathing piece on 4 November 1984, just about a year after Galloway's arrival. Adrian Needlestone wrote: 'The head of War on Want, one of the charities spear-heading aid for starving Ethiopia, is at the centre of a row over a £187 restaurant bill.' It went on to explain that Galloway had charged expenses to War on Want's credit card while on a trip to Israel on behalf of the Labour Middle East Council. Galloway explained that the bill had been reasonable and he had always intended to reimburse War on Want; and in any event, it was sorted out when Labour MP Don Concannon said the Labour Party were happy to pay. The story was a storm in a teacup, but perhaps someone ought to have looked in the bottom of that cup and read the leaves.

At the height of the War on Want infighting in late 1986 the issue of Galloway's expenses was deeply damaging. It consumed weeks of management time and many in key positions weren't talking to one another any more. A consultant called Mr Thorpe, appointed in April 1987 to assess how they could work better, reported on 'a breakdown of mutual trust with and

between staff and management and the Council of Management . . .
suspicion seems to take the place of reasoned discussion.'

In early September 1986, while the investigation into Galloway's expenses
continued, a few weeks ahead of the key audit meeting, it was decided that
Julian Hopkins, the finance officer, and Galloway would put forward
proposals for new expense claims guidelines. Then, on the eve of that audit
meeting, one of many break-ins that have dogged Galloway occurred. The
police were informed and it was noted that Galloway's secretary's door had
been smashed in and papers strewn all over the office.[1] A video recorder was
stolen, but it seems unlikely that the burglary was motivated by petty theft.

The audit meeting went ahead, chaired by Vivienne Lukey and with
Galloway, Hopkins, Ken Ritchie, and Frank Weinberg, an auditor from the
firm of Somers Baker, present. Weinberg reported that as the charity had
grown so much, previous structures might not be good enough and they
didn't want to be left open to the accusation of abuse. It was agreed that
Hopkins would compile a report on all staff expenditure. Galloway said he
could account for every penny of his own expenses.

Over the next few days, Hopkins then called on all staff members to co-
operate in the task of checking through every single claim and expenditure.
Hopkins remembers that he placed a copy of his final report in the safe of the
accounts office, and took home a copy, which he planned to send to Lukey
on Tuesday 30 September. The information in that report was of immense
value to both sides in the dispute.

The report was handwritten and is dated 29 September 1986. It revealed
that Galloway (whose salary was £20,000) had spent £22,048 on travel,
subsistence and vehicle hire in the financial year 1985/6. His expenses alone
came to almost a quarter of the entire expenses bill for an organisation of
seventy-odd people that was supporting projects around the globe. The four
programme officers, the deputy general secretary and the consultants
involved in specific projects together billed £51,996.

Sometime on the night of the 29th–30th there was another break-in at
War on Want. Though the building itself seemed not to have been entered
by force, Galloway's office was broken into, papers scattered about and his
own safe emptied of some travellers' cheques and Luncheon Vouchers. But
what was more perplexing was the fact that the finance office safe, where

the key expenses report had been placed, had been dropped down the stairs. It was found near the front door, with its own door wide open. However, on closer inspection by Hopkins, Stocker and others, it appeared that the safe door hadn't been broken open in the fall and the lock worked perfectly well.

When Lukey received her copy of Hopkins's report on the Monday she was shocked at the amounts of money being spent by Galloway. She asked Galloway to meet her informally to discuss it on the Wednesday, but when the day arrived he claimed he had to go to the Labour Party conference in Blackpool and hadn't time. Lukey then sent a letter to Galloway, formally requesting a meeting with him on Saturday 4 October to discuss finances with Ritchie, Martin Plaut and Louise Carmi. At 10.00 they convened in the War on Want offices at London Bridge Street, SE1. Half an hour later, as Galloway had failed to appear, they decided to start without him.

After much discussion, they adopted this resolution:

> Further to the observations of War on Want's Auditor in relation to the 1985/6 accounts and having considered the special report from War on Want's Finance Officer . . . detailing the expenditure incurred in the use of War on Want's credit cards, petty cash expenditure, and in the use of vehicles, for the 1985/86 year and the period April to August 1986, and having been seriously concerned that there appeared to be prima facie evidence of questionable expenditure incurred by the General Secretary of War on Want over this period, it was decided to request Somers Baker to conduct an immediate enquiry, with the following terms of reference. . .

They then listed a number of questions they wanted cleared up, including

> to list and review all expenditure incurred in the use of the American Express card and the booking of mini-cabs through Express Cars by War on Want's General Secretary . . . to assess whether such expenditure is of a level and nature likely to be considered appropriate and necessary for a charity . . . to indicate whether there are instances of impropriety, and if so, to document the evidence available.

On the same day, Lukey then wrote to Galloway and copied in Ben Birnberg, the company secretary:

Dear George

As you know from the meeting we had on 25 September, we have serious concerns about your use of War on Want finances and resources . . . We had intended discussing this with you today at the meeting of the officers which I instructed you to attend. In your absence we had no alternative but to proceed and I have to inform you of the decisions taken.

Lukey then went on to tell Galloway about the audit, about an extraordinary meeting of the council of management she had called to discuss it all, and that they had also decided to withdraw all credit card and car hire facilities for all staff for the length of the audit.

She continued:

I am therefore instructing you:
1. To make all information requested of you by the auditors available to them on request next week, including your diaries.
2. . . . of your right to be accompanied by a representative of your choice.
3. To immediately hand your War on Want credit card to the Finance Officer, and to desist from making any expenditure of War on Want finances without specific prior authorisation from the Treasurer.

The reaction of Galloway's supporters was unanimous. At a separate meeting, which the 'Gang of Four' didn't attend because they thought it had been cancelled, the minutes documented: 'The actions of Lukey, Carmi, Plaut and Ritchie . . . were unequivocally condemned . . . Full confidence in the General Secretary was recorded.' Yet, in total contrast to that vote of confidence, the senior staff were about to deliver their verdict on Galloway in an independent letter to the council of management. If Galloway had wanted to portray this as a vendetta by a small clique of four, this document appeared to undermine that case. These people were in most of the key positions and included John Denham, who would later become a Labour MP and minister of state.

WAR ON WANT

The Campaign Against World Poverty

Three Castles House
1 London Bridge St.
London SE1 9SG
Tel: 01-403 2266
Telex: 24784 WOW G

George Galloway,
General Secretary,
War on Want.   4/10/86

Dear George,

As you know from the meeting we had on 25th September, we have serious concerns about your use of War on Want finances and resources. Subsequent to that meeting, and upon receiving the report commissioned at that time we have sought legal advice.

We had intended discussing this with you today at the meeting of the Officers which I had instructed you to attend. In your absence we had no alternative but to proceed and I have to inform you of the decisions taken.

1. A special audit will be undertaken commencing Monday 6th October, the terms of which are set out in the copy of the letter attached. This investigation will be completed by the end of the week.

2. An extraordinary Council of Management meeting has been called for Saturday 11th October, to consider and act on the report resulting from this audit, and specialised legal opinion.

3. The Finance Officer has been instructed to take immediate steps to implement controls on expenditure, and to prevent such expenditure without prior authorisation. In this context he has been instructed to withdraw all War on Want credit cards for the duration of the special audit.

As a result of these decisions I am therefore instructing you:

1. To make all information requested of you by the auditors available to them on their request next week, including your diaries.

2. To be available at the meeting of the Council of Management at 11.00 am on Saturday 11th October, and to be prepared to answer questions about your use of War on Want finances and resources. I have to advise you of your right to be accompanied by a representative of your choice.

3. To immediately hand your War on Want credit card to the Finance Officer, and to desist from making any expenditure of War on Want finances without specific prior authorisation from the Treasurer.

War On Want is a Company Limited by Guarantee Registered No. 2599 ... at 103 Borough High St, London SE1 1NN
Company Secretary is Benedict M Birnberg. War On Want ... Nat West Southwark Branch 8 50 03 A/C No 2900820

In conclusion, I still require a satisfactory written explanation of your failure to attend the meeting of the Officers today, despite clear instructions from myself.

Yours sincerely,

Vivienne Lukey,

Vivienne Lukey,
Chairperson, War on Want

cc Ben Birnberg.

Vivienne Lukey's letter to Galloway (see p. 123)

Of all the documents in the battle for War on Want under Galloway's leadership, that letter is perhaps the most clinical and hard hitting. It starts:

> This document summarises our main concerns about the current crisis in War on Want and about the General Secretary, George Galloway's role in this crisis. We recognise the General Secretary's talents in dealing with the media and in contributing to the higher profile of War on Want. This talent and his skilled promotion have given the impression to many that the General Secretary has proved to be a major success for War on Want. The reality in our opinion is very different. We believe that the General Secretary's influence has been to fundamentally corrupt the basic ideals and principles of the organisation. We believe that he has failed to provide the sound management the organisation needs so that problems fester without resolution, hence the poor morale and the recent spate of resignations. We believe that War on Want has stayed on its feet and continued to achieve successes even over these last few difficult months to be in spite of the General Secretary rather than because of him.

The senior staff then go on to list their six main concerns: his level of expenses; his management techniques; his unilateral decision making; his relationships with other aid agencies; his attitude to internal elections; and his overly flattering portrayal of himself and highly critical portrayal of his internal critics. They conclude:

> We are no longer prepared to stand by silently while War on Want's work . . . degenerates further into a lack of direction and unhappiness which we have witnessed so painfully over the last few months. We believe the General Secretary's interest in the campaigns and programmes of War on Want has been inextricably mixed up with his interest in his own political career to the detriment of the organisation. For these reasons we feel compelled to communicate our loss of all confidence in George Galloway as General Secretary of War on Want, and that we regard him as no longer suitable to fill this responsible position.

The document is signed by Helen Allison (women's officer), John Cunnington (programme officer, Asia), John Denham (national campaigns officer), James Firebrace, Julian Hopkins, Sarah Mitchell (appeals officer), Jenny Rossiter (programme officer, southern Africa), Luis Silva (programme officer, Latin America & Caribbean), Simon Stocker and Alison Whyte (press and publicity).

It is remarkable that Galloway stuck it out and fought on, given that the four most senior members of the council of management and ten most senior members of the staff had all declared their opposition to him on a number of different counts. It says a lot about his determination to win, which seems to get more focused the bigger the problem he's in.

With so many staff and management determined to have Galloway removed from office, the internal investigation of his expenses by War on Want's auditor was awaited with bated breath. On 9 October Frank Weinberg wrote back to Lukey:

> I . . . feel it would be inappropriate for me to carry out any further investigations at this stage . . . in the absence of adequate documentation . . . I would point out that my interview with the Gen Sec was most amicable and he appeared only too pleased to answer the questions posed. However, he did point out that in the absence of [details of his American Express card payments and taxi bookings] he was not prepared to make his diaries available to me for

the purpose of attempting to reconcile some of the charges incurred with notes and appointments in those diaries.

Weinberg did not insist on seeing Galloway's diaries, as he was instructed to do and which should have helped considerably in deciding whether the expenses claims had been legitimate or not. Nevertheless, he says: 'This lack of documentation as and when such expenses are incurred is obviously an area of weakness within the system of control of War on Want.'

If Lukey and the others had hoped for a definitive conclusion from Weinberg's report, they were to be disappointed. He goes on: 'On the evidence available, I am unable to comment one way or another as to whether, in my opinion, all the expenses incurred by the General Secretary were wholly and exclusively on behalf of War on Want.' He concludes: 'If you require any further information please do not hesitate to contact me. I would point out that I will not be available from about 11 o'clock Friday morning until 8 o'clock on Tuesday.' This was of little use in a letter delivered by hand in the middle of the day, on the Thursday before a meeting on Saturday.

The crisis was building a real head of steam now and at the specially organised meeting that Saturday at War on Want headquarters, Galloway brought two legal representatives to help him defend himself. He also had many of his supporters on the council with him.

Ritchie delivered his report on the expenses under a barrage of interruptions shouted at him, to the point that a resolution had to be made that he could continue unabused.[2] Speirs recalls: 'I had a background in the TUC and had been close to the peace process in Northern Ireland, so after that, WoW meetings were not difficult. I remember acrimonious meetings.'

The minutes of the meeting state that Ritchie outlined that Galloway's expenses were running at some £500 a week; that there was a lack of supporting documentation on many American Express vouchers; that £1,430 'reimbursable' expenses hadn't been paid back; that Galloway had been using taxis at the rate of £200 a month in 1985/6 and this had increased to £300 a month in 1986/7; that Galloway's claim for removal expenses hadn't been approved. A sum of £1,414 had also been cited as money owed by Glasgow Hillhead Constituency Labour Party (CLP) to War on Want for expenses charged to War on Want by Galloway while on Labour business.

Ritchie also specifically referred to several American Express payments that, according to the minutes,

> did not seem to relate to costs appropriate to War on Want, viz.
>
> (a) £186 expenditure during a visit by the General Secretary to Athens
>
> (b) £180 expenditure on the retirement of Alex Kitson
>
> (c) Expenditure in a gift shop in Tunisia
>
> (d) 20 week-end journeys to Scotland during the 17-month period from April 1985–August 1986.

In his detailed reply Galloway raised a number of issues that appeared to undermine the case against him: his paperwork to support his claims had been the same as in previous years, when there hadn't been any questions raised; he filed his expense accounts every month and they should have been checked by Ritchie; there was a lack of evidence on any claims of his misuse of funds; since he worked 'seven days a week' on War on Want business there was nothing underhand about expenses on bank holidays; the visit to Athens was on business; Alex Kitson, the deputy general secretary of the TGWU, had given substantial help to War on Want and the party was therefore justified; the gift shop claim was for two bottles of whisky for Palestinian leaders helping War on Want; his visits to Scotland were on business; he thought the £1,414 owed to War on Want by Hillhead CLP and the TGWU had been paid back already; he'd never been asked to justify his cab accounts before.

The meeting finally ended at 6.30 p.m., after they managed to agree a resolution to ask the auditors to complete their investigation of Galloway's expenses; to appoint an independent legal advisor 'to liaise with the auditors and to investigate and report to the Council on the circumstances and propriety of all expenditure by the General Secretary'; to withdraw the use of credit cards and Express Cars, pending new control measures.

On the Monday morning following, Hamilton wrote to Julian Hopkins expressing surprise that money was owed by Glasgow Hillhead CLP to War on Want.

On the Sunday night, 12–13 October 1986, War on Want's offices were broken into again, for the third time in the space of a month. This time there was no sign of burglary and no petty theft was reported. Hopkins's safe was tampered with again, only this time it failed to open. The old key, which had gone missing some ten months before, was found broken off in the lock. After the last break-in Hopkins had had the lock changed. Galloway sent round a memo to the council of management the following day, telling them about the break-in. 'I have to inform you that the office was once again entered by intruders last night. Nothing appears to have been stolen . . . The police have been called to investigate.'

So it was against this backdrop of mistrust, name-calling and strange break-ins that the council of management elections were held, with the Electoral Reform Society called in to supervise for the first time in War on Want's history.

At the council of management meeting on 27 October 1986, War on Want's dedicated chair, Vivienne Lukey, and the two vice-chairs, Martin Plaut and Louise Carmi, all revealed that they would not stand. Ritchie did stand but was not elected. Though they remained on the council of management, they were now out of the powerful inner circle that made all the key decisions and they were also one step removed from the ongoing investigation into Galloway's finances and the conduct of the charity's elections.

The new chair, Simon Fanshawe, said the decision to replace the four was unanimous, and confirmed that the investigation into Galloway's finances was continuing, an investigation that would also look at the way that Galloway appeared to have used his War on Want credit card to pay for expenses on Labour Party business.[3] Other changes from the election saw Hamilton and Jenny Young, both from Hillhead Labour Party, voted on to the council.

The new treasurer, Mike Phillips, who took over from Ritchie, was asked by the Charity Commission inquiry about his appointment.

> *Q:* Can you tell us at this stage what your experience was to lead to your election as Treasurer?
>
> *A:* I do not know. I had no qualifications as such in accountancy or any other financially related subjects. It is possible that the council of management felt that in the absence of anybody else . . . and I was not aware of anybody else who had those sorts of qualifications . . . I might be as good as anybody.

While Ritchie came in for criticism by the Charity Commission inquiry, on paper he seemed far better qualified than Phillips for the job as treasurer, with a background in mathematics, financial planning experience in industry and previous employment at another charity.

The day following the removal of the 'Gang of Four', the then political reporter Alastair Campbell made the front page of the *Daily Mirror* with a big exclusive. 'WAR ON WANT BOSS IN EXPENSES PROBE,' shouted the headline, continuing underneath: 'Famine charity boss is being investigated over claims that he spent £20,000 expenses enjoying a life of luxury.' Galloway denied all impropriety and Campbell quoted him saying: 'I can justify every penny and shall do so when I see the auditors.' The internal investigation later cleared Galloway completely of any dishonesty, but Campbell's life-of-luxury line has stuck to Galloway, rightly or wrongly, fairly or unfairly, ever since.

Campbell, informed by someone on the inside at War on Want, probably didn't know all the details. Even at that stage, it looked as though Galloway's enemies were doomed to fail in their attempt to force him out. There simply wasn't the paper trail they wanted to find.

The staff, meanwhile, had come into work to find that the council of management had changed and that the general secretary's expense claims were all over the front page of the *Daily Mirror*. Luis Silva, the Chilean refugee who ran the Central American aid projects, delivered a message from the staff to Galloway and the council. 'The Shop is deeply concerned about . . . the very future of War on Want as a Third World Aid and Campaigning Agency. We are very concerned about the work we do and the safety of our jobs.'

The next day it only got worse, as all the other papers got into the story too. Galloway fought back, claiming that he hadn't had his credit card taken away, but all War on Want credit cards had been blocked during the audit. It was reported that he'd been around the globe, visiting fifteen countries in the eighteen-month period under investigation. In the *Sunday Times*'s News in Focus piece that weekend, Galloway was quoted: 'I reject the glorification of amateurism. They knew the sort of man I was when they appointed me.'

Ritchie, Lukey, Martin Plaut and Louise Carmi, now all deposed from their key places on the War on Want council of management, still had questions. Though he was no longer the treasurer, Ritchie was still entitled as a council member to ask questions and expect answers and he was also in possession of a considerable amount of information. On 16 November of that year he wrote to Frank Weinberg with a more detailed breakdown of Galloway's expenses, to help with the ongoing inquiry. That letter and its appendices revealed some of the truth of what had been going on, but other facts were missing. Ritchie asked Weinberg to find out more:

> Over the past 18 months the GS has, in a personal capacity, attended a number of Labour Party/trade union meetings to seek nomination as a prospective parliamentary candidate, and he has attended selection meetings in Dumbarton and Hillhead (Glasgow). I would suggest that the dates of these meetings be ascertained (in order that we can be quite certain that War on Want money was not used in travelling to them).

Galloway is adamant, indeed there is no concise evidence to the contrary, that these expenses were all incurred on legitimate War on Want business. According to a local press report of the time, Glasgow Hillhead residents had indeed noticed an increase in War on Want leaflets coming through their letter boxes, which tended to feature prominent photos of Galloway himself. Richard Mowbray of Hillhead SDP claimed he'd received a leaflet each month for three months, all featuring Galloway's picture and name. Galloway also told Campbell: 'In the past seventeen months I have performed 290 public engagements for War on Want.' In Weinberg's report to the members of War on Want, dated 27 February 1987, he says:

> With reference to the expenditure incurred in connection with motor, travel and subsistence, the system of control and documentation over such expenditure upon which we could rely for purpose of our audit was insufficient. We were therefore unable to obtain all the information and explanations we considered necessary. Consequently we were unable to satisfy ourselves as to accuracy of the expenditure under this heading.

The information Weinberg did have on paper makes fascinating reading. Galloway claims these days that most Friday nights he likes a curry, like a lot of British people. His constituency flat is just off Brick Lane, so he has a lot of choice. Back in the 1980s, when he lived in Bloomsbury and then Blackheath, he preferred to eat in one of the most prestigious Indian restaurants in the country, the Red Fort, in Soho. It was, and still is, a very impressive place to entertain guests. Galloway conducted a lot of meetings there, and charged some of them to War on Want, as would be correct for a business expense. From March 1985 to the middle of February 1986 Galloway claimed £922.87 as War on Want expenses for meals in the Red Fort: twenty-two visits paid for with War on Want's American Express card in just under twelve months.[4]

Another of his favourite places to entertain was Mr Kong, a Chinese restaurant also in Soho, and from May 1985 to the end of January 1986 Galloway charged the charity's card £450.30 for meals there. That was seventeen visits in nine months. Then there was the Thai restaurant Chiang Mai, which he clearly didn't favour as much, for he charged War on Want's card for meals there only nine times in the eleven months between April 1985 and the middle of February 1986, though he did run up a total bill of £435.20. And finally, at La Spezia between May and July 1985 he charged the card £206.20 over eight visits.

In 1984/5, the last on the alphabetical list of War on Want's acknowledged supporters and donors was Frank Weinberg, whose efforts in going through Galloway's expenses all those months later would turn to the use of Express Cars. Express Cars held War on Want's taxi account and Weinberg was also provided with the details of Galloway's journeys. Some of these receipts were for trips made between London E8 and London SE3. Galloway's London home was in SE3, the postal district that covers Blackheath, but there was no address with direct connection to War on Want in E8. Of course, these were just the trips made on Express Cars' account. There were many more petty cash claims for taxi rides, on an ad hoc basis.

Weinberg was also provided with figures by Ken Ritchie and Julian Hopkins concerning Galloway's hotel bills charged to his War on Want American Express card, and between April 1985 and February 1986 he ran up a total of £1,032.70. Apart from one stay in the Queen's Hotel, Eastbourne, they were all for hotels in Scotland. Galloway had a lot of contacts in Scotland who he was cultivating for War on Want business. He also had meetings to attend at Scottish War on Want. Out of thirteen hotel stays, nine were in Glasgow, where he was adopted as Labour's prospective parliamentary candidate in November 1985.

By the time all his expenses claims were being raked over by his enemies at War on Want, Galloway was gearing up for the election he had to fight, which was looking imminent. On 19 February 1987, just three months from the general election, Weinberg delivered his 'Special Report into the General Secretary's Expenditure'. The conclusion to that report was as follows:

> Expenditure charged to American Express through the General Secretary's company credit card during the period April 1985 to August 1986 amounted to £17,000 and the charges on Express Cars' invoices apparently attributable to him for the same period amounted to £3,800 inclusive of service charges and non-recoverable VAT.
>
> It would appear from the investigation that we have carried out that there has been some expenditure by the General Secretary which has not been incurred wholly and exclusively in connection with his employment. It must be stated, however, that in our opinion this situation has arisen through inadequate internal financial controls and guidance and lack of supervision and not through dishonesty, bad faith or any deliberate attempt to defraud by the General Secretary.
>
> We feel that further investigation by us into this area would still prove inconclusive and the additional cost of ascertaining any further positive information would outweigh the ensuing benefit derived from that information.

Simon Fanshawe, the new chair of the council of management, wrote to all the council members on 25 February, enclosing the above conclusion. The full report, he explained, would be made available at the extraordinary general meeting to be held in Cardiff on the 27th. His letter went on:

> I intend to allow a reading period in the committee room before the meeting starts. I have taken this decision quite simply because information about the EGM has already been sent anonymously to the papers and I am not prepared to put the organisation at any risk whatsoever.
> Simon Fanshawe, Chairperson.

So the elected members of the charity's management council, the equivalent of the board of directors of a company, were not allowed to be sent a copy of the full investigation of the general secretary's financial dealings. When the council sat down at the Crest Hotel, Cardiff, to read the full report, they found it was on purple paper, rendering it almost impossible to photocopy; each copy was numbered; and they weren't allowed to take them away at the end of the meeting.

Suspected of being the source of the leaks to the press, the four deposed leaders were watched. Martin Plaut says: 'I was escorted to the toilet by Steve Morgan, the membership officer.' Louise Carmi had been so distressed by the prospect of having to go to the meeting that she had taken some Valium to calm her nerves. She recalls that 'we were not allowed to take notes. I did smuggle some out, however.' Though she remembered the meeting as 'awful', Christine Hamilton, batting for the other side, recalled it as an occasion with people 'commenting in cold terms'.[5] Also at the meeting were Campbell Christie, Charlotte Cornwell, Jill Evans, Bill Gilby, Sarah Hayward, Vivienne Lukey, Mike Phillips, Ken Ritchie, Bill Speirs, Sarah Veale, Jenny Young and Pam Zinkin. Observing were Andrew Shaw and Julia Collier.

The following is taken from Louise Carmi's contemporaneous hand-written notes of the meeting:

> Once the council members had digested the auditor's report, Galloway addressed them, talking of the high price that he had paid personally and that they had all paid, that he had learned a lot from the process, that he was aware of the damage it had caused. He said that the only way forward was to reach some agreement or compromise, for the good of War on Want, and that the organisation had stabilised since the inquiry.[6]

In the discussion following Galloway's address, Martin Plaut proposed that, in the light of the report, the council of management immediately ask for the general secretary's resignation. Fanshawe ruled him out of order, but Plaut pressed on to explain that he believed Galloway was guilty of gross misconduct, which was an instantly dismissible offence. This was heavily defeated by eleven votes to two, with five abstentions.

At the end of the meeting, it was agreed by a majority vote of twelve to five, with one abstention, to put forward the following motion:

> The Council notes the Somers Baker report. It also notes the decision to call for the report was controversial, but nevertheless feels that its decision has been vindicated insofar as it has:
> 1. Yielded the need to radically overhaul the financial controls and systems of the organisation and
> 2. Shown that there are no issues of dishonesty or bad faith on the part of the General Secretary.
> We note the conclusion that 'It would appear that there has been some expenditure by the General Secretary which has not been incurred wholly and exclusively in pursuit of his employment'.
> Council proposes that in the light of that conclusion to instruct the Chair, the Treasurer and the General Secretary to meet with the auditor as soon as possible to ascertain the exact nature of that expenditure and what needs to be done about it. Council instructs the Chair to report back on this.
> Having taken decisive steps to introduce new financial controls, supervision and systems, Council will assure itself that nothing like this can happen again.
> In this connection Council makes clear to the General Secretary that it is primarily his task and responsibility to ensure that War on Want can never be accused of extravagance or non-charitable spending again. Council makes absolutely clear to the General Secretary the need for great care in the oversight of his responsibility in this regard.[7]

Fanshawe looks back at the events and says:

> He failed to make the right judgement about what you did and didn't spend expenses on. If you don't lay down strict criteria for staff and the general secretary on what you can and can't spend money on, you say effectively that 'we're relying on your judgement' . . . You can't then say 'you shouldn't have spent the money'. You can say 'well, we ought to change the rules' and that's what we did.[8]

Ken Ritchie, Martin Plaut, Louise Carmi and Vivienne Lukey went through the mill over Galloway, partly because they had been determined to get answers to some unresolved questions. They wanted to know how much money Galloway had given back to War on Want and when, in the light of the advice of the auditors, Somers Baker. As they were members of the management council, and trustees, that seems reasonable. A chief concern of the four was that a resolution had been passed by the council of management to have an independent legal report conducted into Galloway's behaviour, but that it hadn't ever been done. Ritchie, who had instructed the solicitor Stephen Mayer of Reynolds Porter Chamberlain to carry it out, had written to him after being deposed as treasurer, but had been told that Mayer wasn't allowed to talk about it to him.

Plaut and Ritchie had asked Fanshawe for the answer to their simple question, but he declined. They had also reminded him that the auditor's report had identified expenses that should have been reimbursed to War on Want by Glasgow Hillhead Labour Party. They asked him to tell them how much had been paid back and how much remained unpaid. Fanshawe refused to disclose the amounts and when Ritchie and Plaut wrote formally to request that information again on 13 April 1987, they received this back from him, dated 22 April 1987:

> It is my intention to move us forward on all of this and to resist all attempts to rake over old coals . . . I have no doubt that the Charity Commission will consider itself to be satisfied when they see the full report and the other documentation, such as the new financial controls which we have instituted. Now that we have set our house in order and have a system of monitoring which is actually operated, I feel happy that no Trustee could let any situation of doubt arise again.[9]

When the Charity Commissioners finally reported on the chaos at War on Want they cited 'serious failings of management and financial control' among a litany of other faults, all of which were at odds with Fanshawe's claims. They were oddly brief about the repayments. Out of the 100,000-word report, extending over some 200 pages, they managed just one small sentence: 'Certain monies were repaid to War on Want.'

In George Galloway's reign so little had actually been known about the finances of their own charity that the management and directors hadn't realised their accounts weren't adding up properly. When the Charity Commission looked into it all, it found that the accounts had been 'materially mis-stated' from 1983 to 1989 and that the auditors, Somers Baker, had 'failed to discharge their functions adequately and themselves relied upon unwarranted assumptions'.[10]

Galloway rightly points out that he had left two years before the boat ran aground, but the problems could be seen as going back to his era. The Charity Commission's conclusion was that 'War on Want was consistently mis-managed during the period of our review', from 1984 to 1989. It also severely criticised the infighting of Galloway's era: 'During 1986 and 1987 these disagreements were so serious that the attention of the staff and members of Council of Management was diverted from the overview of the fundamental activities of War on Want and from its financial reporting.'

The commission inquiry found that the financial troubles stemmed from a failure to separate the huge amounts of money they were looking after for the Horn of Africa charities from their general fund: 'Considerable sums of money that should have been held for those special trust and other charitable purposes . . . had been expended.' In other words, they'd spent other charities' money, probably because for years Galloway and War on Want's management council didn't know exactly how much money they had. Under Galloway's stewardship they had bought new premises for £435,000, which later they would have trouble trying to sell to try to pay off their debts. When they came to the Charity Commission to borrow money, the whole sorry story was revealed and it led to the inquiry.

In 1990 nearly all the staff of War on Want were made redundant, leaving just a core of administrative staff. It teetered on the edge of liquidation, but kept going against all the odds with the help of some other generous charities and an unexpected legacy of £100,000. Questioned about the state of War on Want when he left it, Galloway told Clive Anderson in 2005:

> By the time I got to it in 1983 it was very ramshackle, very small, and an extremely impecunious organisation, and when I left it just four years later, it was very greatly increased in size, increased in wealth . . . and in fact I drove last night past the building that I caused to be bought by it for £400,000,

which is now a block of luxury flats, worth, I would have thought, many, many millions of pounds, it was quite a good bit of business that I did there . . .

The other damaging internal disagreement in Galloway's time had been who exactly was or wasn't a member of War on Want. This was crucial because members were entitled to vote for the people who ran the organisation. The register of members was the equivalent of the electoral roll, yet the inquiry found that 'the Register of Members of War on Want has been inaccurate and its compilation not supervised by either Company Secretary . . . This called into question the validity of the election of members of the Council of Management at a crucial time.'

How the council of management was elected was thrown into doubt, but so was why certain key members got their jobs, when they seemed to have few relevant qualifications. Glenys Kinnock would later tell the inquiry that the management and officers had insisted things had never been better when they were actually on the verge of insolvency.[11] Treasurer Mike Phillips had not known why he had been given the post, beyond the fact that no-one else had seemed to want it.[12] The less stringent attitude to the appointment of people who oversaw millions of pounds of other people's money, donated to help the world's poor, reflected on everyone involved at War on Want's senior levels. In the light of the mis-management of War on Want, one of the Charity Commission's recommendations was that charities over a certain size should have a minimum number of board members with 'proven financial or legal expertise and experience in charities'.

Few escaped criticism in the Charity Commission report of 1991, but the auditors must have found it particularly sobering reading. The accounts were deemed to have been incorrect for five years in a row from 1985. They were later sued by War on Want, under its new general secretary, Giampi Alhadeff.

George Galloway left War on Want and went in 1987 to take his seat as Labour MP for Glasgow Hillhead.

11

Westminster heaven, Fleet Street hell

In the early 1980s Glasgow Hillhead was said to contain the most educated electorate in Britain. At that time its boundaries enclosed Glasgow University, the BBC and a collection of genteel Georgian terraced streets, full of media luvvies, professors and professional middle classes. It was a deeply conservative place, which worked in favour of the sitting Tory MP, Sir Thomas 'Tam' Galbraith, who had held the seat since 1948.

Hillhead was the final Conservative seat in Glasgow, Galbraith hanging on with a slender 2,002 majority. Then, after holding the seat for thirty-three years in his respected hands, Galbraith died in 1982 and during the subsequent by-election it looked like the little Tory Alamo, surrounded but determined to go down fighting. His successor, Gerry Malone, was up against both the Labour Party and the Labour Party's erstwhile grandee, former Labour Chancellor and Home Secretary Roy Jenkins, by then one of the all-new Social Democratic Party.

Jenkins's marketing strategy was put succinctly in one of his election posters, which read: 'Glasgow needs a voice that will be heard.' He'd decided to flatter the posh burghers of Hillhead that they deserved a national figure, not just any local johnny, or Gerry. Of course, he didn't have much choice about that, given that he was Welsh.

The Labour candidate was a portly councillor called David Wiseman, who was undermined by being portrayed as a Bennite. Bizarrely, Labour activists put up another candidate called Roy Jenkins, to confuse voters, but it didn't work and in a close campaign the 'real' Jenkins ran out the winner with 33 per cent of the vote. The SDP had won, claiming it hailed a new era in British politics. Just a year later, in the general election, Jenkins increased his share to 36 per cent and won again, against the backdrop of Scotland's growing realisation that it couldn't stand Margaret Thatcher, even though she had just got back the Falklands, with their close Scottish connections. Jimmy Allison, Labour's national organiser, helped the 1983 Labour candidate, Neil Carmichael. 'I remember there were CND posters all over the place, in windows. But they voted SDP, whose policy was to keep nuclear weapons.'

While the Thatcher and SDP factors were key in 1980s Hillhead, changes in its boundaries would prove equally important, right up until they scrapped the constituency while George Galloway was the MP. In 1983 the first of these changes started to undermine Jenkins's middle class power base: Hillhead would now include the safe Labour areas of cool Kelvingrove and the concrete jungle of Anderston.

War on Want's general secretary, meanwhile, was still looking around for a Scottish constituency. After his failure to get the nomination in Rhondda in 1983, in March 1985 Galloway was in Dumbarton, supported by the TGWU, competing with the Co-op's John McFall. It was really no contest. McFall was the secretary of the local party, had been educated in Dumbarton and had been a teacher in the area. He had the local members behind him, plus the Co-op. It was almost the definition of a shoo-in, and Galloway lost.

Although the chances had been minimal of Galloway succeeding in Dumbarton, he had to show willing and get himself about. He was determined to get into Westminster, as he'd always planned. The irony is that his escape tunnel from the troubles at War on Want would surface in Glasgow, where politics often punches below the belt and he was obviously unlikely to find any great relief. But could he get selected? Dave Stark was Galloway's agent for Rhondda, Dumbarton and now Hillhead. He remembers: 'It wasn't hard to get George selected. Alec Mosson and I persuaded the constituency Labour Party. We'd known him over the years and could vouch for him.'

Until Galloway threw his hat in the ring, there were others who might have stood. The vice-chairman of the constituency Labour Party, Bob Winter, was going to be in the running, but decided against it. Another local activist, Maria Fyfe, wanted the seat but when it was clear that Galloway had a lot of support, she was happy to go over to the neighbouring constituency of Maryhill. In the end, a local councillor and convenor of planning, Patricia Chalmers, stood against him, but with the union nominations in Galloway's favour and good support among the ordinary members, she was outgunned and lost. Galloway was adopted as prospective parliamentary candidate in November 1985, aged thirty-one. Winter recalls:

> The thing about George was that he was a great orator. He took the SLP conferences by storm. He was the darling of the Labour left and most of us at that time were in the Labour left. I voted for him and I worked phenomenally hard for him during that first campaign.

Despite the backing of the TGWU and the Civil and Public Services Association (who were promoting him in the background), Galloway hadn't been an easy choice for the Hillhead hierarchy, as he was known to be controversial. They needed an interesting candidate to take on Jenkins, but Galloway has to be seen as a risk.

After his selection, Galloway wasted no time in trying to build further. At the 1986 Labour Party conference at Blackpool he stood for the National Executive in the constituency section. A bold step, but as he'd been chair of the Scottish Executive, he went for it. Out of eighteen, he came second to last. The successful ones were Tony Benn, David Blunkett, Tam Dalyell, Michael Meacher, Jo Richardson, Dennis Skinner and Audrey Wise. It had been an interesting attempt, and raised his profile a little, but was seen by some as impetuous.

With a general election on the horizon, the key business for the party was to decide finally on policies that would end up in the manifesto. In the debate on economic policy, Galloway ran up against Roy Hattersley, the shadow Chancellor. Reacting to Hattersley's declaration that Labour would not bring back exchange controls, because he feared a flood of capital out of the country, Galloway accused Hattersley of making up policies as he went along. Hattersley's plan instead had been to have a tax-based scheme, which would have penalised pension funds and insurance companies which keep large sums invested overseas. These institutions would keep their tax advantages only if they repatriated their funds and supported the proposed national investment bank, which Labour wanted to set up to back long-term industrial investment.

The resulting manifesto, which would form the basis of Labour's general election campaign the following year, contained policies that Galloway and other Labour candidates in Scotland must have found much more effective than those offered under Michael Foot, although they could hardly have been worse. In the manifesto Neil Kinnock was keen to stress that a vote for the Liberal/SDP Alliance was a wasted one:

> No party other than Labour can possibly win enough seats to form a government. The Liberals and SDP know that. Their hope is to profit from confusion. To divide the non-Conservative vote in such a way as to make them the 'hook' in a 'hung' Parliament and have power far beyond their responsibility.

There was a commitment to reduce unemployment, invest in industry, increase pensions, reduce prescription charges, put more police on the beat and remove US nuclear missiles from the UK. Galloway may have played down the pledge to reverse tax cuts, and given his stand against the right to buy in Dundee, Kinnock's commitment to keep that piece of Tory legislation might have stuck in his throat. The big plusses for all the Scottish Labour candidates were firstly, the policy to 'legislate in the first Parliamentary session to establish a democratically elected Scottish Assembly in Edinburgh. This will have a wide range of powers over health, education and housing and over significant aspects of industrial and economic policy'; and secondly, the promise to 'abolish the Rates Act and repeal the legislation which established the poll tax in Scotland'.

So all was set for the June election. Galloway was up against an odd list of candidates, as Stark recalls, with his own little bit of spin. 'That election in Hillhead was the first time in history that there were all Labour names on the ballot. Bill Kidd was the SNP candidate. There was Roy Jenkins, obviously, and that bouncy party set up by George Harrison.' Kidd had been Labour at one stage, so certainly all the serious people were Labour.

The actual campaign went extremely well, thanks to some excellent organisation. Stark remembers:

We had a good election team at the time, computer databases, lists of phone contacts, and Wendy Alexander, George's PA, was a very clever girl. I'd take George out on the streets and get him to meet people. George is actually a pretty shy guy when it comes to doing that kind of thing. So I'd do the introductions and he'd get talking. They really took to him, it made it personal and familiar.

Glasgow Labour pulled together. Galloway and Donald Dewar, the sitting MP in Glasgow Garscadden, fought side by side. They went around in an open-topped bus, calling out for support. And they got the results they wanted. Though the 1987 general election saw Labour gain twenty seats overall and the Conservatives lose twenty-two, it still left Margaret Thatcher with a huge 375 against Kinnock's 229. In Scotland Labour now had fifty seats to the Conservatives' and the Liberal/SDP Alliance's ten each.

Christopher Mason, chair of the Scottish Liberals, was running the SDP/Liberal Alliance election campaign. He recalls: 'It was a stunning victory, largely made by the hard-working team, some of who were giving up their holidays to work for George.' The reaction of the voters to Galloway was very positive. 'He was thought of as young, radical, with an intellectual edge. The identikit Hillhead candidate. Not a typical union or local government type. But I don't believe he got elected because of what he did. In 1987 there was a huge swing to Labour because of Kinnock, that's what got him in.'

On the TV footage of the election night, Galloway and the other candidates are standing in the usual line-up behind the returning officer, with a young-looking Galloway stage left. When the announcement is made he moves smartly up to the podium to thank the other candidates for a fairly fought campaign. He is clearly making huge efforts not to punch the air, or similar. Instead he keeps his composure and looks like it was all meant to be.

It was one of those iconic victories, to rank with the defeat of Michael Portillo in 1997. It seemed to mark the end of another phase of British politics, as the SDP's leading light crashed out, together with Shirley Williams and Bill Rodgers, who both lost that night as well. Galloway polled 17,958, with Jenkins in second place with 14,707. Brian Cooklin, the Conservative, managed only 6,048 and the SNP a rather pathetic 2,713.

George Galloway won the election for several reasons. Kinnock had made

Labour more electable and also there was a lot of tactical voting. Some Liberal and SDP people voted Conservative because they thought they had a better chance, but all that did was split the Alliance vote. There was also a big anti-Thatcher feeling and that brought Labour supporters to the polling stations. Whatever the excuses and possible reasons, Jenkins, the founder of the SDP in 1981, son of the Welsh miner's leader and Labour MP Arthur Jenkins, talked of as a possible next Prime Minister in a hung Parliament, was down and out in Glasgow. The Labour rebels had been defeated and the left had won.

Galloway was on his way to Westminster, at thirty-one, with a left-wing and Scottish agenda that was illustrated in the August/September edition of *Radical Scotland*:

> I believe there's certainly the makings of a constitutional crisis . . . when the governing party of a state which contains several nations is so bereft of support in one of those constituent nations . . . then I think there is definitely a crisis. Add to that the fact that 76 per cent of the electorate supported parties with a definite commitment to a Scottish Assembly . . . and add again the anger . . . of so many people in Scotland that we have got a government that we didn't vote for, for the third consecutive time, then I believe that there's a responsibility on the political leaders of the Scottish people to make a crisis.

In the same interview Galloway conjured up the image of dark powers waiting in the wings:

> If the present anger is not used properly, if it is not led properly in a noble campaign, then there is a danger that sections of the Scottish people may become totally alienated, and that anti-democratic forces might emerge. Any violence would be pernicious and dangerous, and apart from anything else I suspect that Malcolm Rifkind wouldn't want that as a legacy of his holding the office of Secretary of State for Scotland. It is imperative therefore, that we are able to demonstrate mass support for major changes to the structure of the state and to the way that Scotland is governed.

The sort of demonstration of mass support he was talking about would emerge a couple of years later when he was involved in the Glasgow campaign against the poll tax. That noble cause, which brought together many sides and extremes of the left, was a long way from coming to a head. Before that Galloway would spend huge energies in a return to the sort of internal feuding that had characterised his time in Dundee and at War on Want.

In the weeks after his June victory, he had to find a way to settle up with the charity. Could he extricate himself with some dignity and any semblance of camaraderie? His departure was a double-edged sword for the staff. They all knew Galloway had to leave now and, save for a few of his diehards, overwhelmingly they wanted shot of him. But they were now facing a period of uncertainty, as their boss was almost inevitably going to be directing a major part of his time to constituency business in the closing months of his tenure. After the destruction of morale that the Charity Commission report would later refer to, it was essential that his successor was untainted with past associations.

His last few months were unlikely to be peaceful. In July 1987, ten council members took the remarkable move of writing an open letter to the acting chair, Campbell Christie. The ten were the so-called Gang of Four, plus Ben Crowe, Hermione Harris, Peter Oakley, Jenny Pearce, Andrew Shaw and Trish Silkin, and their letter said:

> Council is now operating in such a way as to make it impossible for us to have objective debate and fulfil our responsibilities as trustees of the charity . . . Fighting world poverty with radical and imaginative programmes has ceased to be the primary concern of Council. Indeed it is many months since we discussed in detail the work of the organisation in the Third World: something that was once the central focus of Council meetings.

To add to the new MP's troubles, in early September 1987 BBC Scotland ran two reports which referred to the expenses row, which Galloway had hoped had been forgotten about. So, at the press conference in Glasgow on Monday 14 September 1987, called to announce that he would be standing down from War on Want to concentrate on Parliament, a pack of reporters from all over the UK, but with a large Scottish contingent, was waiting. Most of them had been briefed about the expenses investigation; some believed this was their chance to settle old scores.

The BBC TV archive recording of this incident makes strange viewing. Galloway looks dog tired and older than his thirty-three years, as he faces down the questions. Sitting on Galloway's right hand is a stony-faced Fanshawe, in big 1980s glasses. Further over to the right, which must have felt odd for him, was Bill Speirs, very seldom to the right of anyone.

Galloway delivered a statement from notes on the table in front of him. On the point of the taxi fares at odd hours and from locations that it had been alleged were nothing to do with War on Want, Galloway revealed that he had paid back £850. He also told the assembled journalists that he had paid back £194.65 that he'd originally claimed as expenses for the union leader Alex Kitson's retirement party. Galloway's original American Express expenses bill for Kitson's retirement party in Edinburgh, to which he had travelled up from London by rail in June 1986 and then stayed overnight, had come to £246.05. It had included £12.25 on flowers from Chivers Flowers.

On the issue of his many restaurant bills, Galloway said he'd paid back £150. He qualified this by saying that the sum was for claims he'd made for unofficial guests, which War on Want had paid for. He said of the auditor, Frank Weinberg, 'I accepted his ruling, pointing out that it was harsh.'

Then proceedings really got interesting, as Galloway turned to a trip he'd made to Greece in 1985. John Nairn, a freelance newspaper reporter based in Scotland, was poised with questions. He'd travelled to the press conference with Louise Carmi and remembers that 'when I walked in with Louise he almost fainted. He looked a worried man.'

Carmi recalls: 'When George had moved out of my mother-in-law's flat in Bloomsbury I went over there to tidy up and found a plastic bag behind the door with all sorts of stuff in it, including some pictures of George in Greece with Lilian Grewar.' She'd let Nairn look at them and he was determined to ask Galloway about them. Lilian Grewar, fellow Dundonian, was Galloway's girlfriend for some years in the late 1980s, after he had broken up with his first wife, Elaine. They had also been close companions for some time before the split, as was evidenced by the photographs.

How the photographs got into Carmi's possession is disputed by Galloway. He claims there was a burglary at Lilian's home, and that negatives were stolen. This story was doing the rounds at the time of the press conference, but in an interview in 1991 with the *Scotsman* he said:

'Before that press conference negatives of photographs had been stolen from Lilian's house in a break-in. They were not compromising in any way, but they were photographs of me taken by her, or her taken by me, at places like the Parthanon, so clearly together in Greece.'[1] Carmi regards the idea of being behind the break-in as 'laughable'.

Nairn's relationship with Galloway went back a little way. He had been based in Dunbartonshire and at one stage during Galloway's campaign to get selected to stand for Labour there, Nairn had interviewed him. 'I'd asked him if he'd ever taken a penny and he said to me: "I will never repay a halfpenny, because I have never taken a halfpenny." '

In 1985 Galloway had travelled to Athens at a time when some at War on Want had believed he was on leave. Galloway disputes that and claims that he had told Vivienne Lukey and Martin Plaut that he was going to attend a conference while he was there. Leave or no leave, conference or no conference, there is no record of a claim to War on Want for his air fare to get there.

When his American Express expenses came back, they totalled £186.30 and included a bill for a meal on Mykonos, an island some way away from Athens. Just how far away and how long it took to get there became the subject of journalists' intrigue. At the press conference Galloway explained that his trip to what he called a 'seminar organised in Athens in May or June of 1985' had been part of a top secret diplomatic initiative. 'We were involved in a major international effort to which we had recruited the German statesman Willy Brandt as the head of that initiative to convince the Ethiopian government to desist from its practice of forbidding food and emergency supplies to cross Ethiopian government lines.' He then explained further about the fact that Ethiopia was a communist state and that they had been meeting Cuban and other diplomats in London, and that the Soviets were changing their position on the Horn of Africa. Eventually Galloway got round to the fact that he'd been invited by someone in that diplomatic circle to go to Athens for the conference. He didn't say who, and seemed to spend a long time implying that it was all too top secret to be revealed.

Galloway then explained that he had made it clear he was going before he went and that he had reported back afterwards:

What is contested now is that they now say, yes, I raised this meeting with them before going, and yes, I raised this meeting on my return, and that they thought for some strange reason I had gone to a conference in Athens for five days at my own expense . . . I had gone to a conference in Athens on the Horn of Africa with eastern European apparatchiks at my own expense. Now I take the view, frankly, that if you believe that you would believe anything.

Finally, he got to the issue that the bemused hacks, most of whom probably knew little about apparatchiks and the Horn, had come to hear about: the money. 'Because this was being made the subject of personal and political controversy I decided, under no pressure from anyone and against the representations and advice of many, I decided to pay those expenditures myself, which I have now done.'

At this point Nairn piped up: 'Could I ask about the Mykonos trip, George, because amongst other things, besides being a journalist I am also interested in geography?' He was trying to establish from Galloway how much time he'd spent on Mykonos, having already found out that it was at least a six-hour journey there and six hours back. To do that as a day trip would have been impractical. Today there is a hydrofoil that does the journey in three hours or so, but in 1985 that wasn't running.

Galloway replied: 'It is a couple of hours' sail from Athens.'

'Two hours' sail from Athens?'

'I said a couple of hours. That is generally regarded as two. [Some laughter from Bill Speirs at this point.] The Mykonos trip, which was one expenditure, one expenditure, was made, was a lunch on the island of Mykonos, following a couple of hours' sail, which the participants in the seminar made during the course of that seminar.'

'In the course of that seminar' sounds as if they took a break and got back to work. Nairn knew that to go for lunch to Mykonos from Athens was absurd, unless you wanted to leave at, say 7 a.m., arrive at 1 p.m., have lunch for exactly one hour and then get back by, at the very earliest, 8 p.m. That's assuming the journeys took exactly six hours and that you ate immediately on arriving for an hour, got back on the boat on the dot of 2 p.m. and sailed straightaway. The idea of this having been a day trip to Mykonos was hard to believe.

Nairn went on: 'So I take it from what you are saying that you left from the seminar and did, what, a day trip to Mykonos and back?'

'I beg your pardon?'

'Did you do a day trip to Mykonos and back?'

'A day trip to Mykonos with other people on the seminar and came back afterwards, yes.'

'What, the same day?'

'No, actually, it was the next day.'

'The next day. I thought that. It's about a six- or seven-hour boat journey according to the Greek tourist office.'

'No, no, no. The boat journey is a couple of hours.'

So, just to recap, these 'eastern European apparatchiks', bent on serious discussion of how to save thousands of lives in the Horn of Africa by getting together with the Soviet Union to persuade the communist Ethiopian government to let aid through their battle lines, went off to Mykonos on a day trip from Athens, for lunch. However, Galloway at least stayed on for the night and returned later.

Nairn was about hitting his stride by now. His next target was to find out more about who Galloway had been with on the seminar, or meeting, or conference. He went on: 'Interesting. Could you tell me whether you were accompanied by any War on Want member on the trip to Greece?'

There was a long pause here, which some have timed at eight seconds. If you look at your watch and count eight seconds, you'll be surprised just how long that is. Eventually, Galloway replied: 'No, I wasn't accompanied by any War on Want member on the trip to Greece.'

'Were you accompanied by anyone?'

'I was accompanied by a large number of participants at the seminar.'

'Surely you met them there.'

'Sorry?'

'Surely you met them there.'

'Met who there?'

'These participants at the seminar.'

'No, some of them were actually on my plane. But if what you are getting at is did I meet anyone I knew whilst I was there, yes, I did, but that's nothing

"It gives me great pleasure."

"CALL BACK LATER! I'VE GOT WANTS OF MY OWN AT THE MOMENT!"

to do with you and is nothing to do with War on Want and didn't cost War on Want any money.'

Slowly, but surely, Galloway was coming out with the fact that he had been on Mykonos with someone he knew. . . But so what? Why did that have to be dragged out of him? Nairn went on: 'Is that person standing for the council of management?'

'I met a number of people, one of whom, yes, is standing for the council of management. Do you work for the *Sunday Sport*, or is it the *Daily Star*?'

'Your snide comments don't cut any ice with me.'

'Carry on anyway. I'm answering all your questions.'

'Would you like to tell us the name of the person?'

'No.'

What Nairn was driving at was that Lilian Grewar, who lived in London while Mrs Elaine Galloway lived in Dundee, had been on the trip to Mykonos, and further-more, was standing in the War on Want council of management elections.

I'm sure in retrospect, Nairn might have liked the opportunity to carry on a while longer, but he passed to Brian McCartney, Dundee correspondent of the *Daily Record*, who took up the question of Galloway's sex life. It led to one of the oddest stories in Fleet Street's history.

McCartney asked: 'Obviously, there is some interest that you travelled to Greece in the company of presumably someone else, presumably a female. Is that the case?'

'Actually,' Galloway replied, 'I travelled to Greece and was in Greece with lots of people, lots of people.'

'You know precisely, George, what the question is.'

'Well, I think you should state it. I think you should state it. I travelled to, and spent time in, Greece with lots of people, many of whom were women . . .'

Fair enough, nothing controversial there. He still seemed to be giving nothing much away. Then, remarkably, he carried on uninterrupted: '. . . some of whom were known carnally to me. Some of whom were known carnally to me. I actually had sexual intercourse with some of the people in Greece . . .'

Simon Fanshawe at this juncture looked like a rabbit caught in headlights.

He had instantly frozen and looked like he might never move again. Roadkill on the Galloway highway.

Galloway carried on: '. . . and if the British public and BBC Scotland think that's of interest they are welcome to broadcast it.'

Nairn, without missing a beat, carried on: 'You mean while you were in Greece, or previously?'

'While I was in Greece, actually. While I was in Greece, actually. But whether the Scottish public are interested in that kind of garbage I have my doubts.'

Fanshawe moved ever so slightly and uttered something about 'that being a moot point'. In front of him all the journalists, tabloid or broadsheet, BBC or STV, good, bad, ugly or indifferent, thought they'd died and gone to Heaven. George Galloway MP had just admitted having sex with people on a trip to Greece.

Years later Galloway told Colette Douglas-Home of the *Scotsman*, for a feature published on 3 June 1991: 'I said I had sex with more than one woman in a futile attempt to take the heat off Lilian.' How making his sex life open season would take the heat off her is hard to fathom. However, it did mean that the rather difficult-to-report business of his expenses was overlooked by many journalists, whose editors wanted all the salacious details of the sex-in-the-sun story.

Another journalist asked: 'Just to lay it on the line, did you go with a lady friend, from London, this woman who is standing for the council?'

Galloway replied: 'I went, I went with a lot of people to Greece, but it . . . but . . . but War on Want didn't pay for any of them and I really don't think that I should . . . I mean, I think that I have been quite blunt. I mean, I have said that I have had sexual intercourse with some of the people at the conference.'

When Galloway was interviewed by Clive Anderson for BBC Five Live at Christmas 2005, he claimed he had not had sex with more than one person in Greece and that he had been misreported. He explained that he had been referring to past sexual liaisons with delegates, not multiple ones in Greece.

Whatever he meant, whatever the details of his sex life really were, it took the heat off the money issues and the next day's papers were full of 'Bonking for Britain'-type stories and cartoons of Galloway with semi-naked girls, cavorting around the War on Want offices. While it was trivial stuff on one level, some contrasted Africans starving while Galloway was having a whale of a time, quaffing bubbly and chasing women.

Nairn still had one more go for more answers on the expenses at the press conference, though. He was aware that if Galloway had flown to the conference with others from London and stayed for some days, including a night on a Greek island, then he may well have charged War on Want money for flights and hotels. Of course, the expenses may well have been picked up by those, whoever they were, who organised the whole affair.

Galloway's American Express expenses from the conference were:

14/6/85	Kalokeriou Tavern, Athens	£28.15
15/6/85	Attica Palace Hotel, Athens	£30.31
15/6/85	Alabatros Rest, Mykonos	£24.25
19/6/85	Lengo Restaurant, Athens	£11.79
19/6/85	Chang's House Rest, Athens	£16.49
20/6/85	Attica Palace Hotel, Athens	£75.31

That would be consistent with someone checking out of Athens on 15 June 1985, going to Mykonos, staying for a number of days there, then coming back to Athens on or before 19 June, and lastly checking out of their Athens hotel on 20 June. Whatever the details, after the auditor's report was shown to the management council, Galloway agreed to pay back £525.42 for his total Athens/Mykonos trip.

On 25 September 1987, War on Want's annual general meeting opened in Brighton with all this unhappiness as the background. It was a weekend conference, with speakers booked of the stature of Gerald Kaufman, then Labour's shadow Foreign Secretary. Apart from debates on Britain and the developing world and fund-raising workshops, the results of the 1987/8 elections for the council of management were to be announced.

Chair Simon Fanshawe had to constantly call for quiet as Galloway's opponents were hissed and jeered to put them off speaking. At one stage a man had to be held back as he strode forward aggressively, shouting at a speaker. Several people cried as they spoke. Speaker after speaker came forward to criticise Galloway and explain what had been going on. John Denham gave what is remembered as a calm, collected and devastating critique , telling the meeting: 'The best and most committed people I've ever worked with have been subjected to intimidation, abuse and vilification . . . on a scale which is absolutely unbelievable.'

In the hall were around 160 people and when the votes were taken, the majority of those present voted against the motion, but when the proxy votes were cast, Galloway ran out the winner. In almost his final act at War on Want Galloway's faction had won, with the help of around 200 votes from members who hadn't heard a word of the debate, and the ten anti-Galloway members were voted off the management council.

The news in the autumn of 1986 that War on Want was conducting an internal audit of Galloway's expenses had worried some in Hillhead Labour, but the momentum of the predicted election and then the campaign itself had made everyone pull together. However, the press conference admission of carnal knowledge of more than one of the women on the Greece trip created uproar among the genteel folk of the Hillhead constituency office. The developing anti-Galloway group pressed for, and got, an extraordinary meeting to discuss whether any more money was owed to War on Want. Furthermore, the women of Hillhead Labour were made even unhappier by the reports in the papers of Mrs Galloway's anger and upset at the press conference admission. Conducting extra-marital affairs was not a popular quality for MPs, though the deputy political editor of the *Daily Record*, Dave King, seems to put this down to feminism:

> The women's section of the constituency Labour Party was strong at that time. George was unpopular for failing to answer summons to the constituency; he was seen as a bit arrogant and then, after the War on Want episode, it escalated to a full-blown row and that was also to do with Johann Lamont, who was a feminist campaigner and very prominent in the CLP.

On 18 October 1987 the party management committee met at Transport House in Glasgow to discuss Galloway's expenses and to decide if Hillhead had to pay back some more money to War on Want. Galloway left the meeting and briefed the press that the issues had been resolved.

Galloway was struggling to keep his enemies in the local party at bay, but there was worse to come. He'd weathered the War on Want storm, as well as bad publicity, and some controversy about his sex life he could handle as well. The next barrage was going to come from far more prominent and powerful organisations: Scottish Television and Channel 4.

12

In the Red

Most MPs in their first few months at Westminster are too busy trying to find their way around and somewhere to live in London to have time for any more than one or two interviews with the constituency media. George Galloway, however, had been dealing with an incredible amount of damaging press coverage. No new MP has ever faced such embarrassment as cartoons in the tabloid press depicting them half naked and supposedly 'bonking for Britain'.

Towards the end of October 1987, while the bonking cartoons and questions about his expenses were still drying on the page, Galloway became aware of another story that was likely to cause concern and problems for the new MP. A crew from Scottish Television (STV) was digging up the buried remains of the financially ruined Dundee Labour clubs. A dogged reporter called Mike Mulford had spent the best part of a year investigating the ins and outs, comings and goings, give and take of the social clubs at Whitfield, Ardler and Menzieshill. Mulford now works for the RAF as a press officer, but back in those days was a leading light of the TV company and had developed a story of such interest that Channel 4 commissioned a forty-minute programme to air across the UK. It was to be the first ever *Dispatches*, which would become a flagship strand for the network, renowned for its campaigning investigative journalism.

Mulford had gained the help of James Martin, a former member of Galloway's inner circle and ex-manager of Whitfield Labour Club, who was going to talk on camera about the financial arrangements between the Labour Party and Dundee's Labour clubs. He named names and provided documentation. The programme also interviewed former members of the clubs, who were angry about the way they had been run. When Galloway had been asked for an interview, he had referred the programme team to his solicitor, who had told them that the matter was too serious to be dealt with by a television programme. His solicitor was his old friend Frank Doran MP, whose name and picture featured in the actual programme. Doran later told the *Sunday Times*: 'STV made a number of allegations of a very serious nature and I took the view that a TV programme wasn't the proper place to investigate them.'[1]

The programme was highly critical of the Labour Party's financial links to the Labour clubs, yet there are thousands of social clubs all over the country that donate money to their parties, including Liberal Clubs and Conservative Clubs. The tone of the programme was accusatory, but the wording in the documentary did not amount to any allegations of impropriety. Yet Galloway and his comrades felt that, in his words, 'the imputation was very clear, that a number of leading Labour politicians had something to do with large sums of money that went "missing"'.[2]

Mulford's commentary stated that by 1981, Whitfield Labour Club's management were

> systematically switching club profits into the local Labour Party. At that time it was taking in over £5,000 a week from the bar. Yet the club was piling up debts and unpaid bills . . . In February 1981 the club had failed to make a VAT return . . . and the VAT man wanted immediate payment of £13,500 . . . Tayside Regional Council were owed £3,200 rates . . .

Though Galloway had said on Radio Tay that 'precious little' money was going from the clubs to Labour, the question was whether any should be going from Whitfield when the club was struggling to pay its bills.

By 1984, Whitfield, Ardler and Menzieshill were each suffering financially. Some blamed the poor local economy for reduced takings at the bar and at functions, while others thought they were being mismanaged. It took a while for the ordinary members of the clubs to get access to enough information to make a judgement, but by early 1986 the Whitfield club committee members had seen a set of accounts and were on the warpath. They called a meeting with the management to discuss why the club seemed to be having money problems, but didn't get the answers they wanted and became so concerned that they went to the Dundee solicitors McGinlay,

Milne and McDonagh to seek advice. They then reported their suspicions of 'financial irregularities' to the police on 28th March.

Whitfield had been in trouble for a couple of years before that. According to Martin, STV's key witness, the club had planned an extension, but the finance fell through when it changed brewers. This left it with cash flow problems and when its new brewers, Scottish & Newcastle, who had loaned the club £154,714.34, asked questions about the finances, they opened up a few cans of worms. Things looked so bad they insisted that no more donations were to be given to the Labour Party and that accountants Arthur Young & Co (now Ernst & Young) should be brought in to conduct an audit of the books. What they found must have left them all reaching for a drink.

Martin had left his post as manager in September 1985, claiming to be sick of the whole business. The club had a reported turnover of around £250,000, but was making a loss, and the 750 members couldn't understand, when the place was full and bar takings were good, how the club had run into problems. By the time the *Dispatches* programme was transmitted Whitfield had debts of £160,000.

On 7 April 1986, a few days after the members had found out that the club was in a deep financial mess, one of the managers, Labour councillor Robert Phillip Grubb, known as Phil, claimed that his set of club keys had been stolen in a burglary at his house. That very same night, £4,000 went missing from the safe. This was the final straw for the members, who then passed a vote of no confidence in their committee of twelve on 20 April. Even though the committee had already gone to the police themselves, the members now did the same to make a formal complaint about the committee. The Fraud Squad was called in.

Though the police had proved themselves more PC Plod than *Miami Vice* when they'd taken on J. L. Stewart, there was a feeling that this would be an easier nut to crack. Superintendent Jim McKay led the investigation with Detective Andy Crook. They pulled in Martin for questioning under caution and held him for three days.

Martin was in a sticky situation. As manager of the club's day-to-day running, it looked as though he was holding the baby. But he wasn't going to go down without a fight and it's important to remember the history of the Martin family at this point. Both James and his older brother Jack had been in the NEDS, the centre of the clique that ran Dundee Labour. Jack had got together with Willie McKelvey to give vital information on J. L. Stewart to *World in Action* all those years ago. Now James thought he might do the same as his big brother and he started to co-operate with Mulford, to try and use the media to his own advantage.

The following month the plot started to thicken regarding Whitfield's finances. On 11 May the *Sunday Mail* confronted Galloway with copies of his own cheques, cashed at Whitfield Labour Club but which had bounced. They were for £135 and £110 and Galloway explained that he had subsequently honoured them: 'One for £110 was drawn on my account at the Co-op bank in Laidlaw Street, Glasgow. That's so long ago the bank is no longer there.' When asked about the one for £135, he reportedly replied: 'I paid that to the former club treasurer weeks ago. And I paid £11 interest.' These same cheques would later become part of the *Dispatches* programme, and were shown on screen.

James Martin gave interviews on camera, and was kitted out with a hidden camera to try to get evidence from Colin Rennie, who'd succeeded Galloway as the boss of Dundee Labour. Mulford and his crew tried to get interviews with Galloway and the others, but they declined to take part. They did manage to confront Ken Fagan, and filmed him looking at several cheques that had been cashed over the bar at Whitfield. The cheques were his and also from members of his immediate family. Like Galloway's, they had initially bounced when they reached the bank. Fagan repeatedly explained that he had honoured the cheques some time afterwards and that there was not a problem therefore. When Mulford accused him of having a 'banking arrangement' with the club, a very calm and seemingly patient Fagan explained that this was not true.

Of course, this TV investigation and the slower-moving, but worrying, police inquiries came at a very awkward time for Galloway. In 1987 he was fighting an election, had just been featured in controversial TV and newspaper coverage of his expenses and was still in a tremendous battle for control of War on Want. The last thing he needed was a film crew door-stepping him and making all kinds of allegations about his conduct over clubs he had left behind in Dundee several years before. So when Mulford, his producer Paul Murricone, and the director Scott Ferguson, made several failed attempts to film interviews with Christie in public places, it was clear that the MPs had to do something. It was decided that Frank Doran, as both a solicitor and a concerned Labour Party member, would go to see the boss of STV, Gus MacDonald, to get him to stop the production. In the meeting he also asked MacDonald to hand over any evidence, 'so that those involved could be brought to justice'. Not surprisingly, he was told that wouldn't be possible.

Having failed to get the programme stopped at source, Galloway and Doran then went to the broadcaster, Channel 4. With the transmission getting ever closer, a meeting was set up in London on 1 October 1987, between STV, Channel 4, Doran and Rennie. To give an idea of the serious-ness and mistrust with which this was approached, the entire proceedings were taped and copies given to each of the parties. Channel 4 and STV kept theirs, while Doran claimed he had given his to Tayside Police. The outcome of the meeting was the same as the one with MacDonald: there was no way they were going to stop the transmission, or give all their hard work to the police.

The pressure didn't let up on Channel 4, right up to the wire. On 5 November 1987, the day before transmission, Galloway was still trying to have the programme pulled. The press had assembled for a special screen-ing, but had to wait an hour while Channel 4 consulted their legal team, after one more complaint from Galloway and Doran. Nonetheless, the assembled press were eventually allowed to see 'In the Red' and prepare their articles for the following day. The revelations in the programme, that clubs set up by Galloway and involving other key Labour figures had gone bust and that money was unaccounted for, were now guaranteed to be all over the papers. The four Dundee MPs whose names appeared, Galloway, Doran, Ross and McKelvey, were angry and determined to counter the claims. In a later letter to the commercial TV watchdog, the Independent Broadcasting Authority (IBA), Galloway, Ross, McKelvey and Doran complained at length over many pages about the quality of the journalism. Oddly, they also stated in their letter that there were no outright allegations against anyone. So what were they so worried about?

'In the Red' is a flawed programme in many ways. Ferguson now says that 'it was structured strangely', and it certainly does jump around from one subject to another in a disorientating fashion. Not only does it cover the Labour club finances, it also touches on the NEDS story, the financing of the *Dundee Standard* and the sale of the Labour Party's headquarters in Dundee. Mulford seems to have had so much information that he didn't know what to do with it all, though it also has the feel of a programme made by a committee, which is not surprising as lawyers were crawling all over it, under pressure from Galloway.

The programme featured some interesting confessions from James Martin, who said: 'I took responsibility as senior member of staff for losses of some £9,500. That money disappeared and I took responsibility to replace it . . . I borrowed money to put it back.' Though today Martin is a chatty fellow with a good sense of humour, in the interviews he seems subdued, resigned to some unseen fate lurking behind the camera. He went on that he was 'disillusioned with things . . . feeling that so many had benefited from this little club empire. In the end the clubs themselves had been left in a real financial mess.' At the time, he was still under police investigation, and Galloway would later be highly critical of the programme makers for not making this clear.

Martin then went on to describe how he had cashed cheques for people over the bar. Some of these cheques then bounced at the bank and had to be sent back several times, before they were eventually honoured. The practice of cashing cheques is perfectly legal and safe, as long as you are sure that they will be honoured. If they aren't, it can be hard to get the money back from the person who signed the cheque. That's why you won't find it easy to do at your local pub, or club. In the days before the now ubiquitous ATMs and debit cards, cashing cheques was often the only convenient way of getting cash, and it seems that a culture built up where Dundee councillors and others who were trusted by Martin cashed cheques at the Whitfield bar.

When Galloway was confronted by Mulford (and the *Sunday Mail*) over the unhonoured cheques, he had first explained that they had been honoured, so there was nothing wrong. He then complained to Mulford, via Doran acting as his solicitor, that the reason they had bounced in the first place was that Martin had been late in presenting them to the bank. Galloway said that because they had been late, he had no longer got the funds in his account to cover the amounts. However, 'In the Red' put on screen pictures of Galloway's cheques that clearly showed that they had been sent off to the bank in a reasonable, normal time by Martin, in fact within a matter of days.

The shocking conclusion of 'In the Red' was that the three clubs were, at the date of transmission, in debt by £650,000, with £100,000 seemingly missing from the accounts. Exactly how so much money had gone missing was not explained. Apart from Galloway's and Ken Fagan's bouncing personal cheques, the programme also showed a cheque signed by Galloway on the account of Dundee Standard Publications, the limited company set up to own the newspaper. This cheque for £500 had also bounced, to be honoured some time later.

In the course of making the programme Mulford and the STV team had got access to some of the financial records of the clubs, but not all. For example in the case of the Ardler club, in one year an amount of £4,450.10 was entered as 'donations', but it was unclear to whom. They wanted to establish just how much money had been given to the local Labour Party, and so did the members of the club, who claimed they had been kept in the dark. The firm of accountants called in by the members to investigate, W. A. Findlay, had found an Ardler cash book with pages cut out and £30,000 unaccounted for, so it was proving a hard task.

Meanwhile, as part of the process to try and clear his client's name, Martin's solicitor, Andrew Lyall of Simpson, Boath, Lyall and Co., had requested access to the Labour Party accounts. Martin and his lawyer wanted to try and check the 'donations' listed in the Whitfield accounts by reference to the, presumably, well-audited Labour Party ones. Unfortunately, these accounts were not going to be available. When Lyall talked to Doran, the Labour Party's solicitor, he was told that he was more than welcome to come down and look at any accounts they had, but sadly the ones for the years 1979–82 had been destroyed in a fire. Annoyingly for all concerned, these had been the most important ones.

There is only one documented fire that affected the Dundee Labour party offices at that time. The Dundee Fire Department records showed that on 2 December 1982 at 1.27 a.m., a unit had attended Dundee Labour Party's headquarters in Rattray Street to deal with what they believed was a case of arson. Petrol had been poured through the letter box and set alight. However, it seemed from the fire officer's report that it hadn't reached very far into the building. The report read: 'Other than severe heat damage to the doors and facings, there was no damage to the fabric of the buildings or its contents.' This is corroborated by a BBC reporter, Neil Mudie, who interviewed Galloway about the fire the day afterwards, in the very office. He remembers that the office 'had a little smoke damage, but that's all'. Galloway was also quoted in the local paper, the *Evening Telegraph*: 'Fortunately, there was little damage to our paper-work and files.'

So, it seemed that the Labour Party accounts would remain a mystery, and in subsequent years they have become a Holy Grail for Dundee's conspiracy theorists and journalists. There are stories of another set being held somewhere in Perth, and of hard men knocking on doors in the dead of night asking for their whereabouts. Whatever happened to them, a hint at their contents emerged on 'In the Red'. The programme revealed what they claimed to be the Labour Party's year opening and closing balances for 1981/2 and 1982/3. These had been provided by Martin, from summaries:

Closing balance 1981/2: £1,489.99   Opening balance 1982/3: £148.88
Closing balance 1982/3: £611.76   Opening balance 1983/4: £1,636.39

You don't need to be an accounting genius to realise that the balance at the close of one year ought to be the same as the balance for the opening of the next. So why these figures were different is another mystery. Meanwhile, 'In the Red' claimed that the closing balance of 1982/3 and the closing balance of 1983/4 are the same, at £611.76. Mulford said in the programme that this is a million-to-one chance.

Channel 4's story of the drinking clubs concluded with the sobering facts that a report into Whitfield's accounts by Arthur Young from 1984 had found that £34,680.00 was missing. They said: 'The amount of the total accumulative deficit indicates not only a lack of control and poor trading performance, but also casts doubt on the accuracy of previous accounts.' 'In the Red' also revealed that Ardler had closed with debts of £212,000 and Menzieshill had closed with debts of £270,000. Overall, a staggering

£100,000 could not be accounted for among the three drinking clubs. Cock-up or conspiracy, that's a lot of beer.

In the aftermath of the transmission, Galloway and Doran, plus the hardly mentioned Willie McKelvey and Ernie Ross, hit back. Galloway claimed that 'tricks and lies were the whole substance of the programme from start to finish'.[3] Doran told the *Sunday Mail* that 'anyone guilty of, or involved in, dishonesty is not wanted in the Labour Party'. Following up their complaints that the whole saga needed to be investigated by the police, not a TV programme, Galloway and Doran contacted Peter Fraser, the Scottish Solicitor General, and asked him to look into the affair.

By 19 November, the four MPs were reported to be about to sue and Doran was alleging that the whole affair was 'the product of a long-standing vendetta conducted by J. L. Stewart'.[4] There is no doubt that Stewart and other Galloway opponents were making the most of all the fuss. Tom McDonald even asked if he could arrange to screen the programme in a Dundee cinema for interested locals who'd missed it first time, or perhaps who'd enjoyed it so much they wanted to see it all over again, with popcorn.

An anti-Galloway poet, calling himself Nemesis, went into print with a leaflet called 'In the Red Flag', which treated the lucky burghers of Dundee to an original song that was supposed to be sung to the tune of *Jailhouse Rock*:

> Bye bye, Georgie, bye bye
> Don't cry, Frankie, don't cry
> The prison van that takes you –
> Away from here – you'll never know how glad it makes me
>
> Pick up Christie and Ken
> To lift fat John takes ten men.
> Here them all wail
> They're off to the jail,
> When they reach Saughton Prison
> They will each get a pail
> Bye bye. Georgie, bye bye
> Don't cry, Frankie, don't cry.

In reply, a supporter of Galloway, calling themselves 'Minerva', wrote and distributed these verses:

> There's an element in oor toon
> Determined to bring oor cooncil doon
> Their inspiration's a bitter wee man
> Who seeks revenge any way he can.

> That twisted wee baillie, known as J.L.
> Who languished a while in a prison cell
> Still schemes and plans wi' crooks galore
> To disgrace the toon as he did before.
> Five years he got for his corruption
> And he's still determined to cause disruption.

On 21 November it was reported that there would be a writ issued against the *Sunday Times* for an article following on from the programme, and that Galloway would be issuing one the following week. However, despite their many complaints, no legal case was ever pursued against STV or Channel 4 and David Scott, the programme's executive producer, says now that Galloway and his fellow MPs received no payment out of court either.

The four MPs were determined to pursue their complaints with the commercial television watchdog, the IBA. They wrote a joint letter on 17 November, on House of Commons stationery, in which they complained that: Frank Christie had been accosted outside a nursery school while holding his child, and then embarrassed in front of other parents; there had been a campaign against Colin Rennie, who then lost his seat to David Coutts of the SNP; Stewart had vowed revenge in prison; James Martin had been paid £10,000 and had been fitted with hidden tape recorder (claims that Martin strenuously denied and which seems to be totally unsubstantiated. He said at the time that he had been paid nothing but a couple of lunches in the STV canteen).

The letter made a case for a continuing vendetta by Stewart against the left-wingers in the party, saying: 'Three of these MPs were instrumental in bringing Mr James Lumsden Stewart to justice.' It also said that they were aware that Gus MacDonald had been executive producer of the *World in Action* investigation into Stewart.

The four alleged that Martin had come to Rennie to ask him for a letter, which showed that £27,000 had been donated from the Whitfield club to the Labour Party. Rennie was said to have been astounded and to have immediately informed Doran. Rennie also claimed that Martin had said he needed the letter for the VAT man and that he wanted no record made in the Labour Party books. The IBA complaint goes on to claim that Rennie was 'informed' by persons unknown that there 'was proof that Martin was responsible for money missing from the Whitfield club', and that a fraudulent loan had been made to Martin.

What Galloway seemingly didn't know was that the IBA had viewed the programme before transmission and, although it had asked STV to take legal advice over it, had given it a green light. So it was not surprising that the regulator wrote back on 27 January 1988 to say: 'The proper procedures were followed in preparing this programme both at Scottish Television and at the IBA . . . We are satisfied that Scottish Television approached the issues honestly and with proper regard for due impartiality.' The IBA didn't go into the detailed allegations made by the MPs, but it did pass on from STV that 'you are wrong in claiming that payments of up to £10,000 were made to the informants: Scottish Television state that informants were paid no more than travel and meal expenses, which amounted to no more than £250.00'.

The programme was to make life even more difficult for Galloway in his new job as MP for Glasgow Hillhead, but the police investigation continued and it would be Martin who faced the worst consequences. As for the clubs, on 8 December 1987 Dundee Council decided to demolish Menzieshill, which had been lying vacant for several months. When the demolition men moved in they found two sacks in the club's cellar which contained cheque stubs and membership applications. They handed them to the police, but in the end no-one was ever brought to justice over the missing money. The only thing to survive from Menzieshill Labour Club is the commemorative plaque, which had been placed on the wall to remind the members that Neil Kinnock had opened the place in much happier times.

Martin, who was running a chip shop at the time, was feeling the heat. He claimed he received two With Sympathy cards through the post, each with a bullet enclosed. He told the author:

> I had two bullets sent to me: one at home and one at the chip shop. I sent the one from the shop to the police. I also had an incendiary device put under my car. My neighbour saw something and told me and when I looked under the car, there was something a bit like a candle, burning. I grabbed it and removed it. I didn't go to the police but went to the papers and the *Sunday Mail* ran a story on it.[5]

According to Martin, the first bullet arrived about a week before his first trial date, which was then postponed a couple of times.

In May 1990 Martin was charged with embezzlement of £9,325.07 from Whitfield Labour Club between 16 April 1984 and 10 September 1985 and with obtaining loans from Citibank and William Ross Devaney under false circumstances. The trial was delayed for several months when one of the accountants involved had a heart attack. So, the anticipation level was high when Sheriff McInnes opened proceedings on 29 April 1991 at Dundee Sheriff Court. Boyle had named Galloway, Rennie, Christie and Phil Grubb to give evidence, as well as James Guild, a former bar steward.

But the charge of embezzlement was not the biggest story. The element that excited everyone was that Martin's lawyer, Billy Boyle, was going to pursue a defence of 'incrimination' and call senior Labour figures to accuse them of the offences he was charged with. It's the legal equivalent of saying, 'It wasn't me, it was them what did it, guv.'

The prosecution laid out their case, claiming that Martin had been in charge of Whitfield and had siphoned off money for himself from the cash income of the bar. For the defence, Boyle claimed that the clubs had been 'systematically looted' and that Martin was 'a patsy holding the ball'.[6] Grubb took the stand and claimed that he had only ever received a bottle of spirits at New Year. When asked why he'd left the club, he said that he had been dismissed from the job of treasurer after the theft of £4,000 from the club safe. He said: 'I was just there as a figurehead . . . The idea was to have a club in Dundee to raise funds for the Labour Party.' When asked if he had been aware of how much money had gone missing from the clubs, he said he'd thought it was about £6,000 until the police had told him it was around £60,000. Despite being treasurer, Grubb told the court that Martin had had sole responsibility for finances and that he, Grubb, had known nothing of bounced cheques until he was shown them by the accountants. He claimed that when the accountants had ordered no more payments to the Labour party for two years, they continued 'most likely behind the backs of the accountants'.

Christie's testimony was likely to be even more interesting, given that he had been the financial controller of Whitfield and the manager of Ardler and had helped out with the books at Menzieshill. He told the court that after the payments from Whitfield to Labour had been stopped by the auditors, bingo sessions were organised to raise money for the party. When Boyle put it to him that the clubs had been 'systematically looted' and that the payments had 'started for honourable reasons, but it degenerated and you were all at the trough taking what you could get', Christie had replied: 'That is untrue.' Boyle then passed him a transcript of the Radio Tay broadcast and when asked if he agreed with Galloway's statement that 'precious little' money had passed to Labour, he said: 'I would disagree with that.'

But after only a few hours the whole trial collapsed. Boyle, still a leading lawyer in Dundee, says: 'The prosecution never thought they had a good case, but were instructed by the Crown and had to show willing.' Boyle found that on the day of the trial the case against his client disappeared into thin air very quickly. 'I had lined up several members of the Labour Party to appear as defence witnesses, to answer questions about where the money had gone. Among them were George Galloway and Ken Fagan.' Instead of a trial lasting a week or so, the prosecution case folded on the first day and Martin was acquitted.

In reply to Galloway's calls for a full investigation into the running of the clubs, in October 1991 the Crown Office announced that no action would be taken: 'Following upon the disposal of the case against James Myles Martin it has been decided that there shall be no further criminal proceedings in consequence of the investigation arising from allegations relating to Dundee Labour clubs.' Galloway continued his spat with STV and considered that they owed him a retration. That same week, in *Scotland on*

Sunday, Galloway's PR man, Ron McKay, and Kenny Farquharson wrote a piece that quoted Galloway accusing STV of a '£1 million smear' against the four MPs. Galloway was demanding a meeting with Gus MacDonald and they withdrew co-operation from STV, saying that until David Scott was removed from his job they would give no interviews. They accused STV of 'gross dishonesty' for not making it clear that the man at the centre of 'In the Red' had been charged with theft, even though he was subsequently acquitted. For several years afterwards Galloway would not co-operate with STV, but was finally persuaded when the management changed.

And what of the clubs, and the local folk who needed them? The clubs had disappeared years before the case ever got to court. Alistair Joss, Whitfield's treasurer from 1987, summed it up when he said: 'We were just left to pick up the pieces.' Unfortunately, there weren't many pieces left: Menzieshill and Ardler closed, as we have seen, and even Roseangle, in some ways the inspiration for the whole enterprise, folded in early 1987. Ironically, Whitfield Labour Club still exists, despite having been left £160,000 in the red in 1987.

13

Hillhead Civil War

The fallout from Channel 4's *Dispatches* documentary affected Glasgow Hillhead constituency Labour Party. In the next few days, the already developing pro- and anti-Galloway factions became polarised around the programme, while over the following weeks and months the political Geiger counter would go off the scale.

The damaging row was played out in the press as well as in private. Susan Singerman, a committee member, told the *Sunday Times* on 8 November 1987: 'We will be having a meeting of the executive to discuss our next move. George Galloway has some more questions to answer,' while from Galloway's camp Christine Hamilton replied: 'This is something that happened in Dundee a long time ago.' Behind closed doors, it was suggested that there were moves afoot to get Galloway. Some elements wanted to propose a vote of no confidence in their MP, who'd only been in the job for four months.

The splits were all the more bitter and complicated because the five wards in the constituency had different political flavours, ranging from almost SDP to Militant. When the fighting started, positions were entrenched over class and political lines, because the two sides gravitated towards the wards where they had more natural support. Galloway's left-wing supporters found it easier going in run-down and working-class Partick/Anderston for example, whereas the moderates had more control in the more affluent Scotstoun, Kelvinside, Kelvindale and Broomhill. As the row continued, Galloway was quoted saying he regretted the class divisions in the constituency, yet still announced plans to move his office to his power base in Anderston, away from the traditional site in upmarket Byres Road. This only had the effect of reinforcing the divisions.

It was in Scotstoun where the movement to get rid of Galloway started. A move to have a motion of no confidence was initiated very quickly and the members gathered to discuss their reaction to the sex and money publicity. On 7 December 1987 they released the following press statement through the chair, Tom Jess: 'Owing to the errors of judgement and controversy surrounding George Galloway, this branch believes that the credibility of the Labour Party in Scotstoun has been brought into disrepute. We therefore have no confidence in our MP.'[1] The motion had been the result of three hours of what those present described as 'heated debate'. The outcome had been as close as possible, running out just sixteen to fifteen against Galloway. This must have been a terrible blow to the young MP, particularly as he was still under tremendous pressure from the continuing fighting at War on Want. He tried to play the vote down, saying, 'I've always had a number of opponents in this branch,'[2] but the question was: would the resolution go to the overall Hillhead General Management Committee? At the time, each Labour MP had to go through a compulsory reselection process in their constituency and if there was a vote of no confidence at that level, then he knew at the very least he faced months of hard work to gather enough support to keep his nomination for the next election.

If some of his 'comrades' were scenting blood, then the press pack was already snapping around his heels. Following up its reporting of the Scotstoun vote, the *Sunday Times* conducted a straw poll of Hillhead party activists, in which 80 per cent were found to be against Galloway.[3] Unscientific straw polls should not be relied on, but it added to a climate of hostility towards him that may well have influenced his decision to read a letter addressed to someone else, which caused an even bigger row.

Back in October, at the Hillhead party executive's meeting to discuss Galloway's expenses, it had been decided to ask War on Want to provide more details of his credit card spending, so that they could establish if any more money was owed by them to the charity. At the meeting Galloway had said that he was sure there was no outstanding debt to War on Want over the Labour Party expenses that he'd put on the charity's credit card between 1985 and 1986. However, it had been decided that a thorough check would be made to kill the matter off for good. Galloway's supporters suspected that this was a politically motivated move to discredit him further. Susan Bhaumik, the Hillhead constituency secretary, had then written to Julian Hopkins, War on Want's finance officer, asking for information. In reply, on

27 November Hopkins sent a letter marked 'private and confidential' to Bhaumik at Glasgow Hillhead Labour Party, containing the details of Galloway's spending. It never arrived.

On 6 January 1988, Galloway wrote to Bhaumik asking if the party had asked for details of his spending and why:

> I have been sent a document addressed to you which troubles me greatly . . . The document is a total list of all expenditure made by me from April 1985 to September 1986 on my War on Want American Express card . . . The document I have retained, but enclose a copy of its covering letter . . . Did you request this information . . . and if so, why? On whose instructions and pursuant to what decision of which committee of Hillhead CLP?

These questions seem odd, given that the decision was taken at a meeting which Galloway had attended, but accounts of this meeting differ. Galloway's recollection, as told to Peter Jones of the *Scotsman*, was that it had been agreed to 'demand a letter finally closing the account from War on Want, and of course I agreed to that'. That is not necessarily at odds with what happened; it may be that the contents of that letter had been not clearly enough defined at the meeting. He went on:

> What I did say at the meeting, three times, but nobody even listened, which is an indication that the vote was nothing to do with the letter, was that I would pay for the treasurer to fly to London [to] let him study the documents and he could take away from those documents anything that he thought was relevant to the Hillhead Labour Party.

The passing of information surely had to go both ways, so that Hillhead and War on Want could cross-check Galloway's expenses to see if there were any sums that needed to be queried. Hillhead had therefore sent a file of expenses claims to War on Want, and vice versa. One of Hillhead Labour who was involved spoke to Hopkins, who said, 'Our priority is to see that War on Want survives.'

Galloway was understandably annoyed that the whole business of his expenses had been raked up again and asked to know on whose authority

A cheque reimbursing War on Want for expenses claimed for Labour business on the charity's credit card.

they had been passed to Hillhead. To clear up the matter, War on Want then released a statement saying: 'Julian Hopkins sought and gained permission from the chair of War on Want to send the relevant information which had been requested by Hillhead Labour Party. Simon Fanshawe has written to Hillhead to explain the situation.'

The danger for Galloway was that the arguments and perceived uncertainty would undermine him at the looming AGM and would leave him facing a newly elected management committee who wanted rid of him. To complicate matters, in the lead-up to the AGM there was anger directed at Galloway's TGWU ally Alex Mosson, who was standing against the stern but respected Janey Buchan in the reselection process for her seat in the European Parliament.

There was also unhappiness politically with Galloway and Mosson that had set them against the influential women's group in Hillhead, who disagreed with them over abortion. At the time the Alton Bill was going through Parliament. Proposed by the Liberal MP David Alton, to cut the length of time during which it is legal to abort a pregnancy, this emotional issue was debated and discussed informally, where it became apparent that

173

neither Galloway nor Mosson were keen on fighting the Bill. In the end, Galloway abstained in the Commons vote, when the women's group felt strongly he should have voted against. The tensions already there between him and Buchan and the women of Hillhead must have been rising. To try to defuse some of this bad feeling, Galloway reassured them that he would be concerned more with local than national issues over the next twelve to eighteen months, and that he would be in Glasgow rather than Westminster much of the time.

The AGM took place on Monday 25 January 1988 and Galloway was under a lot of pressure to justify his pronouncements about his sex life and to explain what he intended to do to heal the party divisions. One branch, Broomhill, had voted by a massive twelve to one to ask Galloway to 'give a full explanation' of how he acquired Hopkins's expenses letter, which had never arrived. Pressed on this, he said he had not forwarded it on because a mole or moles had previously passed on private documents to 'scum reporters' in the press. This was clearly a reference to a file of Galloway's expense claims that had ended up at *Private Eye*. Galloway complained that this was private information that only War on Want had the right to see.

The internal dispute had changed the atmosphere at Hillhead, as the then vice-chairman of the Constituency Party, Bob Winter, recalls: 'We'd had the best Labour Party and a very strong active membership. When George arrived there was a marked and fast atrophy.' Winter also remembers that party activists from the two sides were not talking to each other by this stage, just six months since the election victory. The infighting was in danger of getting in the way of business, as it had done at War on Want and in Dundee.

At the AGM they also had to decide who would be the chair of the party. A thirty-year-old English teacher and Scottish NEC member, Johann Lamont, was elected, unopposed. She was regarded as a neutral at that stage and in her acceptance statement she declared: 'Victory in Hillhead at the general election has been followed by the stuffing being knocked out of our people. My priority is to create a sense of purpose and commitment, restore morale, keep the party profile high, and get to work on issues.' Ostensibly forward looking, the implication of lack of morale and of issues having been forgotten was also a signal that the fighting wasn't over. If there were thoughts of the AGM being the start down the road to recovery, they were misplaced. Many on the new executive committee were deeply unhappy with their MP and there was going to be blood on the walls. They would move against him just two weeks later at their first meeting, when they did just what Galloway had hoped they wouldn't.

On Monday 8 February a vote of no confidence in Galloway was proposed. It was clear cut in favour of the motion by fifteen to eight. It could have been a lot worse if Galloway's six union backers hadn't voted for him. The ordinary activists had been almost unanimously in favour of no confidence. The press soon found out about it and asked Galloway if this meant he was going to resign. He held firm and announced that resignation was not on the agenda. 'I'm not the quitting type,' he declared.

The left wing does love a committee, which is a good thing if you like jaw-jaw and, perversely, can work if you like war-war. Hillhead's Executive Committee vote of no confidence was followed by another vote, this time from the larger and controlling General Management Committee. If this went against him, it would be big news and make life extremely difficult for him. So it must have been devastating when, on Monday 22 February 1988, they passed a motion of no confidence in Galloway by fifty-four votes to forty-four. The way the vote was split is key to understanding how the party had become divided. Galloway had gathered the majority of his support from the unions and from the solidly working-class Partick/Anderston branch. Only three out of twenty-five union votes had gone against him.

Immediately after the vote, Lamont made a statement to the press: 'The constituency has expressed its condemnation of the behaviour of the MP. All his actions have done is to damage and discredit the Labour Party in Hillhead.' Galloway replied: 'I've got absolutely no thoughts of resigning at all.' A lot of other people had, though, including those at the *Scotsman*, which wrote a long editorial on him under the headline 'Time for George to go'. His political opponents made the most of it too and a leaflet circulated in the constituency with a reworking of Georgie Porgie in it.

Georgie Porgie, Pudding and Pie
Made Hillhead voters wail and cry
If we vote Democrat in May
Labour might sack Galloway.

Despite all the calls for him to step down, the votes of no confidence and the continual interest of the press in his every move, Galloway never flinched. He always looked as though he was going to fight and fight. After the vote, Galloway retreated to the relative tranquillity of Westminster, where he planned his campaign. He cut a lonely figure, shunned by many in the Labour Party hierarchy: Neil Kinnock told the author for this book that 'Galloway has always been in a party of one, the George Galloway Party'. In those first few months the pattern was set for his time in Parliament. He was an outsider and would remain one, but in contrast to later years, initially he kept his head down, knowing that he still had an ace up his sleeve. Changes to Labour internal voting at the 1987 party conference meant that his solid union support would give him a chance of surviving the reselection battle that he had to face.

Before 1987, candidates were selected by constituency general management committees. The trouble was that the rules governing who was allowed to vote were open to abuse. For example, the smooth-talking, right of centre MP Robert Kilroy-Silk found that one TGWU branch of 263 members had affiliated itself to seventeen Merseyside constituencies, and was therefore entitled to vote in all of them. Though the union delegates had to be local Labour Party members, they could use huge numbers of union votes from people who never went to any meetings and didn't even live in the area.

The other issue was that ward delegates, who are supposed to be ordinary party members, had often been chosen months earlier at thinly attended meetings that did not reflect the views of the local membership. These highly motivated but often unrepresentative folk were then entitled to use their votes for their candidates, even if the majority around selection time was for another candidate.

Opposition to this system had been building and the debate had been around which one to adopt in its place. Neil Kinnock and other modernisers had wanted one member, one vote, which is the system in use today. But in 1987 the party conference decided to go for an electoral college system, where 40 per cent of the votes were allocated to the unions and affiliated bodies, and the remaining 60 per cent to the members. This took some power away from the management committees and gave it to union branch secretaries, who organised and cast their trade union votes. They received ballot papers and voted for whoever they wanted. Fair enough, you may think, but when the people who ran the NEC back then set up the system they didn't insist that the union officials had to be Labour Party supporters or live in the constituency. Also, the ballot was secret, so there was no check to see if the official was voting the way his members had told him. Furthermore, because the same union branch could affiliate to a number of local constituencies, he or she (mostly he) could vote for any number of candidates. The effect of this system was that it worked against people who didn't have the time or connections to build up support among local union branch secretaries. Add to that a tradition in the unions to select the sitting MP and this made it almost impossible for women, or black or Asian people, to win nominations to fill vacancies in Labour-held seats. But it did work in Galloway's favour, because he had great union backing, as Dave Stark, Galloway's election agent, recalls: 'I remember being called to Bill Copeland's house to talk about the move to get rid of George. Other than me, there was Frank Murphy of the GMB and Alec Mosson of the TGWU. We decided that any threat to George was just more bad publicity, it would draw more attention and damage the CLP.' So the unions were to hold fast behind the sitting MP, as was traditional.

Galloway was largely guaranteed the unions' 40 per cent of the votes, but he still needed a small chunk of the members to back him. It would mean a lot of cajoling, recruiting and some help from Labour's Scottish National Organiser Jimmy Allison, who was dropped into Hillhead to sort things out. Stark remembers:

> Jimmy Allison was brought in to knock some sense into everyone. He was a prominent Labour organiser and was very important to events at this time. Ian Finlay, who is now dead, was the treasurer at the time and he'd been left alone, holding the baby, really. Allison's line was that the most important thing was to keep the seat in Labour hands.

Shortly before he died in June 2006, Jimmy Allison gave an interview for this book in which he remembered

I was happy to get involved and help sort it out. There were big splits in the local party, and complaints about the selection process, but I can say categorically that it was all above board. After that I watched George's career and was very disappointed when he eventually had to leave the party. It was a tragedy.

The fighting had left the constituency politically almost paralysed. Without its support the local office was a hostile place to Galloway. He claimed he had the support of 'ordinary working-class people and trade unionists', while his enemies were 'middle class' and 'intellectuals'.[4] Normally tough Glasgow politics was proving harder than usual and Stark remembers that the strain might have been telling on him. 'During the "troubles", I took him back to my house to have dinner with my family and my four boys. My wife served up dinner and he said, "Ooh, that's a lovely bit of fish, Maureen." And she said, "That's not fish, George, it's chicken."'

Despite the difficulties, it wasn't all doom and gloom and Stark remembers nights when Galloway and his comrades would relax in the pub or local Labour club, where there would often be rousing singing. Those nights would be full of classics such as 'Mac the Knife', and hits by Sinatra. Stark reckons Galloway has 'got a good voice' and no doubt he puts his heart and soul into 'My Way'.

Leaving aside the internal problems in Hillhead, another issue for Galloway to get to grips with in his new constituency was the large community from the Asian sub-continent. Galloway admits that he sometimes comes out with odd turns of phrase, but he can also just offend, or upset, or fan the flames with impetuous pronouncements. Later in 1988, for example, Galloway's interest in foreign affairs got him into a little hot water. In August President Muhammad Zia-ul-Haq of Pakistan, an odious dictator in the eyes of many, died. In a break with political tradition, where even the death of the most awful tyrant is normally greeted with at least a measure of faint praise, Galloway went the extra yard and described the event as the 'death of a hangman'. This might not have mattered if he'd been the custodian of a Scottish Highland constituency, but in Glasgow he was trying his luck. The Pakistani community there was vibrant, influential and divided about Zia.

In some quarters there was uproar. Chief Imam Tafail Shah led the prayers of a reputed 1,000 Muslims in Glasgow Central Mosque, and then condemned Galloway for the attack on Zia. Bashir Maan, chair of Strathclyde Community Relations Council, called it 'callous and shameless' and warned Galloway that it might destroy the support he'd received from the Pakistani community. He went on: 'We will not be satisfied until the Labour Party censures Mr Galloway.'[5] In the Galloway corner sat Rahid Zafar, of the Ahmadiyya Muslim Association in Yorkhill, Glasgow, who rose to defend the MP, and catalogued Zia's human rights abuses, which are too numerous to go into here. Lining up for Galloway too was Sibghat Kadri, former president of the Standing Conference of Pakistani Organisations in Britain, who took the literal approach: 'What George said was clearly right because Zia was a hangman. He hanged Mr Bhutto, the elected Prime Minister of Pakistan, and perpetrated horrifying acts of brutality and torture.' The episode was a lesson to Galloway in the power of word of mouth in Britain's immigrant communities. Since then, he has been very careful to cultivate his relations with ethnic groups, particularly in Bethnal Green & Bow.

If Galloway might have underestimated the power of Pakistani nationalism, he has never underestimated the power of Scottish nationalism. In November 1988 it would rear its head in a by-election among the Glasgow shipyards. Govan is a traditional working-class area, full of proud Scots from the same mould as the hard man of football management Alex Ferguson, who was born and raised there. It is just across the river from Partick, so Galloway knew the area well, and when the sitting Labour MP, Bruce Millan, took stewardship of the Chiltern Hundreds (a device that allows an MP to resign) in order to take up a post in Europe, Galloway and others on the left of the party saw trouble ahead. The Govan by-election was a glimpse of the future, and the future was the anti-poll tax movement.

The Conservative Party manifesto of 1987 had included plans to get rid of domestic rates and replace them with the community charge, which had been proposed in a 1986 Green Paper called *Paying for Local Government.* The community charge or poll tax, as it was almost universally known, became the issue that rallied the left against Thatcher, holding them together long enough for them to successfully fight the government rather than each other. On the eve of the new legislation being passed in April 1988, the Labour

Party Scottish conference agreed a campaign against the poll tax, but which would not go as far as condoning illegal non-payment. Many felt they had not gone far enough and blamed Neil Kinnock and his moderates for opening the door to the SNP, who were supporting non-payment, to gather up votes. 'The SNP have got the Proclaimers, while we've got Wet Wet Wet,' said a delegate.

When Michael Howard, the local government minister, announced that the poll tax would be introduced in Scotland in 1989, then in England and Wales a year later, there was tremendous anger north of the border. In hindsight, the Labour Party did react slowly and this let the SNP in at Govan. Jim Sillars, an ex-Labour MP, whose own Scottish Labour Party had foundered, was now in the SNP and made the most of his opportunity. In the election on 10 November he took the seat from Labour with a massive 38.4 per cent swing. He polled 14,677 votes, with Labour's Bob Gillespie coming second with 11,123. The Tories were almost nowhere, with 2,207.

In the aftermath of Labour's defeat Donald Dewar, the shadow Scottish Secretary, said there was hard thinking to do, but dismissed it as a protest vote, while Robin Cook, then the shadow health spokesman, said the people were trying to tell the party something. Michael Forsyth, chairman of the Scottish Conservatives, said: 'Labour has tried to ride the nationalist tiger, but has been eaten by it,' although his opinion is unlikely to have concerned many in Scotland, given the Tories' appalling result.

On the positive side, the Labour Party had time to regroup for the general election, which was at least three years away. Galloway and others complained that the party had been dragging its feet over a National Assembly, despite an agreement to adopt the policy by all the opposition parties at the 1988 Constitutional Convention in Scotland. This annoyed his fellow members of the Scottish backbench devolution committee, who felt they were moving as quickly as they could, and Galloway quit the committee. There is no doubt that the Govan by-election changed Labour's commitment to a National Assembly. They could not afford to be half-hearted about it again and Galloway had been a clear voice on the winning side of the argument.

These were emotional times, particularly in Scotland. In September 1988 a group of MPs and public figures formed a 'Committee of 100', an old name for a new campaign, where 100 Scots from all walks of life would refuse to pay the poll tax. It was launched at a special Scottish Labour Party conference and was backed by Galloway and his fellow MPs Willie McKelvey, Denis Canavan, Dick Douglas, John McAllion and Maria Fyfe, MP for Glasgow Maryhill, among others. Robin Cook and high-profile members of the Scottish TUC, such as Bill Speirs, also backed the campaign, together with members of the clergy. The chair was a vicar, called John Prescott as it happens, who said the tax was immoral because it redistributed wealth from the poor to the better-off sections of the community.

Donald Dewar fought hard to stop a motion of non-payment, but the only argument he could come up with was that everyone would have to wait until Labour got back into power and then they could repeal the law. Galloway told the *Independent*: 'If ever one side comprehensively won an argument but lost the vote, it was those of us fighting for non-payment.' Ironically, MPs couldn't make much of a stand against non-payment, because local authority finance officers claimed they could get their money from the House of Commons Fees Office, which would deduct it from these state employees' wages.

Galloway had been up with the game on a National Assembly, and his strong anti-poll tax views were going to play very well with the electors over the next year or so, as the opposition grew enormously once people had to start paying it. But the biggest issue for him through 1989 would be the fight for his political life in Hillhead. Although it had been announced that the constituency management committee had agreed to put War on Want and the sex stories behind them, Galloway was busy gathering support to out-manoeuvre his opponents and secure his selection as the candidate in the next general election.

In the New Year Johann Lamont, the woman who had announced to the world that the management committee believed Galloway had damaged and discredited the Labour Party in Hillhead, was the first casualty of the pro-Galloway backlash. She was unfortunate to be the convenor of the Partick/Anderston branch, where Galloway's support was strongest. At the January AGM that support gathered en masse. In previous years the turnout had been around twenty or so, but Lamont and the anti-Galloway faction found themselves facing an eighty-strong meeting, where the majority were against them. Faced with a more left-wing branch, other moderates left the meeting and didn't seek re-election. Though Janey Buchan, centre of the anti-Galloway group, complained to the press, they had just been outplayed at a game of which the left is a master. In the end all but two of the eighteen delegates were Galloway's supporters.

In many Labour constituencies, sitting MPs get selected unopposed, for example Jim McFall, the man who had beaten Galloway to be candidate in Dumbarton. This was never going to be the case for Galloway. Trish Godman, a strong-minded and bright Glaswegian, who was deputy chair of the local party, looked like the ideal candidate. Godman had brought up three kids in a tough part of the Pollok area of Glasgow after her first marriage had broken down. Unlike Galloway, she had a career outside politics, as a social worker, and she was well known in the area as chair of the Easterhouse Committee on drug abuse. She was a hard campaigner, quick thinking and down to earth, and in March she announced her candidacy, saying: 'In the opinion of the vast majority of local party members, the situation has further deteriorated. We continue to have no confidence whatsoever in Mr Galloway.'[6]

Godman's selection to stand against Galloway was a slight problem for the unions, who had a tacit agreement that they voted together as a block. Godman was a member of the Manufacturing, Science and Finance (MSF) union and with two union-backed candidates, there was likely to be some deal making behind the scenes, to sort out whether the block voting arrangement would stand. (Incidentally, her second husband was the Labour MP for Greenock & Port Glasgow, Norman Godman, who was backed by the TGWU, the same union as Galloway.)

Through April and May the local branches held meetings to debate and vote on the candidates. Jimmy Allison, Labour's Scottish 'enforcer' of the time, spoke for Galloway and helped his campaign enormously. However, in the initial ballots it was looking close. Galloway's Partick/Anderston base went for him by thirty-seven to seventeen, but that was down to the union block votes, and he'd been beaten by a ratio of two to one amongst the ordinary members. Godman, on the other hand, had polled ninety-six to fifty-three in the other branches. The whole process was undermining Labour in the area, with the factions briefing the media against each other. Dave Stark of the TGWU said of Galloway's opponents: 'Democracy means nothing to these people. They don't even wait until it's time to put nominations forward before they are off running to the papers with their stories. There is a very deep split in the party which these people have helped to generate.'

In the run-up to the all-important vote, some TGWU members complained that they wanted to vote for Godman, but that only the name Galloway appeared on their ballot papers, though there is no suggestion that Galloway knew of this. In the light of the complaints, the union decided that members would be allowed to vote in their branches this time, though normally the vote was at the higher, district level.

On 26 June the final results were declared. Galloway had been reselected with 62 per cent of the vote. He'd taken nine-tenths of the union votes and of the remaining 60 per cent, Godman had got 208 and Galloway 155. The 40 per cent union vote had been in the hands of forty-four delegates, of whom over half were from the TGWU and the MSF.

After his success, Galloway promised 'a summer of peace and reconciliation', but it may come as no surprise to discover that this wasn't the case. For a start, there was a lot of bad feeling surrounding the election process, which was the fault of the collegiate system of the time. Godman and her backers complained that it was undemocratic to use other political party members to vote in Labour Party elections. Just how many union members voted Tory is not known, but there were certainly many Communist Party members and Scottish Nationalists who'd had a say in the way that the Labour Party had chosen its Hillhead MP. Michael Forsyth criticised the 'archaic brute force' of the union block votes which had got Galloway reselected. The voting had confirmed everything the Tories loved to see in Labour, because it was such a vote loser in the wider British public.

Dave Stark recalls: 'After the deselection bid failed, Johann, Trisha, Bob Winter and so on refused to work for George in the next election. Our position was: "Fine, you don't have to work for anyone you don't want to."' So there was precious little reconciliation. Bob Winter, formerly the CLP vice-chair, decided to give up completely:

> I wouldn't say I was put under undue pressure at the time, just the kind you'd expect in a divided party. It came down to whose side you were on . . . I left

the constituency Labour Party. I was still a card-carrying member but, not just because of Galloway but for several family reasons, I didn't carry on at Hillhead.

Winter had worked for years for Hillhead, but the Galloway selection had changed the constituency. 'The CLP was left disappointed to the point of disaffection,' he claims. So, in late August twelve of the local party resigned, saying they had 'no confidence in the integrity of George Galloway'. That's almost half the executive committee of twenty-six and included Johann Lamont, Godman and Susan Bhaumik as well as Winter. Lamont declared: 'We note that, contrary to the promises made in the reselection process and his acceptance speech, he has done nothing to build bridges with the members of the executive who opposed his selection.' She told the *Guardian*'s Peter Hetherington: 'Since reselection I have had no contact with the MP at all. The quarrel we have is all about accountability, and democracy . . . working in harmony, rather than any personal matters.'

In Galloway's camp there was jubilation. 'There was a joke running around at the time that they left by the "freedom tunnel", because the Clyde tunnel runs from Hillhead to Glasgow South West, where many of them went to work,' according to Stark.

Despite having written a report claiming he was approaching people over the summer to reconcile differences, ironically the news of the resignations reached Galloway on one of his many trips to the Middle East. He was in the West Bank, with Benazir Bhutto's Pakistan People's Party for a week or so and was reported to have remarked 'Bloody hell!' when told. Winter remembers: 'Galloway got the constituency Labour Party he wanted, a compliant party. When those activists who had suspicions failed to deselect him, that set the tone for the future, they left and his supporters filled the ranks.'

14

Romania

As the Hillhead Constituency Labour Party argued about who should be their Member of Parliament, a strange little advert appeared in the soft left newspaper *Tribune*, in the classified section. It was designed to stir up trouble and read: 'LOST ONE MP Balding Answers to name of George but also known as Gorgeous. Last heard of in Romania . . . Reward for information about current whereabouts . . .' This is the ad that propagated the ironic title of 'Gorgeous George' for Galloway, but the important thing is that word 'Romania'. Galloway's relationship with Romania goes back to Christmas 1989 and appears to involve all the ingredients that go to make up a Galloway mini-saga: a good helping of media coverage, a dictator, a smattering of unfortunate children and unfounded allegations of financial controversy.

While Galloway's Mariam Appeal is often talked of, little is remembered or was ever known about an equally intriguing money-raising episode of his from the early 1990s called the Romanian Child AIDS Appeal (RCAA). Like the later Mariam Appeal, this was not a charity, and that's a crucial distinction. Charities have to open their finances to public scrutiny in a lot of detail, but appeals do not. Appeals are only governed by the rules of ordinary companies, though they sometimes do not have to pay so much tax. Anyone could start an appeal tomorrow for what they believed was a good cause, asking for donations to be sent to them by cheque through the post. They would then be entitled to spend that money on the cause for which they'd advertised. Appeals are ideal for responding quickly to natural disasters and emergencies, avoiding having to jump through the hoops required to form a charity.

According to the journalist Christopher Silvester, in December 1989 the Hillhead MP had become interested in Romania when he had dealt with an application for British nationality on behalf of one of his constituents, a

Romanian exile. Silvester quotes Galloway: 'In our meetings together . . . we would spend five minutes discussing his case and fifty-five minutes discussing the state of Romania.' The timing of those conversations was a happy coincidence, because that very month, after nearly twenty-five years in power, Nicolae and Elena Ceauşescu were deposed in the Boxing Day Revolution.

Silvester wrote an article in the *Independent* about Galloway's book on Romania, *Downfall*.[1] In the article he recounts that it was the constituent who first raised the subject of a visit. 'At first Mr Galloway politely declined, but he became so fascinated by events in Romania that a couple of weeks later he changed his mind and made the first of several trips there.' Galloway went over with Bob Wylie, an ex-Militant journalist who now works for BBC Scotland. The two are close and on the journey over they came up with a plan to write about the Ceauşescu, among other things. *Downfall* includes many interviews with witnesses to the revolution and the tragedy of post-war Romania, including Ceauşescu family members, senior government figures and Ion Iliescu, the Romanian President immediately after the revolution.

Galloway has been supportive of Iliescu and just as critics are divided over the former President, so they are divided over Galloway and Wylie's book. The head of the BBC's Romanian service, Petru Clej, was highly critical of it to me and is passionate in his condemnation of what he felt was qualified support for the action of the Romanian miners, who in June 1990 marched through Bucharest and indiscriminately beat people up in the streets.[2] They were rallying to the side of Iliescu, after anti-government demonstrations and some violence that had seen the police headquarters and the interior ministry attacked and had involved the riot police in running street battles. An estimated 10,000 miners from western Romania surged into Bucharest at dawn to crack down on dissent, but six people were left dead, dozens of people were assaulted, some clubbed, others butted repeatedly by the helmeted miners. They took control of the city and few police and soldiers were visible in the capital, while the miners, carrying cudgels and with their faces and work clothes still smudged with coal dust, were apparently left to maintain order as they chose.

The unrest had been going on for months before it came to a head in June. Public pressure had forced the authorities to replace the defence minister, to change the head of state television, and to enter a power-sharing arrangement with the opposition. Back in February, Galloway had witnessed some of the troubles and had got caught up in an anti-government crowd in Bucharest. He later reported that he had seen protesters take over the headquarters of Iliescu's National Salvation Front, then watched as 'troops in special headgear stormed the building and expelled at gunpoint many hundreds of the crowd who had occupied the headquarters'.

The anti-Iliescu protesters were complaining about the number of former Communists in his government, a lack of reform and his dictatorial approach. He is now under investigation for possible human rights abuses in his time as leader. Though Iliescu was supported by the West, broadly speaking, the USA withheld aid for a time to send him a signal that they believed he had instigated the miners' rampage. The protest spiralled out of control and the miners ransacked the university and various public buildings, including museums, claiming that these were decadent institutions.

The British government was very critical of Iliescu's reaction as well, and protested formally about his 'use of vigilantes to crush the opposition', as Foreign Office minister William Waldegrave put it in a House of Commons debate on 11 July 1990. He went on: 'It was the very disturbing methods used by Mr Iliescu at the first challenge that worried us so much because they were just the same methods as Ceauşescu used to use.'[3]

Galloway was standing firm behind Iliescu, however. On 28 June in the Commons he had described what he had seen of the troubles and declared: 'The government completely misjudged the dramatic events that unfolded in the capital, Bucharest, earlier this month, and . . . as a result they seriously over-reacted in a way that was inimical not only to our interests but to those of the Romanian people.'[4] Galloway took the view that Romania had been on the cusp of an attempted coup by right-wing anti-democratic elements and recounted his view of the riots, describing the protesters who had ultimately been driven off the streets by the miners as 'ultra-right, racist and anti-Semitic'. The problems of anti-Semitism in Romania are dealt with in *Downfall* and were referred to by Galloway in the Commons on 22 February that year too, when he remarked that 'the Jewish community is worried, for example, about some of the broadcasts on the Romania service of the BBC'.[5]

In the end, the newly elected Romanian government didn't fall and the country came through to join NATO and has now become an EU member state, notwithstanding concerns about corruption. Many people's efforts to help Romania under Iliescu were affected by corruption too. On his second visit to the country Galloway met officials from the Romanian Health Ministry and the World Health Organization (WHO) to discuss what needed to be done. In a later article,[6] Bob Wylie wrote that 'a plan was established' by Galloway on this trip, in co-operation with the ministry's AIDS committee secretary, Dr Nicolae Beldescu, who is now at the Bucharest Institute of Hygiene. The plan was to raise money in the UK and link up with British AIDS experts, who would then give advice to the doctors in Romania, but the situation in the country was to get more complicated than that.

Unlike the 'liberated' Iraqis, the Romanians had got rid of their psycho-pathic dictator themselves and the world had come in after, to see what all the fuss had been about. Without exception, the foreign aid workers, politicians and journalists who made the trip were horrified at the con-ditions, particularly for the sick, the mentally ill and the many orphaned children. The worst of all the sights to greet visitors were the scores of children with AIDS, infected by contaminated blood in a regime that had declared the disease a capitalist plague and therefore not possible in their perfect socialist state. Doctors and medical books weren't allowed to mention AIDS and there were no precautions taken against its spread.

Galloway's second visit was as vice-chairman of the Foreign Affairs Committee of the Labour Party. He later reported back to Gerald Kaufman, the shadow Foreign Secretary, on the prison conditions that Ceauşescu's family were being held under, and the state of the opposition groups. How-ever, the trip was overshadowed by a visit to an AIDS ward in the southern Romanian port of Constanţa. The city had been particularly blighted by HIV/AIDS, probably because of the large prostitute population who served the visiting sailors. Emaciated orphaned children lay, two or three to a cot, with hardly any blankets, while an ignorant nursing staff were powerless to help them and were even too afraid to touch them, unless wearing gloves and overalls. They had no toys, little food and were just left there to die. The pictures of these children and others like them from around Romania created a world-wide stampede to get them help.

This was the first time a European country had been shown on our TV screens suffering in a Third World way and the effect was unprecedented. Literally hundreds of highly motivated but often badly organised appeals started up, with lorry loads of clothes, food and even used hospital equipment being driven overland to Bucharest, Constanţa and other Romanian towns. Soon the situation was so chaotic that allegations of waste, corruption and even of dumping useless equipment surfaced. Many of the initial appeals folded in acrimony.

Patrick Colquhoun has been running a successful Romanian charity since the early 1990s and saw it unfold. He says:

> Romanians got fed up with being a rubbish dump in the nineties. I was there when a charity from Glasgow had sent a truck full of stuff that was used, or half used. It had been sent by a medic who hadn't wanted to see things thrown away, but it was almost useless . . . I went over in September 1990 for the first time and it was horrific. The orphanages had been state run, so any criticism of them would have led to a visit from the Securitate secret police . . . At the start there were between 450 and 500 charities operating in Romania. There used to be a body called the Romanian Information Service, which did a lot to help co-ordinate the work, but it had its funding taken away by the Department for International Development, which we were all very angry about.

Trying to get the right kind of help to the people who needed it was extremely difficult, and many failed. The country was chaotic, partly due to lack of money and infrastructure, but also because the population was so worn down by Ceauşescu's controlling brand of communism that they had lost the ability, or were too afraid, to take any initiative for themselves. Dealing with them was frustrating for the relief workers because clothes and equipment were being stacked up and ignored. But the factor that really hindered help getting to the hospitals was the corruption of the Romanian medical profession. Colquhoun remembers:

> In the early 1950s they decided that the country needed doctors, but they were only prepared to pay them the same as road sweepers. The authorities decided

to turn a blind eye to bribes from patients to do the job. Presents were given, not money, because people didn't have money. Then after the break-up it carried on and still is a huge problem. It's the doctors who are building the biggest houses . . . In 1998 a woman told me: 'The anaesthetist said that unless I gave him enough money before the operation, he would not wake me up afterwards.' In 2002, the same anaesthetist told another patient: 'I would rather let you die than give you an anaesthetic, if you do not give me enough money.'

On 18 February 1990, Galloway went to a Bucharest hospital named after Victor Babeş, a nineteenth-century Romanian physician, where he witnessed the terrible state of around eighty children with AIDS, nearly all between one and three years old. 'I have seen some appalling sights. I have walked through the killing fields of the famines of Ethiopia and the Sudan. But I have never seen a more distressing scene than Ward B1 of the Victor Babeş Hospital in Bucharest, where eighty tiny babies stricken with AIDS are lying waiting to die,' he later recalled in the House of Commons.[7]

While he was on the trip, Galloway rang the *Guardian* journalist Seumas Milne (see p. 194), who wrote about it in the following day's paper, under a picture of an emaciated little boy. 'Gaby, aged 13 months, is expected to die within the week at the Victor Babes clinic in Bucharest, another victim of the escalating infant Aids epidemic in Romania.' Milne took up the cause of these children and went to Romania later that month. He wrote an emotional piece on 28 February that focused on little Gaby. It opened with: 'Whatever you might have seen on television or read in the papers, nothing can prepare you for ward B1 of the Victor Babes Aids clinic in Bucharest. In six rooms on the second floor, 82 children between the ages of one and three are infected with the Aids virus.' At the end of the piece an appeal was launched in the paper, which asked the British public to send what money they could to help.

The appeal read:

The *Guardian* is launching an emergency appeal to raise money for drugs and medical equipment to take to Romania as soon as possible in association with the British Terrence Higgins Trust. We will be guided by Aids specialists here and in Romania as to what is most urgently needed. It may be too late to do anything for Gaby, but urgent action can make a decisive difference for thousands of other Romanian children . . . The Guardian Gaby Appeal is raising money for drugs and medical equipment for the child victims of Aids in Romania. Donations should be sent to The Guardian Gaby Appeal, c/o The Terrence Higgins Trust, 52–54 Gray's Inn Road, London WC1X 8JU. Cheques payable to The Terrence Higgins Trust (Gaby) Appeal.[8]

Because it had no experience of running a fund like this, the *Guardian* had decided to join forces with the very high-profile AIDS charity the Terrence Higgins Trust (THT), which had decided to depart from its usual focus on UK AIDS victims, to run a fund for Romania's children with AIDS. According to Martin Eade, the THT's chief executive of the time, the first cheque it received on announcing the fund was from Diana, Princess of Wales. 'It was for a substantial amount of money.'

The THT had an experienced fund-raiser called Liz Davies, who did a superb job and raised £82,772 in February alone. It sent off £10,000 of medical supplies with Medical Aid for Free Romania, a charity based in Sussex, almost straightaway and formed links with the WHO and the Red Cross. The trust planned to send trained paediatric staff to relieve the pressure on the Romanian authorities. Even the British government gave money to its fund, in addition to the £5.8m directed from the Foreign Office through government departments. Into that large pot of money also poured £50,000 from the Gaby Appeal, just in the first month, and more would follow.

The combined efforts of Galloway, Milne and Bob Wylie, who were all sending back gripping reports from Romania, were fantastic and helped generate a tremendous response from the British public. Of course, they weren't alone and lots more was done by the TV pictures and emotional radio reports. But Wylie's pieces particularly, for the *Observer* in Scotland,[9] the *Independent* and others, were impactful and heartfelt and he would return many times to the country. In a piece for the *Independent* on 20 May 1990, he described a visit to the AIDS hospital in Constanţa, in which he interviewed Dr Margareta Ilie and wrote that '73 children have died here since the beginning of the year from AIDS-related syndromes, and testing for HIV

191

positive shows Constanta has more than 300 children under five in that category.' In the same piece Wylie describes some of the surrounding area, giving some 'colour' to the article, and refers to the long history of wine growing in the region that goes back to Roman times.

Some of the pieces by Galloway and Wylie started to include references to an appeal fund for the children, with an address quoted for donations.[10] It was 64 Elderslie Street, Glasgow, G3 7AL, Galloway's constituency party headquarters in Hillhead. The money went into an account at the Westminster branch of the Co-op Bank. Galloway then contacted one of the UK's leading experts in child AIDS, Dr Jacqueline Mok, who is based in Edinburgh, employed by Lothian Health Board. She was keen to help and they agreed to go to Romania later in June to see how best to proceed.

In the run-up to the Romanian elections of May 1990, Galloway wrote in the *Scotsman* and the *Independent* that right-wingers were on the rise in Romania and that they were anti-Semitic.[11] He tipped Iliescu's National Salvation Front to win, and referred to opposition remarks of a return to power for Communists as slurs. 'Of course many of the Front's ministers are former Communists – many of the opposition are too – anyone who wanted to work in a professional job in Romania under the tyrant had to be in the Communist Party,' he wrote on 6 May. On 20 May Iliescu won the first elections since the Second World War.

In the second week of June, Mok and an Edinburgh nurse, Sister Chris Rafferty, arrived in Constanţa to see for themselves the situation on the ground and to give some badly needed advice on AIDS treatment. Mok and Rafferty discovered a ward with more than seventy little patients and a very high incidence of child AIDS locally, with 300 out of 700 tested being found positive. The funds for the week-long trip were raised 'through the Romanian Child AIDS Appeal', according to Wylie at the time.[12] On the same trip Galloway and Mok visited Dr Radu Dop, the deputy health minister, who recalls now that 'I met George Galloway, who came across as a senior figure, with high prestige and warmth. He came to see me in my office at a time when I was trying to co-ordinate chaos. There were dozens of NGOs, all moving in by themselves, acting by themselves.' Dop looks back on those times as 'wonderful' and a time of new hope.

As part of Galloway's general pleas for more help for Romania and the

AIDS crisis, he also spoke in the House of Commons to ask the UK government to give more aid. Meanwhile, Galloway and Wylie's own small effort to raise aid was getting more serious and they even took out ads in the *Glasgow Herald* on 30 June and the Scottish *Observer* on 1 July 1990:

CEAUSESCU'S CHILDREN
Do you know that
1 in 2 of the children with AIDS in Romania live in the town of
Constanta?
Did you read the story of the work of the Scottish Medical Staff, with the
AIDS children of Constanta in *Observer* Scotland last week?
Can you send a donation now to help the stricken children?
The Romanian Child AIDS Appeal
c/o Elderslie St Glasgow G3 7AL

As the public's enthusiasm for helping the Romanian AIDS victims saw money rolling in to many charities and appeals, the brutal suppression of the country's opposition by the miners had led to the British government threatening to withhold financial aid packages. In late July Galloway stood up in a Commons debate on Romania, to argue against this and plead for the strengthening of trade between the two countries. He started his speech by declaring 'although I have no pecuniary interest in Romania, I am writing a book on the history of the Romanian revolution. I am advised that I should declare that as a potential interest; I certainly hope that it will become one.'

Then in August 1990, Galloway's appeal received a tremendous bonus when the THT/Gaby Appeal decided to donate £31,000 from their now enormous £300,000 fund. Billy Harrow of the THT announced that the money would be given in two batches of £15,000 and £16,000 and that a trip was planned for September,[13] when Mok and a group of nurses would go over to Romania. Mok was reported as saying: 'It is wonderful news. There is so much which needs to be done and this money will make a concerted effort possible.'

Although some questions were being asked about where exactly the money raised by the myriad of appeals was going, Galloway was bullish about the campaign:

It may be that with some projects money is going astray. I cannot comment on that since I have no direct experience of it . . . We know the money raised by the Romanian Child AIDS Appeal will be spent on the stricken children of Constanţa, not just because of our own direct involvement, but because Dr Dop, the Romanian health minister, and Dr Baldescu, the co-ordinator of the AIDS programme in Romania, have given their approval and know exactly what is going on.[14]

Dop doesn't remember much of the detail of those times and the specifics of the appeal. He says now: 'I don't ever remember dealing with any money. We took materials, medicines and disposable equipment, as well as advice from foreign experts, not money.'

The record of the accounts of Galloway's RCAA has not been made available, but in August 1990 Wylie claimed that £25,000 had been raised. In that case they had at least £56,000 (including the £31,000 from the THT/Gaby Appeal).

Reports in the *Guardian* at the time were full of praise for the paper's own efforts. On 8 August 1990 Chris Stephens in Bucharest wrote that 'at least £31,000 is going to the worst hit Romanian city, the port of Constanta, where 49 per cent of children in institutions under five have the HIV virus'. Stephens also reported that £50,000 had been raised from readers and that this was being spent with £150,000 from the THT:

The joint Gaby/THT fund has supported nine separate projects in Romania, where local resources cannot cope with the scale of the child Aids problem . . . Money from the Gaby/THT fund is being used to fight the spread of the infection: £20,000 has been spent on setting up blood screening centres in the cities of Brasov, Timisoara and Arad.

The THT now has no records of the money it raised, or the amounts it gave to the RCAA, set up by Galloway and Wylie. Nick Partridge, who at the time was in a senior management role, and who is now the boss, confirmed via their press office that 'we donated money to George Galloway's Romanian Child AIDS Appeal. We didn't supervise it after that. These days we don't do that. It's a very different organisation. We might give out grants these days, but we don't give money.'

Though the THT may not have kept detailed records of the Romanian fund, at the time this is what they and the *Guardian* Gaby Appeal claimed they had done with the money:

£10,000 has been spent on emergency supplies for the Victor Babes Hospital in Bucharest, including milk powder, nappies, soap, 20,000 disposable syringes and an industrial washing machine. £30,000 has been allocated to a nursing and Aids training programme at the Colentina Hospital in Bucharest, run by Health Aid. Drugs have also been sent to the hospital. £15,000 has gone on setting up an HIV blood-screening unit at the regional transfusion centre in Brasov, organised by the Brasov Distress Fund. £25,000 has been spent on a Red Cross Aids education programme for nurses, auxiliaries and the general public in the Romanian Health Service.[15]

With the £31,000 given to Galloway, that accounts for around £100,000 out of the quoted total of over £210,000.

The *Guardian* too has failed to keep records of its fund raising. In reply to inquiries for this book a spokesperson wrote:

We remain confident that the money sent in by readers in response to Seumas Milne's original article in February 1990 was properly spent. Being an expert in neither Aids nor voluntary sector funding, the *Guardian* – as you are already aware – took the responsible step of asking the Terrence Higgins Trust, which was skilled in both areas, to administer the funds on its behalf. The newspaper naturally had representation on the committee set up at THT to disburse the funds and the *Guardian* has never had any doubt that the THT selected its recipient charities and organisations wisely. Although the THT appears to have retained no detailed records from that period, it is our understanding that the Romanian Child Aids Appeal, the charity to which you refer, was awarded £31,000 by the THT but in the end required and drew down only £15,000 for its projects – the remaining £16,000 being reallocated by the THT to another international Aids charity working in Romania.

In October 1990 Galloway's constituency newsletter described how well his appeal had been going in the fight against AIDS. He wrote that it had

Oct 1990

The overwhelming feeling amongst the delegates was against any serious rocking of the boat when a crucial General Election is looming.

ROMANIA

The other issue in which I remain involved is Romania. As I earlier reported, I am co-writing a book on the Romanian Revolution and negotiations are well advanced for its serialisation in a major national newspaper. I remain active too in highlighting the plight of the children with AIDS in Romania The Romanian Child AIDS appeal which I co-founded some months ago has already made a significant contribution towards helping to deal with this problem. Now working in conjunction with the Terence Higgins Trust and the Royal College of Nursing and with a board of trustees which include Scotland's leading Child AIDS specialists, Dr Jaqueline Mok and Sister Christine Rafferty and Romania's leading Child AIDS doctors, the R.C.C.A has sent drugs, toys, money, and Scottish expertise to help the Romanians. In conjunction with Olivia Harrison's Angels Appeal it is hoped soon to establish a research laboratory in the Municipal Hospital Constanta under Dr Mok, to study the pathology of Child AIDS in Romania. The R.C.N. are

proposing the steady supply of Nursing help to the Constanta hospital where one in every three child AIDS cases in Europe is being cared for.

SURGERIES

Lastly, my weekly surgery - every Saturday at 10 am in the Office at 64 Elderslie St, Anderston - continues to be busy with constituents seeking my assistance. The surgery on Saturday 29th was the busiest for over two years.

CONTACT

Should any members need to talk to me at any time I restate the appropriate tel and fax nos

London office 071 219 4084, Glasgow Office 204 1465. Carole Hughes 0475 54 267. My home telephone number is 041 248 2972

FAX :

0475 54 458

George Galloway's Hillhead constituency newsletter of October 1990

'already made a significant contribution towards helping to deal with this problem'. The newsletter claimed that Mok was on the board of trustees and that they had 'sent drugs, toys, money, and Scottish expertise to help the Romanians'. It also claimed that 'in conjunction with Olivia Harrison's Romanian Angels Appeal it is hoped soon to establish a research laboratory in the Municipal Hospital, Constanta under Dr Mok, to study pathology of Child AIDS in Romania'.

Mok would not be interviewed for this book, but confirmed under the Freedom of Information Act, via the Lothian Health Board, that she went to Romania on 'two or three occasions' at the invitation of the Galloway appeal and Olivia Harrison's Romanian Angel Appeal, but she couldn't remember exactly how many times. She says now that 'no formal research was undertaken', only data collection with a Dr Rodica Matusa, a Romanian paediatrician. Matusa is now retired, but remembers that Galloway's was one visit of many from all over the world.

Dr Sorin Ruginâ, the manager of the Constanţa Hospital for Infectious Diseases, remembers Galloway and Bob Wylie being in Constanţa in 1990. He also remembers Mok very clearly and that they engaged in an exchange of experts. It is some indication of the poor state of their health service that he recalls a humble microscope being offered by the Edinburgh medics. Interestingly, Ruginâ remembers that there was a plan to build a children's hospital in Constanţa, but that nothing came of it, despite an agreement being signed. The idea had been for the Edinburgh doctors to get the funds for its construction. He is disappointed because he believed it was a 'good project'.

Galloway's efforts in raising money and awareness of the problems in Constanţa were acknowledged by the authorities in the city. In the *Scotsman* on 23 November 1990, the mayor of Constanţa wrote a public letter, saying:

> I am delighted to offer my grateful and warmest thanks to all who sent their kind contributions to the 'Romanian Child AIDS Appeal' run by George Galloway MP and Bob Wylie. I express my full gratitude for the drugs and material donated to ease the care of AIDS children in our town. No less appreciated is the collaboration with the staff of our hospital for the scientific study of AIDS.
>
> A. Manole, City Hall, Constantza, 12 November 1990.

Adrian Manole is still living in Constanţa and remembers Galloway coming to Romania.

As well as trips to Romania from the UK by Mok and Chris Rafferty, some Romanian doctors were brought over to the UK to study. Ruginâ's wife was one of them. Dr Claudia Ruginâ, who also works at the Constanţa Hospital for Infectious Diseases, spent a month in Edinburgh with a Romanian biologist, Elena Gorun. This was from 2 February to 2 March 1990. Gorun recalls now that she visited around half a dozen hospitals and learned enough about HIV/AIDS to form the basis of a doctorate she studied for later.

Running an appeal is time-consuming work and it cannot have been practical for Galloway to stay closely involved with every detail of this project; he states that he passed over the RCAA money and its ongoing projects to the much bigger Romanain Angel Appeal, which is still operating. According to Mok, for the trips she made to and from Romania, all her accommodation and other costs were met by the Romanian Angel Appeal, who organised them for her. Frank Clark, who was the chief executive of Lothian Health Board at the time, confirmed that no money was given to, or received from the RCAA.

15

Poll tax battles, the first Gulf War and meeting Saddam

In the midst of the infighting of Glasgow Hillhead, there were conflicts over policies that went hand in hand with the arguments over George Galloway's style and his extra-curricular activities. When he wrote in the *Scottish Trade Union Review* that fellow Scottish MPs should mount a campaign of civil disobedience against the poll tax,[1] it went down like a lead balloon with the Labour MP Norman Buchan. Like the vast majority of Labour's MPs, Buchan wanted opposition to the poll tax to be exercised through legal means.

Galloway had been quoted in the *Scotsman* that he wasn't going to pay the tax.[2] He attacked Buchan for being a left-winger who had moved to the right. 'Left-wing wolves from the sixties now wearing their umpteenth coat of sheep's clothing,' he declared.[3] It's a tactic he has used against Christopher Hitchens, John Reid, Alastair Darling and a host of others who he likes to portray as having abandoned their principles, their working-class roots or the working people who need them. It implies that he has not done any of those things himself. Galloway believes he has remained true to the original ideals. He describes himself as 'the Ghost of Labour Past' for the same reason, and claims that Respect is the new champion of working people, now that New Labour has abandoned them.

Galloway campaigned against the poll tax in Parliament. On 28 November 1988 he spoke of its unpopularity:

So the poll tax, rejected by four out of every five Scots, had to go ahead . . . wanted by no one who is anyone in Scottish education circles and supported by not a single leader writer, serious journalist, person outside the Scottish Conservative Party, nor even by many members of the Scottish Conservative Party.[4]

In June 1989 he attacked its impact on the poor: 'There are people in Scotland who are pretty nearly going hungry, and this poll tax and these mean-spirited regulations will make it even harder for people living on the breadline to make ends meet.'

Galloway warned that 'Labour's unwillingness to lead Scots willing to engage in struggle against the enemy' might lead them to the SNP. The irony was that over the issue of the poll tax, some elements of the Labour Party were drawn closer to the now expelled Trotskyite Militant, who were a leading element in the Anti-Poll Tax Federation. After their formal expulsion by Neil Kinnock in 1985, Militant members had been hunted down and chased out of Labour all over the UK. By the early 1990s the Militant Tendency had started to call itself Militant Labour, or Scottish Militant Labour. The All Britain Anti-Poll Tax Federation, which claimed 1,500 affiliated local groups, was led by Glasgow councillor and Militant supporter Tommy Sheridan, who was sent to jail for refusing to pay.[5] Sheridan said the accusations of being a front for Militant were 'an insult . . . This is a participative campaign. It's the first issue for years where people think they have got a wee bit of power.'[6] Galloway was not a close ally of Sheridan by any means, but they did share this common bond of opposition to the poll tax. (Sheridan was later to feature in a much-reported libel case in 2006, which he won.)

Galloway has a much better working relationship with Bob Wylie. Wylie is well known to Scottish TV viewers as a reporter for the BBC, but back in the 1980s and 1990s he wrote for Militant and was very active in Glasgow's anti-poll tax campaign. Despite working with Wylie and Sheridan, Galloway never supported Militant, nor agreed with its methods. However, he did oppose its expulsion from Labour in 1984 and he did write an open letter to the *Glasgow Herald* to say that the organisation had supported him.

Labour's concern about the possible renaissance of their *bête noire* was pointed up by Tony Benn, who claimed: 'The Labour Party is more frightened of the anti-poll tax campaign than of the poll tax itself.' The press was full of reports of how Militant was using the poll tax as a way of getting back into Labour and in Militant's official history of the times, it reminds readers that: 'The *Sun* compared us to football hooligans: "The Militant Tendency is Labour's own Inter-City Firm".' While the popular press was using Militant to hit Labour over the head again, Malcolm Rifkind, the

Secretary of State for Scotland, tried to play down the crisis: he told the Scottish Grand Committee, made up of all seventy-two Scottish MPs, that 90 per cent of Scots were paying the poll tax.

Galloway's declaration that he would not pay, and his backing of the 'Committee of 100' high-profile non-payers, never extended to a call for non-payment by others. Benn, however, called for the next Labour government to grant an amnesty for non-payers. Labour's leadership of course rejected the idea of a pre-arranged amnesty for law breakers, but Benn was right on the money when he said: 'If enough people stand firm against the poll tax we can compel the government to withdraw it.' The proof of that was the mass demonstration that followed. It was the pivotal moment in the poll tax 'rebellion', as Sheridan and Militant called it. On 31 March 1990 an estimated 200,000 anti-poll tax demonstrators marched in London. Unlike on the previous day, when some 50,000 had done the same very peacefully in Glasgow, the march ended in the worst riots seen in the UK for at least a decade. Galloway shared a platform with Benn in Trafalgar Square and later witnessed elements in the crowd attacking first the police, then anyone who got in their way. A significant number climbed on scaffolding and hurled missiles down on the crowd, while police charged and beat innocent and guilty alike. The images went round the country and the world and it was a pivotal moment in the UK's history. The tax was now all but dead, as was Margaret Thatcher's administration.

Galloway, reportedly shocked, rounded on the extremist elements that had caused the violence, as well as the creators of the poll tax:

> It was a well-organised demonstration, but these lunatics, anarchists and other extremists, principally from the Socialist Workers Party [SWP], were out for a rumble the whole time . . . If they didn't exist, the Tories would need to invent them . . . The police were clearly repeatedly and viciously attacked with weapons ranging from sticks to blocks of heavy masonry and whatever violence they themselves dished out was clearly retaliatory and frankly necessary to save their own lives.[7]

It's interesting that he chose to single out the SWP as the troublemakers. The SWP had kept its distance from the Anti-Poll Tax Federation because of a long-standing disagreement with Militant. Though they are both Trotskyite groups, the SWP didn't agree with Militant's 'entryist' tactic of infiltrating Labour, and instead believed in a strong, open, separate party.

Though those comments show that Galloway was keen to distance himself from the 'rumble', as he put it, he waded into the political debate that followed in the House of Commons. It was a bad-tempered afternoon in the chamber and the Home Secretary, David Waddington, backed by shouting Tory MPs, accused 'up to thirty Labour MPs' who had publicly backed non-payment of the poll tax of behaviour which could have been interpreted as inciting violence: 'Do they really expect those they seek to influence to draw a neat distinction between one sort of law breaking and another? Do they really expect the people they seek to influence to stop just trying to break the tax and don't in fact encourage them to break policemen's heads?'[8] Later in the debate Galloway warned: 'If the government doesn't change course on the poll tax, it is going to be a long hot summer,'[9] in response to which Waddington shot back: 'The hon. Gentleman's latter remarks do him no credit at all because they could easily be interpreted by people outside the House as an incitement to violence.'

Lumbered with a tax that nobody wanted and civil unrest on a huge scale, Waddington and the Conservative Party chairman, Kenneth Baker, were left with only the Militant straw to cling onto. They hit back at Labour, claiming that their Militant infiltrators had been 'orchestrating violence', using 'bully-boy' tactics and manipulating the All-Britain Anti-Poll Tax Federation. Waddington told the House he would make inquiries into claims by Dave Nellist, the Militant Labour MP for Coventry South East, that the organisers of the rally had asked to change its venue from Trafalgar Square to Hyde Park but had been refused. Nellist called for a general election over the poll tax, but nobody was listening.

Following the riot Galloway continued to campaign against the poll tax on its link with hunger, poverty and illness. In the Commons a few weeks later, he criticised the continuing debate for not showing any sense of the 'popular revolt' in Scotland over the poll tax and cited an estimated 36,000 throughout Strathclyde who were said not to be paying because they just couldn't afford to. In late June he staged a short fast in support of ten anti-poll tax hunger strikers who were campaigning against the policy of taking benefits from people who wouldn't pay the tax. Galloway stood in the Glasgow rain with Sheridan and their picture was taken by the papers.

At its June 1990 conference, the All Britain Anti-Poll Tax Federation issued a statement expressing support for 'the peaceful civil protests that have been organised, including occupations of sheriffs' offices and DSS offices, lobbies of courts and boycotts of employers putting pressure on their workers to pay the poll tax'. Yet there was an angry tone in the speeches, with comments such as 'in Scotland, the sheriffs' officers are facing war' and 'we are the infantry of the Labour movement and we will win'.

Over the next year, the protests continued and Galloway was one of several MPs who refused to pay, including Harry Barnes, Jeremy Corbyn, Ken Livingstone and Tony Benn, and from Scotland Dennis Canavan, Dick Douglas and Ron Brown. The late Tony Banks paid the equivalent of his rates bill instead of the poll tax, and several Scottish MPs, including Brown and Douglas, even had their bank accounts 'arrested'. They all believed that they were beating not just the poll tax, but Thatcher at the same time, and they were probably right. By November 1990 she was gone and John Major had arrived in her place.

The poll tax may have changed the country's political geography, and certainly helped firm up support for Galloway and other Scottish Labour MPs, but another conflict was to prove the bigger influence on Galloway's career. On 2 August 1990 Saddam Hussein ordered the invasion of Kuwait. America's reaction would harden opinion on both sides in the Middle East, with huge Muslim opposition to the consequent foreign armies in Saudi Arabia, but secular support for putting Saddam back in his box. When Operation Desert Storm was launched on 17 January 1991, Baghdad state radio broadcast Saddam declaring that 'the great duel, the mother of all battles, has begun'. Although that particular campaign would be lost very quickly, the First Gulf War was just the beginning of a wider conflict between the United States and the Muslim world, so perhaps in the longer term Saddam's words were prophetic. Galloway, who would later meet Saddam and form strong links with others in his regime, saw Iraq and its people as yet more victims of US empire building.

Galloway has been consistent in his interest in the Middle East, but as soon as Saddam invaded Kuwait, everything changed for him. Up until then, he'd been standing somewhere over to stage left, but suddenly the spotlight was on him and the causes he knew well. He campaigned against the US-led invasion of Kuwait, and at the end of the ground war he argued against the imposition of United Nations sanctions. In the House of Commons debate on Iraq and Kuwait at the start of Desert Storm, Galloway condemned allied air raids as 'mass murder'.[10] At Prime Minister's Questions he said the idea of surgical bombing was a 'fantasy of the armchair strategists in their sandpits in TV studios'. In a taste of things to come, the war was setting Galloway against the mainstream of his own party, which was to side with the US and UK governments.

Iraq was growing as an interest for Galloway, but he had yet to visit the country. Over the years, his trips to other parts of the Arab world have been numerous and paid for by a variety of sources, including the PLO, or interested bodies in the UK, and possibly by himself. In July 1989 he visited the West Bank, Gaza and East Jerusalem 'as a guest of the Jerusalem Cigarette Company', according to the House of Commons Register of Members' Interests. In 1990 he was a guest of the PLO in Tunis. These trips have helped Galloway consolidate his ties in the region, where he is now regarded as a hero.

Of course, these visits were all built on the initial relationship with Nablus, where friction between Israel and Palestinians is often intense. In February 1991, during the Gulf War, he visited the city and was held at gunpoint by an Israeli soldier who Galloway later described as 'psychopathic'.[11] He was walking through the occupied town with Bill Speirs, who was then the deputy general secretary of the Scottish TUC, and two others. Despite explaining that he was a British MP, Galloway was held for some time and treated like a terrorist. When he later complained to the authorities, he received a message from the Foreign Office that there had been 'some linguistic difficulties'.

It would be wrong to give the impression that Galloway was just making trips to Arab countries. In December 1991 he went to Kosovo as a guest of the Democratic League of Kosovo (DLK),[12] the largest political party in the country. At the time, the DLK had formed a 'shadow government' within Milošević's idea of Yugoslavia and tried to break away from Serbia in 1992 by electing a president. It wasn't until 2002 that they formed Kosovo's first democratic government, and they have been in power ever since.

Back at home in 1992, there was the matter of a general election to contend with. It was the first serious opportunity to get back in power since before 1979. The First Gulf War didn't have an impact as most opinion was in favour and therefore it wasn't an election issue. The issue was the economy, with taxation and higher prices successfully portrayed by the Conservatives as 'Labour's Double Whammy'.

Neil Kinnock's foreword to the Labour Party manifesto read: 'This general election is a choice between a Conservative government paralysed by recession, and a Labour government determined to get on with building recovery.' In fact, it was an election more about whether the public trusted Kinnock to run the country. On the day of polling, 9 April 1992, the *Sun*'s front page showed his face inside a light bulb, with the headline 'If Kinnock wins today will the last person to leave Britain please turn out the lights'. That together with a triumphalist rally in Sheffield, as well as the image of Kinnock on the beach, falling over with his wife into the surf, probably consigned him from here to eternity.

Galloway had no problems getting re-elected in the 1992 election and ran out a clear winner with 38.5 per cent of the vote in Hillhead. A month or so before the election, he had excelled himself in the *Glasgow Herald* by describing Scottish Tory MPs as 'the drunk, the stupid and the unemployable',[13] which played well with his supporters and is a fairly typical example of the sort of language he has often used to attack his opponents. Roy Jenkins did not stand again and Galloway increased his majority to 4,826 over the Liberal Democrats' Christopher Mason. However, the increased majority hid changes in the vote, as Galloway's fell by 4.4 per cent, and the Liberal Democrats' dropped by 8.9 per cent, while the Conservatives' went up by 2.7 per cent and the SNP by fully 10.0 per cent.

The lead-up to the election had seen Labour ahead in the national polls, only to be beaten quite badly in the one that matters. It was a tremendous shock and even led to pollsters changing their methods. In the UK at large, the Conservatives took 336 seats, with 41.93 per cent of the vote, while Labour got 271 seats with 34.39 per cent. In Scotland the SNP held onto only the three seats they'd won at the 1987 general election, as Jim Sillars lost Govan. Sillars quit politics with a parting shot describing the Scottish electorate as 'ninety-minute patriots', referring to the length of a football match. The defeat of Sillars and the weakening of the SNP led to Galloway making subtle overtures to the members of that party. He appeared at a few of their rallies.

After the election, with Kinnock gone, a sea change was happening, and the modernisers were about to take over. It was a crossroads for the party and for its members, who had to choose to go with the new leader, John Smith, or not. Many chose to just hold their tongues, but not Galloway, who let his unhappiness come out in various and sometimes odd circumstances.

Over the years Galloway has won substantial amounts of money from newspapers as wide ranging as the *Daily Mirror* and the *Daily Telegraph*, and when journalists ask questions about his lifestyle he will sometimes jokingly refer to the help he has had from Fleet Street. Galloway claims he bought his classic red Mercedes sports car with the proceeds of a libel win against the *Daily Mirror* in 1992. The case came about because the *Mirror* and Scotland's *Daily Record* had unjustly and unfairly accused him of exploiting and abusing parliamentary privilege. He won a substantial amount of money, including costs, and he didn't just buy a car, he also bought shares in Mirror Group Newspapers. Galloway had made comments in the House of Commons about Robert Maxwell, accusing him, under parliamentary privilege, of helping to betray Mordechai Vanunu, the Israeli scientist who had revealed details of Israel's nuclear weapons programme. In fact, Galloway's run-ins with Maxwell's *Mirror* have some history. It had been the *Mirror*'s Alastair Campbell who had broken the story of Galloway's expenses claims at War on Want in the 1980s, so there was no love lost there.

Galloway was further to burn his bridges with New Labour in October 1992 when he complained loudly and at length that he had been unfairly prevented from standing as an MEP. He claimed that 'Walworth Road bureaucrats whose names I don't know' had decided he couldn't stand for the European Parliament.[14] In reply Labour's Jack McConnell pointed out that the party rules had been strictly enforced and no sitting Westminster MP is allowed to stand in European elections. Galloway's only option under Labour rules would have been to stand down as an MP. One reason for Galloway's interest in becoming a Euro MP, apart from his commitment to the EU, was believed to be that the Boundary Commission was rumoured to have decided that there was one MP too many in Glasgow. All the sitting MPs, including Galloway, must have been worried about what this meant to them. Though the official announcement was timetabled for late 1993, the pressure was on and it could have meant yet another reselection battle for Galloway.

In the summer of that year the big issue for many with an interest in international affairs was the effect on innocent Iraqis of the UN sanctions imposed during the Gulf War. These had been in place since 6 August 1990, just after the Iraqi invasion of Kuwait, but when the war ended, the UN continued the sanctions under a different resolution. Under the new mandate, they were linked to the giving up of weapons of mass destruction, but the effect on the people was the same. Though Saddam's critics blamed him for channelling Iraq's foreign earnings away from his people, UNICEF believes that some 500,000 Iraqi children died as a direct consequence of the sanctions, from lack of medicines and safe drinking water. The Iraqi economy suffered generally, because the amount of oil the country was allowed to sell was restricted.

A number of prominent MPs and campaigners were trying to find out more about what was happening in Iraq. Information was difficult to get, because it was hard to get in and out of the country. Galloway linked up with Tam Dalyell, the former Labour MP who became a household name during the Falklands War when he was given evidence that the government had sunk the *General Belgrano* when it had been outside the total exclusion zone and steaming away from it. Dalyell had long been a determined Scottish maverick, of a different kind to Galloway, but they found common ground in Iraq and in the summer of 1993, they travelled there together. Dalyell recalls how it happened: 'In 1993, I wanted to go to Iraq. Tim Llewellyn, then BBC Middle East correspondent, was also interested. Because I was going, George asked if he could come. I said yes because I always thought he was very serious about foreign affairs and one doesn't say no to one's colleagues.'

The man who organised the trip to Iraq in 1993 is Riad Al Tahir, who describes himself as an 'oil man'. He, Galloway, Dalyell and Llewellyn stopped off in Jordan and Dalyell remembers: 'It was like an Anglo-Iraq friendship society. I remember George said: "Of the eighteen people in this room, I'm the only one who hasn't been to a British university." ' They met Tariq Aziz, the Iraqi Foreign Secretary, with whom Galloway would later strike up a friendship. 'In our meeting with Tariq Aziz, [Galloway] was much more forthright than I was, saying that the West was very concerned about the situation of human rights in Iraq.' Dalyell thinks that Galloway was far more critical of Iraq than he was at the time. 'I think George's intention was to fact-find and he developed a great sympathy with the Arab people.' Llewellyn too recalls that Galloway was far more circumspect than Dalyell, 'who was very critical of the British government. He was too adulatory of Saddam's rebuilding of the country, whereas George was pretty canny and was obviously learning as he was going.'

Al Tahir knows the Iraqi oil industry under Saddam and under sanctions in detail. He traded in oil under the UN's oil-for-food programme. Although he lives in the UK, he is a Ba'athist who supported the invasion of Kuwait and had the contacts in Iraq necessary to make the trip happen, including a personal friendship with Aziz. He recalls:

> I contacted several MPs and Tam Dalyell was one of them, I got to know him quite well. I tried to get Tam to go, and he was receptive, but he didn't want to go alone . . . I didn't know George Galloway at all but he said yes, and he invited me over to the House of Commons. When he introduced himself, he said: 'Everyone knows me here as Gorgeous George.'

Al Tahir remembers the trip very well. 'Tam got to the airport very punctually. George Galloway came late and then insisted he had to buy some shoes and he tried to find some. I said: "You're going to Iraq, it's under sanctions." He didn't find any in the end.' Al Tahir thought Galloway's behaviour on the trip was odd and Llewellyn thinks the two men fell out pretty quickly. 'They had a blazing row in the hotel once,' he recalls. 'Al Tahir was trying to control everything, which annoyed me too, but George showed it.'

Llewellyn had been the BBC's Middle Eastern correspondent from 1976 to 1980 and then again from 1987 to 1992, so he knew the region very well. He remembers being impressed by Galloway's knowledge of the politics and also that, despite being taken around by their minders, they felt they were getting a true picture of the terrible conditions for ordinary Iraqis. 'In Basra the children were playing in sewers still not repaired since the war. It was running in sewage.'

While they were there, Llewellyn, Dalyell and Galloway visited a children's hospital in Baghdad, where the effects of the sanctions were shown to them by the Iraqi regime. Dalyell says: 'We were greatly moved by what we saw: the lack of medicine, the state of the children. It was absolutely appalling, all these deformed children without medicine. It was an extremely modern hospital and George and I were very greatly moved.'

In the course of their travels they had been meeting various officials, including health ministers, education ministers and Tariq Aziz, but there was a question mark over whether they should ask to meet Saddam. Dalyell recalls: 'Our attitude was, and we shared it, we were in Iraq and we didn't ask to see Saddam, but if he asked we couldn't refuse a head of state.'

Galloway's trip to Iraq had been an indisputable success for him personally and was the first of several. He would later write that he had fallen in love with Iraq as a man falls in love with a woman,[15] and it was not long before he was back in her arms again. The following year, 1994, he made perhaps the most controversial of all his foreign visits, and certainly conducted his most controversial meeting. It was with Saddam, and despite its brevity, no more than ten minutes, it has taken up thousands of column inches and hours of airtime.

His political opponents have cited his greeting to Saddam as proof that Galloway is not just for the Iraqi people, but also on the side of Saddam himself; Galloway has always been keen to point out that he did not support the dictator. What is often quoted is the rather verbose section where Galloway says: 'Sir, I salute your courage, your strength, your indefatig-ability. And I want you to know that we are with you *hatta al-nasr, hatta al-nasr, hatta al-Quds* [until victory, until victory, until Jerusalem].' When this is juxtaposed with the photo of the two men shaking hands, or if you see the video clip of them facing each other, about three feet apart, it appears to be a very personal, if formal, address. Galloway claims that this quote has been taken out of context and is part of a longer salute to the Iraqi people, not just the dictator.

So here is the full transcript of the address, as broadcast and picked up by the BBC's monitoring service in Caversham. Although no-one would have expected Galloway to greet the Iraqi leader with 'Yo, Saddam', it does seem a little over the top, even for the Arab world.

> Your Excellency, Mr President, I greet you, in the name of the many thousands of people in Britain who stood against the tide and opposed the war and aggression against Iraq and continue to oppose the war by economic means, which is aimed to strangle the life out of the great people of Iraq.
>
> I greet you, too, in the name of the Palestinian people, amongst whom I've just spent two weeks in the occupied Palestinian territories. I can honestly tell you that there was not a single person to whom I told I was coming to Iraq and hoping to meet with yourself who did not wish me to convey their heartfelt, fraternal greetings and support.
>
> And this was true especially at the base in the refugee camps of Jabaliyah and Beach Camp in Gaza, in the Balatah refugee camp in Nablus and on the streets of the towns and villages in the occupied lands.
>
> I thought the President would appreciate knowing that even today, three years after the war, I still met families who were calling their newborn sons Saddam; and that two weeks ago, when I was trapped inside the Orient House, which is the Palestinian headquarters in Al Quds [Jerusalem], with 5,000 armed *mustwatinin* [settlers] outside demonstrating, pledging to tear down the Palestinian flag from the flagpole, the hundreds of *shabab* [youths] inside the compound were chanting that they wish to be with a DShK [machine gun] in Baghdad to avenge the eyes of Abu Jihad [the late Palestinian leader Khalil Al Wazir, who was killed in Tunisia]. And the Youth Club in Silwan, which is the one of the most resistant of all the villages around Jerusalem, asked me to ask the President's permission if they could enrol him as an honorary member of their club and to present him with this flag from holy Jerusalem.
>
> I wish to say, sir, that I believe that we are turning the tide in Europe, that the scale of the humanitarian disaster which has been imposed upon the Iraqi people is now becoming more and more widely known and accepted.
>
> Fifty-five British members of Parliament opposed the war, but 125 are demanding the lifting of the embargo. And this does not include the invisible section of the Conservative Party who must also be moving in that direction.

And Sir Edward Heath is being a very persuasive advocate inside the Conservative Party.

It is my belief that we must convey the very clear picture that 1994 has to be the year of the ending of the embargo against Iraq. Otherwise, famine and all the awful consequences, including acts of despair by Iraqis, will be the result. And this is the message we must convey to civilized opinion in Europe.

Sir, I salute your courage, your strength, your indefatigability. And I want you to know that we are with you *hatta al-nasr, hatta al-nasr, hatta al-Quds.*

Galloway's speech was translated for Saddam, so how do we know exactly what Saddam heard from the translator, Saad-Oun Al Zubaidi? According to Anas Al Tikriti, a friend of Galloway's and spokesman for the Muslim Association of Britain:

I saw the video way, way before he left the Labour Party. I saw the footage before he entered the room. I understand Arabic and it was taken completely out of context. When he said 'you' he meant the Iraqi people, he was saluting their indefatigability, their resolve against sanctions. Even the interpreter got it right and, in Arabic, says 'salutes the stand of the Iraqi people'.

So it seems likely that Saddam thought that Galloway was addressing the entire Iraqi people (including Saddam himself, of course) when he said 'your courage, your strength and your indefatigability'.

The question of Galloway's attitude to Saddam won't go away and when it is raised he will cite his campaigning work against the dictator in the late 1970s and 1980s. He states he stood outside the Iraqi embassy protesting, while the British government was inside selling arms to them, but it's unlikely that he knew precisely what was being done inside the embassy. However, it's worth just drilling down into this claim of Galloway's a little more. There is one organisation in the UK that led the way in the campaign against the brutal treatment of the Iraqi people and that's the Committee Against Repression and for Democratic Rights in Iraq, or CARDRI. On more than one occasion, it has been claimed that Galloway was a 'founder member'. What exactly is meant by this is unclear.

Fran Hazelton, its first honorary secretary, was at the London meetings which founded CARDRI and holds the extensive archive of its life until it folded in 2004. She says: 'I never met George Galloway and I don't know of any work he's done for CARDRI.' So what is the story of CARDRI and what part, if any, did Galloway play in it? Hazelton writes:

> First, on the meaning of 'founder member': there were three capacities in which people became involved with CARDRI.
>
> 1. Sponsors: Lords, MPs, trade union leaders, academics and other 'names' who gave the campaign its respectability and political identity. They were the speakers at CARDRI events.
> 2. Organisers: These people were the committee accountable to the sponsors. They were Iraqis and Brits who met regularly to run the campaign, i.e. organise meetings, release press statements, produce and distribute the newsletters, maintain relationships with other organisations, e.g. Amnesty International or the Campaign Against the Arms Trade.
> 3. Individual affiliates/supporters: these were people who signed petitions, bought the newsletters, wrote letters to the press, moved resolutions at trade union, student union or Labour Party branches, came out on marches or pickets, and attended CARDRI conferences. Some filled in the affiliation form included in almost all CARDRI printed material and paid a small affiliation fee. Others were simply on the mailing list.
>
> There is no written record of and I have no memory of Galloway as a founder member/Founding Member from the beginning of my involvement with CARDRI as its honorary secretary in 1979 and throughout the 1980s.

CARDRI was founded in a series of meetings in Manchester and London in late 1978 and early 1979, when Galloway was the boss of Dundee Labour Party and already very interested in the politics of the Middle East. And here we have to distinguish between the people who founded CARDRI and what Galloway refers to as a 'founder member'. According to Hazelton, those most entitled to think of themselves as CARDRI's founders would be those who met regularly in Manchester and London in 1978 and 1979 and were mostly affiliated to an anti-imperialist campaigning umbrella group called Liberation. 'CARDRI grew out of Liberation. It was driven by Iraqis in the UK and I said I'd be secretary, and I stayed with it ever since.'

The reason Hazelton doesn't recall Galloway's involvement in CARDRI is because it was at the grass roots level in Dundee. In 1979, news of the beginnings of this Iraqi exile/Trade Union/Labour left supported organisation reached Galloway and he moved the Dundee party's affiliation. In the spring of that year, the CARDRI sponsors were Lord Fenner Brockway; thirteen MPs including Frank Alaun, Stan Newens and Audrey Wise; and six trade union leaders including Alex Kitson and Jimmy Milne. Galloway knew Kitson and Milne well, and probably would have heard early about the establishment of CARDRI. Galloway later moved Dundee Labour's reaffiliation and gave regular reports on CARDRI's activities to the party Management Committee and the local branches, circulating CARDRI newsletters. However, there is no record held at CARDRI of Galloway signing up as an individual member.

CARDRI gained widespread support on the left and conducted a co-ordinated campaign against the brutal Iraqi regime, as Hazelton recalls:

> Over the next two years the increasing support for CARDRI was demonstrated by hundreds of protest letters and phone calls to the Iraqi embassy, dozens of pickets and solidarity events, petitions signed by thousands of delegates to trade union, student and Labour Party conferences, scores of resolutions passed, and meetings held in committee rooms of the House of Commons. These events and activities took place in towns and cities throughout the UK including Manchester, London, Birmingham, Nottingham, Swansea, Cardiff, Glasgow, Aberdeen, Stockport, Liverpool, Aston, Loughborough, Newcastle, Blackpool, Warwick and elsewhere. CARDRI's supporters included Neil Kinnock MP and David Aaronovitch, then the president of the National Union of Students.

Galloway also had strong contacts with Iraqi communists, who had fled Saddam's purges and were closely involved in the setting up of CARDRI. The development of British anti-Saddam groups took on a new importance when they became a way for Iraqi exiles to get together for protection. After Saddam took power in 1979, he began to seek out his enemies abroad, and many universities, including Dundee's, found a new kind of Iraqi student on campus. These were Ba'athists, with money and flash cars, who kept an eye on the opposition Iraqis, some of who had settled down with British wives and girlfriends. Fran Hazelton and CARDRI were well aware of the problems being experienced by Iraqis in Europe. 'One or two were killed in Europe. They fed them rat poison and one actually died in this country, though he was probably poisoned abroad.' Saddam thought it suitable to kill his enemies with rat poison.

CARDRI was sponsored by between fifty and sixty MPs; its first two chairmen were Stan Newens, Labour MP for Harlow, followed by George Morton, Labour MP for Manchester Moss Side. The left-wing Labour MP Ann Clwyd ran it from 1983; they had trade union support; and they were repeatedly outside the Iraqi embassy, protesting. Arthur Scargill was at the first national conference in 1981, together with other union leaders and the respected academic Professor Peter Slugett, then of Durham University. That first conference was a huge event, with 400 delegates. It was held on 21 March 1981 at the Conway Hall in London and because of worries over Ba'athist disruption, Hazelton and the other organisers didn't let anyone in whose name wasn't registered. All the names of the delegates are still held by Hazelton, with their original applications. Galloway's name does not appear, though Dundee Labour Party sent a delegate.

Hazelton says, 'There is no doubt that as far as the Labour left was concerned we were the people doing it. We met regularly to plan the campaign and had regular meetings in committee rooms at the House of Commons attended by MPs and other supporters.' When he later became an MP in 1987 Galloway still wasn't very visible in CARDRI, despite his previous support via Dundee and the established connections with Labour MPs.

CARDRI annual conferences continued throughout the 1980s. According to their records, Galloway was never a speaker and there is no record of his participation as a delegate. However in 1982, the CARDRI newsletter *Iraq Solidarity Voice* reported that 'the ruling Labour Group of Councillors on the Dundee District Council have written to the Iraqi Ambassador asking for the whereabouts of people who have disappeared'.

Whatever work Galloway did for CARDRI, he refers to it often. He stood up in Parliament on 13 December 1993 and said, 'For the record, I am a founder member of the Campaign Against Oppression and for Democratic

Rights in Iraq.'[16] He may have made a mistake over the name or perhaps it could be an unusual error of transcription by Hansard. When John Humphrys interviewed him for Radio 4's *On the Ropes* in 2003, Galloway claimed work for CARDRI too:

> I was a known opponent of the Saddam Hussein regime. I used to be demonstrating in the square outside the embassy when British businessmen and ministers were inside selling them guns. I was one of the founders, one of the founder members, of the Campaign Against Repression and for Democratic Rights in Iraq in 1978, when Tony Blair was just an ugly rumour. I was active against the Ba'ath regime in Baghdad.

Officially CARDRI was the Committee, not Campaign; however, some refer to it as a campaign, so perhaps he was just using an informal term for it. There is no reason to doubt his opposition to the Iraqi government, particularly as he knew Iraqi communists back in Dundee in the 1970s. These communists were enemies of Saddam and had influenced Galloway enormously, like the Palestinian students had done. However, it wasn't just communists who were against Saddam and these links were narrow compared to the wider and longer-standing links to other exiled Iraqis. These came out of the Movement for Colonial Freedom, which (in 1963) had given birth to a well-run Parliamentary Committee for the Defence of the Iraqi People, which in turn evolved into CARDRI in the early 1980s. That's why it's called a Committee, not a Campaign.

Galloway stresses his campaigning against Saddam, and contrasts that with the arms dealing done with the British government's consent, but Iraq's major suppliers were the French and the Soviets, according to the Campaign Against the Arms Trade (CAAT). In a report on Iraq's trade with the UK, they state there was

> apparently contradictory action by the British government. It allowed the export of military equipment which it categorised as non-lethal and invited Iraq to the 1986 British Army Equipment Exhibition . . . the Department of Trade and Industry (DTI) does not appear to have investigated and/or taken action on reports that these machines and other equipment were being used

for military purposes. On the other hand the UK appears to have played a leading role in controlling the export of chemicals that might be used in weapons.

CAAT also has evidence that the government research station at Porton Down sold cultures to Iraq from 1985 to 1987 which could have been used in the production of biological weapons. This justifies a campaign to bring this trade to light, as well as to draw attention to the persecution of Iraqi citizens by the tyrant Saddam.

Galloway has always stated that he was working hard against Saddam, even before he had ever visited the country. It became increasingly important for him to keep referring to this, to counter the rather simplistic implications by the right-wing press and his political opponents that he was a supporter of Saddam. For example, in a House of Commons debate of November 1990, in the run-up to the First Gulf War, he stood across the chamber from Douglas Hurd, the Foreign Secretary, and argued not to attack:

> I have no truck with Saddam Hussein, and I hope that the Foreign Secretary accepts that. However, on the day when Saddam Hussein has asked President Bush for talks, will the Right Hon. Gentleman accept that the Iraqis and millions of Arabs across the area who agree with them have a point of view and that it might be useful to sit down and talk about that before the place goes up in flames and our young men and many hundreds and thousands of others are killed?

After the US-led coalition had started to bomb Iraq, Galloway argued that it was the Iraqi people who were suffering:

> In so far as Saddam Hussein is a brutal dictator, does it not follow that his own people are by definition his victims, just as much as the hostages and the people of Kuwait? Does it not give the Prime Minister a moment's pause for thought that those are the very people who, as we speak, are being dragged dead and mutilated out of the rubble of the centre of Baghdad?[17]

On 15 March 1991 he emphasised again in the chamber that he was anti-Saddam:

> There are those of us, such as myself, who have been Saddam Hussein's bitter opponents for as long as he has been in power in Baghdad. There are people, such as myself, who have marched, petitioned, written, railed and ranted at the dictatorship in Baghdad, and it is bitterly difficult for us to see the attitude of those Conservative members who did not want to hear what we were saying and who wanted to say little and do even less about the bestialities that were committed by the dictatorship in Baghdad. For them, the dictatorship was merely a bloody good customer. That is the truth of the matter . . . No one ever argued that force against a dictator such as Saddam Hussein was not justified. We argued whether such force was wise and whether the cost of the use of that massive force would outweigh the good that it would do . . . The liberation of Kuwait was not achieved at the cost of only a handful of lives.[18]

Galloway's strident opposition to the US and British policies on Iraq hardened and became more focused with the awful impact of sanctions. When George Bush Senior ordered a Cruise missile attack on Iraq in January 1993, Galloway made a telling prediction for the country in the Commons:

> The radicalisation and Islamicisation that is occurring across the Arab area and the broader Muslim world will be greatly intensified by what will be regarded as Western double standards, whereby the West is ready, at a moment's notice, to pulverise Iraq, but unable, over decades, to do anything about Israel's rejecting and ignoring international law and international standards, or to do anything to save the lives of the tens of thousands of Bosnian Muslims who have died in the current campaign in former Yugoslavia. Is not the Secretary of State aware that, across the Arab world, Saddam Hussein has been made into a hero by those double standards, and that the blunder and crime that was committed this evening will come back to haunt us in years to come?[19]

On 13 December 1993 Galloway announced in Parliament that he was going back to Iraq to find out more about the state of the country under the UN sanctions:

> I visited Iraq in May. In a couple of weeks, I am going with Ahmed Ben Bella, the former Algerian leader, Mr Ramsey Clark, the former United States Attorney General, and members of Parliament from France, Greece and elsewhere on a mission to study further the devastating impact that the war, its aftermath and the economic embargo and blockade are having on the people of Iraq . . . We visited hospitals where there was no medicine and no spare parts for the medical equipment. There was no electricity for operations and women were having caesarean sections without anaesthetic because none was available . . . The minister knows about the tremendous increase in marasmus, kwashiorkor and malnutrition of all kinds, as well as in polio and cholera, which is a result of the poisoned water that Iraqis in urban and rural communities have to use. Iraq is a developed country which is being de-developed by the United Nations with our participation, using our funds to support the United Nations' effort.[20]

So Galloway went off to Iraq again, this time paid for by the International Campaign Against the Embargo,[21] a body largely financed by Greek trade unions and the governing Greek Pasok party. It was the trip that put him in front of Saddam, to utter the immortal 'Sir, I salute your courage, your strength, your indefatigability . . .' address. George Galloway was finally at the centre of the world stage.

16

MP for Kelvin

'I believe that if George Galloway stood for election in any Arab country, whether for the Presidency or as an MP, he would win.' These are the words of Sabbah Al Mukhtar, a UK-based Iraqi lawyer, who helped set up the Mariam Appeal with Galloway.

Galloway's trip to Iraq in January 1994 raised his profile enormously in the country itself, and around the Arab world. Since then he has become a familiar face from appearances on Aljazeera, Abu Dhabi television, Syrian television and all the other major stations across the region. His greeting to Saddam certainly raised his profile in Britain too. The Labour Party hierarchy was unimpressed and when Galloway got back he was closely questioned by them.

The whips and some other Labour MPs were also annoyed because he'd missed a couple of votes, something that has often been raised with Galloway. His attendance in the chamber to vote in 2006 was 'well below average amongst MPs', according to the Westminster monitoring organisation They Work for You.[1] In 2006 he only attended 16 per cent of the votes and only spoke in four debates, but he has complained that the Speaker doesn't come to him, and he doesn't have to vote if he 'pairs up' with another MP.

Galloway has spent a lot of his career since then defending his stance on Iraq and on Saddam. He has been accused of being anti-American, rather than pro-Iraq, and in his Senate appearance took great delight in pointing out that he had met Saddam just as often as the US hawk Donald Rumsfeld, who met the dictator in 1983 and 1984. The subject can bring out strange reactions from him. For example, on the BBC discussion programme *Dinner with Portillo*, Galloway replied to the insinuation that he was anti-American by bragging: 'I'm not anti-American. I'm a world authority on the American Bob Dylan.'[2] A liking for Bob Dylan, a notable critic of US policy down the years and someone who many Americans might cite as hardly the most obvious example of pro-Americanism, is no proof of not being anti-American. Interestingly, according to his friend Ron McKay, Galloway knows everything there is to know about Dylan and may well be a world authority, though it is an odd boast. However, he may have had the opportunity to show this knowledge when he was lined up to be on the prestigious BBC TV show *Celebrity Mastermind* with Dylan as one of his specialist subjects. In the end his appearance was cancelled.

In the summer of 2004, Galloway was contracted by the BBC and a fee agreed. He was all set to be grilled by John Humphrys on the history of the Labour Party. As the October studio record dates and also his libel trial with *The Daily Telegraph* approached (see Chapter 19), he claims he then received a phone call from the production team querying the subject, so he volunteered to take the life and work of Dylan instead. After some discussion, the BBC eventually came back to him and said that his appearance had been cancelled. A BBC spokesperson confirmed for this biography:

> George Galloway was initially considered to appear as a contestant on *Celebrity Mastermind*. Closer to the recording, the production team looked at the mix of guests and there were a number of politicians already confirmed to appear. As it is important to get the right balance of guests for an entertainment show, a decision was taken to stand down Mr Galloway.

Despite not appearing on the programme, Galloway was paid anyway, as their statement goes on to explain: 'With any programme, when a celebrity has been booked and they are stood down at a later date, it is only fair to honour the contract and pay them for their time, which is standard procedure.' Though Galloway was disappointed not to be on *Celebrity Mastermind*, he had far more important things to deal with than have to revise his knowledge of Bob Dylan. By this stage in his career, he was terminally at odds with the Labour hierarchy.

The falling out with Labour in 1994 over his meeting with Saddam was just a taste of things to come. In the end his comments over the invasion of Iraq would get him expelled from the party, but he would also spend his remaining years in New Labour as an intermittent critic of Blair and Brown over their economic and social policies. For instance, he was in favour of keeping Clause 4 of the Labour Party constitution and fell out further with members of Labour's up and coming new blood as a consequence. 'That's when he fell out with John Reid, who wanted change and helped deliver the UNISON vote,' remembers Dave Stark, Galloway's election agent. Stark was Galloway's right-hand man from the TGWU, which opposed change, along with the GMB union. 'George and the Euro MP Alex Falconer spoke against changing Clause 4 at the Scottish annual conference in Perth. It was one of his best conference performances.'

After Tony Blair had won the nail-biting vote to change Clause 4 of their constitution, unburdening Labour of the commitment to government ownership of the means of production, the traditional left of the party needed to regroup. In August 1995 Galloway joined others from the Labour Party in Scotland in their Campaign for Socialism, to fight for a left agenda. 'We lost the Clause Four battle but we are far from losing the war against the idea that there is no other way to run our society than the rotten and corrupt way of capitalism,' he told the *Glasgow Herald*.[3]

At the Camp for Socialism conference organised by Glasgow councillor Bill Butler, Galloway nailed his anti-New Labour colours more firmly to the mast. Like others on the left of the party, he was highly critical of centralised policy making: 'Tony Blair has to realise that policy is made by the Labour Party conference, not by the issuing of press releases.' In the *New Statesman* of August 1995 two of Galloway's close allies, Falkirk West MP Dennis Canavan and Birmingham Northfield MP Richard Burden, called Blair a democratic centralist, a charge normally levied at those who ran Scotland's Labour politics. In the same edition Galloway himself set out his grounds for battle with New Labour, or at least set out his own agenda. He wanted a minimum wage at 50 per cent of the adult median wage, which would have been £4.15 per hour at the time. He also wanted a commitment to full employment, even if that might be at the cost of inflation, which he saw as a price worth paying to bring two million off the dole. And he also wanted to see comprehensive education defended and an end to the NHS internal market and the legions of associated bureaucrats.

At the same time as laying out his socialist credentials, on 8 December 1993 Galloway formed a company called Glassable Enterprises Ltd,[4] which became Hawk Communications Ltd on 1 March 1994, and four weeks later was renamed Hawk Communications International Ltd. According to Galloway's House of Commons Register of Interests, the company was formed 'to assist democratic development in the Middle East and the Indian Sub-Continent'. It was intended that it might help organisations such as the Palestinian Authority to better their links with trade unions and political organisations. In January 1994 Galloway registered that he had an unpaid consultancy in Glassable/Hawk, prior to becoming a director and shareholder later that year.

The company failed to file accounts for a couple of years. Then, on 14 December 1995, Hawk Communications' solicitors filed dormant company accounts (because the company had not been active) with Companies House and indicated that the company was being closed down. Companies House now lists it as dissolved on 26 November 1996. Galloway claimed a few years later that the company never served any function and was wound up because the Middle East peace process ran into difficulties. Though the Oslo declaration of September 1993 had raised hopes of a more peaceful era, these had been dashed when Yitzhak Rabin was assassinated in November 1995. When the House of Commons Standards and Privileges Committee looked into the company in 1997, they agreed that it had never traded.

There were quite a few people involved in the company at various times, though. Basem El Masry, a Palestinian from the Diplofoundation, an international organisation to promote the use of new technology in diplomacy for poorer nations, held the posts of director and secretary from 21 December 1993 to July 1995. Another company was listed as a director initially, a way of getting advice as a start-up. Interestingly, when the *Scotsman* looked into this company, Instant Companies Ltd of Bristol, they found that it 'specialises in channelling profits from offshore companies into foreign tax havens. In its publicity material it entices potential clients with the offer to transfer import/export profits to offshore jurisdictions where the tax rate is 'lower or nil'.

A few others were involved in Hawk. In January 1994 Lynda Ann Pettifor, a Labour activist, joined as director, followed by the then Glasgow councillor and former Pakistani People's Party activist Mohammed Sarwar in May 1994. He joined to help build relations with India and Pakistan. That same month Galloway's girlfriend, Amineh Abu Zayyad, a Palestinian biologist, became a director too.

Hawk seemed to have prospects, but nothing came of them. For example, the *Financial Times* of 26 August 1995 ran a feature that gave it some good publicity. Their reporter James Henderson went with Galloway to Jericho, Gaza and the West Bank, and at the end of the report it gave a good plug, as follows: 'Tamara Travel (tel. 0171-724 1666) and George Galloway's Hawk Communication work together to arrange a variety of trips to "Occupied Palestine" and the Middle East.' Henderson is now a travel writer who specialises in the Caribbean, but back in the mid-1990s he freelanced all over the globe and had sold the idea to the *FT* of covering this interesting holiday package. He remembers that Galloway was mentioned by Tamara Travel from the start and that Galloway himself seemed to have had a big hand in the itinerary. Though Galloway wasn't exactly the tour leader, he was there on the week-long trip to give comments and chat about the political issues to the tourists. Galloway was not with the tourists all the time, as they had half-days here and there by themselves, but he was clearly a major part of the whole package. 'We went to the Gaza Strip, to Jerusalem, Tel Aviv and also drove past a refugee camp. That was shocking, because people had been living in makeshift huts for thirty years. We were advised not to go in, and in fact a few rocks were thrown at us as we drove past,' says Henderson.

Of course, this was a very illuminating trip for those interested in the plight of the Palestinians, but one wonders what Galloway was thinking of, spending days with a small group of tourists, when MPs are normally using their precious time trying to influence millions via TV, or persuade world leaders behind closed doors.

Hawk Communications, or Hawk Communications International, may just have faded into obscurity, but it became the subject of a complaint to the Parliamentary Standards Committee by the Tory MP Charles Hendry in 1996. The complaint wasn't upheld, but it is interesting to follow what happened. All the details are on the House of Commons website.[5] The complaint is described thus:

In a letter dated 22 May 1996 Mr Charles Hendry made a formal complaint alleging that Mr George Galloway failed to declare a relevant interest during an Adjournment Debate speech on 24 January. The debate was on Saudi Arabia and, at the time, Mr Galloway had an entry in the Register of Members' Interests as a director of Hawk Communications International Ltd – described as a communications company established 'to assist democratic development in the Middle East and the Indian Sub-Continent'.

The background to the complaint was that Galloway had been helping a Saudi opposition group, based in London, called the Committee for the Defence of Legitimate Rights. CDLR is run by the Saudi dissidents Dr Saad Al Fagih, and Professor Muhammed Al Mass'ari. Al Mass'ari fled to the UK in 1994, after being held and tortured by the Saudi secret service. The CDLR is an Islamic pressure group, fighting to remove the Saudi government and in 1995 Galloway had organised a speaking tour for Al Mass'ari and was paid around £5,000 for expenses incurred in booking venues and organising a House of Commons reception.

The committee's final report continued:

> Although Mr Al Mass'ari refers to payments to Mr Galloway of around £1,000 a month, he repeatedly maintains that this was to cover costs and not to provide any personal gain. Among the costs referred to are the services of a bodyguard and a part-time secretary, hotel bills, a lunch at the House of Commons, travel and advertising material. He also made it clear that the financial arrangements were wholly or largely in the hands of Dr Saad Al Fagih, who has separately confirmed that no personal reward was involved.

The report concluded:

> I do not believe that the evidence in support of the complaint is sufficient to validate the allegation that there has been a breach of the rules of disclosure. Indeed I have no grounds for challenging Mr Galloway's own version of events and I recommend that the Committee should find accordingly. I have discussed these findings with Mr Galloway, who agrees with the facts and the balance of presentation.

Although the main allegations were successfully refuted, Galloway was criticised for acting as a 'financial intermediary'. In its draft report of March 1997, which refers to the use of credit cards and 'incomplete evidence', and which can also be read in full on the House of Commons website, the committee stated:

> Mr Galloway's relationship with the CDLR was as an individual rather than through Hawk Communications. He described his role as attempting to 'professionalise' the operation of the CDLR by providing advice on effective campaigning, identifying professionals whose services would assist in this, finding administrative staff, organising travel and accommodation around the UK, advising on publications and, in two cases, negotiating the provision of research by academics.
>
> Mr Galloway strenuously maintained throughout his evidence that he received no taxable, nor registrable, benefit from or for any of these actions. He also told us that many of the payments were made directly by Dr Al Fagih, who was 'in sole charge of the organisation's financial affairs' although he also made some payments directly. Mr Galloway provided evidence that he paid for some of the services using his credit card and he gave us copies of some of the bills he had paid by cheque. He said that the credit card statement and the bills represented the sum total of the payments he had made and that he was reimbursed for this expenditure by Dr Al Fagih in cash. On two occasions he had acted as an intermediary for Dr Al Fagih in making cash payments to academics for reports they had written for the CDLR. Mr Galloway did not keep a record of the payments made to him. He told us: 'I had no reason to keep records of the reimbursements because I was not requiring them for income tax or any other purpose,' and: 'There is no record of them reimbursing me.' Nor did he hold out any hope of such a record being available from Dr Al Fagih. To this extent the evidence before us is incomplete.
>
> We note that Mr Galloway accepted that 'the regime which obtains now in the House is different from and better than that which obtained' at the time he was acting as the CDLR's intermediary in the provision of services and that 'it would certainly have been better not if I had kept better accounts, but if I had had nothing to do with the money at all, that I would have insisted that they open a bank account and that they sent cheques in the post like everyone else. That would have been undoubtedly better . . .'.

It is undesirable for a member of Parliament to act as an intermediary for third parties in such circumstances as those described in this case. In particular it is unacceptable for any member to be involved in recycling cash between third parties . . . It is also highly undesirable for any member to act on behalf of any organisation where no full record is kept of all financial transactions with which the member is associated. It is bound to be susceptible to misinterpretation and risks bringing the House into disrepute. We consider it to be fundamental to the House's system of declaration and registration that whenever a member has a pecuniary relationship with an outside organisation which requires declaration or registration, the member should ensure that this relationship is adequately documented.[6]

Galloway's reaction to the Mass'ari/Hawk controversy was to point out in a newspaper article:

Hawk Communications has not existed for a long time and I had no remuneration, no expenses or reward of any kind from the Saudi opposition. I did all that I did and still do because I am determined to help the overthrow of the corrupt Saudi regime, not for any financial reward. Last year the Saudi opposition hired a hall at Westminster, and as the MP sponsoring it I had to pay for the hire . . . They then paid me that money back. Those are the only circumstances in which a single penny changed hands.

Galloway's connections with the Muslim world were not just from over-seas causes. Muslims are the second largest religious group after Christians in the Greater Glasgow area. Although they account for just 2.4 per cent of the total population, they are in far greater numbers in Galloway's old constituency of Hillhead and in the redrawn Kelvin, where ethnic minorities as a whole form over 7 per cent of the total. Dealing with the concerns of his Asian constituents took up an increasing amount of time for Galloway and seemed a natural progression from his established knowledge of the issues of the Middle East and Pakistan. Dave Stark remembers: 'He often spoke at the Glasgow Central Mosque. We had great meetings there, and always got a good curry afterwards.'

Many Asians in the UK are great football lovers but they have felt alienated from the culture of football, and Galloway's Asian constituents were no exception. This has something to do with its history of nationalistic thuggery, but also there have been few examples of Asian players, managers or owners to show the way. But with growing economic power, it would seem only a matter of time until a football club became Asian owned and for a fleeting moment it looked as though Galloway was going to be involved.

Partick Thistle, 'The Jags', is one of the best-known teams in Scottish football. It was formed in 1876 and is the local team for Kelvin. In August 1995 there were numerous press reports that Galloway was attempting to take it over as part of a consortium of Asian businessmen.[7] The 1994–5 season had not been good and they were struggling on and off the pitch (the following season they were relegated from the Premier Division to Division One). The club had debts that were threatening to put it out of business completely. At the beginning of the new season, in late August, it was reported that Partick's chairman, Jim Oliver, took a phone call from Ron McKay, who explained that there might be a bid for the club that would help them out of their mess and that he ought to meet with the interested parties.

The following day, 25 August 1995, the *Glasgow Herald* reported details of a 'working lunch' to discuss the possible creation of a consortium of Asian businessmen, which would buy the club and bring money and new blood to Partick. The report continued that the meeting was attended by a local restaurant owner called Charan Gill, Galloway, McKay and Imran Muneer, the editor of the *Scottish Asian Voice* newspaper. The *Herald* piece said that the deal would all be in place by the end of the following week and that they had a good idea of what the price should be. When Galloway was asked later for his comments he was reported in the *Herald* as saying: 'We can provide a shot in the arm: Asian capital, Asian entrepreneurship and Asian interest in the sport, including through the gates.'

Despite the fact that no bid had been received and that the club was not for sale, according to the man who owned and ran it, a deal was still being talked of as though it was a possibility. Meanwhile, the partners in this increasingly odd enterprise were not happy. Gill, now an MBE and owner of the largest chain of Indian restaurants in Europe, announced that he was not interested in taking any further part. A little later that day, Galloway called a press conference and said he and McKay were pulling out, but wished everyone involved good luck. There was no mention of the fact that Gill had already withdrawn. So that was it: the consortium was finished, the 'bid' was off.

The effect on Galloway's standing among the locals is hard to gauge, but Stark, who was a season ticket holder, remembers taking Galloway to a game around this time: 'George went up to get the pies at half-time and I remember he had a bit of a *tête-à-tête* with one of the supporters who wasn't too pleased.' Glasgow journalist Dave King puts it all down to Galloway's impetuosity: 'I don't think he was ever particularly serious about that. It was just another one of his brainwaves. "Let's go along with it and see what happens." '

The Partick Thistle saga had been just a little light relief compared to other far more serious issues on the go at the time, which included the crucial question of whether Galloway would have a constituency or not at the next election. Gradually, he was gaining the support he needed to get selected to be Labour's candidate in the new seat of Glasgow Kelvin. His opponent was a bright young lawyer called Shiona Waldron, at the time a deputy procurator fiscal from Dumbarton and a former member of the breakaway Scottish Labour.

The new constituency was named after the icy river Kelvin and the Scottish scientist Lord Kelvin. Galloway and Waldron were competing for a great opportunity to grasp a far more working-class area than Hillhead. The boundary changes had shunted the middle-class Jordanhill out of the renamed constituency and brought in part of the old Glasgow Central, full of potential Labour voters. Waldron's camp made much of their distaste for what they called Galloway's 'idiosyncratic style'. They pointed up his unpopular meeting with Saddam Hussein and accused him of being preoccupied with international issues.

The way the election worked was that if one candidate got enough votes in the different wards that made up Kelvin, they would go forward as Labour's candidate, but if there was no clear majority of two-thirds or more, the contest would come down to a one member, one vote ballot of all Labour members in Kelvin. Waldron was keen to get to that stage, as she thought she had a good chance if union block voting didn't play a part. In early November 1995 the wards had their meetings and Galloway won

Scotstoun/Broomhill and Kelvin West, but lost Hyndland/Hillhead and the women's section. There was no clear majority, but despite protesting to the national party organisers, Waldron was unable to get the ballot she felt entitled to.

The labyrinthine workings of the Labour Party had kicked in again at this stage and the Kelvin General Management Committee (GMC) decided that a full ballot wasn't necessary because of another rule that stated that a sitting MP could be selected by a committee vote. Although this was a new seat, Galloway was ruled to be technically the sitting MP. Yet again, the party rules had worked against a strong female challenger and on 19 November the GMC voted by twenty-six to twelve to recommend him as the sole nominee on the candidates' shortlist. Galloway was safe, home, dry, and certain to become the MP for Glasgow Kelvin.

One of many British Pakistanis that Galloway calls a friend is Mohammad Sarwar, elected MP for Govan in the 1997 Labour landslide and Britain's first Muslim MP. Galloway's links to Pakistan and British Pakistanis are complex and fascinating. He counts Benazir Bhutto, twice Prime Minister of Pakistan, as a friend and has strong relationships not just with his old constituents in Glasgow, but all over the UK. So close is he to Bhutto that in 1990 she awarded him the country's highest civil honour, the Hilal-e-Quaid Azam award, for his services to Pakistani democracy. There is no doubt that Galloway is an iconic figure for Pakistanis, Bangladeshis and Muslims in general across the country, seen largely as a lone figure expressing their views in Parliament. It's a remarkable phenomenon for a white Scot of Irish ancestry.

Pakistani politics is a treacherous arena and Galloway had upset some when he called President Muhammad Zia-ul-Haq a hangman on his death in 1988. (Zia had hanged Benazir's father, Zufiqar Ali Bhutto, who had been President and Prime Minister of Pakistan; see p. 179.) Over the years Galloway has made no bones about the fact that he is a fan of the Bhuttos, who claim they have been persecuted by the succession of military hard men who have run the country. In 1990 he questioned Margaret Thatcher over security for Benazir Bhutto during the Pakistan elections, after Bhutto had been dismissed as Prime Minister after just twenty months in the job, under what many observers considered to be trumped-up corruption charges.

So, in 1996, when Galloway announced he was setting up a newspaper aimed at the Asian public in the UK, it seemed to be a natural step for all concerned. The paper was called *East* and was run from an office above a Chinese restaurant in Tooley Street, south London. The editor was Nadene Khan Gouri, who now works for the BBC, but the power behind the throne was Ron McKay, now Galloway's spokesman and the former editor of the *Dundee Standard* (see Chapter 5). Galloway and McKay were directors of the company Asian Voice Ltd, which owned *East*, and another partner in the enterprise was the Pakistani diplomat Wajid Hasan. Galloway listed Asian Voice in his House of Commons Register of Interests as a company from which he earned money for media work. The funding for the paper was in part from the government of Benazir Bhutto, which was not referred to in the House of Commons Register of Interests.

Saeed Shah, a journalist on the paper who now works for the *Independent*, remembers one of his first jobs in the media as unconventional:

> One of the sub-editors was a chap called Stuart Christie, who'd been in the Angry Brigade and claimed he'd tried to blow up General Franco . . . Galloway used to bring Middle Eastern businessmen and his friends in and show them round the office, but he didn't talk to us much. He was flamboyant and charming.

The paper was aimed at the professional Asian market, but there seemed to be a problem with distribution and though it was supposed to be available in corner shops across the country, Shah remembers that it was almost invisible. 'The distribution was dreadful. It just wasn't available anywhere. It was supposed to be in shops, but I never saw any. We needed to have business managers, but there weren't any.'

East seemed unconventional to some of its key editorial staff. Nadene Khan Gouri claimed to the BBC that she had waited for her salary to arrive, but that her first wages were paid in cash.[8] 'A courier turned up at the door with £2000 in cash . . . I called George's secretary and said "What's this?" She said, "That's your wages".'

They also had an unconventional ad campaign. And the best thing that could have happened to it did happen. In November 1996 their controversial poster got banned, giving them even more publicity. The problem was that it showed a turbaned Asian youngster kicking a white skinhead between the legs under the banner 'The East Fights Back'. When it was referred to the Committee for Advertising Practice, it ruled that it breached four clauses of its code of conduct, including ones about race and the encouragement of violence. Though Galloway described the poster as 'tongue in cheek' and was reported denying that it would make Asian youths go out and beat up skinheads, the Commission for Racial Equality said it thought the ad might 'provoke racial disharmony'. In the end the poster was reshot and the final version featured an Asian woman wearing Dr Marten boots under traditional dress, walking along with a bulldog on a leash.

And that was about as high profile as *East* got, with one exception. With the benefit of hindsight, we can see that *East*'s real moment of glory came when they scooped an interview with the then hardly known Islamic terrorist Osama bin Laden. No-one on the paper knew anything about it and, according to Shah, 'it just appeared in the paper'.

The paper came out weekly, for six months, and McKay spent one or two days a week in the office, but was based in Glasgow. *East*'s main competition was *Eastern Eye*, a more downmarket publication, so there may have been a gap in the market. It is notoriously difficult to start a paper from scratch, but Galloway had got it right by finding good backing. The trouble was that as soon as *East* started, Benazir Bhutto was booted out of government for the second time. It amounted to a coup and it threw everything up in the air at the newspaper. Remarkably though, this important news story for *East*'s target audience was only covered very briefly on the publication's page 11, although they did run an opinion piece by Galloway. Nadene Gouri told the BBC that Galloway had called her to give his opinion that the story wasn't to be covered at all, but she insisted.[9]

After Bhutto's removal from office, Shah remembers that the money soon dried up. 'One morning in 1997, most of the staff were sacked by phone. We got no redundancy, which seemed ironic.' Shah and Gouri called in the National Union of Journalists' in-house lawyer and took action against Asian Voice. They got their money in the end.

The paper wasn't quite dead by then, but it was in debt and had to move to cheaper offices off London's North Circular Road. Galloway meanwhile was trying to raise money and in May 1997 he wrote to the Prime Minister of Pakistan, Nawaz Sharif, asking for money. The letter, written on House of Commons notepaper, was addressed to Sharif personally and asked for £150,000. It read:

Your Excellency, Dear Prime Minister,

Alas I must draw your attention to a critical issue which risks gravely embarrassing Pakistan and Labour on the threshold of a new victory. The government of Pakistan – in the shape of the then Foreign Secretary – promised to pay the costs for February, March and April, totalling £150,000. None of these instalments arrived. Consequently, I now face creditors to the tune of £141,000. Now that Parliament is back, they are literally coming through my door at Westminster demanding money. My dear Prime Minister, if these creditors are not paid, they will take me to court on a winding up petition. This level of debts cannot be quietly forgotten. Events thereafter would be disastrous for me, probably your best friend in the new Parliament, and would badly damage the reputation of Pakistan.

I beg you, Sir, to please instruct the high commission in London to honour the country's commitments. There are literally, only days to spare.

This letter would later come back to haunt Galloway when the BBC's *Newsnight* got hold of a copy,[10] as well as some cheques made out to Asian Voice Ltd. In a heated exchange by telephone, the *Newsnight* journalist Richard Watson was confronted by McKay, who was recorded saying he would come and see him and 'fill him in', which was later claimed to refer to giving Watson more information. *Newsnight* claimed they had a copy of a cheque for £135,000 made out to Asian Voice. The programme also had an interview with a Pakistani official who claimed that the Pakistan government had also agreed to pay a further £189,000 to keep the paper going until the next election. After the transmission, Galloway made it abundantly clear that he had received no personal financial benefit, and dismissed the programme as 'a farrago of distortion, half truths and innuendo . . . The paper never promised to follow the line of the Pakistani People's Party and as even this programme had to concede, it never did so.'

These minor controversies didn't affect Galloway's popularity and when it came to the 1997 general election, he ran away with victory in Kelvin, amassing 16,643 votes, 51 per cent of the total. The SNP came in next with 21.4 per cent, followed by the Liberal Democrats on 14 per cent and the Conservatives with just 10.8 per cent. The Boundary Commission had created a very attractive Labour stronghold for anyone lucky enough to get selected to stand. In the UK as a whole it turned out to be a famous landslide for Labour, though when they got in and took on the spending plans of Kenneth Clarke, the outgoing Tory Chancellor, some on the left wondered which party they were now in. Galloway was one of them. In the Scottish Catholic paper *Flourish* he described the plans of his old enemy Brown, now Chancellor, to cap spending limits in the first two years as 'not acceptable' and declared that 'every Labour MP I have spoken to feels the same'. The Tories' Alan Duncan took this small crumb of divisive comfort and replied that this would be 'the first of many Exocets from Labour backbenchers which would sink the Labour ship within minutes'.

17

The Mariam Appeal

One little girl with leukaemia came to symbolise both the cruel impact of the UN sanctions on Iraqis and the serious allegations of corruption that swallowed up the UN's oil-for-food programme. Mariam Hamza, a four-year-old Iraqi girl, had been discovered in a Baghdad hospital by George Galloway and Ron McKay in March 1998, and they picked her to represent all Iraqi children, whose medical treatment was being seriously undermined by the sanctions. It's a very effective technique that tabloid journalists have used for generations.

Galloway and McKay came back to the UK with an experienced charity worker, Stuart Halford, and started up the Mariam Appeal, which raised enough funds to pay for Mariam to be flown from Iraq to Scotland to receive cancer treatment. But the appeal was also used to fund a wider political campaign and would become the centre of allegations levelled against Galloway and others involved, none of which has been substantiated in any way. When he stood and fought those claims in his dramatic appearance in the US Senate, the affair shot him to world political superstar status.

How the two men came to visit that particular hospital and choose Mariam probably came down to a passing comment by the journalist Felicity Arbuthnot, a friend of Galloway who is so well connected that she has sometimes been involved in negotiations to release hostages in the region. She says:

> I'd left the day before he arrived. I thought I could never be shocked but I'd been round a hospital and left a message for George saying, whatever else you do, go to this hospital. Mariam was designed for maximum publicity, but you'd save one life if you could . . . George said Mariam was the first child from the first bed in the first hospital he saw.

Arbuthnot was a tireless campaigner against sanctions and would later help in the Mariam Appeal. 'Before the sanctions, people would go to Iraq for health care from Kuwait. By 2000, the UNICEF *State of the World's Children* report listed Iraq below Malawi.'

McKay has stated that immediately after seeing Mariam and the other children in the ward, he and Galloway were both on the verge of tears and 'George said, "We have to do something about that." '[1] Mariam was not just an example of the effect of sanctions, she was also an example of the consequences of the allies' use of nuclear arms in the First Gulf War. She came from the south of Iraq and probably contracted leukaemia through the radiation from the uranium-tipped weapons used by the allies in that war.

Before this particular trip to Iraq, there had been talk among Galloway's circle of how best to put across the case against sanctions. The group called themselves the Emergency Committee on Iraq, and it included Iraqi expatriates such as Dr Mudafar Amin, Sabbah Al Mukhtar and Burhan Al Chalabi. Amin was a representative of the Iraqi government, Al Chalabi was the chairman of a pressure group called the British Iraqi Foundation, and Al Mukhtar is president of the Arab Lawyers Association. When Galloway came back from his trip to Iraq with the plan of bringing Mariam over, they agreed that it would be a great idea.

The day before he first saw Mariam Hamza in mid-March 1998, Galloway had told reporters that the sanctions were a crime against humanity. When he returned to the UK it was reported that he applied to the Department of Trade and Industry to get permission for a humanitarian flight to bring Mariam back and to the Foreign Office for her visa. Then on 8 April Galloway and McKay went back to Baghdad and two days later, on Good Friday, visited her in hospital, where pictures were taken and later appeared in the press. A week later Galloway told the *Scotsman*: 'I want Mariam to be a focus for the suffering of all the children in her position.'

When telling the story of Mariam's journey to the UK and the raising of the money for the medical care, McKay makes it sound like quite a risky financial enterprise. In an interview with me in November 2005, he said:

> We hadn't any way of paying for that and obviously it would have to be done privately. He was asked by the hospital in Glasgow for sick kids who was going

to pay for it and straightaway he said he pledged to pay for it. The bills came to over £70,000 and she was in the country for about six months being treated.

The funding of the Mariam Appeal would later become the subject of conjecture and speculation, driven by Galloway's political opponents and made more complicated by the fact that it was not a charity, and when its accounts were taken to Jordan, there was no legal power to get them back. Galloway's friends maintain that they did look into registering it as a charity. Al Mukhtar remembers the discussion of exactly how the appeal should be run:

> I advised that it should have a constitution, regulatory body and members. We discussed the issue of whether it should be a charity at length to start with. I advised to set it up as an incorporated body, a bit like a neighbourhood watch or something like that. Others thought we should register it as a charity. But I knew we wouldn't be able to. At that time, the Charity Commission would not have registered it, as it didn't fall within their categories of homeless, education, religion or assistance to the poor. At that time, even Amnesty wasn't registered as a charity until they changed the rules in 2003/4.

There are several names which crop up in relation to the Mariam Appeal, but the key one is Fawaz Zureikat. This Jordanian businessman had been a close friend of Galloway's second wife, Amineh Abu Zayyad. Zureikat donated several sums of money to the Mariam Appeal and also traded in Iraqi oil options (see Chapter 21). Zureikat was very well known to the media and to Western governments, and has never made any secret of his oil dealings. His success as a businessman prior to the sanctions has been questioned by some, including Riad Al Tahir, who recalled: 'Originally he was a small contractor, not doing much. He had made enquiries to the Iraqi government about small contracts. If you're dealing with 5,000 barrels and then you go to millions, it makes a great deal of difference.'

Although Zureikat has been described by the Senate as a rather mysterious figure, McKay observes that he was well known in Iraq, and had good contacts:

The BBC, Jon Snow, Channel 4, they all know him so the idea of him being shadowy is preposterous . . . He traded with the old regime, as many, many people did. He traded the oil-for-food programme. He was a representative of French and American companies, in Jordan and in Iraq, so he was a big and very well-known businessman.

Without access to the appeal's accounts it is impossible to ascertain all the funding details, but according to McKay,

very little came from the British public. It all had to be done in a hurry, obviously, but very little came from the British public. The principal bulk of the funding came from the now deceased ruler of the UAE, the present King of Saudi Arabia and a Jordanian businessman. That would be about 90-odd per cent of the funding and it was about in the region of £1 million that was raised.

When the US Senate Permanent Subcommittee on Investigations looked into the funding of the Mariam Appeal, it stated in its report of 25 October 2005 that the major donor was the government of Abu Dhabi:

Over the life of the Mariam Appeal, approximately £756,116 was deposited into the Mariam Appeal account at Lloyds, and approximately £622,693 was deposited into the Mariam Appeal account at National Bank of Abu Dhabi, amounting to a total of £1,378,810 (over $2.4 million) in deposits. The deposits made by the government of Abu Dhabi accounted for approximately 37 per cent of all deposits made to Mariam Appeal accounts, making it the largest 'donor' to the Mariam Appeal. Zureikat's total deposits account for approximately 33 per cent of all deposits into the Mariam Appeal accounts, making Zureikat the second largest 'donor' to the Mariam Appeal. Other major deposits into the two Mariam Appeal bank accounts include those made by the Royal Embassy of Saudi Arabia (£20,000), Wajed Hakem Sultan (approximately £50,000) and an anonymous deposit from 'one of our clients' (£33,475.21). Galloway identified the Saudi Arabian donor as Crown Prince Abdullah bin Abdulaziz al-Saud.[2]

So the Mariam Appeal was well funded throughout its short life and it got off to a great start with sustained press interest when Galloway returned with the little girl to take her to hospital. It only intensified when it proved impossible to get her into what he described as 'the best cancer hospital in the UK' and she had to be taken to Glasgow's Royal Hospital for Sick Children. Once there, she had private chemotherapy and was cured of her cancer eventually, though she also went on to have treatment in the United States in August 2000. Tragically, when she returned to Iraq they tried to carry on the treatment and she was blinded by an overdose of chemotherapy, but she is alive and, according to Galloway, is now quite healthy.

The Mariam Appeal was just one aspect of the campaigns organised against sanctions. It was connected to a wider collective known as the Great Britain–Iraq Society (GBIS), which held its first meeting on Monday 26 June 2000 in the Grand Committee Room at the House of Commons. Galloway was joined by Tam Dalyell and Scott Ritter, the former lead inspector for UNSCOM's Concealment and Investigations Unit. Ritter had spent years trying to find Saddam's weapons of mass destruction, only to become disillusioned with the meddling of the politicians. He had the sort of in-depth knowledge that they needed, but it perhaps was a controversial move to invite him.

The group considered what its priorities should be and the consensus was that getting the sanctions against Iraq lifted was number one. The fact that Ritter was adamant that Saddam no longer had any weapons of mass destruction, or the capability to make them, bolstered everyone's feeling that this was the battle they must fight. Ritter proposed that weapons inspectors should go to Iraq to confirm the country's disarmament and monitor its progress, with a long term-goal of bringing Iraq back into the international community. Dalyell recounted that Tariq Aziz had told him on the trip the previous December: 'You may think that Saddam Hussein and I are extremists but that is nothing compared to what will follow if the current situation isn't rectified.'

It was decided that the GBIS would publish a newsletter, organise exchange visits and trade missions, and generally help forge links between Great Britain and Iraq. Members paid £25 subscription and the day-to-day running of the society would be taken on by Stuart Halford, at an office in

1 Northumberland Avenue in central London. This was the same address as the Mariam Appeal, of which Halford was also a director and the organiser. According to the House of Commons Register of Members' Interests, within six months of its creation the GBIS had helped fund seven overseas trips for Galloway, to Jordan, Morocco, Lebanon and Ukraine, along with four trips to Iraq.

Lawyer Sabbah Al Mukhtar, of the GBIS, set up the Mariam Appeal. He says: 'I produced the constitution, opened the bank account in Abu Dhabi and at Lloyds; I was a signatory to the account. Then, thereafter, my roles became less.'

It was reported that Galloway sent out letters to prospective supporters, an early one of which read: 'The Mariam Appeal has had to guarantee the costs of her treatment which could be up to £50,000. The appeal's target is £100,000 with the balance being sent back to Iraq in medicines and medical supplies for the children she has had to leave behind.'[3] Her medical treatment ended up being more expensive than that, probably in the region of £70,000 in the UK, plus some American and other bills on top. However, the total costs of her treatment are a drop in the ocean when you consider that the appeal raised £1,378,810. The vast majority of that money was spent on campaigning, with Galloway himself making fourteen overseas trips between September 1999 and January 2002. He visited Jordan, the United Arab Emirates, Lebanon, Hungary, Belgium, the United States and Romania. The various fundings of those trips are set out online in the House of Commons Register of Members' Interests, or on They Work for You's website. The Mariam Appeal and the GBIS provided the majority of the funds, but there were other sponsors too.

The overseas trip that got the most attention kicked off in September 1999 but did not use Galloway's usual form of transport. It used a London Routemaster bus, and it was to travel all the way from London to Baghdad, overland. It took a small amount of anti-cancer drugs for Iraqi children, but its mission was to raise awareness of the impact of the continuing sanctions. And it did a tremendous job of that, through countries including Spain, Morocco, Algeria, and Jordan. Literally millions of Muslims across north Africa met the bus, and scores of millions saw it on television. Although Galloway was a well-known figure before, the trip made him a household name in the region, bigger even than David Beckham. Al Mukhtar says:

> George came up with the idea; he said we must do something to bring
> attention. We thought of the London double-decker, looked into the cost and
> the route. It cost a hell of a lot of money: about £150,000, but Sheikh Zayed,
> then leader of the UAE, donated the entire cost.

On the trip, a small group of activists struggled to get the old bus to limp
its way along. It was an arduous trek, and Galloway hadn't time to be with
the bus the whole way. He would fly into the big cities to meet and greet. Al
Mukhtar recalls:

> He would make speeches along the line of broad Arab federalist ideas. There
> is a cutting from an Arabic newspaper in Tangiers, where he made a speech
> at the port when the bus landed on Moroccan soil; there were about 500
> people there. It read 'the Nasser who came from London', because he was
> effectively saying the things that Nasser used to say, e.g. that Arab countries
> from the ocean to the gulf should be unified; if they were they could be a
> superpower; they had the wealth to be powerful and had more in common
> with each other than the Europeans.

Al Mukhtar remembers that it was a marvellous opportunity for
Galloway, who addressed people in open meetings, in states where freedom
of speech is unheard of.

> He made speeches in dictatorships. In Casablanca there were about 5,000
> people. He called upon the government to give the people of Morocco
> freedom and democracy so that when the government was under pressure
> from the West or its enemies, it would seek the opinion of the public and that
> would make it stronger. An Arab would have been burnt alive.

The culmination of the journey was the arrival in Baghdad, where
millions lined the streets to greet the famous British politician, who they saw
as their voice in the West. Al Mukhtar was overwhelmed: 'I would say that
not the trip itself, but the arrival in Baghdad, is the greatest achievement of

my life. We were going through Baghdad with a million people welcoming us.' The first member of the government to shake Galloway's hand was the Iraqi Foreign Secretary, Tariq Aziz.

Hans von Sponeck was the United Nations' top humanitarian official in Baghdad from mid-1998 to February 2000, when he resigned over the effects of the sanctions on the Iraqi people. He was in Baghdad for the triumphant arrival of the bus.

> George Galloway ran the UK's most prominent counter-initiative. I was based in Baghdad when he arrived in the double-decker bus, and he created a lot of attention. He talked about the wrongdoing of two permanent members of the Security Council, and that was significant. I cannot quantify how much life was saved, but it was an important contribution. There were others – German Physicians Against War, the Austrian Arab Society – but in the UK and US they were voices in the wilderness. The Mariam Appeal was the most successful initiative in western Europe because he was the most outspoken and eloquent in his criticism of double-talk and double standards.

Although the impact of the Mariam Appeal is perhaps hard to quantify, von Sponeck believes Galloway's work was important.

> He was very active in travelling back and forth and challenging a policy that led to the destruction, not the preservation, of life. Peter Hain was there saying that the suffering of Iraqis was totally due to Saddam Hussein. That contradicted the findings of Clare Short in the multi-party committee in 2001. Galloway's contribution was that he verbalised this horrendous violation of humanness.

In later years, when the Mariam Appeal became the subject of investigations on both sides of the Atlantic, the good work that it did in raising awareness of the suffering due to sanctions was inevitably somewhat overshadowed.

Even respected professionals such as von Sponeck found it hard to get a sensible hearing about the conditions in Iraq.

If you started speaking out, you were told to shut up or worse. I tried in the beginning to see Ambassador Greenstock [the UK ambassador to the UN]; he was always kind, they listened, they knew the conditions very well. In the US, if you speak out, you're seen to be in the pockets of Saddam Hussein. I was a UN officer, I wanted to be a bridge builder and help solve conflict. Albright's [Madeleine Albright, the US Secretary of State] staffer, James Rubin, said of me: 'This man is paid to work, not to speak.' We became more and more angry and helpless. I thought, if I continue, I cannot make a difference and I will be part of what happens. I resigned because my side hadn't done what it was meant to under the UN charter.

After the Big Ben-to-Baghdad trip, Galloway remained in Iraq for a few days and had several meetings with officials, including Aziz. He even went to church on Christmas Day with members of the Aziz family, who are Christians. Ziad Aziz, Tariq's son, recalls:

George and my father were just friends. The first time I met him was in Christmas 1999; he'd met with my father when he arrived on the bus . . . I went with him to church on Christmas Day, to the St Mary church in Baghdad where my family went every Sunday. Then he went back to his hotel because he had another meeting.

Ziad is clear in his own mind that Galloway was not a supporter of Saddam, but of Iraq: 'George Galloway supported Iraq, not Saddam Hussein. He worked with my father because of the embargo and the sanctions. He worked for Iraq.'

After the success of the bus trip, they needed further publicity to keep the momentum going. At the time there were no commercial flights from London to Baghdad and the UN sanctions meant that anyone wanting to charter their own plane had to get permission from the UK government and the UN. In March 2000 it was reported that Galloway was refused permission to fly with a group of campaigners, so he instead flew to Amman in Jordan and then drove 600 miles through the desert to Iraq.[4] When he arrived, with a small party of supporters and journalists, a welcoming committee of around fifty met them, holding up placards of Saddam and chanting 'Galloway welcome'. He announced to the assembled crowd: 'We are determined to break the stranglehold the Americans have on the country. One day we will win, because God is great.'

Mark Seddon, the former editor of *Tribune*, was on the trip. He recalls:

> We got to Baghdad via Amman, driving in convoy across the desert. Once in Iraq, we visited schools and hospitals; it was clearly an effort on behalf of the Iraqi government to put forward the case that sanctions were harming people . . . We saw an exhibition in a Basra hospital of the shocking deformities, all laid at the feet of the West because of Desert Storm. But it wasn't clear whether it was depleted uranium or Iraqi dumping, and at the same time, chemicals were used to destroy the marshes so it was impossible to tell what the cause was . . . There was no doubt this was a very nasty regime but sanctions were not the answer. We were aware that the wool was being pulled over our eyes and that the Iraqi regime were presenting a particular picture.

The trip got some minor coverage, but the feeling was that they had to get through the sanctions net and make it from London to Baghdad by air. By November 2000 a group had been assembled who were willing to risk it. Paediatrician Nick Rea, Lord Rea of Eskdale, was one of them. He says:

> I wanted to go and see for myself what the effect of the sanctions on the children of Iraq was. When I got there I was horrified. You see, the problem was that every time a child needed medicine, that case had to be put forward to the UN sanctions people in New York. By the time they had said yes, the child was much worse, or even dead.

Galloway and seven others, including Father Noel Barry, a Catholic priest and former press officer for Cardinal Thomas Winning; Andy Darmoo, an Iraqi-born British businessman; Fawaz Zureikat; Stuart Halford; and a couple of journalists, took a secret flight L2-011 from Manston airport in Kent, ostensibly to a religious conference in Bulgaria, but then went on to Baghdad, via Greek, Cypriot and Syrian air space. Though some reports claimed that they went through the UN no-fly zone to land in Baghdad, that seems an unlikely detour. The flight was perfectly timed to arrive for an international trade fair, full of politicians and businessmen from France, China, Russia, Germany, Belgium and elsewhere, who were all there to try to snap up the contracts to rebuild the country after the Gulf War.

The Foreign Office minister Peter Hain, who had stopped the previous flight, was highly critical when he learned that this one had made it through:

> What these propaganda flights do is give Baghdad a big morale boost, creating the impression that sanctions are being undermined. It also puts off the day when sanctions can be suspended. It's a deeply, deeply irresponsible attitude. He wants to claim that it's a sanction-breaking flight from Britain but the flight was not from Britain.[5]

In reply, Galloway wrote an open letter to the *Independent* on 18 November:

> The flight was bought and paid for in Britain, using a British charter firm, although it is true that it did refuel, necessarily, in Bulgaria. If Mr Hain's ministerial Montego stops for petrol in a Putney service station, does that make it the property of BP? The minister clearly believes so. Hain states that ours was a 'humanitarian' flight. It was not. We carried only passengers and those were dedicated anti-sanctions campaigners . . . his officials knew nothing of the flight and the Department of Trade and Industry did not inspect it. We could have been carrying anything at all, but in fact we carried only our determination and our hand luggage.

Which side benefited in propaganda from Galloway's flight to Iraq is debatable, but there was no disputing that the Mariam Appeal was now the best-known organisation working against the sanctions. And it was expanding its interests. In autumn 2000 it advertised for four full-time brigade co-ordinators, each at a salary of £20,000, who would be spending three months on site in Iraq. The advert said:

> The Mariam Appeal, which campaigns for the lifting of sanctions on Iraq, is sending a series of International Work Brigades to Iraq to build an

International Friendship Village that will be used as a centre for international friendship and solidarity with the people of Iraq. The village will symbolise 'reconciliation through reconstruction' and will upon completion be used by Iraqi children for recuperation, rest, education and play. The project will enable people from all over the world to express solidarity with the people of Iraq, who have suffered grievously under the 10 year embargo. The brigades will perform light construction duties (under the guidance of Iraqi tradesmen), hold discussion and education sessions and enjoy a variety of cultural and social activities.

Interested? Think you have what it takes to organise international brigades? Then please contact us!

The letter was signed by Halford, but had shades of Galloway's style. In the Spanish Civil War, international brigades had come to the aid of the Spanish people, and the Mariam Appeal was invoking their memory to galvanise a new generation of young helpers. It aimed to send around sixty volunteers to the village in Iraq between May and October 2001. These young people were to get themselves to Amman and then be picked up by Mariam Appeal staff and taken to the site, south-west of Baghdad, but difficulties were encountered and the scheme folded.

Galloway was regarded by his colleagues in the old days of the Scottish National Executive Committee as a leading figure, the sort of person you'd look to for an opinion. The Dundee Labour MPs had seen him in that light. All these years later, at the turn of the century, in the very different surroundings of Baghdad, he was still at the leading edge. Hans von Sponeck went, as an observer, to a conference at the Iraqi Foreign Ministry, where a number of delegates from around the world were speaking, including Galloway. He says:

I came away thinking that the right issues were being discussed but I was not comfortable with what the government was trying to do. By this time, I'd already become a liability to the UN in speaking out. It was a very leftist gathering: communists, a few far-left groups and even some right-wing groups. The wife of Le Pen in France was there. It was fanatical, quite extremist . . . George Galloway was the key figure in the whole thing. There

245

were delegations from Cuba, Russia and southern Europe: Spain and Italy. There was no one from central Europe, no Germans or Scandinavians, and Galloway was the climax of the meeting for the foreign delegates . . . When Tariq Aziz came into the room, it was clear where he went first to shake hands, to Galloway.

Galloway was an eloquent talker on this occasion. Von Sponeck continues:

> The meetings were of a poor quality: language was poor, papers were terrible and then Saddam gave the most horrible of speeches. In this circumstance, eloquence has a special niche. Some of those who came to the meetings were genuine, with a concern for the Iraqi people, others were there out of pure economic self-interest, no other interest than getting into the business of things. Like hounds, bloodhounds, trying to get a piece of that Iraqi oil cake. [But] George was highly critical of the government's policies and he called for anti-sanctions measures. He used words that I wasn't comfortable with back then, talking of violations of the genocide convention. In that way, he was ahead of the game. Now I'm much more comfortable with those allegations because I've learned the extent of it; then I thought it was a lack of timely action. He was the one who first spoke of the 'Security Council contributing to the suffering of the Iraqi people'.

Galloway is often seen as wanting to provoke a reaction in his supporters and he loves to discredit the opposition. On 4 November 2000 he stood up in Parliament and named four of the UN's weapons inspectors as Israeli spies. Von Sponeck, who agrees with Galloway's aims to some extent, believes his tactics undermined him in Iraq: 'It was clear that George was considered by the Iraqis as an important player and was given all the freedom that he needed: to get around, to speak to everyone. He spoke at annual anti-sanction meetings . . . He was impressive in giving a powerful voice to those affected by sanctions. From my vantage point of the time, I felt that his closeness could have been misinterpreted, which in fact it was.'

The way Galloway's campaigning has been interpreted, whether against UN sanctions, or for the Palestinians, or against the 'War on Terror', has set him against large sections of the media. His reaction to people asking more searching questions can be unparliamentary, to say the least. This from *The Times*:

> Mr Galloway is keeping secret who paid for his trip to Baghdad last August, when he provided a propaganda coup for Saddam by meeting him and praising Iraqi diplomacy. The MP dodged questions from *The Times* about his foreign expenses. He sent *The Times* an e-mail yesterday stating: 'I regard you as a whore writing for a pimp. The *Sun* is in the sewer, you merely in the gutter; no doubt looking up at the stars (and stripes). Not only will I not speak to you, I feel tainted merely writing to you. Please do not attempt to contact me again.'[6]

There is no other MP in this country who would reply to a question in this extraordinary manner. In fact it's hard to believe that any public figure would write in those terms.

Galloway's usual method of defence often seems to be attack. It's a technique he used brilliantly in the Senate and one that he has used again and again in open debate, and if used well it can win the day. Over the years he has used personal insults, an aggressive style, flamboyant vocabulary. That kind of behaviour is a useful weapon, but it can get blunt with too much use, unless the context changes. But after 11 September 2001, everything changed. War was declared by George W. Bush and Galloway's stock-in-trade performance was suddenly the best show in town, entertaining and galvanising crowds from Baghdad to Basingstoke.

18

Stop the war against terror

In 1998 President Bill Clinton had made it US policy to get rid of Saddam Hussein and install a democratic government, using the words 'regime change'. That same year the USA and the UK bombed Iraq in July, November and December, as part of their campaign to get Saddam to remove the weapons he was allegedly hiding. The last of these 1998 attacks was on the eve of Clinton's impeachment debate. After this large bombardment, Saddam ordered the UN weapons inspectors out of the country and they were not allowed back in. This ban became the focus of Iraqi–US animosity and though inspectors were allowed back, in November 2002, it was too late to stop the invasion of Iraq by the USA and UK in March 2003.

There were also bombing raids on Iraq in 1999 and 2000 and there was a history of the country being an easy and popular target, so when Al-Qaeda attacked on 11 September 2001, it was no surprise that the USA tried to apportion some blame on Saddam for what had happened, even though their own investigation later found that there had been no link between Iraq and 9/11. In the run-up to the invasion around 40 per cent of the American public believed Saddam had been involved and George W. Bush would later say: 'In the war on terror, Iraq is now the central front.'

In a House of Commons debate soon after the September 11th atrocities, George Galloway stood up and warned that the UK shouldn't write the USA 'a blank cheque' for retaliation: 'The only test that matters in this is the test of whether the action will make matters better or worse. If you launch a devastating attack upon a Muslim country, killing thousands, you will make 10,000 bin Ladens rise up instead.'[1] His argument didn't cut much ice in a House of Commons packed with pro-war Labour and Tory members and it must have just added to Galloway's belief that this was no longer a forum that was going to be at all helpful to him. In December 2005 he told Clive

Anderson in a BBC radio interview that Westminster was now a place where only the most trivial of decisions are made, 'like what colour to paint Whitehall'. This disillusionment with our democratic institutions can be seen as the backdrop to much of Galloway's post-9/11 career.

More than ever, people power, based on the anti-war movement, is now the key to Galloway's approach. The hard left claim that they are in touch with the ordinary man and woman of the UK, in contrast to the cynical and arrogant Labour Party and Tories. John Rees, a co-founder of the Stop the War Coalition and chair of the Respect party, is a close comrade of Galloway's.

> The political class is not representing the people and that has crystallised around the issue of the war, but I don't think that can explain the scale of the anti-war demonstrations. You can't understand that level of mobilisation without understanding that what poured into the war was obviously concern about that issue, but a lot of wider feelings about disenfranchisement, about alienation from a political process, about an inability to express yourself in establishment and party politics. And what we did was express and give a forum for expression for that, and George was central to that . . . he understood that problem in politics . . . so 'cometh the time, cometh the man', really.

Galloway, Rees and others on the left moved quickly in the wake of 9/11 to form an opposition to Bush and Tony Blair's concept of a War on Terror, which the Yale Cowboy once described as a 'crusade', seemingly without knowing that this was an old idea that might have offensive and unhelpful implications. The Stop the War Coalition would see trade unions, the Socialist Workers Party, CND, some left-wing Labour MPs and the Muslim Association of Britain all came together to focus public support against a military solution. The question remains, even after the coalition gave birth to a political party called Respect: is this whole movement a one-issue cause? They would argue not, but their election successes have been in areas where their anti-war stance has keyed in with large elements of the electorate for whom that is a major issue.

The Stop the War Coalition (STWC) was formed on 21 September 2001 at a public meeting of around 2,000 people in London. Those present included Tony Benn, Tam Dalyell, Tariq Ali, Jeremy Corbin, Trevor Phillips and Rees, among others, and their manifesto was recorded as

> to stop the war currently declared by the United States and its allies against 'terrorism'. We condemn the attacks on New York and we feel the greatest compassion for those who lost their life on 11th September 2001. But any war will simply add to the numbers of innocent dead, cause untold suffering, political and economic instability on a global scale, increase racism and result in attacks on civil liberties . . . We call on all peace activists and organisations, trade unionists, campaigners and labour movement organisations to join with us in building a mass movement that can stop the drive to war . . . We are committed to opposing any racist backlash generated by this war. We will fight to stop the erosion of civil rights.[2]

Andrew Murray, a TGWU officer and Communist Party member who later became chair of the STWC, recalls:

> George and I were both at the earliest meetings, where Lindsey German was the convenor and Tariq Ali was elected as the chair. George's role is extremely important. He has two distinguishing features from other MPs: an understanding of the Middle East and his anti-imperialist views. They endeared him to the Muslim community.[3]

The hard left are well represented in the STWC. German and Rees are both in the SWP, and the Communist Party of Britain and International Socialist Resistance are both affiliated organisations. However, there are a large number of more mainstream left-wingers involved and the grass-roots supporters are from every political hue. And it was the ordinary folk who made the movement so powerful and remarkable in the political history of the UK. The STWC motivated millions to get involved, to march in public demonstrations of feeling on a scale never seen before. People who would not consider themselves to be political became politicised, even if just for a few months. Galloway played a central role in generating that support and motivating local activists to co-ordinate the movement, as Rees remembers:

We spoke in town after town, city after city, together on anti-war platforms building the Stop the War Coalition. It was George's joke at the time that it was the nearest we'd ever get to being in a rock and roll band, because you did one gig one night, then another and another . . . and we got to know each other very well in that period. It was, and still is, a tremendously dynamic and challenging period politically and we were at the forefront of building an absolutely huge mass movement. And that's the kind of experience that, you know, you don't get very often in life.[4]

These were exciting times for left-wingers, who felt they were 'mobilising' a group of almost revolutionary size and that this was a renaissance of the left. Rees continues:

He's a great public speaker and we built the Stop the War movement out of those great rallies, really. It was a journalistic commonplace that the public meeting was dead before that, but in actual fact we built that movement and I would say transformed public opinion in this country on that issue through that tried and tested mechanism. We didn't have access to the media. We didn't have the ability to practise what's become regarded as central to modern politics . . . the management of the media. That wasn't an option available to us, so we did it the old way and George is a fantastic practitioner of that art.

Whether or not they were the key factor in 'transforming public opinion' is debatable, but the STWC meetings were the perfect vehicle for Galloway, whose speaking style had been formed in the Dundee School of Hard Knocks, where 1970s and 1980s union rallies had demanded grand emotions, simple messages and clear calls to action.

The Iraqi lawyer Sabbah Al Mukhtar was impressed:

I saw George speak at many conferences around that time, on depleted uranium, on sanctions, on genocide. He's an orator, a real orator even by English standards, even by the standards of the House of Commons. Even if you disagree with what he says, he always has his principles and addresses people's concerns.

251

Over the course of 2002, Galloway, Rees and others were on tour, while the USA was planning its longer-term response to 9/11 and hunting for Osama bin Laden. They had already bombed and invaded Afghanistan, which had been top of the hit list. The Taliban's spiritual leader, Mullah Mohammed Omar, had tried to argue that Al Qaeda wasn't to blame, knowing that bin Laden was hiding in his hills. He accused the Americans of making him the 'prime suspect' as a pretext to attack Afghanistan and deposing his Islamic government, which they did. Even after the fall of the Taliban, bin Laden eluded capture and the USA needed a good news story in their War on Terror. Maybe Saddam would be easier to get.

In the House of Commons, Galloway was busy whipping up a storm. On 6 March 2002, in a debate on military action in Iraq, the Foreign Office Minister Ben Bradshaw pushed Galloway too far. This is the Hansard transcript:

> *The Parliamentary Under-Secretary of State for Foreign and Commonwealth Affairs (Mr Ben Bradshaw):* . . . My Hon. Friend the Member for Glasgow, Kelvin made his familiar views known in his inimitable way. Some of the good points that he made on the Middle East peace process would, I believe, carry more credibility if he had not made a career of being not just an apologist, but a mouthpiece, for the Iraqi regime over many years.
>
> *Mr Galloway:* Why do you not give way on that slander?
>
> *Mr Bradshaw:* We are not discussing—
>
> *Mr Galloway:* The Minister is a liar.
>
> *Mr Deputy Speaker (Mr John McWilliam):* Order. The Hon. Gentleman must withdraw that statement.
>
> *Mr Galloway:* The Minister told a lie about me.
>
> *Mr Deputy Speaker:* Order. The Hon. Gentleman must withdraw that statement.
>
> *Mr Galloway:* Why? The Minister told a blatant lie about me. What else could I do? What else can I call it? I demand that he withdraws the allegation against me.
>
> *Mr Deputy Speaker:* Order. The Hon. Gentleman must withdraw immediately.
>
> *Mr Galloway:* An allegation of dishonourable conduct has been made against me by the Minister. It is an assumption in the House that Members are honourable gentlemen and ladies. His imputation that I am a mouthpiece for

a dictator is a clear imputation of dishonour. He is the one who should be withdrawing, not me.

Mr Deputy Speaker: Order. I have no alternative, but to report this matter to the House. I must immediately suspend the sitting for 10 minutes.[5]

As with many of Galloway's disagreements, you have to remind yourself that this is two Labour MPs, having a go at each other. Calling another MP a liar is one of the most serious breaches of the code of parliamentary behaviour, so the debate was suspended, amid much huffing and puffing on all sides. Such was the gravity of the incident with Bradshaw that it was thought likely that Galloway might get suspended, but behind the scenes good sense prevailed and the two later apologised in the chamber. Both their apologies were worded very carefully.

Bradshaw said:

> During the heat of debate, strong feelings are expressed on both sides of the House. I hope in my time here I have always shown proper respect for the chair and observed its rulings . . . As you will be aware, I was not asked by the Deputy Speaker in Westminster Hall yesterday to withdraw my remarks at the time they were made. However, on reflection, I accept that it would have been better if I had not used the phrase that I applied to Mr Galloway and I am sorry for the offence that was caused.

Galloway stood and added:

> In the debate in Westminster Hall yesterday exchanges became frank to the point of being unacceptable and I should like to apologise to the Deputy Speaker in Westminster Hall, to you, Mr Speaker, and to the House for my part in that. I would like to say I am sorry for stepping out of parliamentary order and for my failure to withdraw my remarks when asked to do so . . . The issues under discussion were of grave urgency and importance and were issues which mean a very great deal to me. Exchanges on both sides of the argument were decidedly robust. Nonetheless I would like to say I am sorry for stepping out of parliamentary order and for my failure to withdraw my remarks when asked to do so by the Deputy Speaker. I now do so withdraw them.

This incident was followed by a bizarre one from the American actor John Malkovich early in May of the same year. The star of films such as *Dangerous Liaisons* and *The Killing Fields* had been at the Cambridge Union debating society and had been asked who he'd like to fight to the death. He replied: 'I'd rather shoot them,' and when pressed said Galloway and the respected Middle East reporter Robert Fisk were his top two. Galloway was reported as not being amused: 'In the current climate of terrorism and violence and so on, if it was a joke it is not very funny, and if it wasn't a joke he will be hearing from my lawyers . . . We can have a high noon at the Old Bailey if he likes.'[6]

As the summer of 2002 progressed, it seemed as though the USA and the UK were on an inevitable course to invade Iraq, with the US Secretary of State, the popular Colin Powell, claiming he had proof that Iraq was hiding weapons of mass destruction. The STWC was gathering support throughout the country and one of its leading members, Tam Dalyell, wrote to the Prime Minister urging him to let MPs vote on military action: 'Don't you think you ought to give a straightforward undertaking in the next 24 hours that you will follow the United States and consult elected representatives before participating in an attack on Iraq?'

Meanwhile, Galloway was addressing the other side, on a trip arranged by Saddam for Galloway to see him in Baghdad. On 7 August he had his second of two meetings with the dictator, at which he recounts that he tried to persuade him to let the UN weapons inspectors back in, who had been barred since 1998. It was almost certainly too late at that stage, as the US military build-up was well advanced, and Hans Blix and his inspectors were looking like an irrelevance. After the meeting Galloway told Reuters that the Iraqi leader wanted to find a diplomatic solution to the crisis but would fight if attacked. 'I found him to be calm, very calm indeed, but determined,' Galloway said, adding that war was not inevitable 'but if we are to avert it, we'll have to move quickly'. Saddam wanted more dialogue, and outdid Galloway in his colourful language: 'The forces of evil will carry their coffins on their backs to die in a disgraceful failure . . . they will be digging their own graves.'

Back in the UK, Galloway wrote in the *Guardian*, as war loomed closer:

Picture if you will a bearded gentleman on a recruiting poster, finger pointing imploringly. 'I need you,' it would say. No, it's not the ubiquitous Lord Kitchener appeal, but 'the emir', Osama bin Laden, and he needs you to invade Iraq. If there is one man who wants an Anglo-American invasion and occupation of an Arab country more than the chief of the US defence board, Richard Perle, it's surely the elusive and pious pimpernel of the Tora Bora . . . And in the age of Arab-Sat, every burning building, every scorched corpse, every broken family dragged out of the Iraqi ruins will be viewed in Technicolor from the Atlantic to the Gulf . . . In Saudi Arabia, huge sweeps of oppositionists are a harbinger of turmoil to come. Around the world, anger is exploding, literally, and if the Prime Minister is right, our own capital may be next. For bin Laden and his ilk, Britain is now in the front ranks of the hated.[7]

Shortly after Galloway's meeting with Saddam, Ron McKay pulled off a remarkable scoop when he landed a TV interview with the Iraqi leader, with Tony Benn asking the questions. 'I asked Tariq Aziz personally . . . Tony Benn was ideal and overjoyed when I told him.' The interview was shown on Channel 4, but had been secured as part of McKay's grand plans to start an English-language satellite TV station called Arab TV, whose start-up costs were rumoured to be in the region of £4 million. However, it never got off the ground.

The interview was the first Saddam had given to the Western media for twelve years and exploiting the rights in it would most likely have been very profitable. When he was questioned about doing the interview, Benn pointed out that 'ATV were involved but I don't know anything about them. I paid my own fare and my own hotel bill.' Benn is a calm and confident interviewer and asked straight questions that seemed to get direct answers. When asked about weapons of mass destruction, Saddam replied:

I gave you the freedom to ask me any question directly so that my reply would be direct. This is an opportunity to reach the British people and the forces of peace in the world. There is only one truth and therefore I tell you as I have said on many occasions before that Iraq has no weapons of mass destruction whatsoever. We challenge anyone who claims that we have to bring forward any evidence and present it to public opinion.

Of course one would expect Saddam to say that, but as it turned out, he was probably telling the truth.

If Saddam was giving an interview to the British he must have been getting desperate. He was clutching at straws, but it must have given him some hope that around the democratic world huge demonstrations were taking place, to try to stop the invasion of his country – the sorts of demonstration that he would have sent in the army to quell with live ammunition and gas. The leaders would have been arrested, tortured and executed, as would their families. In the past he had personally executed some of his enemies and his sons had enjoyed killing a few themselves. According to Amnesty International,

> over the years tens, or possibly hundreds, of thousands of people were killed by Iraqi security forces – lined up and shot in their villages, poisoned with chemical weapons and executed in prisons. Many of the victims were targeted simply for belonging to a community seen as opposed to the government. The killing of an estimated 5,000 men, women and children by chemical weapons in the Kurdish town of Halabja in March 1988 was just one example of mass extermination, made notorious only because journalists could reach the border town from Iran. Other methods of political killings included mass executions by firing squads, burying people alive, drowning in rivers, bleeding prisoners to death, and targeted assassinations. Thousands more died in custody in mysterious circumstances.[8]

But not many of those who took part in the anti-war demonstrations of February 2003 were thinking of Saddam's cruelty. They were trying to stop even more people dying and that's the irony. It was a no-win situation for Iraq's people, who were going to get killed by Saddam, or by Bush, or then maybe in a civil war.

Over the weekend of 15 and 16 February there were mass gatherings in Glasgow, Belfast and London, as well as around the globe. The STWC called it 'No War on Iraq, Freedom for Palestine' and in London the police estimated that at least 750,000 took part, while the STWC thought the number was nearer two million. It was hard to gauge, as there were so many routes into Hyde Park and not everyone had the patience to march on the allotted roads. Tony Blair was watching, and shortly before the march started he warned of 'bloody consequences' of not confronting Iraq, and that he didn't 'seek unpopularity as a badge of honour, but sometimes it is the price of leadership and the cost of conviction'.

John Rees, who organised the march, claims a wider issue than war was behind this public action: 'It's essentially the same seam from which Respect emerged. I think even before the war it was clear to anyone that wanted to look close enough that there was a widening chasm between the people and the political establishment, on a variety of issues, not just the war.'

The speakers ranged against Blair in Hyde Park included Charles Kennedy, Rev. Jesse Jackson, Tariq Ali, Mo Mowlam, Ken Livingstone, Vanessa Redgrave, human rights campaigner Bianca Jagger, Galloway and Benn. Even the taciturn playwright Harold Pinter spoke, calling America 'a country run by a bunch of criminal lunatics with Tony Blair as a hired Christian thug'. Andrew Murray recalls: 'The 15 February demonstration was a tremendous expression of opposition to war. We were all fighting to prevent the war and the tragedy was that we didn't manage to.'

In the last few days before the bombing started on 20 March, Galloway made another of many attacks on Blair, when he let rip with 'He is the roving ambassador to the right-wing, born-again, Bible-belting fundamentalist crew'. After the USA and UK attacked, his speeches became increasingly hostile, with more extravagant language, sailing ever closer to the wind in denouncing Blair and Bush personally, and supporting the Iraqis. By this stage it was too late, and now all he could do was try and fight politically what he saw as an immoral and illegal act. How far was he prepared to go in his relations with the party?

19

Expulsion from Labour and press attacks

The invasion of Iraq was a watershed in George Galloway's relationship with Labour. He had been in a dispute with them for years, but from March 2003 he took the gloves off and laid into them with his bare knuckles. It left him in more pain than them.

It has often seemed hard for Galloway to follow anyone's line but his own, and this consistently angered the Labour Party and led him to fall out with its leaders. Michael Foot disagreed with him, Neil Kinnock is known to be vehemently opposed to him, but it fell to Tony Blair to finally get rid of him. When the USA and the UK had bombed Iraq in December 1998, Blair had famously justified the bombings by saying: 'We set out to diminish and degrade Saddam's military capability and we have done so; substantial damage has been inflicted upon his air defence systems; the command and control system for his armed forces; missile production capability; and systems which could be used for chemical and biological warfare.'

When Galloway cleverly threw Blair's words back at him in the House of Commons he turned up the heat on their personal enmity:

> I wonder if you thought, as I did at lunchtime, as the bleeding women and children were carried into hospitals that those who were diminished and degraded were not the Iraqis, but us – diminished and degraded by being reduced to being a tail on this verminous and mangy desert fox?[1]

Blair replied: 'I find it curious that you should attack President Clinton personally and mention not one word of condemnation of Saddam Hussein.'[2]

On 20 March 2003, despite boos and shouting from both sides as he tried to speak, Galloway rounded on the Defence Secretary, Geoff Hoon:

> Will the secretary of state give a straight answer to this question: given the view in the advice of the overwhelming number of unpurchased international legal experts that this action is illegal, what assurance will he give British forces that they will not face prosecution in the International Criminal Court by other countries for the actions that he has ordered them to carry out today?[3]

Hoon replied:

> I will defend my Hon. Friend's right to be heard – as I will also defend the right of the opposition in Iraq to be heard; and I should be much happier if he emphasised that more frequently than he has sometimes done in the recent past. I assure him, as I have assured the House on previous occasions, that the actions of our armed forces are entirely lawful and based on the clear advice of the Attorney General, which has been set out for the benefit of Members.[4]

Since then it has been claimed, though never substantiated that this legal advice was strongly influenced by the Attorney General's American counterpart, on a special visit to the USA.

Although there were other voices of dissent, including Tam Dalyell's, it seemed that Galloway was getting most of the newspaper coverage. On 25 March, referring to the resistance of the Iraqi army, he took on the Foreign Secretary, Jack Straw:

> Is not the government's problem that the weapons of forgery, plagiarism, fabrication and lies that they have fed the people of this country and the world have become boomerangs, which are now cutting, alas, not the bodies of the donkeys who sent our people into battle, but the lions who are having to stand and fight in defence of the British government's lies, forgery and deception?[5]

Straw replied:

> I would find my Hon. Friend's extravagant rhetoric more convincing if only I

did not recall that he used exactly the same rhetoric in respect of the military action in Afghanistan, and predicted that there would be a world war that went on for at least a year or two years.[6]

Galloway didn't seem to like that reply and started heckling Straw, which annoyed the Speaker:

Mr Galloway: You said it would be over.
Mr Speaker: Order.
Mr Galloway: A year ago, you said it would be over.
Mr Speaker: Order. The Hon. Gentleman put the question. I cannot help the reply that he gets. He cannot complain about the reply.[7]

He wasn't just the government's most persistent critic in the House of Commons, he was all over the Middle East's TV channels doing the same. A few days later, he was seen on Abu Dhabi TV being highly critical of Blair and Bush, calling them liars who were acting like wolves, while Iraq was fighting for the whole of Arabia. He also asked if Iraq was going to receive the support of the rest of Arabia, but then backtracked and said this was unrealistic. He disputes the exact phrase used, but he was reported as saying: 'Where are the Arab armies?', a phrase much used in the Middle East as a chant by critics of inaction over Palestine and Iraq. The same day he appeared on ITV News and said that other British soldiers should follow the example of three who had already objected to following what they regarded as illegal orders, and refuse to fight. These three soldiers had been sent home, but no action was taken against them. Various other interviews from around the same time followed those basic lines, but the reason Abu Dhabi TV and ITV are remembered now is because they formed the basis for the Labour Party's two main charges against him when they brought him to account later.

When the *Sun* ran a front page with 'TRAITOR' splashed across it on 1 April, they weren't joking. A sub-heading ran: 'MP blasted over "kill Brits" call'. They reasoned that Galloway's question, 'where are the Arab armies?', was inciting the Arab world to fight our soldiers. The article featured a transcript of the Abu Dhabi interview, which Galloway later accused the government of having provided to them. Adam Ingram, a fellow Scottish

Labour MP and armed forces minister, was quoted as saying: 'Are there no depths to which George Galloway will not sink? I am sure such disgraceful comments will be rightly condemned the length and breadth of this country,'[8] whereupon it was clear that the government/Labour machine was targeting him at least as accurately as one of their heat-seeking missiles.

Under this barrage, Galloway dug in and threw out a few grenades such as 'The wolves are Bush and Blair, not the soldiers. The soldiers are lions led by donkeys, sent to kill and be killed' and 'I didn't call on Arabs to attack the British army, I called on British soldiers to disobey illegal orders, which is an obligation on all armies since the Nuremberg trials.' Both reasonable points, but it was beginning to look extremely serious for him when Blair gave an exclusive interview to the *Sun* on 18 April. In it he said: 'His comments were disgraceful and wrong. The National Executive will deal with it.' By this stage the leaders of the Labour Party must have fervently wanted to get Galloway out; the only question was how would they be able to accomplish this. With Galloway determined to fight 'every inch of the way' it was likely to be a damaging exercise politically.

Blair, Campbell, Hoon and Co. must have been heartened when, on 22 April, just four days after the *Sun* carried its Blair interview, the *Daily Telegraph* claimed it had found documents in Baghdad that showed Galloway had taken money from Saddam's oil-for-food programme. This would later become the subject of a libel trial that Galloway won, but at the time this undermined Galloway and markedly affected sympathy for the anti-war campaigner. On 6 May David Triesman, Labour's general secretary, announced that the whip had been taken from Galloway and that there would be a hearing to decide if he had violated the party's constitution by 'bringing the Labour Party into disrepute through behaviour that is prejudicial or grossly detrimental to the Party'. It was made clear that the newspaper allegations were also a factor in this decision, even though they were being strenuously denied by Galloway and it was looking as though they would be the subject of legal action. The party appointed Chris Lennie, the deputy general secretary, to take charge of a 'thorough' investigation, which could lead to the National Executive expelling him.

What had motivated the disciplinary procedures was the press publicity. The *Daily Telegraph*'s report by David Blair was one of three articles based on documents that had come to light in Iraq in the chaos after the fall of the old regime. The American newspaper the *Christian Science Monitor* and the *Mail on Sunday* had both paid for other bundles of papers, which were quickly proved to be bogus. The *Christian Science Monitor*'s were published on 23 April 2003 and had been provided by an Iraqi general, Salah Abdel Rasool. They both made the astounding claim that Galloway had received $10 million from Saddam. Galloway himself later explained to Clive Anderson for a BBC Radio Five Live interview just how ludicrous these allegations were:

> Within a couple of days of the fall of Baghdad, documents with my name on . . . including some with my purported signature on them, were being bought and sold by right-wing newspapers in Britain and abroad . . . one of them a right-wing newspaper for which I work, which nonetheless bought a set of documents which they imagined showed me receiving £10 million from a son of Saddam Hussein that I have never met, starting a year before I had ever set foot in Iraq, finishing six months after I last set foot in Iraq, with a totally forged signature, absurdly forged signature as it turned out, on them. And an American newspaper published a similar set of documents, but from a different son, on their front page and had to answer for it in the High Court in England.

The *Christian Science Monitor* put out an apology in a piece on 20 June. 'At the time we published these documents, we felt they were newsworthy and appeared credible, although we did explicitly state in our article that we could not guarantee their authenticity,' said the *Monitor*'s then editor, Paul Van Slambrouck. 'It is important to set the record straight: we are convinced the documents are bogus. We apologize to Mr Galloway and to our readers.' It was too little too late and Galloway was intent on reparation. He released a statement:

> I want to know who forged these documents. I am calling on the Prime Minister, as head of the co-occupying power in Iraq, to investigate how this conspiracy came about. As a member of the House of Commons, indeed as a British subject, I have the right to the protection of the British intelligence services from a conspiracy hatched by persons unknown, but whose handi-

work was conducted in foreign territory co-occupied by Great Britain . . . I don't accept their apology. Firstly, a newspaper of their international standing should have conducted these basic checks on the authenticity of these documents before they published them and not more than two months afterwards . . . This internationally renowned newspaper published on its front page that I took ten million dollars from Saddam Hussein, based on papers which have proved to be forgeries . . . They did not even speak to me before publishing these allegations. My legal action against them continues.

In the end the *Monitor* was taken to the High Court in London in March 2004 and quickly paid up an undisclosed 'substantial' sum.

In his 2005 interview with Anderson, Galloway also explained that he had only just stopped the *Mail on Sunday* from publishing different allegations that were similarly fantastical.

> *Galloway:* Yes, and the ones bought by the *Mail on Sunday*, showing another £10m from a different son . . . believe me, I had to work very hard to stop the *Mail on Sunday* running that story, or I would have ended up in the libel courts suing my own employers . . .
> *Anderson:* Well, there may have been a certain satisfaction in that—
> *Galloway:* No, because I have a very good and long relationship with them. But until seven o'clock on a Saturday night I was rushing my passport over to the head office of the *Mail on Sunday* to prove to them I could not have been in Iraq on the date I was supposed to be in Iraq signing for millions of pounds.

Nobody wants to sue their employer, particularly if you get paid between £85,000 and £90,000 a year by them, which was his fee for writing a weekly column, according to his entry in the House of Commons Register of Members' Interests. It was a contract he lost in 2006.

Unlike the *Christian Science Monitor* and the *Mail on Sunday*, the allegations in the *Daily Telegraph* were not going to go away so quickly. Their piece was followed up by every newspaper and TV station in the UK and many around the globe. They were all asking questions about the financing of the Mariam Appeal and if there were any links to Galloway. Despite years of investigation, by journalists and the US government, no connection has ever been found between Galloway's personal finances and the finances of the Mariam Appeal. Equally, no-one has ever demonstrated that any money has passed to him from the oil-for-food programme.

The *Daily Telegraph* case alleged that Galloway had been paid by the Iraqi regime but, crucially, the paper had not paid for the documents, so if there was a conspiracy, it did not involve anyone making money from it. The motives would have to be political, however unlikely or likely that might be. The *Telegraph* was keen to get the story out as soon as it could, and Andrew Sparrow, the newspaper's political correspondent, had the job of finding Galloway over a Bank Holiday, to put the allegations to him. He finally got hold of him at his Algarve holiday home and spent thirty-five minutes talking it through. Galloway said he was 'flabbergasted' and that the allegations were 'preposterous'. According to Sparrow in court, he immediately said that the documents must be forgeries. 'Maybe it's the product of the same forgers who forged so many other things in this whole Iraq picture,' he said. 'The truth is, I have never met, to the best of my knowledge, any member of the Iraqi intelligence. I have never in my life seen a barrel of oil, let alone owned, bought or sold one . . . It would not be the Iraqi regime that was forging it. It would be people like you, and the government whose policies you have supported.'

Despite his complete denial of the story, the next morning the *Daily Telegraph* ran the story across its front page, with the headline 'Galloway was in Saddam's pay, say secret Iraqi documents'. Inside they had the memo in Arabic and English, with Galloway's denial. As the final nail in, as it turned out, their own coffin, they printed an editorial, 'Saddam's Little Helper', which used the word 'treason'.

As soon as he'd put the phone down on Sparrow, Galloway had swung into action, to mount a counter-offensive. He issued a press release and started giving interviews saying the *Telegraph* had 'either been party to it, or been hoodwinked by it', but either way, 'they would answer for it in front of the British courts'. Over the next few days, as an indication that he had no hidden money, he said he was considering selling everything he had to fight the case. Then on 23 April he appeared on the BBC's *Newsnight*, claiming he was prepared to open the Mariam Appeal's accounts to scrutiny. Had these accounts been made available, Galloway's troubles could have been quickly resolved. Unfortunately, they had been taken to Jordan by the appeal's chairman, Fawaz Zureikat, and to date the scrutiny has not happened.

A couple of days later the Charity Commission announced that it had received a complaint about the use of the Mariam Appeal's funds and that it was going to conduct an inquiry. Lord Goldsmith, the Attorney General, had also received a complaint and was being asked to investigate allegations 'that funds raised for medical care had been used by the MP for travelling expenses'. Galloway wrote an open letter to him in which he said he'd always made clear that the appeal was also a campaign against sanctions:

> The Mariam Appeal, which I founded, has been involved in highly publicised, highly political campaigning against the government's policies for some years without a whisper of complaint from anyone in your department . . . Even the Foreign Office, whose policy we were directly challenging, has dealt with the Mariam Appeal on the basis that we were a political campaign . . . For you now to respond to this atmosphere of witch hunt against me in the way which has been reported would be unworthy of you.

He went on to say that his own travel costs had been declared in the Register of Members' Interests.

In April of the same year the Parliamentary Commissioner for Standards received complaints that Galloway should have declared the money that he was alleged to have received from the Iraqi government. The Standards and Privileges Committee was being asked to look into whether Galloway should have declared the very large alleged payments each year. By December it had decided it could not report on this matter, because it was felt that any reporting might prejudice the libel trial. The committee postponed its inquiry.

So by the summer of 2003, Galloway had a lot on his plate. He was pursuing libel cases against the *Daily Telegraph* and the *Christian Science Monitor*, and he was being investigated by the Labour Party, the Attorney General, the Parliamentary Commissioner for Standards and Privileges and the Charity Commission. Added to that, the *Sun* was claiming that it had served a 'notice of treason' at a London magistrates' court calling for his prosecution under the 1351 Treason Act. Then on 27 July, he arrived back at his converted farmhouse in the Algarve to find that there had been a break-in and that a computer had been stolen. He reported to the police that the burglars had also taken his desk and chair, and that they had cut his phone line. If the burglars had been looking for something interesting on his computer, he said they were 'doomed to disappointment' because it only contained his memoirs. That was uncharacteristically self-deprecating of him; surely his memoirs would be sensational.

The Labour Party National Constitutional Committee (NCC) held its hearing into Galloway's conduct on 22 October 2003. His submission to what he would later call 'a kangaroo court' makes fascinating reading, and it can be found in full on the Stop the War Coalition website. Anyone who thinks that Galloway was trying to get thrown out of the party to make a point about the war, or Labour's drift to the right, ought to read this submission, which goes into enormous detail in his own defence.

The case against him was being brought by Labour's National Executive Committee, but would be heard by a panel of three NCC members, who were to sit and hear the evidence from both sides, then decide on a verdict and sentence. The NCC is a body of twelve Labour stalwarts, which had been set up in 1986 under Neil Kinnock when Labour was expelling Militant. The idea was to make it legally watertight so that those expelled had no comebacks. Galloway's three panellists were Noel Jenkins, Rose Burley and Lee Vasey. They are all rank-and-file Labour people: Vasey is a magistrate and councillor in Darlington, Burley is a councillor in Walsall and Jenkins is a teacher in London.

The charges that Galloway faced were as follows:
- He incited Arabs to fight British troops
- He incited British troops to defy orders
- He incited Plymouth voters to reject Labour MPs
- He threatened to stand against Labour
- He backed an anti-war candidate in Preston.

The case for the prosecution was being put by Chris Lennie, who opened on the Wednesday, with Galloway calling his witnesses on the Thursday. Lennie's major allegations relied on a transcript of the interviews Galloway had given to Abu Dhabi TV. There were three problems with that, as

Galloway saw it. Firstly, the transcript was an English translation from an Arabic translation of his original interview. Because he'd been interviewed in English, the Arab TV station had faded down the sound of him talking and put their translator's voice over his pictures, so that the audience could under-stand what he was saying. This Arabic version had then been translated back into English. So the tribunal was arguing over his use of words, when they were relying on two different translators being 100 per cent accurate. Secondly, the recording of the interview had been impossible to hear in parts and 'words indistinct' had been inserted. Lastly, the prosecution had been using an edited version, rather than the full transcript. The full transcript, taken from the STWC website, is below, with the sections edited out in italics.

> Well, let me say first of all that Iraq is fighting for all the Arabs. Why don't the Arabs do something for the Iraqis? [*You speak about the dignity of the Iraqi people and their support.*] Where are the Arab armies? [*Even if it is not realistic to ask a non-Iraqi army to come to defend Iraq, we see Arab regimes pumping oil for the countries (words indistinct). Today fifty-one Iraqi civilians were killed in Baghdad by a missile fired from an Arab country (words indistinct).*] We wonder when the Arab leaders wake up? When are they going to stand by the Iraqi people?

When Galloway had asked the prosecution to see a video of his interview, they had to admit that they hadn't got one, and had based their case on the above version, translated by, as he put it, 'a person unknown'. Galloway also argued that they should be proving beyond all reasonable doubt that he was intending to incite Arabs to fight British soldiers, and that the above statements didn't support that contention. In particular he drew the tribunal's attention to the fact that he had said 'even if it is not realistic to ask a non-Iraqi army to come to defend Iraq' and argued that this was proof that he had not been calling for them to attack British troops.

On the second charge, that in an ITV news programme he had called on British troops to disobey orders, he asked the tribunal to look at the context of his remarks, which had been left out of the prosecution's submission. A fuller transcript of his ITV interview is below:

[The government's own principal legal advisor in the Foreign Office resigned from her job for precisely that reason and Kofi Annan, the Secretary General of the United Nations, who are [sic] in charge of international law, has stated that this is an illegal war. So there isn't much controversy about it being an illegal war and the idea of obeying illegal orders died at the War Crimes Tribunal at Nuremberg at the end of the Second World War.] So three British soldiers are already on their way back to England to face court martial for refusing to obey illegal orders and the others should do so too.

Presenter: [But I mean, let's be real about this . . . that they're not going to do that, are they? The thousands of personnel over there are not going to just suddenly lay down their weapons and say: 'Well, we're not going to obey our commands.']

GG: [Well,] three of them *[just have and they]* were right to do so.[9]

Galloway's written submission to the tribunal went as follows:

As can be seen I called for British troops to disobey 'illegal orders'. This call is predicated on the basis that I (and others) consider the war to be illegal. Such a statement was a natural extension of my opinion that the mobilisation of British forces against Iraq was an illegal act of war. I specifically did not say that soldiers should not obey any orders, rather that they should not obey 'illegal' orders. Orders to fire on civilians would fall into this category. If the war on Iraq was itself illegal, as I believe, then it is arguable that orders for British servicemen to fight in Iraq were also illegal . . . Principle IV of the Nuremberg Principles of International Law (recognised in the Charter of the Nuremberg Tribunal and in the Judgment of the Tribunal and adopted by the International Law Commission of the United Nations in 1950) states: 'The fact that a person acted pursuant to an order of his Government or of a superior does not relieve him from responsibility under international law, provided a moral choice was in fact possible to him.' Since Nuremberg it has been the duty of every soldier to disobey an order that he considers to be illegal. By obeying an order that is in fact an illegal order, armies, and therefore individual soldiers, run the risk of committing a war crime and being tried for such a crime.

Looking at the above evidence, it appeared that Galloway was building a well-reasoned case, particularly when you consider that the ex-Cabinet

Minister Robin Cook, who had resigned as Foreign Secretary over Iraq, had called for British troops to be pulled out of Iraq as soon as they had got there. The other, lesser, charges would clearly never have been brought against an MP who had not already fallen out with his bosses. As well as his own submissions, Galloway also called some very powerful character witnesses to plead on his behalf, including Tony Benn and TGWU leader Tony Woodley, and even had advice from Michael Foot, who he has not always seen eye to eye with.

Though it was claimed that it was not a foregone conclusion, on 23 October 2003 at around 3 p.m., Galloway was expelled from the party by unanimous vote and by the next morning letters had already arrived on doormats explaining the fact to Labour members, which was pretty quick work. He had been acquitted on one of the five charges: urging voters in Plymouth not to back Labour. However, he was found guilty of inciting Arabs to fight British troops, inciting British troops to defy orders, threatening to stand against Labour candidates and backing an anti-war candidate in Preston against the official Labour candidate.

Galloway's immediate reaction was: 'This was a politically motivated kangaroo court whose verdict had been written in advance in the best tradition of political show trials. It was a travesty of justice.' He accused Tony Blair of being

> a conspirator and a liar . . . Blair's response to the mistake of the war is to attack those who stood against the war and root them out of British politics. I think that's a very serious mistake . . . The anti-war movement is not going to go away and we will continue to hold him to account for a war crime and a blunder of extraordinary magnitude.

His friends and comrades rallied to his side. Benn commented: 'What hope is there for the Labour Party if the public think that when you join you just become a private in Mr Blair's army and have to obey orders or be thrown out of the party? That is what is really worrying.'

The party hierarchy were unequivocal. Ian McCartney, Labour's chairman, who had many years before travelled up from Dover to Dundee to be defeated in a unanimous vote by Galloway and his supporters, said any reasonable person would have been 'disgusted' by the comments and that the NCC was right to expel him: 'The issue here is a very simple one. George Galloway incited foreign forces to rise up against British troops at a time when they were risking their lives. He was the only Labour MP to do this and he has never taken back or apologised for these comments.'

The former *Tribune* editor Mark Seddon, a National Executive member, supported Galloway throughout:

> George has been consistent on the Palestinian/Arab cause. Essentially, on Iraq and on the sanctions, he was right. I opposed his expulsion from the party. My argument on the Executive was that people are innocent until proven guilty in court and, at the time, he was challenging the charges through a defamation case. I told them he would be made a martyr . . . He's very intemperate . . . but I didn't think he deserved to be expelled.

There were many others in the party who thought he'd been treated unjustly, but perhaps Willie McKelvey, the man who'd signed him up in the first place, deserves the final word on it: 'The process wasn't right. There was no appeal. George was very bitter about it, but I'd say he was on the brink. He was enjoying being on the edge and got so involved with it. I think he enjoys that brinkmanship.' He might have been on the brink, but now he'd passed over onto another side, and although he was still an MP, the independent member for Glasgow Kelvin, he was no longer in the organisation that had made him. From thirteen to forty-nine, man and boy, he'd been a Labour Party member. The party had cushioned him, given him opportunities, helped form his opinions, and now he was out. The truth was that it had moved on, or to the right, and he hadn't. Unlike others who had gone with the flow, Galloway always seemed determined to do things his way, swimming against the tide.

20

Respect

In the days following his expulsion from Labour, George Galloway appeared on speaking platforms as part of his continuing work for the Stop the War Coalition. He was free of party restrictions now and if there had ever been anything holding back the insults for his enemies, there wasn't any longer. At various meetings he dubbed Tony Blair George W. Bush's 'monkey'[1] and the US President an 'imbecile'. To standing ovations, he called for protesters to join the national demonstrations that were being organised to coincide with Bush's visit to Britain in November. If the Labour Party had wanted to silence him, they had failed, and all they had done was increase his pulling power and authority with the anti-war movement. Andrew Murray of the STWC saw how Galloway's expulsion put him on another level: 'It was a fiasco for the Labour Party and the government. George's prestige was higher than ever.'[2]

In many ways it was business as usual for Galloway, but was he going to stay in Parliament? Would he want to fight on as an independent? Might he form a new party? Though he'd thrown himself into the fight to save his Labour membership card, the idea of a new political party had already been talked about with John Rees, who had been one of the founders of the STWC. Rees recalls:

> We talked about the possibility, though we didn't have the name or anything, but we knew there was a gap between what people thought and the Labour Party, and particularly on the question of the war. And very sharply after the 15 September 2003 demonstration of one million, we were being asked at meeting after meeting – there was no meeting that we did, whether it was 10 people or 10,000 people, where somebody wouldn't get up and say: 'Well, what are we going to do at the next election? Who are you saying we should

vote for?' And we'd conceptualised the need for such a thing, as with the formation of Stop the War Coalition. It came very strongly as a kind of rank-and-file thing.[3]

He claims that the idea had begun to take real shape as far back as the end of 2002:

> We talked about it a lot . . . I think the decisive conversation happened in Cairo. We were both at an international peace conference in Cairo in December 2002, I think, and we had a long conversation and we agreed that there was a vacuum after Thatcher had moved to the right and that had been endorsed and continued by Blair, but that the majority of Labour supporters and very definitely the majority of Labour activists in the Labour movement just weren't going there.

On 29 October 2003, Galloway announced: 'I am launching this evening a coalition, a unity coalition, which will seek to unite the left, the peace movement, the anti-war cause, the Muslim community in Britain, persuading people of all parties and none to fight New Labour in the European elections in June.' At first it fell short of being a political party, as he wrote in the *Guardian*:

> I will now seek to challenge New Labour at the polls. In the European elections next June, I will be part of a list – in a proportional representation contest – which will seek to unify the red, green, anti-war, Muslim and other social constituencies radicalised by the war, in a referendum on Tony Blair . . . We will not be a political party, but a coalition around which we hope many will rally – some perhaps only for the day, merely lending us their votes – to show the true colours of the British people.[4]

On 19 November he continued his headline-grabbing tactics by comparing the fighting Iraqis to the British resisting Adolf Hitler. At a press conference he said: 'Iraqi resistance will continue against all foreign forces. They have a legal and moral right to oppose occupying forces in their country,' just as if 'Hitler had crossed the Channel'. He also warned that Iraqi resistance would mean that many more Americans and British would be coming home in body bags and that it was ordinary Iraqis who were giving their support to the resistance movement and sustaining it. This message was repeated on stages around the country, in the company of speakers as wide ranging as the US Vietnam veteran Ron Kovic (the man on whose life the film *Born on the Fourth of July* was based) and Harold Pinter. All the way, Galloway's message was clear. To John Humphrys on BBC Radio 4's *On the Ropes* he said: 'I don't recognise the concept of "my country, right or wrong". I don't regard my country involved in an unjust war as having anything to do with me, except in as much as it places a special responsibility on me to oppose it.'

Although Respect – the Unity Coalition had not started as a political party, it soon became a de facto one. Its name is an acronym for Respect, Equality, Socialism, Peace, Environment, Community, Trade Unionism, and in its constitution it describes itself as 'a political coalition of groups, parties, organisations and individuals who support Respect's Founding Declaration and the decisions of its annual conference'.

That founding declaration included some very straightforward statements that made Respect a strongly anti-war party:

> Tony Blair's New Labour has taken us to war five times in the last six years, each time with calamitous consequences. The bloodshed, the waste of precious economic resources, the lying and hypocrisy that have accompanied the attack on Iraq have brought many to the conclusion that they must rethink their traditional political allegiance.[5]

However, it was also keen to stress its other policies. Among other socialist commitments, Respect wants:

- an end to all privatisation and the bringing back into democratic public ownership of the railways and other public services;
- an education system that is not dependent on the ability to pay, that is comprehensive and that gives an equal chance in life to every child, no matter how wealthy or poor their parents, from nursery to university;
- a publicly owned and funded, democratically controlled NHS, free to all users;
- pensions linked to average earnings;

- the minimum wage to rise to the European Union decency threshold of £7.40 an hour;
- to tax the rich to fund welfare and to close the growing gap between the poor and the wealthy few;
- the repeal of the Tory anti-union laws.

In the constitution it set itself up as an anti-New Labour party, saying:

> We recognise that the current New Labour leadership has fully embraced the neo-liberal agenda of radical marketisation. It has supported US imperialism in its invasion of Iraq, its so-called permanent war on terrorism, and its attacks on human rights. Its racist attitude towards migrants and asylum seekers has bolstered the far right. We also recognise that it has changed the constitutional position within the Labour Party to ensure that this right-wing path cannot be reversed from within.

Much of Respect's philosophy sounds like 'old' Labour, so to what extent is it the party of turning the clock back? Rees leaves the door open to nationalisation:

> It might be that if you ask about renationalisation you get one answer, but if you ask about continued privatisation you get a very different one, and certainly it isn't hard to imagine that two steps down the road people may say: 'Well, if privatisation isn't working then we have to discuss public provision in some form.' Neither they nor we want to have the old nationalised industries return, but we do want democratic public provision of essential services, and I would say there is a very, very large constituency for that view.

Respect would build and crystallise around the one-man headline generator, George Galloway, and over the next few months he kept on working the speaking platforms, while polishing his memoirs into what he called an autobiography, though it was very limited in scope and spent more time on his anti-war thoughts than his actual life story. It came out later in 2004, with a title that refers to one of his musical heroes, John Lennon. *I'm Not the Only One* is a line from Lennon's 'Imagine': 'You may say I'm a dreamer, but I'm not the only one.' But what was Galloway dreaming of? The answer, as with another man forced out of Labour, Robert Kilroy-Silk, was Europe.

Respect – the Unity Coalition declared that it was fielding candidates across the country in the European elections of 2004 and that Lindsey German, a campaigner for the Socialist Workers Party and the STWC, would be running for London Mayor. It was an enormous commitment for a new organisation, but as it was an alliance, it called on the ready-made candidates and machinery of the SWP and other STWC-affiliated organisations. Even with that network and the support of the Muslim Association of Britain, when June came it brought a pretty miserable result. Whereas the suntanned Euro-critic Kilroy-Silk and his party got twelve seats, the suntanned New Labour critic and his party got none. Despite, or perhaps because of, putting his name on their ballot papers so that the forms read Respect (The George Galloway Party), they got fewer votes than the British National Party. Respect's proportion of the national vote was just 1.7 per cent, but there were a few glimmers of hope. In the London borough of Newham it took 21.41 per cent, and in Tower Hamlets Respect received more votes than any other party. Meanwhile, German came fifth in the London mayoral election, just beating the BNP's candidate.

Even though Respect had not won a seat, there were signs that it had something to build on in certain areas, and in a few weeks it would be given a golden opportunity to capitalise. Away from the polls, though, Galloway was bracing himself for the results of the investigation into the Mariam Appeal. After a year-long inquiry, on 28 June 2004 the Charity Commission delivered its verdict. It was a mixed bag. While the commission ruled that he and the other trustees should have set the appeal up as a charity, and that Stuart Halford and Galloway's wife's salaries had been 'unauthorised payments', it concluded that there was no evidence that the funds had been misused. The Charity Commission's director of operations, Simon Gillespie, said: 'The commission's thorough inquiry found no evidence to suggest that the large amounts of money given to the Mariam Appeal were not properly used.' Galloway announced that the inquiry had been a waste of time and money and had been politically motivated by the Attorney General, Lord Goldsmith.

Sabbah Al Mukhtar, who had helped set up the Mariam Appeal, agrees with him: 'The "investigation" into the Mariam Appeal was one of the clearest politicisations of law, whereby the Attorney General instructed the Charity Commission to investigate.' There were raised eyebrows that the Charity Commission had been asked to look into the appeal at all, given that it wasn't a charity, but judging whether an appeal is a charity or not does come under the commission's remit. More pertinent to Galloway's complaint of political manoeuvrings perhaps was the relationship between the Attorney General and the Charity Commission. The official line from the commission was: 'The Attorney General and the Charity Commission have concurrent powers in ensuring the proper administration of charities. The commission, however, as the statutory regulator of charities, is better placed to take this matter forward ... The Charity Commission will keep the Attorney General informed of the results of its enquiries.'[6]

On the issue of 'unauthorised payments' to Halford and Galloway's wife, the inquiry concluded that they had been paid salaries from appeal funds, which was not allowable, but that the services provided by the paid trustees were 'of value to the appeal', so no further action would be taken. The conclusion was that the Mariam Appeal had in effect been a charity all the time, but Galloway, Halford et al. had been 'unaware that they had created a charity'. The commission also reported that although some of the appeal's activities were political, this was allowable because the trustees 'could reasonably have formed the view' that lifting the sanctions against Iraq would have enabled the treatment of sick children.

So Galloway had been cleared of any wrongdoing, and had been operating quite legally within the existing framework. The case did throw up the fact, however, that there may be a weakness in the whole system of appeals. Unlike for registered charities, there is no obligation on an appeal trustee to open the appeal's books to anything more than a summary inspection. Exactly how the public's money had been spent was impossible to find out, as the Charity Commission had stated in the detail of the report:

> 12. The Commission has been unable to obtain all the books and records of the Appeal. Mr Galloway, the first Chairman of the Appeal, has stated that this documentation was sent to Amman and Baghdad in 2001 when Fawaz

Zureikat became Chairman of the Appeal. Mr Galloway has informed the Commission that this documentation is no longer under the control of the original trustees of the Appeal and cannot be located by them. Mr Galloway confirmed that the Appeal did not produce annual profit and loss accounts or balance sheets.

13. The Commission received assurances from Mr Galloway that the monies received by him from the Appeal related to expenses incurred in his duties as Chairman of the Appeal.

14. The Commission established that Dr Amineh Abu-Zayyad and Stuart Halford, two of the original trustees, received unauthorised benefits in the form of salary payments from the Appeal's funds. The information provided to the Commission suggests that the Executive Committee considered these payments were necessary and were unaware that they were unauthorised. The Commission accepts that none of the Executive Committee acted in bad faith and that the services provided were of value to the Appeal.

Al Mukhtar says:

The Mariam Appeal wasn't a charity so we had no statutory duty. We provided the books and records that the Mariam Appeal had but it was extremely limited because it was a loose organisation. It was a joint venture and so it was eventually moved to Jordan and run by Zureikat, because there were so many blocks in the UK in getting anything over to Iraq. Jordan became the stepping stone, the middleman for all activities of that kind . . . All the major expenditure was accounted for because it's all in the banking records. There was some money taken out in cash to pay for expenses, rent and accommodation, Mariam and her family.

While the funding of the Mariam Appeal would keep Galloway occupied in time-consuming battles for years, it was onwards and upwards for the Respect coalition. It may have been unsuccessful in its European campaign, but it had learned from its defeat. There had been a strong Muslim vote for Respect, particularly in Tower Hamlets. So, when a by-election was declared close by just a few weeks later, it put everything behind its campaign in the consequent by-election. Josh Peck was the Labour Party chair in

Bethnal Green & Bow, the constituency that includes the contested ward, and must have watched the election closely, because he knew that Respect was looking like a threat in the area for the general election. He says: 'St Dunstan's & Stepney Green is a very mixed community, with many white and Bangladeshi residents. It had been Labour's strongest seat, but Respect took it and it was a sign of things to come.' Respect's Oliur Rahman won the ward and became its first elected representative anywhere. He recalls:

> The election was fought like a parliamentary campaign, George was there, Oona [King, then Labour MP for Bethnal Green & Bow] was there. I became the first Respect councillor in the country. It was Oona's agent, Liam, who told me I'd probably won at the count. It felt like a victory for working-class people of Tower Hamlets. I come from a working-class, trade union background and it was for them.

Peck remembers that the campaign amounted to a referendum on the invasion of Iraq:

> Respect has a car that they drove through the streets with megaphones. A woman was speaking: 'Every vote for Labour is a bullet in the back of an Iraqi child. Vote for Labour and you will have blood on your hands and on your conscience' . . . I remember Galloway on the election night. He stood outside, on the low wall next to the candidate, Oliur Rahman, a local trade union activist. Galloway spoke first, a rousing speech. He said then: 'Oona King, Jim Fitzpatrick – today Stepney & St Dunstan's, tomorrow we come for you.' That's when we knew for sure he'd stand but, at that stage, he only wanted to secure the defeat of Labour.

If Galloway had shone on the stump in St Dunstan's, Peck recalls that he showed his steel at the count:

> There were five or six council officials present. I was sat next to Galloway, watching the ballots being counted. It's standard to call any ballots that have irregularities to see if they are disqualified. I called one that had a 'Yes' next to Respect rather than a cross. Galloway spat at me: 'The intention is clear.'

It wasn't all gravy for the new party. In the Hartlepool by-election of September that year, Respect came fifth with 572 votes and lost its deposit. But then Hartlepool has few Muslim voters. It was another signal that they had to think strategically and play to their strengths. It also may not have helped that Galloway had called Bush and Blair 'terrorists' on a variety of Arab TV stations in early August and kicked up a storm. He also hinted at his 'where are the Arab armies?' comment when he said the Iraqi resistance was not just defending Iraq but all Arabs: 'Two of your beautiful daughters are in the hands of foreigners: Jerusalem and Baghdad . . . and the Arab world is silent. And some of them are collaborating with the rape.'[7] When Labour MP Eric Joyce, a former Army officer, said that 'passing comments like this puts the lives of British soldiers at risk and devalues the lives of the British soldiers',[8] Galloway hit back with: 'The people who have put British troops' lives at risk are the people who sent them to war on a pack of lies.'[9]

Better news came from the Isle of Dogs, a mere stone's throw from Bethnal Green. Respect did reasonably well in a September council by-election, and managed to beat Labour back into third place in the Millwall ward. Ironically, the effect of Respect's strong showing was to split the Labour vote and let the Conservatives in. But the result had been another small achievement and as the end of 2004 approached, the Respect engine was building a head of steam and the question everyone was asking was whether Galloway would be standing for it in the general election. But before that decision could be taken, there was the small matter of the *Daily Telegraph* libel trial to contend with.

Normally libel trials are held in front of a jury, but because this was going to rest on an interpretation of the law, it was held in front of one judge at the High Court, Mr Justice Eady. Galloway's legal team, led in court by Richard Rampton QC, claimed that the *Daily Telegraph* had libelled him, not because they had published the contents of the Iraqi Foreign Ministry documents, but because they had concluded from them that Galloway had solicited and personally taken money from Saddam. When the case opened in the High Court on 15 November, the arguments boiled down to whether the *Daily Telegraph* had reported the documents and their contents in a neutral and responsible manner. For its part, the *Telegraph* maintained that it had done that and therefore had a right to publish the documents under what is known as the Reynolds qualified privilege defence. This gives the press the right to publish allegations in good faith, if they are of sufficient public interest, and was derived from a libel case that the former Irish Prime Minister Albert Reynolds had brought against the *Sunday Times*.

In its story, the *Telegraph* had alleged that Galloway had secretly received something in the region of £375,000 a year from Saddam, and that he had diverted money from the oil-for-food programme and had used the Mariam Appeal as a front for his personal financial gain. All these allegations were vehemently denied by Galloway, who said they were grossly defamatory and, if he didn't make a stand against them, were likely to ruin his career.

It was a fascinating battle, with Galloway's counsel claiming that the *Telegraph* had been waging a 'vendetta' and wanted to 'terminate' him as a public figure. Neil Darbyshire, the executive editor of the paper, had to stand in court and protest that they had never 'hated' Galloway:

> Hatred is very corrosive and exhausting. It doesn't work like that. We don't have figures we hate . . . We wouldn't agree with everything Mr Galloway said, but newspapers tend to like political bruisers because they are colourful and provide copy . . . I am sure that the *Guardian* or *The Times* would have published it.

When Darbyshire was asked if he thought the paper should have waited until it could contact Fawaz Zureikat, Galloway's successor as chairman of the appeal, he said the newspaper had contacted Galloway himself. The trouble was that it appeared that Galloway hadn't been told the full extent of the allegations and the judge felt that he hadn't been given enough opportunity to reply to them. The other crucial issue for the *Telegraph* was that they had also run a leader comment, which hadn't been put to Galloway either, which referred to 'treason' and 'taking money from the oil-for-food programme'. However, in the paper's defence, Darbyshire had pointed out that the leader had only said 'if' the allegations had been proved true.

Although the question of whether or not the documents were genuine was not part of the trial, the *Telegraph*'s barrister, James Price, QC, told the judge: 'The effect on the claimant's reputation arises from the publication of the documents.' He claimed that they were the 'centrepiece and essence' of the *Telegraph*'s reporting.

On the question of privilege, the *Telegraph* argued that the publication of the documents was 'one of the most important stories of a most important time', and therefore the public interest had given them justification: 'It is not, and never has been, any part of the *Telegraph*'s intention to suggest guilt or to suggest guilt could be established other than by most careful investigation using powers which a newspaper lacks.'

It had always been an uphill struggle for the *Telegraph*, who had surrounded the good work of their journalist David Blair with hasty and ill-judged opinion. When the judge delivered his verdict on 2 December 2004, it was firmly in favour of Galloway. Mr Justice Eady ruled that 'the nature, content and tone of their coverage' was not neutral reportage and that the paper was not covered by the qualified privilege defence because it hadn't given Galloway enough time to respond to its allegations. This is one of ten factors that have to be looked at under the Reynolds ruling. Calling Galloway on the evening before publication hadn't been sufficient, Eady said:

> If the documents had been published without comment or serious allegations of fact Mr Galloway could have no complaint since, in so far as they contained statements or allegations of fact it was in the public interest for the *Telegraph* to publish them, at any rate after giving Mr Galloway a fair opportunity to respond to them.

Outside the court, Galloway and his placard-wielding supporters were triumphant. He declared that the judge had given the *Telegraph* 'a judicial caning' and that it gave him no pleasure to receive the £150,000 damages.

After the celebrations and questions outside the High Court, he headed over to Brick Lane in the East End and held a press conference to announce that he would be standing at the general election in Bethnal Green & Bow. John Rees recalls how they had decided on that constituency:

> By the time we'd come to make that decision we'd already stood in the 2004 Euro elections and the GLA [Greater London Authority] and the mayoral,

and we'd had the vote breakdown and the East End of London and particularly Tower Hamlets was our strongest vote in the country. In addition, it had an MP who had the great virtue of being absolutely pro-war, an absolutely dog-loyal Blairite, and was unpopular in her own constituency and had only been narrowly selected by the Labour Party itself, and so we simply put it together: our best candidate in our strongest area, against one of their weakest opponents. You don't have to be a strategic genius to work out that that was a good thing to do.

In the general election of 2005 the strategies of both Labour and Respect would be called into question, in what became known as the battle for Bethnal Green & Bow. Such was the atmosphere of confrontation in the constituency that police officers guarded polling stations on 6 May. The sitting Labour MP, Oona King, with a 10,000 majority since 2001, had inherited a traditionally strong though turbulent Labour area in 1997.

The area has issues and a cultural context that makes it almost unique in the UK, as a local businessman and friend of Galloway's, Azmol Hussein, explains: 'People round here are not living in England. You have to persuade them to allow their kitchen staff to be educated. It's unbelievable, not good.' The ethnic mix of the constituency was the key factor in 2005. Around 36 per cent of the population describe themselves as Muslim, and most of those are Bangladeshis. Their strong objections to the war against terror, the invasion of Iraq, the Bush/Blair support for Israel and the perceived double standards in the treatment of Muslims were hugely important factors in the election. Sitting on what she must have thought was a comfortable majority, King had consistently voted with the government on Iraq, despite a large slice of her constituency being totally opposed to the policy. What she hadn't been able to predict was that Labour's rebel Galloway and Respect would become a powerful force in the area.

One unusual aspect of the campaign was that Galloway had announced right from the start that he would only stand in the Bethnal Green this one time, and after that he would stand down to give a Bengali a chance to be an MP. Mohammed Chowdury was King's assistant during the election. 'Oona was a hard-working MP but she took Bethnal for granted. She never publicised the work she'd done. When we were canvassing, the white people would say, "well, we can tell there's an election because you're here" and Muslims just couldn't forgive her for voting for the war. She made a misjudgement, she thought she could vote for the war and get a ministerial post, but once George offered an alternative there was no chance.'

Josh Peck remembers that King had been on the back foot from well before the election:

> Before the election, we'd hold general community meetings in which Oona would answer questions. The biggest issue was always Iraq. There was great upset and Oona was faced with a real dilemma in voting for the war. She had done a lot of work on human rights in Iraq and at that time felt she had to vote for the overthrow of the regime on humanitarian grounds.

The large SWP contingent in Respect coloured the campaign tactics from the start. This Trotskyist group brought hard-line tactics to bear on the very soft King, using the kind of approach that had earlier been employed in Dundee and Glasgow. Meetings were packed with SWP members who would try to stop King talking. Right from the start this was evident, in a public meeting where King and Galloway had agreed to go head to head over the issue of fire brigade services. Peck was there:

> There was an announcement that one of the fire engines was going to be removed . . . Oona and George both agreed to speak in a public meeting, the first head-to-head. There were about twenty residents and another forty or fifty Respect supporters who booed, heckled and jeered Oona whenever she spoke. Galloway was cheered to the rafters. It's a very effective technique . . . There were another couple of teachers who were well-known SWP activists. They said things like: 'If it wasn't for you killing Iraqi babies, we could afford to keep that fire engine.' Even this came back to the war. When we left, about half of the audience were selling SWP newspapers outside . . . After that we decided to do no more head-to-heads. It wasn't an edifying view of politics. At the front of the crowd were a few old East End ladies who'd turned up to hear about their fire engine and found themselves in the middle of this baiting session. It was very intimidating.

Glyn Robbins, the chair of Tower Hamlets Respect, is a long-serving SWP supporter. He says:

> The SWP is part of the Respect family; they were fundamental to the formation of Respect. I would no more turn my back on them than on a relative or a friend. Without their effort and energy, their skills and organisational powers, Respect would never be where it is . . . We were new, there's lots of people that don't understand Respect and it's had a very negative presentation in the media. We're basically still a volunteer army against much bigger and wealthier parties.

So what part does Galloway play in the Respect coalition? According to Robbins, 'on the whole, George is very much a unifying force. He demonstrates it. If he comes along to a Respect members' meeting, he reminds people what it's all about. He's so good at manning the arguments, if we're having a petty argument over standing orders, George gives perspective.'

Azmol Hussein is one of Galloway's key men in the area, a wealthy local landlord and restaurant owner. He is described as Galloway's right-hand man in Tower Hamlets Respect and says of himself: 'I am more than closely involved in Respect here.' He is now a good friend of Galloway's and remembers how they first met: 'I saw him outside during the campaign. He came in, I liked him and I gave him the keys to a building in Hanbury Street, a three-floor building, and he set up Respect there.' Hussein is bullish about the future: 'I've brought a lot of followers to Respect. A lot. And more are coming. We will take over the council, I know that for sure.'

King was undone by Tony Blair's foreign policy, even among her own local party members, and Labour has acknowledged that some of their own people didn't fight as hard as they might for her because of Iraq. Some even switched sides, such as Gulham Moortusa, a Labour councillor who defected to Respect at the time, but who is now back with Labour. He says: 'People don't think of the Bangladeshi community as defiant but we can be. Lots of people were on the fence and when people like me changed sides then others felt they could too.' He maintains that there was a lot of opportunism at play on the Bangladeshi side:

We knew that we wouldn't be able to sustain it, though. He used us and we used him. It was win-win . . . When Galloway expressed an interest, we found someone with whom we could beat Labour. It was tactical on our part too. People were unhappy with the Labour Party, that was the real issue. They were fed up with the housing situation, with educational underachievement. Then Iraq was the last straw.

It is hard to overestimate the Iraq factor, according to Moortusa. 'Oona's vote for the war was disgusting. A hundred and forty MPs voted against it. She could have done so too. She would have been a hero here. She would have guaranteed her re-election. With a little we could have been very happy.'

Galloway brought the different sides of the Bangladeshi community together too, as Gulham Moortusa explains: 'Galloway got support from the religious and secular parts of the Bengali community. That's something a Bengali could never do. We're not a lump that can be moved together, there are big splits. But we could unite behind a white general.'

In contrast to Labour's rather lacklustre performance, Respect had real momentum, as Peck admits. 'Respect knew how to stir up that feeling. They went round with their battlebus, creating a carnival like atmosphere, and they generated a lot of excitement.'

According to Moortusa, the two sides had very different approaches:

Respect didn't have any roots so it was all people to people, mouth to mouth. Oona was there with all her posh leaflets and persuasive arguments. But Galloway relied on people getting the word out. We used the Bengali media, the *East London Advertiser*, they all supported us . . . He managed to get old and young behind him. There are a lot of people who fall into the category of 'NEET' round here – neither employed, in education or in training. They want to find something exciting and new and he gave that to them.

With religion at the heart of the Iraq issue, another important battle was for the support of the local Muslim groups. King's researcher, Mohammed Chowdury, recalls:

The people on the mosque committees had been told that they shouldn't campaign on behalf of any party, but many openly did so on behalf of Respect. And, for those that didn't, there was no hope anyway because the congregation or the people that used the community facilities had already been mobilised. Respect did look a lot more representative.

Dilwar Hussein, director of the East London Mosque, adds:

The East London Mosque has a congregation of around 5,000 to 6,000, and most of them are under thirty. So all the parties wanted our support. We had to be very careful and not be seen to vote for any party. In the end, it's true that many people voted for Respect.

Peck acknowledges that Respect did a good job of gathering support in that way:

They forged strong alliances with the mosques. The mosque committees always said they didn't support any particular candidates. But it was clear that Respect got their support. They felt angry that they hadn't been listened to, that they'd been taken for granted. Galloway gave them a voice. They also had good links with community organisations, they ran a network for young Bangladeshi women and a football team.

Many commentators during the election period saw the concentration on the Muslim vote as short-termism which had longer-term implications. Peck believes that

politicians who understood the history of Tower Hamlets appreciated the need to work with all communities . . . Respect ran their campaign almost exclusively in Bangladeshi areas. The SWP had a few stalls in Bow, a predominantly white area, and they leafleted all over. But Galloway devoted most of his time to the Bengali areas. I don't think that's in anyone's interest. You've started to see letters in the *East London Advertiser* saying: 'Galloway only represents one part of the community, what about the rest of us?'

The media descended on Bethnal Green & Bow in the 2005 general election like a pack of foxhounds deprived of a hunt. Few other places offered anything like as interesting a story, and with so much coverage the hacks fanned the flames of controversy even more. Mohammed Chowdury says:

> I remember one day a journalist called [King] up and started asking her about animal rights. She said she was against the deliberately cruel treatment of animals. Then he asked if she was against halal meat. The next day, the *East London Advertiser* led with 'Oona wants to ban halal meat'.

This kind of report led to rumours going around the tight-knit community, where word of mouth quickly propagates myths that are hard to dislodge. It became common 'knowledge' that King was meant to be against halal meat. With Labour relying on traditional press manipulation methods, they were left powerless to stop the bad stories, as Peck explains: 'It was all Chinese whispers, all unaccredited. Which made it impossible to respond. It was all word of mouth rather than the traditional means of press statements and replies.'

Apart from using the wrong overall tactics in their media campaign, Labour also shot themselves in the foot not just once but twice. Chowdury recalls:

> At one point in the campaign, we had two leaflets. One directed to the Muslim voters with issues such as Palestine and religious discrimination, and the other without. Respect gave us hell over this and we got into trouble and had to withdraw one. But then, before the election, Galloway went to Bengal and was photographed with all the dignitaries. They made this leaflet, *Respecting Bengal*, all in Bengali, total hypocrites. But a savvy move.

The second major gaffe, which had more serious implications for King personally and also showed another side to her campaign, was the decision to use Galloway's time at War on Want against him. King personally spoke to several former directors of War on Want, as well as former staff. She and her team also gained access to its files from the late 1980s. From these documents and conversations, she compiled a rather naive press release making allegations that could not be substantiated. Galloway sued her and won an out-of-court settlement. The idea had been badly conceived and executed, and left her open to attack.

Rather than dirty tricks, King's better tactic was a sense of humour, which often deserts Galloway when he needs it most. Peck remembers:

> In one radio debate, George was getting hot under the collar and Oona joked: 'Hey, just calm down, George.' He couldn't take that because he's got no other gears than soapbox oratory. Humour deflates him, he doesn't like being laughed at. After that, we used to sit in the audience, look him in the eye and laugh at him to put him off.

In a campaign so focused on race and religion, the question of King's own ethnicity came into play to an extent as well. Her father, Preston King, is an African-American civil rights activist, who married her mother, a Jewish teacher, while he was in the UK at the London School of Economics. (Incidentally, her uncle was Martin Luther King's lawyer and her grandfather a founder of the National Association for the Advancement of Colored People, the USA's key civil rights group). In reply to King's assertion that she was interested in human rights in Iraq, Galloway would refer to Labour's policy in Iraq having led to the deaths of people 'with blacker faces than hers'. Having an American father and a Jewish mother clearly wasn't going to add to her appeal in Muslim Bethnal Green & Bow.

In the campaign, abuse spilled over into physical threats and actual violence, on both sides, though there have never been any suggestion that Galloway or King knew about the tactics, or approved of them in any way. King's car was pelted with eggs, and eggs and vegetables were thrown at her and a party of Jewish mourners at a memorial service. John Prescott was egged on a trip to the constituency too. King would be followed around by groups of Respect supporters when she went out to meet and greet people. According to Peck, 'It had started in the local council elections at the Brick Lane Festival, when one man followed King down the street with a megaphone, saying: "This is your MP, look at the blood dripping from her." It's an effective tactic for paralysing and stopping interaction.' At a meeting of a tenants' association in Spitalfields about six weeks before the election, a group of teenagers wearing Respect stickers came and pounded on the doors, shouting abuse. Peck says:

> When we arrived we saw one of the Respect organisers in the background, a man, who disappeared when he saw us. Later, when we were walking around the estate, we were egged. That happened a few times. And then the tyres were slashed . . . It made everyone in Labour very cautious. In the end, we wouldn't go door knocking with less than five or six people and a car nearby to make sure Oona could get away. On the one hand, it was only kids and it was often done in quite a jovial manner but when you've got groups of eight or ten kids following you round it's intimidating.

According to Dilwar Hussein, a leading figure from the East London Mosque:

> Galloway was fantastic at getting young Muslims involved. It did get a bit ugly but only because the issue was so sensitive. Young people are more likely to get upset and angry. We tried to calm down the situation, to condemn the egging, that it wasn't the civilised way to protest. Our volunteers went and spoke with the lads who did it.

Gulham Moortusa, who had changed to Respect from Labour, plays down the trouble. 'I think the tension was exaggerated. There were a few incidents, a few eggs, but it's part of the Bangladeshi political culture to throw eggs. It wasn't that bad.' Nevertheless, just before polling day, King and Galloway went to see the borough police to talk about security. Moortusa recalls: 'We didn't want a situation, as we'd seen in Leicester, where twenty or so Respect supporters would hover round polling stations in Labour areas. Galloway was utterly charming, totally won us over.'

King and Labour were still playing into the hands of their opponents, however. Their lack of judgement led to another own goal when they accused Respect supporters of beating up an old Labour chap in the street, an allegation that proved unfounded.

As polling day approached, the heat got turned up again when Galloway claimed he had been targeted by a radical Islamic group who threatened to hang him, as Moortusa explains: 'They thought he was manipulating the Muslim voters, being a false prophet.' At the time it was thought that they might have been the fundamentalist Hizb-Ut-Tahrir group, but both Respect and Hizb-Ut-Tahrir denied this later. From the accounts of Galloway and bystanders, it was a pretty frightening event, as a gang of thirty Muslim fundamentalists surrounded him and his supporters. According to Galloway, they said they were 'setting up the gallows' for him and warned any Muslim who voted for Respect that they faced a 'sentence of death'. The two sides fought openly in the street, until the police intervened. 'I heard shouting and looked out into the street to see a large group of Asian men. Many of them were fighting,' said a local. 'There were punches and kicks thrown, then a large number of police arrived and broke up the riot.' Galloway, who had his daughter, son-in-law and baby grandchild waiting for him in the car, was reported in the *Evening Standard* explaining: 'They were claiming I was representing myself as a false deity and for this apostasy I would be sentenced to the gallows.' Respect now claim that 'the attack was carried out by an organisation called al-Ghurabba, an offshoot of the dis-banded al-Muhajiroun, who subsequently invaded another of our meetings in Luton'. This was never substantiated.

Galloway became the MP for Bethnal Green & Bow on 5 May 2005, with 15,801 votes, 35.9 per cent of the total. King came a close second with 14,978 and 34 per cent, with the Conservatives trailing a long way behind on 6,244 and 14.2 per cent. Labour had made Galloway walk the plank, but he'd simply leapt off it into a meaner, sleeker ship called Respect.

The election had been a remarkable event, not just because the new party had taken the seat, but because a coalition of some atheists from a far-left Trotskyist group had collaborated with a group of working-class, religious believers. Alibour Chowdry reflects: 'It's worrying because young people were manipulated. Respect is full of some far-left lunatics. It's worrying to see Socialist Workers inside the mosques and youth centres, people who'd previously been ignored. In essence, many of them are anti-religion.'

That was the 2005 Bethnal Green & Bow election: a tale of abuse, mobs, smears and general bad feeling. Labour had started out looking like losers and had stayed that way. It is probably a sign of their complacency and lack of connection to the constituents that it wasn't until polling day that the possibility of defeat began to dawn on their campaign manager, Tim Nuthall:

> I didn't think we were going to lose until the afternoon of polling day. I was back at HQ and the first indicators were coming through. They didn't look good. I rang round all the campaign offices and told people to get out on the street. It was about 7 p.m. and I was out knocking doors. A sad, desperate sight! I had Oona's husband and Mohammed [Chowdury]'s mum with me. I walked into one estate and a lad came up to me and said: 'What the fuck are you doing here? Go away, it won't work.' I went and knocked on the doors of people who'd promised to vote for us. Many of them couldn't look me in the face and I knew the boy had been right, it was a waste of time. And as I left the estate, the Respect battlebus came up the road; the kids were on the deck shouting and celebrating. There was a festival atmosphere. They started pointing down at us and chanting 'murderer, murderer, murderer'. And there was Mo's mum, holding up her Oona banner. So tragic! I thought, God, put it down. And the kids started coming out of the house and joining in. Imagine!

21

I am not now, nor have I ever been

The dust had hardly settled on the battleground of Bethnal Green, when on 12 May 2005 the United States Senate launched the political equivalent of a transatlantic Cruise missile at George Galloway. They had pressed the start button back in April 2004 when Senator Norm Coleman had instigated an investigation into alleged 'abuse and misconduct related to the oil-for-food program', and now the findings were published. They were so grave that within a week Galloway was on a plane to Washington, to reply to the accusations and deliver blow after blow against US policy on Iraq. From the Atlantic to the Pacific, the TV footage showed how a plucky little Briton was taking on the Bush machine. On anyone's judgement, he had turned defence into attack in brilliant and audacious style.

The *Report on Oil Allocations Granted to Charles Pasqua and George Galloway* claimed that Saddam Hussein had misused the oil-for-food programme to reward people he hoped would work against UN sanctions. Galloway strongly denied the allegation that he personally had profited from this. 'I have never profited from anything related to Iraq . . . This cannot possibly be called an investigation,' he said. 'This is a lickspittle Republican committee, acting on the wishes of George W. Bush.'

The Senate Permanent Subcommittee on Investigations, which is made up of both Democrats and Republicans, alleged that Baghdad had given Charles Pasqua, a French politician, the right to buy eleven million barrels of oil, and Galloway twenty-three million. (It claimed that middlemen dealing in options in oil could collect commissions of between three and thirty US cents per barrel.) These allegations were based on an analysis of documents drawn up by the Ministry of Oil under Saddam and interviews with 'high-ranking Hussein regime officials'. Galloway has always strenuously denied them and there is absolutely no evidence that he has ever benefited from any Iraqi oil deals.

The oil-for-food programme had been set up in 1996 to allow Iraq to sell some of its oil, but only if the profits were used to buy food, medicines and other essential supplies. The question of how much of the money actually went to the people and how much to the leaders of the regime is disputed between each side of the political argument, but the overall damage to the Iraqi quality of life cannot be disputed. Hans von Sponeck, the UN's top humanitarian official in Iraq between 1998 and 2000, resigned over the sanctions because he believes they were inhumane. He says: 'During the whole oil-for-food programme, the total figure of benefit that each Iraqi civilian got was 51 cents per day; that was to cover health, food, water, agriculture, education and, by 2000, telecoms and communication too. That's $185 per year.'

The Senate's report summed up the way the oil-for-food programme worked:

> The arm of the Iraqi government that managed the sale of Iraqi crude oil was the State Oil Marketing Organization, commonly called 'SOMO'. In order to manage the volume of oil flowing through its pipelines, Iraq divided its oil supply into discrete units, typically ranging from 1 to 10 million barrels. It then allocated these units to prospective oil purchasers, essentially giving those recipients an option to purchase that allotment of oil. These options are typically called 'allocations'. Assuming that SOMO and the purchaser could agree on other contractual terms, such as the loading schedule, the purchaser would contract with SOMO and proceed to buy the oil . . . The Iraqis repeated this allocation process for each of the 13 six-month phases of the Oil for Food Program.

Von Sponeck is damning of the whole scheme, which, he explains,

> relieved the Iraqi government's control of its assets and turned the money over to a bank in Paris with a UN treasurer. The government of Iraq was free to order what they thought was needed. It was in a way a farce because they

identified inputs into various sectors and assumed that the government of Iraq would have enough to finance them, through the sale of oil. But no one could anticipate the market price for oil and it fell very, very low.

This left Iraq without the money its people needed to buy their essential goods. The US Senate committee later accused the Saddam regime of making more than $21 billion through smuggling oil and from kickbacks in breach of UN sanctions, in an effort to keep the economy afloat. The committee claimed that about $13.6bn came from selling oil to some of Iraq's neighbours, and that about $4.4bn was creamed off through bribes on food, medicine and so on supplied through the oil-for-food programme. Many involved on both sides had been caught in the crossfire: even the son of the Secretary General of the UN faced criticism concerning his behaviour.

According to Galloway's spokesman, Ron McKay, he and Galloway were told nothing about the investigation and first received the news that the Senate was about to reveal their report from an American journalist. The journalist claimed that the date of publication was going to be the day of the 2005 general election. McKay says:

> Probably because they realised that it wasn't a very good publicity coup to perhaps influence an election, it was held back . . . George had not been questioned in any way and all of a sudden, a few weeks later, out comes this report, which effectively claims that he had been a party to receiving money, kickbacks, from the oil-for-food programme. So the report appeared and the first thing he did was to . . . complain he hadn't been given a chance to put his point of view, hadn't been summoned, hadn't been asked for his evidence, hadn't been phoned, hadn't been written to, hadn't been emailed – what kind of justice was this

Pasqua denied receiving any money and has never been to Washington to dispute the claims, but McKay says that Galloway decided very quickly that he had to:

> So he immediately said: 'Right, we're getting on a plane. We're going to

Washington and we're going to demand to be heard, and we're going to make a fuss about it. We're going to make sure they can't ignore us. I'm going to have my say; this is a travesty of justice from a man who is supposed to be a lawyer.' So that was it. No invitation. George's office told the Senate that George was going to be coming. They eventually said: 'Well, OK, we can fit you in on a particular day, for a couple of hours.' So that's it, off we went to the Senate to fight the battle.

Galloway's Respect comrade John Rees was more concerned:

> I thought that he should do it but I was worried about him because there's one of him and half a dozen Senators . . . I remember Ron McKay saying to me: 'But he's innocent.' I said: 'I know that, Ron, but so were the Hollywood 12 [*sic*]. It didn't stop them being out of work for a generation either.' Being right and willing to fight doesn't mean you come off best. But in the end we all thought there wasn't an option. If you have this huge bit of this administration against you, if you don't confront it on the same scale, then you're going to be living under its shadow forever.

(Rees is in fact referring to the Hollywood Ten, a group of writers and directors who refused to give evidence to the House of Representatives Un-American Activities Committee.)

They weren't travelling alone. The British media went with them in force, some on the same plane, many others on different flights, some to join their colleagues already working in the United States. McKay remembers:

> It was a circus. There were people, camera crews on the plane as we went. Camera crews as we left, camera crews at the other end, camera crews following us in, a scrum, a huge media scrum on the pavement, inside the building, in the Senate Committee room, and afterwards it was an utter press jamboree.

Even before Galloway had set foot inside the Senate building, he started another row, with the British US-based journalist Christopher Hitchens. Like those in the Labour Party who have moved from hard left to right, and who get the rough edge of his tongue, the fact that Hitchens used to be on the left but now isn't clearly cause Galloway intense annoyance. On the steps of the Senate building Hitchens approached and claims he asked him about Saddam's support for suicide bombers in Israel, but only received abuse in return. Calling Hitchens a 'drink-sodden ex-Trotskyist popinjay' has since passed into legend, but what is not mentioned so often is that a few years before Galloway had called him 'that great British man of letters' and 'the greatest polemicist of our age' when he and Hitchens appeared to be on the same political side. Hitchens was keen to get Galloway to talk about letters that the MP had claimed he'd written to the Senate the week before, in which he asked to be allowed to clear his name. So, shortly before Galloway took the stand that day, Hitchens tried to get him to talk, but was rebuffed by McKay and Galloway, in an exchange caught by the BBC. It went like this:

> *Galloway:* This is a bloated, drink-sodden, former Trotskyist lunatic, who is just walking around as a sort of bag lady in Washington.
> *Hitchens:* Just enquiring . . . I just wondered. You said you'd contacted the committee by letter, by email. Did you bring copies of the letters with you?
> *Galloway:* Has anyone got any sensible questions?
> *Hitchens:* Or the email?
> *Galloway:* You're a drink-soaked, bloated—
> *American reporter:* Are you going to answer his question? The substance of his question?
> *Galloway:* I'm here to talk to the Senate.

Galloway and Hitchens together became a sort of sideshow later that year when they had a head-to-head debate in the United States, which sold out and was broadcast around the UK and America. For the time being, however, Galloway had more pressing things to think about. He had the Senate report to read, as McKay explains:

> This was the first time that we had even seen what purported to be these documents that the Senate inquiry was supposed to be based on, and we were only handed a bundle of the report and several appendices, including these documents, on the day, as George waited to go in front of the committee.

When we flicked through it seemed rather curious that what they said were original documents circulated within the Iraqi ministry all happened to be written in English. Of course it transpired that these were American translations. George was promised that he would be given an opportunity to examine forensically the original documents, but that's never happened. They've never done that. And they've subsequently issued another report, again without talking to George. Just the usual summary justice from the Republican-controlled committee.

In the Senate's second report, published on 25 October 2005, which McKay was referring to above, there is a reference to Galloway being invited to submit further evidence, to back up his appearance on the witness stand. It reads: 'Galloway's response to Subcommittee's interrogatories: Mr Galloway declined to be interviewed by the Subcommittee, but did agree to answer written questions. In submitting the interrogatories to Mr Galloway, the Subcommittee informed him that the questions and his answers would be considered a continuation of his sworn testimony before the Subcommittee.' So they claim they invited him to talk, but that he refused and gave written evidence instead.

It's quite likely that Norm Coleman never wanted to see or hear Galloway ever again after his May appearance. It was a tour de force that must have set his teeth on edge, as Galloway spewed out facts like bullets, claiming that if the world had listened to him, Iraq wouldn't have been in such a mess. 'It was all completely off the top of his head,' says McKay. 'He obviously knew what he wanted to say, but he had nothing written down, there was no preparation. It was difficult to prepare anyway, because we didn't quite know what the format was going to be. We didn't know the substance of the supposed evidence that they had until we actually got to the Senate and were actually handed all of the documents . . . He knew how long he had to say it. He didn't have any notes. He knew the ground very well . . . So he just went in and decided that he was going to have his ten minutes and then react to the questions.'

The atmosphere in the room was very different to the quiet of a House of Commons committee, says McKay: 'It's totally unlike the British Parliament. There are cameras everywhere, massive rooms, people coming and going all the time, not the formality, the rigour that there is at the British

Parliament. There were hundreds of press in the room, many, many film crews.' They were all going to broadcast Galloway's tirade against the Bush government, and around the world that performance has gained Galloway millions of admirers. In a political culture that has little confrontation and open debate, it must have been doubly shocking for the Senators who were watching. John Rees remembers the reaction:

> On the day he did it brilliantly, but the interesting thing about that is lots of people said: 'I've never heard it said like that to them, and he was so good on the arguments.' And he was, but I know where that came from . . . That was the greatest hits of George Galloway's speeches to Stop the War meetings for two to three years beforehand. It had been rehearsed in a movement for two to three years before that.

Rees may claim that Galloway was bolstered by a movement, and rehearsed over two or three years, but it needed tremendous guts and self-belief to take on the USA in its own backyard. He did have a nervous moment before he went in, though, as McKay explains: 'We were sitting waiting to be called, and he turned to me and whispered: "Do you know where the toilet is?" And I said: "Yes, follow me," so we all left and hundreds of newspapers and film crews followed us to the toilet.' A lighter hiatus, but overall it was heavy duty and intense, with Galloway ferocious in his denials of the accusations. In football parlance, he took Route One to goal, and it is as well to remember that his performance was a game of two halves: 1. the denials of the Senate's allegations against him personally; 2. the attacks on US policy towards Iraq. His critique of the situation in Iraq, for which they had unwittingly given him the biggest soapbox in history, was devastating. Here are some of the highlights:

> I gave my political life's blood to try to stop the mass killing of Iraqis by the sanctions on Iraq, which killed one million Iraqis, most of them children; most of them died before they even knew that they were Iraqis, but they died for no other reason other than that they were Iraqis with the misfortune to be born at that time.

I told the world that Iraq, contrary to your claims, did not have weapons of mass destruction. I told the world, contrary to your claims, that Iraq had no connection to al-Qaeda. I told the world, contrary to your claims, that Iraq had no connection to the atrocity on 9/11/2001. I told the world, contrary to your claims, that the Iraqi people would resist a British and American invasion of their country and that the fall of Baghdad would not be the beginning of the end, but merely the end of the beginning.

Senator, in everything I said about Iraq, I turned out to be right and you turned out to be wrong and 100,000 people paid with their lives.

Senator, this is the mother of all smokescreens. You are trying to divert attention from the crimes that you supported, from the theft of billions of dollars of Iraq's wealth . . . Have a look at the real oil-for-food scandal. Have a look at the fourteen months you were in charge of Baghdad, the first fourteen months, when $8.8 billion of Iraq's wealth went missing on your watch. . . . Have a look at the oil that you didn't even meter, that you were shipping out of the country and selling, the proceeds of which went who knows where. Have a look at the $800 million you gave to American military commanders to hand out around the country without even counting it or weighing it.

Galloway's denials of the serious and potentially extremely damaging allegations in the report were equally brilliantly put across, and he summed it up very well when he said: 'Now I know that standards have slipped in the last few years in Washington, but for a lawyer you are remarkably cavalier with any idea of justice. I am here today but last week you already found me guilty.' Like all the other inquiries to date that have tried to establish links between Galloway and various funds, the Senate's report fell short. At no stage has any financial record ever been produced that shows that he has personally taken money.

What the investigation showed was that Fawaz Zureikat, a trustee of the Mariam Appeal, had been allocated the right to trade in Iraqi oil. He had been given a letter signed by Galloway, which made him the MP's agent in Iraq on Mariam Appeal work. McKay tried to explain to the author in November 2005:

The allegation is that George somehow colluded with Fawaz Zureikat: that the money was paid, bona fide deals were then struck, and that money was then given as commission to Fawaz Zureikat – all of which is entirely legal – and that then he somehow gave money to George Galloway, which would be, if you like, the point where the legality breaks. But that hasn't [been] and can't be proven. But everything there is absolutely legal. These were legal oil deals. It's whether or not George Galloway knew anything about them, whether he's on these documents and whether he colluded in that. And of course he's absolutely denied that.

Galloway's testimony on 17 May 2005 was designed to push all the right buttons with the media. He even invoked the United States' anti-communist witchhunts (conducted by the House Un-American Activities Committee and also Senator Joseph McCarthy), at which various citizens were accused of being communists, and where the phrase 'I am not now, nor have I ever been, a member of the Communist Party,' came to epitomise proceedings. Galloway started with 'Senator, I am not now, nor have I ever been, an oil trader and neither has anyone on my behalf. I have never seen a barrel of oil, owned one, bought one, sold one – and neither has anyone on my behalf.'

As part of his defence of himself he again referred to his work campaigning against Saddam Hussein. 'I was an opponent of Saddam Hussein when British and American governments and businessmen were selling him guns and gas. I used to demonstrate outside the Iraqi embassy when British and American officials were going in and doing commerce.' He also referred to Hansard as evidence of his stance against Saddam: 'You will see from the official parliamentary record, Hansard, from 15 March 1990 onwards, voluminous evidence that I have a rather better record of opposition to Saddam Hussein than you do and than any other member of the British or American governments do.'

Taking the twelve months from that date, as an example: on 15 March 1990 Galloway stood in the Commons and joined almost the entire House in criticising 'the Iraqi regime' for its 'judicial murder' of Farzad Bazoft, a British-based journalist who had been executed for spying; on 18 April, in a debate about Iraq's 'supergun', he said that all countries in the Middle East, including Israel, should give up their weapons of mass destruction; in November he said: 'I have no truck with Saddam Hussein, and I hope that the Foreign Secretary accepts that,' but said nothing critical; in January 1991 he called Saddam a 'brutal dictator' and complained about the inaccuracy of US/UK bombing of Baghdad. These were all in the House of Commons debating chamber.

At the Senate hearing of 17 May Galloway also complained about other evidence that the sub-committee had included in its report: 'You have my name on lists provided to you by the Duelfer inquiry, provided to him by the convicted bank robber, fraudster and conman Ahmed Chalabi, who many people to their credit in your country now realise played a decisive role in leading your country into the disaster in Iraq.' He was referring to a CIA report into WMD, conducted on behalf of the allies who had invaded Iraq by Charles Duelfer, a former UNSCOM weapons inspector. Duelfer had compiled a list of names of people who allegedly benefited from the sale of Iraqi oil, but the list was discredited when many names were edited out for what Duelfer claimed were legal reasons. Chalabi was also discredited when it became apparent that he had the track record as described by Galloway.

After Galloway's allotted time to put his own case, there followed a question-and-answer session. Senators Norm Coleman and Carl Levin were asking the questions. Here are a few of the more important answers:

- *Galloway:* I can assure you, Mr Zureikat never gave me a penny from an oil deal, from a cake deal, from a bread deal, or from any deal.
- *Galloway:* My point is, you have accused me personally of enriching myself, of taking money from Iraq, and that is false and unjust.
- *Levin:* Did you have conversations with Tariq Aziz about the award of oil allocations? That is my question.
- *Galloway:* No.

Judged on style, Galloway certainly won the day. Some have claimed that Coleman saw his career destroyed in front of him, and if he ever runs for higher office, that footage of him listening to Galloway will surely be trotted out. For his part, he claims that he had to stifle his laughter at Galloway's delivery. Only time will tell for both men what the consequences are of that day, but Galloway's performance will be remembered long after the issues have been forgotten, simply because it's a piece of great theatre. To most it wasn't about right and wrong, or politics, or Iraq, it was just one man versus the machine. When Galloway reviewed his own performance in his book *Mr Galloway Goes to Washington*, which includes a transcription of his evidence, he wrote: 'I can only say that God gave me wings that day'. He flew, but some may wonder if, like Icarus, one day he will get too close to the sun.

The title of his book refers to the Frank Capra movie *Mr Smith Goes to Washington*, starring James Stewart, where an innocent country bumpkin is accused of corruption in Washington. The make-believe and drama of Hollywood seems to suit Galloway. There is perhaps something Hollywood about his vision of himself. That must have been helped when, not surprisingly, he became the most sought-after speaker on the anti-Bush circuit. He did a tour of ten dates in twelve days and found himself feted by the USA's celebrity anti-war elite. When Ron McKay and Galloway were in San Francisco, actor and director Sean Penn invited him to lunch, then Warren Beatty and Annette Bening had him over to their house in Mulholland Drive, Los Angeles, one of the most prestigious and expensive locations in America. Galloway really had hit the big time.

Meanwhile, his acquaintance Tariq Aziz had hit an all-time low. He had been arrested after the invasion and was now in a US jail, with no prospect of release. His son, Ziad Aziz, says:

> Galloway only visited us in Amman in April 2003. He said he was sending a letter to ex-friends of my father to make a petition. He did it for a while but he stopped. He said, 'I will try to work hard for your father,' and he had worked hard for it but I don't know why it stopped . . . Since then, he's sent his regards to us through friends but we've had no contact with him for two to three years. I am not disappointed with George Galloway himself. Since my father was arrested, lots of friends went, they did not ask about us as a family. A lot of them were gone with the wind. Galloway was the same.

The Senate investigation had thrown some light on Galloway's relationships with Tariq Aziz and Fawaz Zureikat, but also on his relationship with his wife, Amineh Abu Zayyad, a friend of Zureikat's. When he first went public over her, in 1995, they gave an interview and even arranged a photo shoot. After that, they kept it out of bounds to the press, until Amineh's name came up in the oil-for-food scandal and she also sued for divorce, citing numerous affairs.

They first met in 1991 at a Partick political meeting where Galloway was speaking. The Jerusalem-born Palestinian, who is twenty-three years younger than him, says that she is a cousin of not only Yasser Arafat (see Chapter 6) but also Said Abu-Rish, a biographer of Saddam Hussein. Another close relative, Ziad Abu-Zayyad, had been a Cabinet minister under Arafat. Amineh was studying cell biology at Glasgow University at the time she and Galloway met. She completed her doctorate in Glasgow and has spent much of her time since studying the effects of depleted uranium on the people of southern Iraq, a quest that may have led to her contracting leukaemia from that radioactive material.

The new happy couple gave a joint interview to the *Daily Record* in November 1995, declaring their love. In it Amineh talked of her brother, who had been jailed and her uncle killed 'as they campaigned to reclaim the Occupied Territories from Israeli control'. In the same piece Galloway claimed that it had been love at first sight back at that Glasgow meeting. He had made a beeline for her and that was it. He later said: 'The night I saw her changed my life. I saw this beautiful young woman in the audience and made sure I was introduced to her . . . as soon as I met Amineh I knew things were different. We started to see each other and fell head over heels.'

Amineh, for her part, told the *Scotsman* in April 2003:

> From the day I met him, he was the most gentle and honest man I have ever known. Once we got serious there were enough people willing to tell me about his past and other women. I didn't care about that. I see the side that nobody else sees. I sometimes see him worried and tired, but I also see how committed he is to his work.

They were married at Lambeth Register Office in March 2000, and made their home at Ambleside Avenue in Streatham, in the house that Galloway had bought years before.

Amineh was a glamorous addition to Galloway's life and it is likely that she helped him with further introductions into Palestinian society, via her father, a businessman, and other members of her family. She has remained close to them and often talked about them, according to Galloway's former chauffeur, Roberto Sinatra, who used to take her shopping on a regular basis, 'where she spent a lot of money on presents for her family'. Her work in the Middle East kept her away from Galloway for long periods at a time and the strain showed. In 2005, just before the general election, she announced that she was seeking a divorce, on the grounds of infidelity. She told journalists that she had received calls from women claiming to have had romantic links with him. 'When he told me his new party was going to be called Respect, I went upstairs and cried. How can he call it this when he doesn't even treat his own wife with respect?' In reply, Galloway issued a statement admitting he perhaps hadn't treated his wife with enough respect, but that he had hoped for a reconciliation, which he conceded was by then unlikely. Riad Al Tahir, who knows Amineh well, thinks she was a little naive. 'Amineh believed Galloway sacrificed a quest for the leadership of the Labour Party to pursue the Palestinian cause.'

Galloway doesn't deny his relationship to Zureikat and confirmed to the Senate investigators that he had written a letter on House of Commons paper headed 'To whom it may concern', which named Zureikat as his 'representative in Baghdad on all matters concerning my work with the "Mariam Appeal" or the Emergency Committee on Iraq'. The letter went on: 'It would be appreciated if all co-operation could be extended to him in his dealings on my behalf' and that 'save for any written permissions from me, no other person should be entertained as acting on my behalf in any circumstances'. Galloway signed the letter as the chairman of the Mariam Appeal and organiser of the Emergency Committee on Iraq.

When Galloway had appeared in front of the sub-committee in May, Coleman had asked him about Zureikat. This is the transcript of that exchange:

> *Coleman:* I am asking you specifically, in 2001 were you aware that he [Zureikat] was doing deals with Iraq?
>
> *Galloway:* I was aware that he was doing extensive business with Iraq. I did not

know the details of it. It was not my business.

Coleman: . . . So in 2003, you are saying you do not know the answer to whether he was involved in oil deals?

Galloway: I told you in my previous two answers, I knew that Mr Zureikat was heavily involved in business in Iraq and elsewhere but that it was none of my business what particular transactions or business he was involved in . . .

Coleman: . . . You never had a conversation with him in 2001 of whether he was ever doing oil business with Iraq?

Galloway: . . . I never asked him if he was trading in oil.

Coleman: So in 2003, when you said you did not know whether he was doing oil deals, were you telling the truth at that time?

Galloway: Yes, I was. I have never known until the *Telegraph* story appeared that he was alleged to be doing oil deals.

Clive Anderson interviewed Galloway in December 2005, a month or so after the second report had been published. This is how the part of the interview ran in which he explained the funding of the Mariam Appeal:

Galloway: I know exactly where the money came from because I'm the one that raised it. And I'll tell you we got £508,000 from the King of the UAE, the now deceased Sheik Zayed, approximately £150,000 from the now King of Saudi Arabia, King Abdul Abdin Aziz, and the balance from a Jordanian businessman called Fawaz Zureikat, whom in 2000 we made the chairman of the Appeal, and who met virtually every British journalist who ever passed through Iraq, sat at his table, him paying the bill, acting in his capacity as the chairman of the Mariam Appeal and as a businessman doing big business with Iraq. And if necessary I will produce a very large number of journalists who took his hospitality in that dual capacity. So far from being a secret benefactor, we made him the chairman of the Appeal. Now interestingly, no-one ever asks me about the two Arab kings, who gave much more money than Mr Zureikat did. No-one ever asks me: 'Did you ask the King of Arabia where he got the money that he gave to the Mariam Appeal?' and I wonder why not. I guess he got that money because he's a King, and I guess Mr Zureikat got his because he's a businessman. I didn't ask either where they got their money from, I was only happy that they were donating it.

Anderson: I suppose the reason why people focus on him is because if he was getting his money from trading in oil, as part of the oil-for-food programme, then it to an extent undercuts the political/moral case that you're making. If you're saying that children are dying because of lack of food or lack of medicine, and part of the reason is because that's due to lack of money, and money is being siphoned off and some of it goes to him, and if that comes back to your appeal, there is a sort of . . . you can follow the moral criticism that goes with it.

Galloway: I, I, I really can't. I can from ignorant journalists, but not from somebody with your intellect, because if you think about that, if, instead of Mr Zureikat buying the oil and selling the oil, Mr BP or Mr Shell had done so, they would have put all the profits from the deal into their shareholders' pockets. Instead of putting it in his own pockets, Mr Zureikat appears to have made some of it available to anti-sanction, anti-war campaigning. So, far from being more reprehensible than the activities of Mr BP or Mr Shell, it's much more morally valid. You know, he ought to be congratulated for not pocketing the profits he made from oil trading in the way that a normal oil trader would have done.

Anderson: Well, you make that point, but of course in the world of politics, if somebody is seen to be benefiting by payments in an indirect route from the people who they are apparently supporting then that's always going to cloud the issue and undercut your position.

Galloway: He was not giving money to me, he was giving money to a campaign. And moreover he was giving money to campaigns from Canada to Cairo.

Anderson: And also involved in this, or alleged to be involved in this, was your wife of the time. Was she receiving money and channelling money as well, or do you say you know nothing of that?

Galloway: Ha ha . . . that's what I call slipping in a rather damning series of propositions. My ex-wife is a scientist who specialised in the very depleted uranium epidemic that probably produced the leukaemia sickness that Mariam and many, many other children suffer from. She spent almost five years, the best part of five years, down amongst the nuclear debris in Iraq studying that whole proposition that the WHO was forbidden by the United States from investigating. So nobody was investigating it. She of course fundraised for her scientific work and I'm aware that she fundraised from

Switzerland and in the Arab world. I knew that she had received some funds. I didn't know how much, or from whom. But she never gave any of it to me, she never used it for her own personal benefit. It was not a gift, it was research funding that she spent on equipment, on the materials that a scientist requires, on the travel around Iraq, on the recruitment of volunteers, and when you count up what the costs of all that would be you see that there's not very much left.

The Senate investigators produced bank records in their report purporting to show monies coming and going from Zureikat's Citibank account. Every transaction in US dollars, anywhere in the world, is registered in a US bank. They claim that these records show the amounts he donated to the Mariam Appeal and amounts paid to him by Taurus Petroleum, an oil dealing company. There is no suggestion that these, or other transactions, in any way involved Galloway, as has been made clear, including by Galloway himself, in his interview with Clive Anderson.

So what was the object of the US Senate's investigating Galloway? Some, such as Sabbah Al Mukhtar, consider that the billions spent invading Iraq, the billions' worth of damage to the country, the billions of dollars that just went missing after the invasion all make the inquiries into the aspects of the oil-for-food programme irrelevant. Al Mukhtar says: 'The oil-for-food allegations are all rubbish, not just about George Galloway, they're all rubbish. The UN spent $15 million on its enquiries, searching for payments of $10,000 or $20,000.' As for the kickbacks to Saddam's officials, there was no choice for those involved, as Riad Al Tahir admits: 'Anyone involved who was not prepared to pay the surcharge would not get any oil. I myself paid the surcharge. It is documented through my bank to SOMO.'

There was no-one closer to Galloway in the old regime than Tariq Aziz. Galloway had numerous meetings with him over many years and got to know his family reasonably well too, well enough to spend Christmas Day with them in 1999. Ziad Aziz believes Galloway acted for the Iraqi people:

Galloway worked against America and he helped the people of Iraq. I know Galloway works for the Iraqi people but I don't know about money or the oil for food. The UN investigators came to see me and asked questions about

307

Galloway. I told them I didn't know. Why do they want to ask about something ten years later?

Of all the allegations levelled at Galloway, the one that understandably infuriates him is that he was Saddam's MP. But what did Saddam himself think of Galloway's work? A very good source, Saman Abdul Majid, who was Saddam's English and French interpreter for fifteen years, wrote in his memoirs, *Saddam Years*, that the tyrant's opinion of Galloway went downhill fast in the late 1990s, when Galloway became more vocal in his condemnation of Saddam under all the pressure not to be portrayed as a stooge. 'Saddam was very sensitive and felt humiliated,' claims Majid, who more than once witnessed Saddam refusing to see the MP and leaving it up to one of his murderous sons, Uday, to conduct the meetings.

22

Big Brother and beyond

Publicity is the oxygen of every politician's career, but George Galloway has filled his lungs at more than usually regular intervals. On occasions he has been in danger of hyperventilating, but it was the media and general public who were rendered dizzy and incoherent when he turned up on Channel 4's *Celebrity Big Brother*.

On the night of 5 January 2006, a rag-tag bunch of has-beens and never-weres that included the depressive former TV host Michael Barrymore, the surgically altered former pop star Pete Burns, the former basketball player Dennis Rodman and a woman from Essex who had to convince the other housemates that she was famous when she just wanted to be, all entered the Big Brother House. The show reveals each contestant, one after the other, with a fanfare of screaming and a halo of neon, in a parody of the sort of showbiz premieres which feature genuine stars. So right from the very start, this is a celebration of irony. The desperate housemates are greeted like the Hollywood A-list, and they then spend three weeks being humiliated at the whim of the producers, in a way that the A-list would never be.

Big Brother's producers build the entrance sequence to fever pitch, and the identity of the last member is the climax. But on this occasion, when the final contestant got out of the limo and made his way along the catwalk, the reaction of the crowd was peculiar. The cheering was subdued and there were even a few boos. The general atmosphere was of slight confusion, as if a good portion of the twenty-something placard-wielding *Heat* readers didn't know who this was. They were looking at a slightly chubby and mildly tanned man in his fifties, sporting a moustache and receding hair, and wearing a long coat. He gave a Churchill-style V sign and calmly walked on down the catwalk. One can only guess at the reaction of the viewers at home, who were being given close-ups of George Galloway's face and explanations from the host, Davina McCall, of who he was. Once the penny had dropped, everyone was baffled. TV critics, political pundits, his friends and foes, the politically interested and the apathetic, were stunned. Why did Galloway, a serving British MP, decide to go on *Celebrity Big Brother*?

His political opponents were quick to make the most of what they saw as an own goal. The actress Helen Mirren, a supporter of Oona King and a constituent of Galloway's in Bethnal Green & Bow, said: 'Where does this guy's ambition go? That's very peculiar . . . I think he's a very disturbing person, I think he's a very disturbing politician. Personally, I feel his interest is a self-interest.'[1]

In a press statement released by Respect the day after he entered the house, he wrote:

> Firstly it was for Palestine. Millions of people vote by premium phone and text lines to choose who should face eviction. A percentage of the proceeds goes to the charity of the participant's choice. My choice is Interpal . . . their humanitarian work amongst some of the most oppressed people on the earth has prevailed. They don't get many opportunities to raise really serious amounts of money. My appearance on *Big Brother* will give them the chance to move up the Premier League.
>
> Secondly, I'm doing it for the audience. The biggest audience I will ever have. Every night on prime-time television millions of viewers will tune in. Almost everyone in the country will see at least a part of at least one episode. In the slow January news month the newspapers will be chock-full of *Big Brother* . . . I hope, within the difficulties of C4's editing of 24 hours down to one hour per day (though E4 will have wall-to-wall coverage), to reach this mass, young, overwhelmingly not yet political audience with our simple case. That war without end, war throughout the world is leading us all to disaster . . . I will talk about racism, bigotry, poverty, the plight of Tower Hamlets . . . I will talk about war and peace, about Bush and Blair, about the need for a world based on respect. Some of it will get through.

When he got out and found that birdsong had been being played when he had been talking politics, completely undermining his main reason for being on the show, Galloway showed his unhappiness. He claimed that the production company, Endemol, had told him that this would be a great platform for his views and that he had been misled by them, an accusation that they deny. The BBC reported that Galloway said:

> Not only did I not know I'd be censored, I was told by the *Big Brother* producers I would not be . . . In fact one of the main points that they made when they met me in the House of Commons to persuade me to do it was that it would be a good place to be effectively a soapbox for my perspective on events . . . And therefore I was very surprised when I got out to hear the birdsong over any political statement that I made.

The fact that Channel 4's most impactful programme takes its name from George Orwell's concept of state censorship gives Galloway's complaints about having his political conversation edited out another layer of irony. In order to get Galloway on the programme, Endemol had sent a high-level delegation to the House of Commons. They had convinced him to appear, but the details of the conversation are disputed by both sides. Endemol and Channel 4 both claim that Galloway knew that he could not air political views that remained unbalanced by other opinions. Peter Bazalgette, Endemol UK's boss, had to explain on BBC 1's *This Week* programme that 'there are these arcane broadcasting regulations. George has been talking about Iraq and the poll tax, but you have to show countervailing views,' while Channel 4 said: 'George was aware that we are bound to operate under the Ofcom broadcasting guidelines.' However, the channel's spokesperson was 'unaware' if Galloway had been told that when he started talking about politics, birdsong would be played. 'I don't know the details of that conversation,' she told reporters.

It had all got very messy, with both sides criticised. Galloway was called naive and Endemol and Channel 4 were accused of having been economical with the truth when contracting him for the show. But the real damage to Galloway was not what didn't go out, it was what did. In the course of the twenty-one days he lasted in the house, he was made to wear a wig, dress up as Dracula, dance in a revealing leotard and pretend to be a cat. The last task he threw himself into with some abandon, and got down on all fours to lick imaginary milk from the actress Rula Lenska's hands, while she stroked behind his ears. He then curled up and put his head on her lap. His pussy act is the one that seems to have stuck with his critics, from all parts of the political spectrum. 'The sad farce of Galloway on *Big Brother*' is how the Trotskyist *Workers' Liberty* described it, while Labour MP Steve Pound joked that he would be welcomed back at the other House, the Commons, with cries of 'meow' and a saucer of milk.

Even his close comrades had serious reservations about his decision to appear. John Rees, of Respect and the Socialist Workers Party, wrote:

> George Galloway has issued his own statement about appearing on *Big Brother*. In it he says he did it to raise money for a Palestinian charity, which he will, and to reach out to an audience turned off by conventional politics ... Nevertheless lots of people feel that it's not an appropriate way for an MP to spend their time. People in their workplaces and communities say that many Respect supporters don't think that this was a good idea ... We didn't know that George Galloway was going to go on the programme until 24 hours before it happened. We didn't agree with the idea, but by that stage the die was cast and the contract signed ... But what matters is the stand George has taken against war and neo-liberalism. That's why we continue to support him and Respect. We stick by our allies, even if we feel they have made a mistake.[2]

The reaction of his constituents was predictably mixed, but the bad publicity his appearance generated was widespread. Even outside the UK it was reported in a negative light by impartial observers. Shane Hegarty of the *Irish Times* wrote on 28 January:

> He came across as arrogant, vain, petty, abusive and hypocritical. He proclaimed himself a defender of the weak, but he did not intervene when other house members were being bullied and he mocked Michael Barrymore's alcoholism. He said he wanted to reach out to youth, but he rowed repeatedly with the younger residents of the house. He will be remembered not for political wisdom but for an extraordinarily cringeworthy sequence in which he pretended to be a cat, purring and licking imaginary milk from the hands of actor Rula Lenska. Or the night he wore a leotard and acted out, through the

medium of robotic dance, 'the emotion of bewilderment when a small puppy refuses to come to heel'. Oddly, it was the same expression he had when he left the house.

In the *Independent* on 18 January, the comedian and commentator Mark Steel was more supportive, but even he felt he had to write: 'Having campaigned for the Respect coalition, I'm finding George Galloway's life in the Big Brother House both compelling and atrocious.' He went on to make the point that Galloway's critics will invent conspiracy and bad faith in everything: 'At some point an American senator will claim he's been paid 2,000 barrels of milk by the Syrian Milk Marketing Board in return for publicising their product as an ideal beverage for cats.'

And what did Galloway himself think of the exercise? In the *Independent* of 22 May 2006 he answered questions from readers. One from a Sarah in Dorset asked: 'How damaging to your career and your causes was your humiliation on *Celebrity Big Brother*, and do you regret being in it?' He answered: 'I don't regret it and I reject your interpretation. I raised a lot of money for a Palestinian charity, my fee went to hiring two additional constituency workers and supporting Respect. And I never say never.'

In the Register of Interests at the House of Commons, Galloway lists his fee from Endemol as being between £145,001 and £150,000. The celebrities' payments for their appearance on *Big Brother* are negotiated on an individual basis, and are not made public. It is not as straightforward as a flat fee for taking part, and a celebrity will be paid more for surviving longer. They also may get a share of the revenue generated by the phone calls and texts to the show by people voting for who gets kicked off each week. Exactly what George Galloway received from Endemol is confidential.

Big Brother raised Galloway's profile enormously among the politically apathetic. Suddenly everyone knew who he was, but it would be hard to find many who thought it was an unqualified success. His opponents made the most of the opportunity to lampoon him and some even attacked his choice of charity. Interpal is a British-based organisation which, according to the Charity Commission, has 'the principal aim of providing aid to the poor and needy, including sick children and widows of those who are missing or detained, and to those detained themselves, as a consequence of civil or military action or national disasters. The charity confines its activities to Palestine and Palestinian refugees.'

Two Charity Commission investigations into the running of Interpal cleared it of any links to terrorism, saying, 'We found no evidence in the charity of any pro-terrorist bias or indeed any bias of any kind.' Yet Israel and the United States treat it as a suspected terrorist organisation and have put the British government under pressure to do the same. As soon as Galloway announced that he intended to give his fee to Interpal, so 'many will eat in the Gaza strip', the *Sunday Telegraph* ran a story referring to Galloway and claiming that the Israeli ambassador was renewing pressure on Britain to restrict Interpal's operations.

Another complaint about his appearance was that he missed vital work in the House of Commons while he was incommunicado in the House of Big Brother. At the time Crossrail, the huge railway development to link east and west London, was being debated in Parliament. This scheme, expected to cost £15 billion or more, is to run in part through Bethnal Green & Bow and has aroused great concern among Galloway's constituents, who are threatened with years of disruption for what Galloway himself described in an earlier Commons debate as a 'commuter service that will primarily benefit the City . . . the residents and small businesses of my constituency will pay the greatest price for a service designed to connect Canary Wharf to Heathrow airport.'[3]

While Galloway was in the Big Brother House the next stage of Crossrail was being discussed, with a vote taken on whether the scheme should be looked at by a committee to discuss the detail. His political opponents claimed that Galloway was missing a key debate and vote, on an issue that directly affected his constituents. Tower Hamlets Labour Party issued a press release on 11 January 2006 saying: 'Galloway absence Day 7: Residents of Tower Hamlets to present "alternative speech" as deserter MP set to miss crucial Crossrail vote.'

However, the proposition that a railway should run from 'Maidenhead in the west to Shenfield and Abbey Wood in the east, with a prescribed number of named stations on its route'[4] had already been decided on the Bill's second reading in July the previous year, and Respect rallied to Galloway's side to explain that 'there is . . . no general or specific debate on the substance of the

Bill and the two motions are what might best be termed technical motions'. Technical or not, there was reported dismay among some in Bethnal Green & Bow, who had expected their MP to be taking every opportunity to represent their views. As it turned out, the vote was carried unanimously, so Galloway's appearance would have been academic.

Just like any other TV 'reality' show, a week after *Big Brother* ended the subject was old news. It had been a good way of raising Galloway's profile among the apolitical masses, but a bad way of getting his anti-War on Terror message across. He had made precious little political capital out of his appearance, but when the dust settled it did look like a watershed for him. *Celebrity Big Brother* can be seen as marking the end of his time as an MP of any serious intent. He has tabled questions in Parliament and done work in the constituency since, but in appearing on that show he staked his claim to a future outside Westminster, perhaps even one that didn't rely on the momentum of politics to carry it along. It underlined his previous declaration that he wasn't going to stand for Parliament again.

While Galloway will continue to argue for what he believes, it is more likely now that this will be with callers into his radio phone-in on TalkSport, where he argues the toss over contemporary issues, or perhaps as a polemical TV host or newspaper columnist. While he will almost certainly continue to appear on political platforms to speak for socialism and the Arab people, his time in mainstream political life is all but over. He won't be an MP after the next election, having said that he will not stand again. He is no longer in a party with any wide influence, and unlike Tony Benn, who stood down but will always be looked to for a left-wing perspective in the mainstream media, Galloway may well spend his remaining years on ever-smaller soapboxes, preaching to the converted.

Galloway's phone-in show and other media appearances may give him a large quantity of airtime, but they don't necessarily guarantee its quality. If he is sought out for an opinion, it will most likely be on the Middle East, where he has a depth of knowledge gained from thirty years' experience of the region. However, Aljazeera and the other Arab outlets where he has become a well-known face will probably use him less when he is no longer a British MP.

There may be more attempts to discredit him by the right-wing press, but he is a canny operator. He saw through the *News of the World*'s 'Fake Sheikh', who tried to entrap him into expressing anti-Semitic views, which he has never held, and absurdly to implicate him in what would have been illegal political funding. You have to get up pretty early in the morning to trick Galloway.

In May 2006 he answered 'yes' to Piers Morgan in *GQ* magazine when asked if it would be 'morally justified' to assassinate Tony Blair in revenge for the attack on Iraq. (He has since stood by these views in many interviews, including on BBC TV's *Hard Talk* with Stephen Sackur in January 2007, in which he described Tony Blair as 'a mass murderer'.) Although he also made it clear that 'I am not calling for it', and qualified his comments by saying that he would expose a plot to kill Blair, on the grounds that his murder would be 'counterproductive', this was unprecedented behaviour. No MP has ever claimed that it would be morally defensible to murder anyone, never mind the Prime Minister. As with so much of Galloway's life, it left more questions than it provided answers. While there was a logic in what he said, which derived from his view that Blair is a war criminal for ordering the invasion of Iraq, the quotes had played into the hands of his opponents. So while Galloway remained true to his belief, did this show a lack of judgement? Or did he calculate that this would play well with his supporters around the world, and to hell with anyone who disagreed?

His *GQ* comments illuminate George Galloway brightly. Firstly, in his world you are either with him or against him; and secondly, he is a compulsive quotemonger. Through his life and career this has been demonstrated over and over. He clearly loves to hit his opponents hard and fast via the media and to rouse his supporters with simple, black-and-white arguments. Even as the ink dries on this biography, there may well be another controversial incident in the pipeline. His enemies will throw up their hands and make as much personal political capital out of it as they can, while his friends will admire him for his guts and for his lack of compromise.

A politician may take on a cause that is unpopular, or so much against the current thinking of the government, or establishment, that they start to get a Jesus complex, to think that they are a lonely voice of righteousness, on a path to martyrdom, or that in some way they are already on the cross, suffering for us all. Some leaders also start to confuse themselves with the movement which centres on them. They think they have become the movement and to criticise them is to criticise the cause. Is there an element of this in George Galloway's makeup? Perhaps.

And what of the future for him? Twenty-plus years in Parliament may have misled him into thinking that he doesn't need to be an MP to have influence, but being an elected representative gives a weight and impact to his work that will quickly evaporate when he is just plain George Galloway again. British politics hardly has room for a third party, never mind a fourth or fifth, and moving from Labour to Respect shifted him to the fringes of politics, despite the hype surrounding their election victories. He may still feel he's at the centre of the anti-War on Terror campaign, but Blair and Bush will soon both be history and Galloway may well become just a small voice drifting off into the wilderness, whose calls we will occasionally hear, like echoes, reminding us that a lot of people once cared enough to march against going to war in Iraq.

Epilogue

The inclement summer of 2007 proved to be an unsettled one for George Galloway. Two separate investigations into his behaviour in connection to the Mariam Appeal came to fruition, one in June and the other in July. It seemed that this episode of Galloway's life just wouldn't go away.

On 8 June the Charity Commission reported on the Mariam Appeal's finances, concluding that 'the charity trustees of the Appeal did not make sufficient further enquiries as to the source of the funding' from one of its major donors, the Jordanian businessman Fawaz Zureikat. The commission concluded that the appeal's trustees should have assessed 'whether it was proper and in the interests of the Appeal to accept these funds'.

Just over a month later, on 17 July, the House of Commons Committee on Standards and Privileges published a report that had been more than four years in the making. It was one of the most critical in its history and reported that Galloway had 'failed to comply with his obligations' under the MPs' Code of Conduct. The committee recommended that 'he apologises to the House, and be suspended from its service for a period of eighteen actual sitting days'. The report also stated that 'we consider that he owes an apology to Mr David Blair', the *Daily Telegraph* journalist who discovered the documents that led to the libel case against the newspaper that Galloway comprehensively won in 2003. This was for comments Galloway had made about Blair in the House of Commons, in which he had called him a liar.

In the course of its investigations into the Mariam Appeal, the Charity Commission looked at how money had derived from the United Nations' oil-for-food programme, and how improper payments, or bribes, had been made to various Iraqi officials involved in the process of dealing in the country's black gold. The report referred to the UN's Independent Inquiry

Commission, which officially exposed corruption in the oil-for-food programme. It quoted the inquiry:

> Some beneficiaries sought the assistance of intermediaries to arrange for oil sales. Others used front companies to enter into United Nations contracts and then sold the oil to established oil companies or traders who bought the oil for a premium over the United Nations' official selling price for the oil. The premium covered the commissions owed to intermediaries and beneficiaries.

From investigations into Fawaz Zureikat's business dealings, the report concluded that 'at least $376,000 donated by Mr Zureikat to the [Mariam] Appeal resulted from contracts made under the [oil-for-food] Programme'.

The Charity Commission's earlier inquiry into the funding of the Mariam Appeal (see Chapters 17 and 21) concluded that 'Mr Zureikat was a major funder of the Appeal' and that he had donated over £448,000 to it. The commission stated: 'These funds were donated to the Appeal in eleven separate payments. The first donation was made on 4 August 2000 and the last on 17 July 2002. The largest single donation to the Appeal made by Mr Zureikat amounted to $340,000 (£224,996.31) on 4 August 2000.'

The commission's June 2007 report concluded:

> The donations made by Mr Zureikat came from improper sources. This calls into question whether these funds were properly donated and there is risk to the Appeal and to the trustees that claims could be made to recover funds improperly given . . . In accepting the donations from Mr Zureikat, the charity trustees of the Appeal, as with all trustees, should have fully considered their legal duties and responsibilities given the particular circumstances prevailing . . . Although Mr Galloway, Mr Halford and Mr Al-Mukhtar have confirmed that they were unaware of the source of Mr Zureikat's donations, the Commission has concluded that the charity trustees should have made further inquiries when accepting such large single and cumulative donations to satisfy themselves as to their origin and legitimacy. The Commission's conclusion is that the charity trustees did not properly discharge their duty of care as trustees to the Appeal in respect of these donations . . . Had the charity trustees done so, they almost certainly would have discovered that there was a connection

between the Appeal and the improper transactions conducted under the Programme. The Commission is satisfied, on the information before it, that Mr Zureikat had actual knowledge of the connection between the Appeal and the Programme. The Commission is also concerned, having considered the totality of the evidence before it, that Mr Galloway may also have known of the connection between the Appeal and the Programme. Mr Galloway has continued to deny that he was aware of any such connection.

In reply, Galloway himself was quoted by the BBC and others claiming that the report was 'sloppy, misleading and partial'. He told the press:

> For the second time the Charity Commission has concluded that there was no misuse of the funds paid into the Mariam Appeal. The claim that the appeal's humanitarian and political campaigning was funded improperly is palpably false. The man who is claimed to be the source of 'improper donations' has never been charged with any wrongdoing, travels freely in the US and continues to do business in Iraq under the puppet government.

The report finished by stating that 'the Appeal is not on the Central Register of Charities, has not operated since early 2003, has no active trustees and holds no assets requiring the protection of the Commission. In the circumstances, the Commission will not be taking any additional action.' It prefaced this by reminding readers that the Charity Commission

> does not have any powers of criminal prosecution. Whether or not, under national or international law, there is illegality in these transactions and breaches of the Sanctions are matters for other agencies and regulators to determine. The Commission has fulfilled its statutory duties in this regard by liaising with other relevant agencies.

When the Committee on Parliamentary Standards and Privileges reported, it referred to the Charity Commission. The Parliamentary Commissioner for Standards, Sir Philip Mawer, explained that he had used the evidence gathered by the commission for its first report into the Mariam Appeal to understand 'how the Appeal came into being, what it did, how it ran and who funded it'. There was a lot more to his report than that, though. It was far more detailed and wide-ranging, and was deeply critical of Galloway's behaviour, not only on the original accusation of not declaring financial interests, but also in regard to his dealings with the inquiry itself. Mawer's recommendations left Galloway looking even more isolated in Westminster, and he was temporarily suspended from the House.

Mawer competed for the post of commissioner with sixty-three other candidates, and his previous jobs include a significant role in the momentous Scarman report into the Brixton riots of the early 1980s, as well as ten years on the Church of England General Synod. His full memorandum on George Galloway is contained in the sixth report of the Committee on Standards and Privileges, 2006/7 session, and can be read on the House of Commons website.

Leaving aside his assessments of the evidence for a moment, Mawer's report was also remarkable for its judgement of Galloway's co-operation with his inquiry. Mawer took time to point out that Galloway had 'consistently failed to live up to the expectation of openness and straight-forwardness in responding to questions and in other dealings which is critical to the continued effectiveness of the House's self-regulatory conduct regime'. He went on to accuse Galloway of

> repeated denial of facts, in some cases only conceded when they cannot be denied any longer . . . constant attack without justification on the motives and conduct of anyone who has in any way offered evidence which might be considered damaging to him . . . repeated attention to issues which in some cases are peripheral . . . Other evidence which is central but inconvenient – I have in mind Mr Thorne's forensic report [of the *Daily Telegraph*'s documents] – Mr Galloway has dismissed as 'an expensive irrelevance' . . . the making of wholly incorrect allegations without any factual basis . . . readiness to argue one way and then argue the opposite when it suits him.

For his part, Galloway replied by pointing out: 'I have been cleared of taking a single penny, or in any way personally benefiting from the former Iraqi regime.' He accused the MPs on the committee, who had relied on Mawer's evidence and recommendations, of being 'a pro-sanctions and pro-war committee of a pro-sanctions and pro-war parliament passing judgement on the work of their opponents'.

So why had the House of Commons decided to investigate Galloway? It all went back to April 2003, when the *Daily Telegraph*'s story accusing him of taking money from Saddam Hussein first surfaced. Andrew Robathan, MP for Blaby, complained to the Standards and Privileges Committee that none of the money mentioned in the newspaper's reports had been declared in the MPs' Register of Interests. A member of the public, Mr Andrew Yale, also made a formal request for the committee to inquire into Galloway's behaviour. As soon as Mawer had received these complaints he emailed Galloway to tell him, and Galloway replied that he'd started libel actions against the *Daily Telegraph* and the *Christian Science Monitor*, arguing that an inquiry by the House of Commons would be prejudicial to those actions. In a letter to Mawer two days later Galloway firmly denied that he had anything to answer for: 'I confirm to you that I have received no income which should have been registered with the Members' Interests and I have no business interests which are unregistered.'

MPs have to be very careful about who they take money from and they must declare an interest not only in the Register of Interests, but also in writing or verbally for each relevant debate. Many MPs will declare an interest as the first thing they say when they get up to speak in the chamber. The key line in their Code of Conduct is: 'No Member shall act as a paid advocate in any proceeding of the House.' It also states: 'Members shall at all times conduct themselves in a manner which will tend to maintain and strengthen the public's trust and confidence in the integrity of Parliament and never undertake any action which would bring the House of Commons, or its Members generally, into disrepute.'

If Mawer's inquiry established that, as he put it, 'Mr Galloway had, recklessly or knowingly, improperly received monies from a foreign government, directly or indirectly, either for his personal gain or in support of his political activities on behalf of policies favoured by that government', then a judgement would have to be made about 'whether he had thereby brought the House as an institution, as distinct from himself personally, into disrepute'. We now know that the inquiry found against Galloway, but how Mawer arrived at that conclusion is fascinating.

By November 2003 Galloway's legal action against the *Daily Telegraph* was gathering momentum and his solicitor wrote to Mawer, saying that he had advised his client not to answer any questions, on the grounds that Mawer's inquiry might be prejudicial. Mawer agreed that this was a possibility, so while the libel case went ahead, he pursued 'other lines of inquiry as were open to me'. A year later Galloway won his case, and £150,000 damages, but, crucially for the Standards and Privileges Committee's inquiries, the truthfulness of the documents that had been at the centre of the *Daily Telegraph*'s stories hadn't been tested. Mr Justice Eady said: 'It has not been part of my function to rule directly upon the truth or otherwise of the underlying allegations [against Galloway].'

For Mawer, however, the truthfulness or otherwise of the documents was a key question. In his report he asked: 'Are they authentic, i.e. are they genuine documents, as opposed to forgeries or fakes? . . . Are their contents credible?' This was a key element in establishing whether or not Galloway had left income undeclared on his Register of Interests. According to Mawer's report, these documents purported to be evidence that, as he put it, 'Mr Galloway received money from the regime of Saddam Hussein through the mechanism of the UN Oil For Food Programme'.

Galloway has consistently argued that the documents relating to him are not to be believed, that there was a conspiracy to create them and possibly to get them to the *Daily Telegraph*. He even went as far as to call David Blair, the journalist who says he found them, a liar, under parliamentary privilege in the House of Commons. He has never gone that far outside. Blair, meanwhile, has always maintained that he found the documents by chance and that he believes them to be genuine. Mawer concluded: 'In the absence of any direct evidence to support Mr Galloway's account of the provenance of the documents, I find Mr Blair's account convincing.'

The discovery of the documents by Blair, the *Daily Telegraph*'s man in Baghdad, is very illuminating. He is an exceptional journalist, with a highly regarded track record of reporting the situation in Zimbabwe that earned him the Foreign Press Association's Young Journalist of the Year award in 2001. He has also reported from Pakistan, Israel and South Africa. The following description of how he found the documents that mention Galloway is taken from his sworn testimony to the libel trial and his evidence to Mawer.

Like many reporters based in Baghdad after the invasion, Blair had looked through some of the ruined buildings of the old regime, in the hope of finding documents relating to Saddam or foreign powers, or just anything to make an interesting story. For example, he had been to the headquarters of the Mukhabarat, the secret service, on 16 April 2003 but it had been looted and nothing remained of any interest. On the following Saturday, the 19th, he went out with just his translator and a driver to look around a building he had often driven past, the Foreign Ministry. This had been the headquarters of Tariq Aziz, whom Galloway had known so well that he had gone to church with his family at Christmas one year. Blair was intrigued and thought he might be ahead of the press pack, because he'd not heard of anyone exploring this building before. When they arrived there were looters taking some furniture away and the area was not at all safe to wander around. Nevertheless, while the driver waited with the car outside, Blair and his translator went in. (Neither the driver nor translator can be named for their own safety because of the situation in Iraq.)

According to Blair's testimony the building was a mess: windows had been broken, small fires had blackened the walls, and larger ones had destroyed the entire contents of some of the rooms. Blair walked down several corridors and in and out of a few rooms until he found the main archive, which had been completely gutted by fire; all that was left was piles of ash. He then found a small, darkened room, through a blackened fire-damaged door, that seemed to have escaped the fire and was full of orange filing boxes. The room looked as though looters had been into it, thrown a few boxes around to check if there were any safes in the walls, then left. The boxes were stacked on three walls, on metal shelving units, four tiers high. Blair estimated that there were around 200 of them.

The boxes were all 'very similar to one another' and contained pale blue folders, stamped with the Iraqi eagle. Blair noticed that the boxes all had small labels on, which the translator told him said either 'Security Council' or 'Political Records' or the name of a country. In that room they came across boxes with 'France', 'Algeria', 'Yemen', 'United States', 'Egypt', 'Tunisia', 'Syria', 'Mauritania' and 'Jordan' written on them. He asked his translator to look for one with 'Britain' on it, obviously, and they both stood on top of a heap of boxes trying to get a better view of all the labels. Finally they got down on their hands and knees and searched under the shelves that the boxes were stacked on, where they found some loose files carrying 'Confidential' labels. Right after that, Blair's translator found another entire box with 'Britain' written on it.

Blair must have been quite excited by this stage, but got his colleague to carry on looking while he opened the box and looked inside. In it, he said, were

> three or four of the pale blue folders. I flicked through one or two of them and saw a mass of Arabic documents and a letter from Sir Edward Heath. I also came across a letter from Mr Galloway nominating a Mr Zureikat as his representative in Baghdad. These stood out only because they were in English but I didn't think much of them at the time. I put the folders back in the box, put it on one side and went back to looking for another box.

The two men then spent some more time looking for other boxes with 'Britain' on them, around the other shelves, and successfully came up with a second, plus another labelled 'Britain and France'. At this point Blair, who was carrying a few thousand dollars in cash, heard some looters walking down the corridor outside and hammering in one of the nearby rooms. These looters were often armed and clearly it was not safe to stay there with so much cash. Deciding to leave, they took the boxes with them back to Blair's hotel room.

Against this account, Galloway claimed to Mawer in February 2005 (and in interviews with the media, including with Clive Anderson for BBC Radio Five Live in December of that year) that he had evidence that the documents were found in different circumstances. Initially, he said he couldn't reveal the details, but that he would tell the House of Commons as soon as he was able. On 8 May 2006, under parliamentary privilege, and therefore with no threat of legal action being taken against him, he said:

> That Mr Blair was not led to those documents but had merely chanced upon them when wandering around a looted and burning building, and that he had found all of the documents published by the *Telegraph* in the same place, at the same time and in the same box, is quite simply a lie.

He went on to claim that he had been contacted by a very senior British journalist, a foreign correspondent on a national daily paper, who had told him that on the weekend Blair had found the documents he had pulled out of a planned trip at the last moment, and had told Galloway's contact that he had been worried about the veracity of the documents, their treatment by the *Telegraph* and its assumption of Galloway's guilt. Galloway claimed that his contact had told him that David Blair had confided in him that some of the documents had been given to him, and he hadn't found them at all. Galloway also claimed that his contact had been told by Philip Sherwell, a journalist with the *Sunday Telegraph*, that he had been through 'the same room in the same building and that everything was fire or sprinkler damaged beyond repair. On Sherwell's prior visit, the box Blair later claimed to have found was not there.'

Both Blair and the *Daily Telegraph* objected strongly to Galloway's claims, and Sir Philip Mawer reported that Blair wrote him a letter, saying that

> everything Mr Galloway had said about him in the House was untrue. He had not planned to travel to the South of Iraq with another journalist as Mr Galloway had claimed; both the documents published by the *Telegraph* on 22 and those published on 23 April had been found by him bound together in the same folder in the damaged former Iraqi Foreign Ministry building; none of the documents had been given to him by a third party; and he had had no conversations of the sort alleged by Mr Galloway with a senior foreign correspondent. He had nothing to add to or subtract from the evidence he had given during the libel action, which had been corroborated in a witness statement by his Iraqi translator.

Mawer continued that, in reply to a letter from him asking for his comments on Galloway's speech in the House, Sherwell wrote

> that his comments had been misrepresented during Mr Galloway's contri-bution to the adjournment debate. He had visited the Foreign Ministry building in Baghdad prior to Mr Blair but had never been aware whether he had visited the room in which Mr Blair said he had found the documents.

Hence he could not comment on the state or contents of the room.

Sherwell added:

> There were scores of rooms on several floors and we did not come close to
> trawling all of them. So when I heard that Mr Blair had found the documents
> in question, it did not surprise me at all and it never crossed my mind that my
> failure to find the same paperwork raised any questions about his subsequent
> discovery . . . I certainly never asserted – as Mr Galloway stated in his speech,
> quoting his journalistic source – that I had searched the same room. Hence by
> definition nor could I have made any observation about the state of its contents
> or whether the box that Mr Blair found was there or not at the time I visited
> the building.

So who was this mystery contact of Galloway's? When Mawer asked
Galloway to provide the name, he declined; however, he did bring forward
a witness to the meeting he'd had with the contact: his friend, former
business associate and PR man, Ron McKay.

Another major aspect of Mawer's report was to examine whether the
documents themselves were genuine, as distinct from the whole business of
how they were found. Galloway has always maintained that the documents
that related to him were either altered or completely faked. In March 2007
he wrote to Mawer, saying:

> I refute the alleged provenance of these documents . . . Whatever [their]
> provenance . . . the contents of them are false. I am not in a position to know
> who wrote them or when or why. They may all or in part be forgeries; they
> may all or in part reflect some corruption within the former Iraqi regime –
> corruption widely acknowledged; they may all or in part reflect the use of my
> name without my knowledge or benefit by other people. In any case the claims
> made in them are entirely untrue.

The key document that Mawer's inquiry centred on is reprinted in full
here, as it is in the Standards and Privileges Committee's report:

In the Name of Allah the compassionate and Merciful
Republic of Iraq
President's Office
Iraqi Intelligence Service
Confidential and Personal
Letter no. 140/4/5
3/1/2000

To: The President's Office – Secretariat

Subject: Mariam Campaign

1. We have been informed by our Jordanian friend Mr Fawaz Abdullah Zureikat (full information about him attached appendix no. 1) who is an envoy of Mr George Galloway because he participated with him in all the Mariam Campaign's activities in Jordan and Iraq, the following:

    a. The mentioned campaign has achieved its goals on different levels, Arabic, international and local, but it is clear that by conducting this campaign and everything involved in it, he puts his future as a British member of parliament in a circle surrounded by many question marks and doubts. As much as he gained many supporters and friends, he made many enemies at the same time.

    b. His projects and future plans for the benefit of the country need financial support to become a motive for him to do more work and because of the sensitivity of getting money directly from Iraq it is necessary to grant him oil contracts and special and exceptional commercial opportunities to provide him with a financial income under commercial cover without being connected to him directly. To implement this Mr Galloway gave him an authorisation (attached) in which he pointed out that his only representative on all matters related to the Mariam Campaign and any other matters related to him is Mr Fawaz Abdullah Zureikat and the two partners have agreed that financial and commercial matters should be done by the last (Zureikat) and his company in co-operation with Mr Galloway's wife Dr Amina Abu Zaid with emphasis that the name of Mr Galloway or his wife should not be mentioned later.

2. On 26/12/1999 the friend Fawaz arranged a meeting between one of our officers and Mr Galloway in which he expressed his willingness to ensure confidentiality in his financial and commercial relations with the country and reassure his personal security. The most important things that Mr Galloway explained were:

a. He stressed that Mr Fawaz Zureikat is his only representative in all matters concerning the Mariam Campaign and to taking care of his future projects for the benefit of Iraq and the commercial contracts with Iraqi companies for the benefit of these projects. But he did not refer to the commercial side of the authorisation he granted to Mr Fawaz for reasons concerning his personal security and political future and not to give an opportunity to enemies of Iraq to obstruct the future projects he intended to carry out.

b. He is planning to arrange visits for Iraqi sports and arts delegations to Britain and to start broadcasting programmes for the benefit of Iraq and to locate Iraq On Line for the benefit of Iraq on the internet and mobilise British personalities to support the Iraqi position. That needs great financial support because the financial support given by Sheikh Zaid is limited and volatile because it depends on his personal temper and the economic and political changes. Therefore he needs continuous financial support from Iraq. He obtained through Mr Tariq Aziz 3 million barrels of oil every six months, according to the oil-for-food programme. His share would be only between 10 and 15 cents per barrel. He also obtained a limited number of food contracts with the Ministry of Trade. The percentage of its profits does not go above 1 per cent. He suggested to us the following: First, increase his share of oil. Second, grant him exceptional commercial and contractual facilities, according to the conditions and suitable qualities for the concerned Iraqi sides, with the Ministry of Trade, the Ministry of Transport and Communications, the Ministry of Industry and the Electricity Commission.

c. Mr Galloway entered into partnership with the Iraqi Burhan Mahmoud Chalabi (available information in appendix 2) to sign for his specific oil contracts in accordance with his representative Fawaz, benefiting from the great experience of the first in oil trading and his passion for Iraq and financial contribution to campaigns that were organised in Britain for the benefit of the country, in addition to his recommendation by Mr Mudhafar al-Amin, the head of the Iraqi Interests Section in London.

3. We showed him that we are ready to give help and support to him to finish all his future projects for the benefit of the country and we will work with our resources to achieve this. But we should not be isolated from Mr Tariq Aziz supervising the project in its different aspects. We are going to make arrangements with him to unite the positions and cooperate to make the work succeed.

4. In accordance with what we have said, we suggest the following:
   a. Agreement on his suggestion explained in article 2 b.
   b. Arranging with Tariq Aziz about implementing these suggestions and taking care of the projects and Mr Galloway's other activities.

Please tell me what actions should be taken.

With regards,
[Signature illegible]
Chief of the Iraqi Intelligence Service 2/1/2000
Confidential and Personal

In the *Daily Telegraph* libel trial some forensic analysis had been undertaken of this and the other documents submitted by the newspaper, but the issue wasn't pursued as it wasn't relevant to the case. Mawer felt he had to establish how likely or otherwise it was that the documents were genuine.

Galloway wrote to Mawer on 17 January 2005 to explain his view of them:

The documents alleging financial wrongdoing on my part are fakes. They may have been forged, like the material supplied to the *Christian Science Monitor* by the *Daily Telegraph* writer Phillip Smucker, which led to an apology in the High Court and the payment of substantial damages by that newspaper to me. Or, like the documents bought by the *Mail on Sunday*, from the same source which supplied Mr Smucker and which were adjudged by Scotland Yard forensic experts to be forgeries, they have been doctored in a way to incriminate me in wrongdoing. Or they are the product of some corrupt scheme involving others and using my name. Whichever is the explanation, I am not yet able to say. The *Telegraph* documents are photocopies (unlike the *Christian Science Monitor's*) and thus, not subject to forensic examination. I am unable to travel to Baghdad to conduct an investigation there since the British and American invasion and occupation has turned the country into a conflagration. These documents are merely pieces of paper with my name written on them. There is no evidence that anything in them is true.

Mawer referred to the expert evidence of two forensic scientists who had examined the documents for the libel trial. They were Mr Oliver Thorne of LGC Forensics, instructed indirectly on behalf of Mr Galloway, and Dr Audrey Giles of the Giles Document Laboratory, instructed by the *Daily Telegraph*. Mawer also decided to commission Thorne, who had worked on behalf of Galloway's team in the libel case, to conduct a more thorough examination for his report.

Galloway pointed out that the documents were photocopies of the originals, and that this undermined the case for them being genuine. Mawer explained that both the forensic experts had agreed that this 'limited the conclusions' that could be drawn from them. However, he went on:

> Mr Galloway has asserted that the fact that the key documents are photocopies means that they are not therefore capable of being subject to any forensic analysis. However, this is to claim more than either forensic expert I consulted indicated would be justified. It was clear from my contacts with both Mr Thorne and Dr Giles that the key *Telegraph* documents were capable of some forensic analysis.

So what could they deduce from the documents? Mawer wrote:

> On the basis of the tests she conducted, Dr Giles concluded in her first draft report: '. . . the physical association between the [key] documents and other documents within the files amounts to strong positive evidence that the [key] documents have been handled within the Foreign Ministry in a manner

similar to other documents stored on the files and which I have assumed are genuine.'

And in his report on all 2,500 documents that came into the *Daily Telegraph*'s possession, whether they related to Galloway specifically or not, Thorne is quoted as concluding:

> In my opinion the evidence found fully supports that the vast majority of the submitted documents are authentic. In my opinion the submitted documents are not all forgeries created at a later time. Whilst I cannot totally exclude the theoretical possibility that all the submitted documents were created during the time that they state but by a non-authentic source such as a 'shadow office', I consider that this is extremely unlikely.

On the documents that actually referred to Galloway, Thorne is quoted in Mawer's report: 'Given that the vast majority of the submitted documents are authentic then, in my opinion, there is a high probability that all the disputed *Telegraph* documents are also authentic. I find no evidence that any are forgeries or altered and I consider this possibility to be extremely unlikely.'

Galloway gave his reaction to this in writing to Mawer: 'To say that I am surprised by your "forensic" report is a gross understatement. As you know I have always maintained that whether or not these documents are "authentic" they are false. Therefore your commissioning of the report is an expensive irrelevance.'

In his extensive report, Mawer also went into substantial detail on the oil-for-food programme and the records of money flowing in and out of Fawaz Zureikat's companies' bank accounts, which are referred to in Chapter 21. He also interviewed other participants in the Mariam Appeal. In drawing all the evidence together Mawer concluded:

> a. There is clear evidence that the *Telegraph* documents [provided by the paper's journalist David Blair] are authentic and, taking the evidence as a whole, credible.
>
> b. The Mariam Appeal was primarily a political campaign. It was, effectively,

directed by Mr Galloway and Mr Fawaz Zureikat was the second highest donor to it.

c. A substantial part of the donations made to the Appeal by Mr Zureikat came from moneys derived, via the Oil for Food Programme, from the former Iraqi regime.

d. Mr Galloway was not directly and personally in the pay of that regime but his political activities conducted through the Mariam Appeal were, in part, funded by the regime via Mr Zureikat.

e. Mr Galloway at best turned a blind eye to what was happening. On balance, it is likely, however, that he knew, and was complicit in, what was going on.

Mawer's report is remarkable for its detail and the persistence with which he pursued his task over more than four years. He interviewed Galloway himself in person and by letter, but was critical of the MP's attitude to such an extent that he added this to his conclusions:

> The evidence shows that Mr Galloway's conduct throughout this matter has fallen short of several of the general principles of conduct (the so-called Nolan principles) which were first articulated by the Committee on Standards in Public Life and subsequently embodied in the Code of Conduct of the House. I have in mind in particular the principles of openness . . . honesty . . . accountability.

Mawer explained:

> Mr Galloway has consistently denied, prevaricated and fudged in relation to the now undeniable evidence that the Mariam Appeal, and he indirectly through it, received money derived, via the Oil for Food Programme, from the former Iraqi regime:
> - 'The money came from Zureikat, it did not come from the Oil for Food Programme. I suspect you may well say he earned this money through his business dealings with the Oil for Food Programme but it is not as true as you think it is.'
> - 'I have never received a penny, directly or *indirectly* [emphasis added] from the former Iraqi Government.'

333

- ... 'There is not a jot or tittle to indicate that he [Fawaz Zureikat] had committed any illegal act.'

He went on to criticise Galloway for his attitude to his accountability, and quoted comments made in answer to the commissioner's enquiries:

- 'With respect, that is none of your business and it is none of anyone else's business' (when asked about the financial record-keeping practices of the Mariam Appeal).
- 'There is no evidence that I ever received any money from any business with Iraq which should have been entered in the Members' Register.'

Galloway's description of the inquiry as being part of an 'attempted political assassination' in a letter to Mawer only made things worse. This, and the previous criticisms of his behaviour towards the inquiry itself, led Mawer to conclude:

I believe that Mr Galloway has breached his obligation under the Code to conduct himself in a manner tending to maintain public trust and confidence in the integrity of Parliament. I am not speaking here of the objectives he pursued, but of the manner in which he has been found to have pursued them.

However, of all the 50,000 words written about Galloway's Mariam Appeal by Sir Philip Mawer, perhaps one paragraph stands out. It says:

The conclusion that Mr Galloway knew what was happening is one to which I find myself driven not only by the weight and consistency of the evidence taken as a whole but by my understanding of Mr Galloway's character. To have been ignorant of what was going on would have required a remarkable degree either of complacency or of naivete. Mr Galloway can in no way be accused of possessing either of these faults.

Not only did Mawer make judgements about Galloway's character, he also took the time to point out that in the MP's second interview for the inquiry, 'Mr Galloway argued in effect that the political end he sought – the abolition of sanctions on Iraq – justified any and all the means he employed to achieve it. That is a dangerous argument for anyone to advance, however noble they believe their cause.' He went on to remind readers that 'it is in part to prevent the excesses and distortions to which such an approach can give rise – and to which the evidence shows they gave rise in this case – that behavioural frameworks like Codes of Conduct exist'.

When Mawer completed his report, he sent it to Galloway for his reaction. In a letter dated 11 May 2007 the MP replied that it had not been proven that he had 'directly and personally, unlawfully' received money from the Iraqi regime and that this should have led Mawer to refute Andrew Robathan's original complaint. He added that the report he'd seen was 'laden with smear and innuendo which the media will be able to report freely, protected by you'.

But the Mariam Appeal saga didn't end there. In the House of Commons debate on whether to impose the recommended ban of eighteen sitting days, Galloway gave a vintage performance, personally attacking the members of the Committee of Standards and Privileges and being repeatedly reprimanded by the Speaker. He said that being lectured by the current House of Commons on the funding of political parties (a reference of course to the cash-for-peerages allegations) 'is like being accused of having bad taste by Donald Trump or being accused of slouching by the Hunchback of Notre Dame'. Having been repeatedly reprimanded and warned by the Speaker, eventually he was 'named' by him and thrown out of the chamber. He had been repeatedly asked to stop attacking the motives of the members of the Standards and Privileges Committee, and when he turned on Ann Clwyd and Andrew Robathan that proved to be the final straw. It had been one of the most heated, personal and confrontational exchanges for years. In the peaceful discussion that followed, members of the committee rose to defend themselves in reply to Galloway's criticisms of their conduct. The motion was passed 'on the nod' after the Speaker ruled that a count of the votes was unnecessary.

The suspension is due to run from the beginning of the new parliamentary session in October 2007. Having repeatedly confirmed that he would not stand again as an MP, Galloway said in the same debate: 'The Labour Party is much preoccupied with which Labour minister I am going to stand against at the next election. All I can say is that he is in the building right now.'

The George Galloway story still has a long way to run.

Appendix: websites for further information

George Galloway's own site
http://www.Georgegalloway.com

Archived historical web pages of Mariam Appeal
http://web.archive.org/web/*/http://www.mariamappeal.com

US Senate Permanent SubCommittee on Investigations
http://hsgac.senate.gov/index.cfm?fuseaction=subcommittees.home&
subcommitteeid=11&initials=PSI
http://hsgac.senate.gov/_files/psireportpasquagalloway.pdf

World Health Organization's Sanctions Assessment Handbook
http://www.who.int/hac/network/interagency/news/sanctions_
assessment/en/index.html

Parliamentary monitoring
http://www.theyworkforyou.com/mp/george_galloway/bethnal_green_
and_bow

Hansard
http://www.parliament.the-satationery-office.co.uk/pa/cm/cmhansrd.htm

House of Commons Standards and Privileges Committee reports
http:..www.publications.parliament.uk/pa/cm200506/cmselect/cmstnprv/
cmstnprv.htm

House of Commons Register of Members' Interests
http://www.publications.parliament.uk/pa/cm/cmregmem.htm

Notes

Chapter 1

1. E.g. *Independent on Sunday*, 23 January 1994; *Observer*, 21 November 2004.
2. E.g. *Sunday Times*, 4 September 2005.
3. Galloway, interview with the *Scotsman*, 3 June 1991.
4. Graham Ogilvy, in interview with the author.

Chapter 2

1. Interviews with Graham Ogilvy, James Martin and Willie McKelvey.
2. *Glasgow Herald*, October 1976; *Sunday Mail*, October 1976.
3. *Sunday Post*, 3 April 1977.

Chapter 3

1. *Sunday Post*, 7 August 1977.
2. *Miltant*, 10 March 1978.
3. Interview with Clive Anderson, BBC Radio Five Live.
4. Ibid.
5. Ibid.
6. Ibid.
7. Ibid.

Chapter 5

1. 'In the Red', *Dispatches*, Channel 4, November 1987.
2. *Scotsman*, 2 September 1980.
3. Ibid.; *Sunday Mail*, 22 March 1981.

Chapter 6

1. Interview with Clive Anderson, BBC Five Live, December 2005.
2. *Dundee Courier*, December 1980.

3.   www.tufp.org.uk.
4.   *Dundee Courier*, December 1980.
5.   Author interview with Graham Ogilvy.
6.   *Dundee Courier*, 4 January 1981.
7.   *Daily Telegraph*, 23 February 1981.
8.   *Sunday Post*, 5 April 1981.
9.   *Daily Record*, 6 April 1981.
10. *Sunday Mail*, 5 April 1981.
11. Ibid.
12. Graham Ogilvy files.
13. *Dundee Courier*, 12 July 1981.
14. Jimmy Allison, *Guilty by Suspicion: A Life and Labour* (Glendaruel: Argyll, 1995).
15. See Allison, *Guilty by Suspicion*.
16. *Financial Times*, 13 March 1982.

Chapter 7

1.   *Scotland on Sunday*, 5 May 1991.
2.   'In the Red', *Dispatches*, Channel 4, November 1987.
3.   *Sunday Mail*, 21 December 1980.
4.   *Sunday Mail*, 26 April 1981.
5.   'In the Red'.
6.   Ibid.
7.   Radio Tay, 7 February 1982.
8.   Hansard, HC Deb.
9.   *Dundee Courier*, February 1983.

Chapter 8

1.   *Sunday Mail*, 12 December 1982.
2.   *Dundee Courier*, 26 May 1982; *Glasgow Herald*, 26 May 1982.
3.   *Newsnight*, BBC2, 20 March 1983.
4.   Mark Luetchford and Peter Burns, *Waging the War on Want: 50 Years of Campaigning against World Poverty – An Authorised History* (London: War on Want, 2003).
5.   Ibid.

Chapter 9

1.   Charity Commissioners of England and Wales, *War on Want: Report of an Inquiry Submitted to the Commissioners 15 February 1991* (London: HMSO, 1991).
2.   Testimony to the Charity Commission.
3.   Ibid.

4. Figures from Charity Commissioners' report.
5. Galloway's testimony to the Charity Commission.
6. Minutes of emergency War on Want council meeting, 22 March 1986.
7. Minutes of War on Want council meeting, 6 April 1986.
8. Testimony to the Charity Commission.
9. Findings of Charity Commissioners' report.
10. Letter of October 1986, quoted in Charity Commssioners' report.
11. Membership records from Charity Commissioners' report.
12. Minutes of War on Want council meeting, 6 September 1986.

Chapter 10

1. *Glasgow Herald*, 30 October 1986.
2. Minutes of War on Want meeting, 11 October 1986.
3. Minutes of War on Want council of managment meeting, 27 October 1986.
4. Expenses details from War on Want's financial records.
5. Charity Commissioners of England and Wales, *War on Want: Report of an Inquiry Submitted to the Commissioners 15 February 1991* (London: HMSO, 1991).
6. Files of Louise Carmi.
7   Minutes of War on Want council of management meeting, 27 February 1987.
8. Interview on BBC Radio Five Live, December 2005.
9. Files of Martin Plaut.
10. Charity Commissioners' report.
11. Glenys Kinnock, testimony to Charity Commission.
12. Mike Phillips, testimony to Charity Commission.

Chapter 11

1. Interview with Colette Douglas-Home, *Scotsman*, 3 June 1991.

Chapter 12

1. *Sunday Times*, 8 November 1987.
2. Reported in *Scotland on Sunday*, 6 October 1991.
3. *Dundee Evening Telegraph and Post*, 7 November 1987; *Sunday Post*, 8 November 1987.
4. *Press and Journal* (Aberdeen), 19 November 1987.
5. Also covered by Kenny Farquharson in *Scotland on Sunday*, 5 May 1991.
6. From transcript of proceedings.

Chapter 13

1. Reported in the *Scotsman*, 8 December 1987.
2. Ibid.
3. *Sunday Times*, 13 December 1987.
4. Quoted in the *Evening Times* (Glasgow), 4 February 1988.
5. Reported in the *Glasgow Herald*, 20 August 1988.
6. Reported in the *Scotsman*, 24 March 1988.

Chapter 14

1. George Galloway and Bob Wylie, *Downfall: The Ceausescus and the Romanian Revolution* (London: Futura, 1991).
2. 'The miners were cheered to the echo on the streets of Bucharest that day for saving democracy.' Ibid., p. 249.
3. Hansard, HC Deb, vol. 176, cols 304 & 306.
4. Hansard, HC Deb, vol. 175, col. 587.
5. Hansard, HC Deb, vol. 167, col. 1130.
6. 'Where babies wait to die', *Observer*, 10 June 1990.
7. Hansard, HC Deb, vol. 167, cols 1129–30.
8. *Guardian*, 28 February 1990.
9. 'Where babies wait to die', 10 June 1990.
10. *Independent*, 20 May 1990; *Observer* Scotland, 25 February 1990 & 5 August 1990.
11. 'Romania, the domino that will be no pushover', *Scotsman*, 18 May 1990; letter to the *Independent on Sunday*, 6 May 1990.
12. *Observer*, 10 June 1990.
13. *Observer* Scotland, 5 August 1990.
14. Ibid.
15. *Guardian*, 29 June 1990.

Chapter 15

1. *Scottish Trade Union Review*, September 1988.
2. *Scotsman*, 12 November 1988.
3. *Glasgow Herald*, 12 September 1988.
4. Hansard, HC Deb, vol. 142, col. 489.
5. Peter Taaffe, *The Rise of Militant: Militant's Thirty Years 1964–1994* (London: Militant, 1995).
6. Quoted in the *Independent*, 6 March 1990.
7. *Los Angeles Times*, 1 April 1990.
8. Ibid, col. 896.
9. Hansard, HC Deb, 2 April 1990, vol. 170, col. 901.
10. Hansard, HC Deb, 13 February 1991, vol. 185, col. 839.

11. *Glasgow Herald*, 21 February 1991.
12. House of Commons Register of Members' Interests.
13. *Glasgow Herald*, 29 February 1992.
14. Quoted in *Glasgow Herald*, 14 October 1992.
15. Quoted in George Galloway, *I'm Not the Only One* (London: Allen Lane, 2004).
16. Hansard, HC Deb, vol. 234, col. 726.
17. Hansard, HC Deb, 17 January 1991, vol. 183, col. 992.
18. Hansard, HC Deb, 15 March 1991, vol. 187, col. 1350.
19. Hansard, HC Deb, 13 January 1993, vol. 216, col. 1022.
20. Hansard, HC Deb, vol. 234, cols 725–6.
21. House of Commons Register of Members' Interests.

Chapter 16

1. Information taken from the organisation's website, www.theyworkforyou.com.
2. *Dinner with Portillo*, BBC2, 18 March 2003.
3. 4 August 1995.
4. House of Commons Register of Members' Interests.
5. Standards and Privileges Select Committee, *Complaint against Mr George Galloway*, second report, Session 1997–98, HC 179.
6. Ibid., Appendix 1.
7. Reports in the *Daily Record*, the *Glasgow Herald* and elsewhere.
8. *Newsnight*, BBC2, 25 June 1998.
9. Ibid.
10. Ibid.

Chapter 17

1. Interview with author, November 2005.
2. United States Senate Permanent Subcommittee on Investigations, *Report Concerning the Testimony of George Galloway before the Permanent Subcommittee on Investigations*, 25 October 2005.
3. *Guardian*, 24 April 2003.
4. *Guardian*, 16 March 2000.
5. *Scotsman*, 16 November 2000.
6. Dominic Kennedy, *Times*, 5 April 2003.

Chapter 18

1. Hansard, HC Deb, 14 September 2001, vol. 372, col. 640.
2. Stop the War Coalition website, www.stopwar.org.uk.

3.   Interview on BBC Radio Five Live, December 2005.
4.   Interview on BBC Radio Five Live, December 2005.
5.   Hansard, HC Deb, 6 March 2002, vol. 381, cols 88WH–89WH.
6.   BBC News Scotland website, 4 May 2002.
7.   'In the hands of the three witches', *Guardian*, 27 November 2002.
8.   'Decades of human rights abuse in Iraq', Amnesty International website, 8 April 2004.

Chapter 19

1.   Hansard, HC Deb, 17 December 1998, vol. 322, col. 1107.
2.   Ibid, col. 1108.
3.   Hansard, HC Deb, 20 March 2003, vol. 401, col. 1095.
4.   Ibid.
5.   Hansard, HC Deb, 25 March 2003, vol. 402, col. 140.
6.   Ibid.
7.   Ibid.
8.   BBC News Scotland website, 1 April 2003.
9.   From Galloway's testimony, on the Stop the War Coalition website.

Chapter 20

1.   Stop the War Coalition rally at Northampton, 27 October 2003, reported in the *Herald* (Glasgow), 28 October.
2.   BBC Radio Five Live, December 2005.
3.   BBC Radio Five Live.
4.   'Why I will stand against New Labour: Blair's hallmark policies of war and privatisation must be challenged', *Guardian*, 13 October 2003.
5.   Respect website, www.respectcoalition.org.
6.   A contemporary press release from the Charity Commission said: 'Following preliminary enquiries into a complaint that the Mariam Appeal may have used charitable funds for non-charitable purposes, the Attorney General has agreed with the Charity Commission that the Commission will carry out further fact finding. The Attorney General and Charity Commission have concurrent powers in ensuring the proper administration of charities. The Commission, however, as the statutory regulator of charities, is better placed to take this matter forward. The Charity Commission will keep the Attorney General informed of the results of its enquiries.'
7.   Syrian television, 31 July 2005.
8.   *Daily Telegraph*, 5 August 2005.
9.   *Herald* (Glasgow), 5 August 2005.

Chapter 22

1. Reported on BBC news, 6 January 2006.
2. 'George Galloway and *Big Brother*', Socialist Worker Online, 14 January 2006.
3. Hansard, HC Deb, 19 July 2005, vol. 436, col. 1154.
4. Description taken from the Crossrail Bill.

Index

The following abbreviations are used in the index:
GG = George Galloway; WoW = War on Want